BEING MĀORI IN THE CITY

Indigenous Everyday Life in Auckland

Indigenous peoples around the world have been involved in ongoing struggles for decolonization, self-determination, and recognition of their rights, and the Māori of Aotearoa/New Zealand are no exception. Now that nearly 85 per cent of the Māori population has its main place of residence in urban centres, cities have become important sites of their cultural affirmation and struggle. *Being Māori in the City* is an investigation of everyday Māori life in the city of Auckland and of what being Māori means today.

One of the few ethnographic studies of Māori urbanization since the 1970s, this book is based on two years of fieldwork among Māori families, and more than 250 hours of interviews. While most studies have focused on indigenous elites and official groups and organizations, *Being Māori in the City* sheds light on the lives of ordinary individuals and families. Using this approach, Natacha Gagné explores how indigenous ways of being are maintained within an urban context, and are even strengthened through change and openness to the larger society.

NATACHA GAGNÉ is an associate professor in the Department of Anthropology at Université Laval.

ANTHROPOLOGICAL HORIZONS

Editor: Michael Lambek, University of Toronto

This series, begun in 1991, focuses on theoretically informed ethnographic works addressing issues of mind and body, knowledge and power, equality and inequality, the individual and the collective. Interdisciplinary in its perspective, the series makes a unique contribution in several other academic disciplines: women's studies, history, philosophy, psychology, political science, and sociology.

For a list of the books published in this series see page 343.

NATACHA GAGNÉ

Being Māori in the City

Indigenous Everyday Life
in Auckland

UNIVERSITY OF TORONTO PRESS
Toronto Buffalo London

© University of Toronto Press 2013
Toronto Buffalo London
www.utppublishing.com
Printed in Canada

ISBN 978-1-4426-4592-9 (cloth)
ISBN 978-1-4426-1413-0 (paper)

Printed on acid-free, 100% post-consumer recycled paper with vegetable-based inks.

Library and Archives Canada Cataloguing in Publication

Gagné, Natacha, 1975–
Being Māori in the city : indigenous everyday life in Auckland / Natacha Gagné.

(Anthropological horizons)
Includes bibliographical references and index.
Includes some text in Maori language.
ISBN 978-1-4426-4592-9 (bound).   ISBN 987-1-4426-1413-0 (pbk.)

1. Maori (New Zealand people) – New Zealand – Auckland.   2. Idigenous peoples – Urban residence – New Zealand – Auckland.   I. Title.   II. Series: Anthropological horizons

DU423.A1G24 2013   993'.2400499442   C2012-905902-1

This book has been published with the help of a grant from the Canadian Federation for the Humanities and Social Sciences, through the Awards to Scholarly Publications Program, using funds provided by the Social Sciences and Humanities Research Council of Canada.

University of Toronto Press acknowledges the financial assistance to its publishing program of the Canada Council for the Arts and the Ontario Arts Council.

ONTARIO ARTS COUNCIL
CONSEIL DES ARTS DE L'ONTARIO
50 YEARS OF ONTARIO GOVERNMENT SUPPORT OF THE ARTS
50 ANS DE SOUTIEN DU GOUVERNEMENT DE L'ONTARIO AUX ARTS

Canada Council   Conseil des Arts
for the Arts   du Canada

University of Toronto Press acknowledges the financial support of the Government of Canada through the Canada Book Fund for its publishing activities.

To Awhina, Gloria, and Misty
Three great Māori women,
For their everyday struggles

Contents

Figures

Acknowledgments

The motivation for the research that led to this book stems from my own experience of being a member of a people whose ancestors suffered the collective pain of colonization. As a Québécoise, I have always been interested in struggles for autonomy, processes of decolonization, the relationships between minority and majority populations, and modes of coexistence.

From a very young age, I also became particularly interested in the struggles of First Nations peoples in Quebec and Canada. I soon realized I was in a strange position. I am part of a people who were themselves colonized. I am also the descendant of French settlers who displaced and took control over indigenous peoples (some of whom are also among my ancestors) until the British took over the business of colonizing. And I am a citizen of a state that has been exercising its colonial power over indigenous peoples since the moment it succeeded the British colonial empire. The provincial state of Quebec and the federal state of Canada – as well as their population – each maintain the colonial situation, since the indigenous peoples who live on "their" territory come today under the shared responsibility of the Canadian and provincial governments.

To gain insight into this peculiar set of circumstances, I thought to look at colonial situations elsewhere, which is how I became interested in anthropology. During my studies, I learnt about (de)colonization, nationalism, power relationships, independence, and social movements. I also had the opportunity to meet Professor Eric Schwimmer who introduced me to Māori studies. Having read his work and engaged in long and stimulating discussions with him, I decided to go to

Aotearoa/New Zealand in the hope of one day coming home with new perspectives and ideas to change our situation in Quebec.

Above all, I would like to thank all the Māori in Auckland and else-where who participated in this research and who so generously shared their time with me for discussions, explanations, and interviews. I am particularly grateful to the Māori organizations, Māori groups, and the representatives of *marae* (traditional meeting place and ceremonial centres) who opened their doors to me, as well as to the *kapa haka* (performing arts) groups that kindly allowed me to join them in learning, practising, and performing their arts. To maintain confidentiality, I cannot greet you personally, but I know that you will recognize yourselves. *He mihi nui tēnei ki ngā tāngata katoa i tautoko, i awhi mai i ahau i roto i taku mahi. Ko te tūmanako ka tangohia e koutou ēnei mihi aroha e tuku atu nei au ki a koutou katoa.* Thank you so much.

I must also say that I am indebted to many people from my Māori language classes at the University of Auckland. These students, as well as the lecturers, were my first real contacts with Māori worlds and some of them accompanied me all the way through my field research. They patiently answered my questions, they introduced me to their *whānau* (extended family), they supported me in my presentations and seminars, they laughed with me and even at me. Some who were very close to me also cried with me, and they were angry and understanding, too, when I went through difficult experiences. I realize that I have been very lucky to have had them around me. I am very privileged to have shared with them what was for them a stressful experience. University is not always an easy world for Māori and many who helped me were parents and workers who, as mature students, were going to university for the first time or who were returning to university after many years.

A very special thank you to the families who welcomed me into their homes and helped me in so many ways. My deepest thanks to Kiri, Andrew, Rangi, Hoani, Manuka, and all the other *whānau* members for giving me a home and a family. All the people in these two households gave me much important practical advice and personal support.

I am particularly grateful to Rangi and Manuka, my research assistants. Both had aptitudes for and some experience with research, as well as a strong interest in research about Māori. They helped shape the research, as we discussed the best avenues for its progress, the things they thought I should learn, and the issues I should address. They corrected and commented on my work in progress and assisted me in interviewing people. They took me around the city and even to the country to visit family and friends. All along, we talked about our ideas as well as my personal learning and new understanding. This collaborative process was both relevant to my research and very enjoyable and I am deeply indebted to both of them.

As well as my Māori and non-Māori friends in Aotearoa and elsewhere, I would also like to thank my family for their deep support and for believing in me and my research; I am sure that you will recognize yourselves.

The research for this book was supported by scholarships from the Social Sciences and Humanities Research Council of Canada (SSHRC); the Québécois *Fonds pour la Formation des chercheurs et l'aide à la recherche* (FCAR); McGill University; the Centre for Society, Technology and Development (STANDD) of McGill University; and the Faculty of Social Sciences of the University of Ottawa. I would like to thank the Canadian Federation of University Women (CFUW) for the Margaret Dale Philp Biennial Award for 2003–4. And the Canadian Anthropology Society (CASCA) selected me as the 2002 recipient of the Richard F. Salisbury Award. Both awards included a financial contribution. I have a special appreciation for Professor Jonathan Friedman who welcomed me as a postdoctoral fellow at the Social Anthropology Department of Lund University in Sweden and at the *École des hautes études en sciences sociales* (EHESS), Paris. My current SSHRC Standard Research Grant (2009–12) has also allowed me to go back to New Zealand for further research in the field.

I take this opportunity to acknowledge the University of Auckland which gave me ethics approval for my fieldwork. Special thanks go to the Department of Anthropology and its members, where I was welcomed as a visiting graduate research student in 2001–2 and as an honorary research fellow in 2005 and to the Department of Māori Studies and its members who welcomed me and offered me office space in 2011 as a visiting researcher. I deeply appreciate their support throughout my field research. I am also pleased to generally acknowledge the advice and support of the members of the James Henare Māori Research Centre and of *Ngā Pae o te Māramatanga*, New Zealand's Indigenous Centre of Research Excellence, of the University of Auckland.

I am most grateful to Professor Joan Metge, who was at the Anthropology Department of Victoria University of Wellington until her retirement, for her comments on my work, for her assurances that I had not lost my way, and for her generosity and encouragement. I wish to extend my deepest appreciation to Professor Éric Schwimmer, who was at the Anthropology Department of Laval University until his retirement, whose passion and intellect were a great inspiration. I thank him for believing in me, for stimulating my intellectual curiosity and for spending innumerable hours in conversation with me. I also extend my warmest gratitude to Professor Carmen Lambert from the Anthropology Department of McGill University, for her support, generosity, and encouragement.

I also thank Robert Bull and Jessica Moore for reviewing the text and Kristen Walsh for reviewing the bibliography and glossary.

Last but not least, I owe very special thanks to dear colleagues and friends (in alphabetical order): Claude Bariteau, Sylvie Poirier, Martha Radice, and Marie Salaün. Their encouragement and support has meant an enormous amount to me over the years.

A Note on Language

Where I think it is important, I have used Māori words in this book; I think that they are necessary to understanding contemporary Māori and Aotearoa/New Zealand worlds, ways, and experiences. Māori use Māori words quite extensively when speaking in English, and many of these words are also in current use by non-Māori New Zealanders (see Macalister 2005; Metge 2010). They give a special colour to the language and reveal, to some extent, the place that Māori occupy in New Zealand society. This book is no exception.

To make the reading easier, at their first occurrence and whenever useful, I will give the English approximation of Māori words afterward in parentheses. A glossary of all Māori words can be found at the end of the book. When I quote from Māori participants, I reproduce the words as they were spoken. Two words will often appear in this book without translation because of their importance and repeated usage: *marae*, which refers to Māori traditional meeting places and ceremonial centres; and *whānau*, generally translated as the extended family but which can also mean the family in a much broader sense depending on context.

I will follow the Māori spelling of Māori words, indicating long vowels with macrons (some authors indicate the long vowels by using double letters, dieresis, or circumflex accents). This method has become standard. The lengthening of vowels (in any of the aforementioned ways) affects not only pronunciation, but often the meaning of the words. The only exceptions to this rule will be "Maoriness," "Maoridom," and "Pakehafied," which are English words formed from Māori words. For this reason, I opt for an English spelling of the Māori part of these words, with no doubling of the vowels. These English words are not in italics in the text, in contrast to all the Māori words, with the exception of "Māori," "Pākehā," and other proper nouns. When quoting authors who do not italicize Māori words, I do not italicize them either and I reproduce the quotes without changes. When quoting authors who use macrons, dieresis, and circumflex accents in their texts, for purpose of standardization as well as for technical reasons, I change them to macrons. For those who do not mark the long vowels of Māori words, I do not mark them either, and I reproduce these quotes without changes.

Because Māori words often possess many layers of meaning, they are not easily defined by an equivalent word or short phrase in English (Metge 2010: 58), and the ontological status of translations varies with the mother tongue of translators (see Schwimmer 2004a). Whenever possible, I use the translations given by different Māori analysts in their texts, glossaries, and footnotes, principally Walker (2004), the James Henare Māori Research Centre (2002), and Tauroa and Tauroa (1986). I also use Metge's (1995, 2010) glossary and definitions when necessary, since she is widely recognized by Māori as a reference and very often quoted as such. I also consulted Ngata's (1995 [1993]) and Williams's (2000 [1971]) dictionaries. Most Māori nouns do not change to become plural (unlike English). The few exceptions to this rule are contained in the small set of words referring to people. Here are two such words that I use in this book: *tangata* (man, person) becomes *tāngata* (people) and *tipuna* (ancestor, grandparent) becomes *tīpuna* (ancestors, grandparents).

A last note: the Māori "wh" is pronounced like the English "f," and the Māori "ng" is pronounced like the English "ng" in "sing."

BEING MĀORI IN THE CITY
Indigenous Everyday Life in Auckland

Introduction:
Māori "Sitting at the Table"

Now in New Zealand, as at no other time, public debates include discussions about constitutional arrangements, emerging multiculturalism, and liberal democracy. In December 2010, the government announced a three-year constitutional review to examine, among other things, electoral issues, the role of the 1840 Treaty of Waitangi[1] and Māori interests, and New Zealand as a constitutional monarchy versus that of a republic with a written constitution. Some Māori individuals and representative bodies, such as *iwi* (tribal) authorities, insisted they have their say in the government review and are also running their own constitutional review process.[2] Māori, with renewed vigour, are stressing their indigenous status and rights[3] to strengthen and counter threats to recent gains in issues of social and historic justice, economic adjustment, and political representation and governance.

In November 2008, the National Party – a centre-right political party appealing primarily to conservative and classic liberal voters – won the election under the leadership of Prime Minister John Key and formed a coalition government with votes of confidence and supply from three minor parties, including the Māori Party created in 2004. This Māori Party won a total of five seats, which was an important breakthrough for a party appealing mainly – if not exclusively – to Māori voters.

Enthusiasm ran high among Māori when I was in the field in the month following the 2008 election. For an external observer, however, the composition of the coalition government as well as the general optimism in Māori circles was at first surprising, considering the National Party had helped fuel racial resentment and tensions between Māori and non-Māori and had voiced some of the more conservative and radical positions on issues concerning Māori in the years preceding the election. What could explain, then, so much enthusiasm and optimism among Māori? Most obviously, observers noted the numerous compromises made by the new leader of the National Party, John Key, who was elected as prime minister in 2008. Another clear answer came when listening to Māori people around me at the time I was back in New Zealand at the beginning of the electoral year 2011. Despite certain disagreements with some of the government decisions that had the support of the Māori Party, I heard a common observation: "It's the first time that we are sitting at the table. This is our chance!" It was indeed the first time a party representing Māori interests and supported by a large Māori electorate was part of the government.

Shortly after the November 2011 election, and following a consultation tour in which members gave their input about the best ways to move forward, the Māori Party – which had managed to secure three seats after a turbulent year[4] – embarked on a new confidence and supply agreement with the National Party. This new agreement meant "the Maori Party will support confidence and supply, but differs [from] the arrangements with Act and United Future in that the Maori Party is allowed to vote on a case-by-case basis" (Cheng 2011).[5] After the election, Tariana Turia, coleader of the Māori Party, reiterated the common observation I had heard earlier in 2011: "you can't make gains unless you're sitting at the table of the government" (One News 2011).

In the last decade, the long struggle for recognition of Māori rights and autonomy has finally resulted in a series of achievements. Recent events have led to the most important Māori mobilization of all time, with daily, less obvious battles being as crucial to success as the public protests and political activism. This everyday combat is the main focus of this book. In particular, I will concentrate on the regular experiences and strategies of urban-based Māori; city life is the reality for the great majority of Māori today. To understand the importance of this everyday struggle, I will first place it in context with a brief overview of the significant political events of the last few years. Because of its effect on change, I will pay particular attention to one set of events known as the "foreshore and seabed controversy."[6]

In June 2003,[7] a New Zealand South Island confederation of tribes, Te Tauihu o Nga Waka, won an appeal to the New Zealand Court of Appeal to be heard by the Māori Land Court. Among other things, they wanted the land below the mean high water mark of Marlborough

Sounds to be declared customary land (which means land held in accordance with *tikanga* Māori, customary values and practices).

The National Party, which then formed the opposition, saw an opportunity to score what Walker (2004: 381)[8] described as "brownie points" and to gain in their support of the electorate. The party suggested that the court's decision meant that customary rights to the foreshore and seabed could be converted into private titles, thus depriving New Zealanders of their public access to beaches.[9] The party also raised the possibility that the decision could open the door for more Māori claims to any part of the coastline. This declaration in response to the decision of the Court of Appeal (Ruru 2004: 57) was a major contributor to polarizing the debate between Māori and the dominant population. The result was an obscuring of the facts, which hindered understanding among the general public (Walker 2004: 381–4). The Māori repeatedly stated that they were only seeking "greater stakes" when sections of the seabed and foreshore were used for commercial operations (such as for marine farms) and not for any restriction of public access. But the National Party ran a vast campaign with the theme "Beaches for All." An irony ignored by the campaign, and as underlined by Walker (2004: 385), is that about 30 per cent of New Zealand beaches were already in private ownership.

Facing a decline in support for the Labour Party, Prime Minister Helen Clark sought a way to reassure the (mainstream) electorate. The government decided to legislate to clarify the Crown's ownership of the seabed and foreshore. This overthrew the decision of the court that gave the South Island confederation of tribes the right to proceed with their claim to the Māori Land Court.

The government decision to stop the legal process generated an indignant reaction among Māori. The affair was interpreted as just another violation of the Treaty of Waitangi. Māori leaders also called it the worst land confiscation ever to occur because no unalienable title of ownership could be claimed under the new law even if continuous usage by Māori groups could be proven (Ansley 2003, 2004; Ruru 2004: 64). This interpretation motivated the huge Māori mobilization that followed in the name of *rangatiratanga* (chieftainship), *tino rangatiratanga* (self-determination, sovereignty), and indigenous or ancestral rights as recognized in the interpretation of the Treaty of Waitangi.

Despite Māori protest, the government went forward with a consultation of Māori communities on *marae* (traditional Māori meeting places and ceremonial centres) across the country. Each meeting saw Māori take various actions of opposition (Walker 2004: 386–7). During the consultation period, Māori also lodged several other applications with different judicial bodies (see Ruru 2004: 65 for details). Finally, on 17 December 2003, the government announced its proposed new bill.

To add to rising Māori dissatisfaction, in January 2004, Don Brash, who had recently become leader of the National Party, gave a speech on the state of the nation in which he accused the government of promoting race-based policies and creating two standards of citizenship (Brash 2004, see also Poata-Smith 2004b). He also pleaded in favour of the "removal of any race-based provisions in existing legislation, the abolition of the Maori seats, and a speedy end to the historical claims process" (Miller 2005: 168).

The speech had the effect of invigorating public resentment over the so-called privileges enjoyed by Māori. It exacerbated a situation already strained over the previous six months by the foreshore and seabed controversy. Brash's speech also increased significantly the National Party's support (Walker 2004: 397; Miller 2005: 166).[10] Since the 1975 Treaty of Waitangi Act, the National and Labour Parties had agreed on the implementation of policies related to biculturalism and the Treaty of Waitangi. But Brash's speech, as underlined by Walker (2004: 403) and Barber (2008), represented an important breach of bilateral consensus. The importance of the Treaty of Waitangi will be raised many times throughout this book.

It is essential to understand that Brash's speech was part of a larger context in which ideas of multiculturalism or pluralism (rather than biculturalism), republicanism, and a written constitution for New Zealand were in the air. The speech also reflected a changing demographic context in which New Zealand welcomed more and more immigrants. This situation worried some Māori, who were afraid that Māori might become one minority group among others (Smits 2010; O'Sullivan 2007). In the mainstream population, Brash's speech accelerated a growing backlash against Māori. For some time, especially since the treaty settlements of the 1990s, increasing resentment had been expressed in "racial" terms (see Miller 2005; Van Meijl 2006a; Walker 2004).

In reaction to polls that revealed that Brash was leading in popularity among voters, the prime minister announced at the end of February 2004 that Labour would review its policies with respect to affirmative action programs for Māori and that the proposed foreshore and seabed legislation would be scrutinized yet again, with the prime minister even suggesting that the place of the treaty within New Zealand's constitutional arrangements could be the subject of an inquiry (Miller 2005: 168).

Facing the government's determination head on, Māori organized a huge *hikoi* (march) that started in Waitangi and culminated at the Parliament Buildings on 5 May 2004 in time for the first reading of the Foreshore and Seabed Bill. With its estimated 40,000 to 50,000 participants throughout the route (Smith 2010a: 511; Sullivan 2010: 545; Mutu 2011: 148), the march was one of the most important public demonstrations since the well-known 1975 Land March and gathered from 15,000 to 20,000 people in Wellington (*New Zealand Herald* 2004a, 2004b; Harris 2004a).

The events led to the creation of the Māori Party.[11] The party was officially launched in July 2004 on the crest of a wave of Māori unity and enthusiasm inspired by the march (which was nonetheless very connected to deep feelings of sadness, disappointment, and anger). Miller (2005: 159) describes the Māori Party as the first one to appeal to mainstream Māori opinion and to cut across tribal and social class divides.[12] At the 2008 general election, as already mentioned, the party secured five seats in Parliament and was part of a coalition government with the National Party and two minor parties. According to the Relationship and Confidence and Supply Agreement between the National Party and the Māori Party, both agreed, among other things, to consider constitutional issues including Māori representation in Parliament and to review the Foreshore and Seabed Act 2004 "to ascertain whether it adequately maintains and enhances mana whenua"[13] (*mana whenua* could be translated roughly as "customary rights, Māori power, and authority over a particular piece of land"). In addition to making the government more flexible over the contentious issue of the ownership of the foreshore and seabed, the Māori Party has been quite successful within government since 2008 in asserting Māori advancement. Among other achievements, they achieved government agreement in 2010 to the Whānau Ora scheme[14] and to support the United Nations Declaration on the Rights of Indigenous Peoples.[15] In March 2011, the Marine and Coastal Area (Takutai Moana) Act finally replaced the Foreshore and Seabed Act 2004 and restored Māori rights to seek customary title on the areas concerned.[16]

The events since 2003, as well as the acceleration of the treaty settlements process – in particular through early direct negotiations, to which I will return – have put in place the conditions for important

Māori mobilizations in public space and a rise of political consciousness among Māori. The feelings of enthusiasm and unity were very
present when I was in New Zealand in early 2005. Symbols of Māori
pride and unity like the *tino rangatiratanga* (Māori sovereignty) flag
were more visible than ever, even among the "ordinary" Māori with
whom I had worked in 2001 and 2002. Māori were keen to mobilize
and go to the streets when necessary. They did so, among other occasions, after the events now known as the "terror raids," a wave of police raids that occurred in October 2007 and focused on Ruatoki in the
Bay of Plenty at the heart of the land of the Tūhoe people, an important Māori tribe in terms of membership and with a strong history of
resistance.[17] In May 2009, another march drew up to 7,000 protestors on
Queen Street calling for Māori seats on Auckland's Super City Council
(Hayward 2010b; Tahana and Orsman 2009; Sullivan 2011). *Iwi* (tribal)
leaders have also been more vocal in recent years and have striven, for
example, through initiatives like the Iwi Chairs Forum created in 2005,
to present a united front.[18] It is reasonable to think that the so-called
foreshore and seabed controversy has been a turning point for Māori
politics through, among other things, the declining importance of internal differentiations, which stimulated the mobilization of ordinary
Māori and allowed for the creation and success of the Māori Party and
other pan-Māori or inter-tribal initiatives.

In recent years, Māori have become viable competitors and competent partners in many fields. There are innumerable Māori success
stories. These include the launch of Māori television channels,[19] many
achievements in Māori education and language revitalization, the increased Māori political representation in Parliament and local government under official bicultural policies, the vitality of Māori arts and
literature, and the creation of successful businesses run by Māori, especially in fisheries, health services, and commercial radio (see Belich
2001; Durie 1998, 2011; Poata-Smith 2004b; Walker 2004). As emphasized
by Sullivan (2010: 541–2), "[a] Māori economy, while still small, is finally emerging and providing the vehicle for tino rangatiratanga, or
self-determination. Māori investment is concentrated in agriculture,
fishing and home ownership (see New Zealand Institute of Economic
Research 2003) and while exposed to the vagaries of the global economy, their asset base is increasing."[20] According to the Māori Economic
Taskforce,[21] the asset base of the Māori economy was estimated at $36.9
billion for 2010 (Nana, Stokes, and Molano 2011: 9). Although these are
only estimates, it's true that the Māori economic asset base has been

rapidly growing since 2001, when the total commercial assets owned by Māori individuals, *whānau* (extended families), *hapū* (subtribes), and *iwi* (tribes) were estimated at $9.4 billion (Nana, Stokes, and Molano 2011: 9). In the last few years, Māori economic ventures and initiatives have multiplied, *iwi* have made cutting-edge investments, and they are now ready for public-private partnerships.[22] One of the defining features of the 2011 election campaign was precisely the privatization of New Zealand public assets and the fear of assets ending up in foreign hands. For tribes, this is a good investment opportunity, and they have shown their desire to invest in state assets. If the Māori Party is opposed to state asset sales, it will still support *iwi* that want to buy shares, a position supported by at least one newly elected Māori MP from the Labour Party (for example, Trevett 2011). The new National-led government has agreed to consult *iwi* about its privatization plans (Bennett 2011).

The recognition of the Treaty of Waitangi and the creation of the Waitangi Tribunal are far from foreign to these successes.[23] There was consensus among the major parties after the Treaty of Waitangi Act 1975, which established the Waitangi Tribunal. The Tribunal redirected attention to the Treaty of Waitangi and biculturalism,[24] which led to the treaty settlements of the 1990s and 2000s. Douglas (1991) attributes to the Waitangi Tribunal the shift from public protests, marches, and demonstrations to a more "introverted" period of conciliation and dialogue between parties. Sullivan (2003: 228) writes that "[overall], the 1980s can be characterised as the decade of recognition and litigation. Historic grievances were recognised and legitimised by the state." As emphasized by Schwimmer (2004a: 246), "the sense of Māori identity since 1975 . . . flowed directly from the change in Pākehā [New Zealanders of predominantly European ancestry] response to Māori claims." Schwimmer thus sees the changes as directly related to transformations in the relationships among the minority and majority populations.

The whole history of Māori protests, struggles, affirmation, and re-sistance[25] also has to be understood in a wider and even global context. The 1970s marked a rise in Māori activism[26] – the decade is recalled for its large protests and land occupations. That period, which continued into the early 1980s, is often called the Māori cultural renaissance. The Māori political activism of the 1970s and 1980s should be seen as linked to worldwide trends in political activism following the collapse of the postwar economic boom. These included movements around the world to promote the rights of black people, indigenous peoples, women, and gays and lesbians, as well as liberation movements in both the so-called third and fourth worlds (Poata-Smith 1996; Smith 1999). The period corresponds also to a resurgence of class conflicts, the appearance of a new Left, the growth of student political activism, and the movement in the West against the Vietnam War (Poata-Smith 1996). The involvement of Māori leaders in the world indigenous movement since its beginning in the 1970s certainly also played a role in Māori mobilization (see, for example, Charters 2007; Coates 2004; Niezen 2003; Sissons 2005; Smith 1999; Tsing 2007), as did Māori urbanization and the disproportionate concentration of Māori workers in the primary sector, which made their marginalized condition more apparent (Pearson 1994; Sissons 1993; Walker 1996; Webster 1998).

In the following period, which some have qualified as "introverted," the general global disengagement from social movements and public protests, the international decline of the working-class movement, and the rise of the new Right as a global political force (Poata-Smith 2004b: 74; Rata 2011a: 342), as well as the national context of conciliation, appear to have affected Māori too. Indeed, Māori were in general less active in social and political groups and movements and resorted less often to public protests, marches, and demonstrations in the 1980s, 1990s, and the early 2000s.[27] They focused instead on the rediscovery and revitalization of Māori culture (a movement accompanied by government actions to legitimize Māori traditions and culture). This coincided with "an emphasis on cultural identity as the determining factor in Māori oppression" (Poata-Smith 2004b: 74), rather than class.[28] They were not disengaged however from the struggle for Māori rights and autonomy. As emphasized by Sullivan (2010: 544), "[e]xercising the democratic right to vote is not necessarily the only or most important vehicle by which Māori choose to participate in politics" and "[p]rotest is only a minor aspect of Māori political activities." Quoting Walker (2004), she adds that the "Māori struggle for social justice, equality and self-determination . . . is fought on a number of fronts" (Sullivan 2010: 544), including peaceful occupations and marches, but also in participation in *hui* (meetings) and celebrations, including those on Waitangi Day (McAllister 2007, 2011).

During this period, mobilization thus took other forms and expressed itself differently. It occurred on an everyday basis at *marae* and in other places in the city that became important meeting sites and places of support and comfort for Māori at all levels (social, economic, cultural, and spiritual). The struggle consisted of (re)learning Māori traditions and language, doing genealogical research, and wearing different signs of Māori identity. By focusing on education, health, justice, and socio-economic conditions, as well as on cultural survival and development, the Māori opened important doors to societal participation and engagement in the larger world. The struggle that took place in that period – and that still continues today – has been part of the creation and widening of places and spaces and the internalization, under contemporary conditions of life, of the various worlds of meaning that allow participation in heteroglossic ways in those worlds.

The struggle was not only to form "ethnic Māori," but also to allow Māori to participate in the larger society as polyvalent and active citizens. And this daily battle paved the way for the many Māori achievements of the past decade, as well as for the vast mobilization of 2004 and the creation of the Māori Party and its success, in particular at the 2005 and 2008 general elections. It is to this Māori everyday struggle, which has been generally overlooked, that I dedicate this book. In particular, this book explores the everyday struggle in the years preceding the foreshore and seabed controversy as I witnessed it and participated in it during my 2001 and 2002 field research. This everyday struggle has been engaged by Māori for the last decades and still continues today even as things are changing quickly.

The last New Zealand national census (2006) showed that the city is the main place of residence for nearly 85 per cent of the Māori population. This study is an investigation of what being Māori today means, and in particular what it meant in the very first years of the twenty-first century. It is grounded in an ethnography of everyday life in the city of Auckland, New Zealand's largest and most multicultural city. This book pays special attention to the ways Māori experience the city, which is often perceived as an alien and colonized site.

My research reveals that for most "ordinary" Māori, and this was particularly true in the years preceding the foreshore and seabed controversy, their place and autonomy within the nation state are not among their more immediate concerns. Rather, what is fundamental is feeling and being comfortable. For many, being comfortable simply means being Māori. Being Māori is not (always) an elaborate discourse or ideology. But it does imply a whole set of everyday relationships and ways of doing things.

Māori experiences of affirmation and resistance in the city are supported by the *whānau* (the extended family) and through certain kinds of "city houses" that follow principles of the *marae* (the traditional

Māori meeting place and ceremonial centre). Māori relationships to the urban milieu are complex, as are the ongoing struggles to (re)affirm Māori identities and preserve aspects of the culture considered important elements of these identities. Māori in the city create places and spaces for themselves. They build networks connecting themselves to Māori and non-Māori. These are all aspects of Māori daily life, and the focus of my exploration in this book.

In contrast to many studies of indigenous cultures and societies that have stressed how urban milieus and global forces exert pressures to assimilate, leading to what they call "culture loss," cultural fragmentation, dislocation, disorganization, detribalization, or even dysfunctionality,[29] this book underlines processes of (re)affirmation. Although this is changing, there are still commentators, both Māori and non-Māori, who do not consider the views and experiences of so-called "urban Māori" as valid and "good enough for real Māori." This study takes the experiences and voices of Māori who live outside their tribal area seriously. What is revealed is that indigenous worlds, visions, and ways of being are maintained and even strengthened through change and openness to the larger society. The main argument of this book is that Māori who live in the city affirm Māori ways of being and identities while working to reconcile the demands of the different *universes of meanings* in which they engage.

In this book, when using the concept "universe of meanings," I mean a set of general principles and values that constitutes a realm of interpretation in which particular principles, values, characters, actors, categories, and identities are recognized, in which particular significance is assigned to certain acts, ideas, and symbols and in which particular outcomes and projects are valued over others. Universes of meanings serve as an "orientational device" (Ramstad 2003) through life, experiences, and practices.

The concept of "universe of meaning" is useful for examining the principles that guide people in their actions and daily interactions and in the way that they engage with places and spaces, as well as in the ways in which they make sense of the world. It takes into account the actors' meanings and representations, their main values, their projections into the future, and the possible worlds they imagine and through which they take part in today's worlds. This term is also less all-embracing than a term such as "culture" and allows for the recognition of the idea that people, individuals and groups, (may) participate or engage in more than one universe of meanings.

Coexistence and interrelation are a necessary mode of existence and this is true for universes of meanings. Many universes of meanings thus coexist, interrelate, and confront each other. They sometimes have elements in common and sometimes have incompatible aspects that create dilemmas for the persons and groups who engage in them. In the case of Māori living in cities today, this book will focus on the interactions and articulations between Māori and Pākehā (New Zealanders of predominantly European ancestry) universes of meanings.

The concept of "universe of meanings" also emphasizes imagination and creativity, and therefore the possibilities for re-orchestration and improvisation. In a dialogical type of approach like the one that I propose here, the actors are seen in "a state of being 'addressed' and in the process of 'answering'" (Holland, Lachicotte, Skinner, and Cain 1998: 169). The "answers" emerge in particular contexts, in practice and through interactions, but always in relation to the universe(s) of meanings in play. Identities are also dialogically formed in these universes of meanings through interactions and practices. Characterized by flexibility and multivocality or heteroglossia, universes of meanings are the products of history as well as of social contingencies and improvisations.

If current expressions of long-enduring or earlier forms of universes of meanings are never precisely the same, their connection to their previous forms and expressions can still be more or less recognized. Continuity is made possible through change. This is exactly what I argue when discussing the universe of meanings of the *whānau*. It has changed through colonization and urbanization but it is still alive and well.

In Canada, the United States, and Australia, scholars have just started in recent years to look at the urban experience of indigenous peoples. This field of study, however, is now attracting more attention and publications have started to multiply. Māori urbanization took place much earlier than that of indigenous peoples in these countries, and considering the importance of the urban setting for Māori today, it is surprising that so few studies have been done on the subject, in particular in anthropology. A few works about Māori urban experiences were published in the 1960s and 1970s (Chapple 1975; Hopa 1977; Kawharu 1968, 1975; King 1975, 1978; Metge 1964; Schwimmer 1968; Walker 1970, 1972, 1975, 1979; Winiata 1967), but they have been the only substantial studies on the subject until recent articles and book sections that deal with specific aspects of Māori urban life by Barcham (1998); Borell (2005); Durie (1998); George (2012); Harris (2004b, 2007–8); Hill (2009);

Maaka (1994); Maaka and Fleras (2005); Rangiheuea (2010); Rosenblatt (2002, 2011); Sissons (2005); Tapsell (2002); Van Meijl (2006c); and Webster (1998); as well as unpublished PhD theses by George (2010); Harris (2007); Williams (2010); and Woods (2002); and a report by the James Henare Māori Research Centre (2002). Among these, to my knowledge, only George, Rosenblatt, Sissons, Tapsell, Van Meijl, Walker, and Webster are anthropologists.

And to my knowledge, only Harris (2004b, 2007, 2007–8); Metge (1964); Walker (1970, 1972, 1975, 1979); Williams (2010); and Woods (2002) have done serious qualitative research about the early urban migration and its causes; the expectations of the newcomers; the first arrangements in the city; the relationships of newcomers with "others" in the city, Māori and non-Māori; their participation in voluntary associations and community life; and their living arrangements (see Rata 2000 and Emery 2008 on the reverse migration and reconnection processes of today).[30] And only Metge and Walker did so from an anthropological perspective – Harris, Williams, and Woods are historians.

Additional recent works have studied urban experiences and organizations. But these are either personal accounts or stories (for example, Grace, Ramsden, and Dennis 2001; Ihimaera 1994, 1998) or they are more of a description of groups/organizations as such (for example, Phillips 1999; Sharp 2002; 2003; Rangiheuea 2010) and their structures, the services they offer, and the socioeconomic characteristics of the population/clientele they serve. While these works are of a great informational value, they lack, in the first case, an analytical synthesis and, in the second case, attention to the people themselves: their experiences, their actions, the reasons for their involvement in such groups or organizations, their expectations, and a description of the relationships among the persons and groups involved and the relationships among those groups or organizations and their neighbours, or the innovations and changes that they have brought about.

A great part of the scholarship also focuses on "traditional" Māori society and culture, including their social structures and belief system. When dealing with other aspects of contemporary life, studies are more quantitative and macrosociological in nature and deal with topics such as the impact of social policies on Māori, Māori health, Māori education and language, Māori art and literature, the Treaty of Waitangi and its implications, and environmental and land issues. In 1998, Webster, writing about researchers from the University of Auckland, thought that this situation was partly due to the particular interests and orientations of the chairs of the departments of anthropology and Māori studies. He also attributed it to the political situation in a period of Māori affirmation. I think this is still true today.

As I describe in this book, a rhetoric of Māori authenticity intensified at the end of the twentieth century with the juridification of Māori property, a process known as "retribalization," and various claims settlements, as well as in reaction to various additional state practices that often required Māori representatives and their presentations, propositions, and projects to be authentic. This situation invites – if not obliges – Māori leaders and negotiators to personify and fight for this essence. The general Māori resistance and struggle for more autonomy, with its strong focus on more traditional spheres of existence as well as on sociopolitical and economic conditions, explains in large part the emphasis on quantitative and macrosociological work. Universities and research more generally are part of the larger political context. This situation has also created zones of exclusion for researchers who do not fit the essentialist definition of a "real" Māori as well as for certain topics or subjects that do not fit what can be seen overall as Māori (Gagné 2008d; George 2012: 445–7). Either as researchers or as the subjects of research, this is the case for Māori who live in the city, who do not necessarily speak the Māori language or have deep connections with their tribe and deep knowledge of Māori traditions. In particular in 2001 and 2002, many participants in my research explicitly expressed their sadness, suffering, and anger at the processes of exclusion brought about by the rhetoric of Māori authenticity as well as by their desire for their experiences to be acknowledged and considered as much Māori as any other. This book responds to this request by exploring important Māori issues and experiences that have been neglected by social scientists in the past.

Māori living in Auckland constitute a varied population characterized by different tribal affiliations, social classes, levels of formal education, types of employment, and levels of participation in city life and in the broader society. Some of them are "leaders" in Māori movements for self-determination. Some are also well-known public figures defending particular political positions while others are not actively involved in political activities or in the public scene. The discourses and public activities of the leaders are well known. Edited volumes have grouped together the opinions of well-known Māori involved in politics (King 1975, 1978; Melbourne 1995; Ihimaera 1994, 1998), and books have also been written about prominent Māori individuals such as Te

Kooti (Binney 1995), King Pootatau (Jones 1959), Te Puea (King 1977), Eruera Stirling (Salmond and Stirling 1980), Amiria Stirling (Salmond and Stirling 1976), Apirana Ngata (Walker 2001), and Ranginui Walker (Spoonley 2009), to name only a few. But very little has been done on what ordinary Māori think and feel, and how they see their worlds and foresee their future.

So the scholarship about Māori in the urban setting, particularly in recent years, is in sharp contrast to a long anthropological tradition in which the focus is on ordinary people, families, communities, and "kitchen-table stories" (Schachter and Funk 2012). The present study, with its focus on everyday life, comes within the scope of this tradition and is an attempt to understand how ordinary Māori live their engagement, express their Māori identity, and see their autonomy in the urban milieu. By revealing how the Māori extended family and city houses are central sites in negotiating relationships with the larger society and engagement in multiple universes of meanings, this study shows the paths followed to create Māori places in the city and to build spaces and comfort for Māori in the various sectors of the larger society.

This book is based on almost two years of fieldwork and more than 250 hours of formal semi-structured interviews. I was in New Zealand from February 2001 to the end of June 2002, from January to April 2005, in December 2008, and again from January to March 2011. The methods I used in my research combined long-term participant observation, unstructured and semi-structured interviews, and informal conversations. While participant observation and informal conversation were always at the very centre of my research, interviews with a total of 108 persons served to deepen my understanding of specific themes and allowed me to collect viewpoints from a wider group of people who were not part of my everyday networks and who had wide-ranging characteristics and positions in Māori society.

I made particular efforts to follow chains of connections starting in varied places and among various profiles of people. By including participants from multiple social settings, I became aware of Māori diversity in Auckland and in Māori places and spaces in the city, escaping the potential disadvantage of the snowball technique – that is, being caught in a narrow social circle (Radice 2000: 21). I purposefully sought to include in my sample people from different tribes, different age groups, and both sexes. I interviewed people newly arrived in the city, people born in the city, and second-generation urban residents. I also sought to interview people from various socioeconomic milieus and differing backgrounds and work experiences. And the participants varied in their knowledge of the Māori language and traditions.

For this book, I selected a limited number of interviewees' voices, chosen on the basis of the complexity of relevant information and the way they could throw light on Māori engagement in various worlds. These voices were selected among the people I met in 2001 and 2002 (see appendix A for profiles of the participants interviewed), since this book focuses on the everyday Māori struggles in the years leading to the foreshore and seabed controversy. They are fairly representative or typical of widely shared Auckland Māori experiences of the time. I have not emphasized a tribal-based perspective since significant tribal distinctions did not stand out in the analysis. This does not mean, however, that tribes, tribal identity and responsibilities, and tribal politics are not important for Māori in Auckland or do not have an impact on Māori experiences of and in Auckland. They do – and several Māori talk about their tribes in this book. If tribal politics was not as important in 2001 and 2002 as it is now – in large part due to the treaty settlement process, to which I will return – Māori people's connections to their tribes and subtribes still carried weight for the participants in my research. In analysing the data for this book, however, tribal differences were not significant in the way Māori experience the city and in their everyday life there. And my methodology, centred on the diversity of urban-based Māori experiences of and in the city, was not intended as an in-depth exploration of tribal-based perspectives (for that, I would have had to focus on tribes and tribal identities from the very start, and choose people according to their tribal connections and participation in tribal life). If I had selected participants from a limited number of tribes, I could have brought out tribal-based perspectives and discussed the relevance of tribes in Māori urban experiences. I could also have sought out, for example, tribal elders' responses to their descendants' experiences and innovations in the city, comparisons between urban and rural/village family life and living arrangements, or a better understanding of the relationships to urban Māori authorities (and urban-based Māori more generally) and the tribes, by basing a significant part of the research in tribal areas. But this would have been another research project altogether. These points, though beyond the scope of this book, are nevertheless relevant and should be further investigated.

I first met people at university where I was enrolled in Māori language courses. Gradually I became quite involved in the life of the university *marae*: *kapa haka* (Māori performing arts) practices, study retreats, graduation ceremonies, morning or afternoon tea, and other activities. As the months passed, I also established a good relationship with a tribal *marae* and its people in the east part of the city, and I participated from time to time in their activities. By the end of my stay, I was also attending another *marae* in West Auckland a few times a week. I occasionally visited other *marae* in the city and in the country for various reasons, like gatherings and meetings, twenty-first birthday or wedding celebrations, visits to family or friends, and funerals. Moreover, I tried to discover the Māori world in the city: in art galleries, markets, conferences, festivals, talks, and in meetings of all kinds. I made a point of going to places Māori talked about, while immersing myself in the general city life and listening attentively for Auckland and Māori stories and news.

I also travelled out of Auckland and visited villages, towns, and sites all around the country that people had mentioned to me. I was always on the move, accompanying people, visiting their families with them, and participating in their activities everywhere they took me. In this, I was inspired by Hastrup (1995), De Certeau (1980), and Rapport (1997), who all plead in favour of an important change in the process of anthropology: a passage from a semantic and fixed vision to a pragmatic vision inspired by people in movement and by itineraries that cross spaces and networks, rather than by maps with fixed coordinates.

During my time in New Zealand, I first lived on my own in a flat near the city centre. Then, at the invitation of a Māori mature student from the university, I moved in with her family in South Auckland and stayed there for many months before moving on to another Māori household, with no connections to the first one, in West Auckland, to get a better feeling of the city and of Māori circles in different areas. Chapters 5 and 6 of this book are mainly about the way of life that I experienced there. In my following stays in 2005, 2008, and 2011, I had the great pleasure of being welcomed again by the same people.

Like all anthropological encounters, my view is necessarily partial, due to both my own positionings and the people I happened to meet. However, I think my view is representative of certain widely shared Māori worlds and experiences. As Abu-Lughod (1999 [1986]: xvii) wrote so well in her book *Veiled Sentiments*, nothing is worse than "my own frustration at the way I had not been able to convey as richly as I would have liked the quality of 'life as lived.'"

In the first chapter, I present an overview of Māori and New Zealand history, which briefly outlines the colonization process but mainly focuses on the period of urbanization, from World War II to the present day. This overview highlights the role of the state in the current Māori situation and the ways in which Māori have reacted to it and struggled from early colonization to the present day.

In chapter 2, I introduce readers to the diversity of Māori in Auckland, to life in the city for Māori, and to how the city is experienced in general and in Auckland in particular. I also begin my examination of places and spaces that are significant for Māori comfort, affirmation, and resistance. I therefore consider the rhetoric about "real" versus "urban Māori" and the notion of "comfort" as used by Māori to speak of their relationships to others, Māori or not, and their relationships to places, including urban ones.

Chapter 3 looks at another significant place for Māori affirmation, the *marae*, the traditional Māori meeting place and ceremonial centre. I first define what a *marae* is and then look at their first appearances in cities where they constitute today an important symbol of identity and continuity with the ancestral past.

The focus in chapter 4 is on everyday life in the *whānau* (extended family) with whom I lived for a great part of my fieldwork. I then discuss their house and other city houses that function like theirs as another significant place for Māori survival and (re)affirmation in the urban setting.

In chapter 5, I examine the different definitions of the *whānau* as well as its major principles or values, which serve as the guiding principles for an important Māori universe of meaning or realm of interpretation. The chapter gives an account of the historical evolution of the *whānau* through colonization and urbanization. I explore the continued significance of the *whānau* in the city, but also its importance as a link between rural and urban milieus, and thus between places and spaces. I also discuss the journeys that some Māori undertake to renew links with their *whānau* network and universes of meanings.

Chapter 6 constitutes a case study of a *whānau* dilemma that helps to illustrate how the guiding principles of the universe of meanings of the *whānau* emerge and unfold in practice as the dilemma is resolved. In this chapter, I also look at the coexistence and interrelation between universes of meanings and at the negotiation and heteroglossia that multiple engagements involve in practice.

Chapter 7 shows the extension of the principles of the *whānau* to non-kin families, the *kaupapa whānau*. It also explores the politics of differentiation at play among Māori and between Māori and non-Māori, and in which the *whānau* plays a very important role. I look at the dichotomy between the worlds of Māori and Pākehā (New Zealanders of predominantly European ancestry) that emerges from Māori narratives in this politics of differentiation. I then explore why the boundaries between these worlds are presented as so clear-cut when in practice they seem rather porous and flexible.

Finally, I specifically focus on how some places and spaces – like specific types of houses where traditional Māori principles and values are applied, *marae,* and the universe of meanings of the *whānau* – are central to survival and comfort and to Māori mobilization and engagement in the larger world. I also look back on how the anthropology of everyday life and experience and the anthropology of "ordinary" people allow for a better understanding of the struggle for Māori affirmation of particular identities and "traditional" universes of meanings, resistance to the larger society, and participation in today's world on their own terms. And I examine how participation in the greater society is achieved through supporting Māori identities, cultural practices, and universes of meanings. This reveals a particular Māori type of engagement in the larger society, which also gives a particular colour to autonomist, self-determining, and decolonizing processes, mechanisms, and visions.

1 An Overview of Māori and New Zealand History

This brief historical overview is designed to give a better understanding of Māori experiences and practices in the city today. It touches on the colonial era but its main focus is on the period following the "urban drift" from the postwar years until the present day. It highlights the relationship of the New Zealand state to Māori throughout history and the state's impact on Māori search for greater autonomy. It is widely accepted that the state and its policies have a direct effect on populations, on social dynamics in society at large, and in urban contexts in particular. Global dynamics and the market forces of capitalism also shape the Māori situation (see, for instance, Bargh 2007a; Rata 2000, 2011a, 2011b; Stewart-Harawira 2005; see Friedman 1994, 2003a on indigenous peoples more generally).

New Zealand is a country of just over 4.1 million inhabitants (2006 Census), located in the Pacific, southeast of Australia. It was colonized by Great Britain during the nineteenth century. Māori originally came from Polynesia, but they had been in Aotearoa for about 1,000 years at the arrival of the British (Anderson 1989; Davidson 1984; Belich 1996).

Bouchard (2008) describes New Zealand as being the most recent and the newest of the nation states created by European settlers. It is the most recent because it is where colonization began most recently – that is, not until after 1830, when British colonization became more intense. It is also the newest because, until quite recently, it embodied the model of the motherland. New Zealand only acquired a distinct character in the last half of the twentieth century – principally through literary and artistic expression.

The colonial situation began to change in New Zealand, as well as elsewhere in British colonies, following World War II (see, among others, King 1988, 2007; Sinclair 1975).[1] New Zealand was by then completely independent by virtue of the Statute of Westminster of 1931, even if this independent status was only recognized by the New Zealand state itself almost two decades later, in 1947, through the Statute of Westminster Adoption Act (Harris 2010: 92). But the process of rupture and distancing from Great Britain was very slow. Even though Great Britain withdrew from New Zealand after the war, Belich (2001: 425) situates this process in the period from 1965 to 1988 and, more narrowly, from 1973 to 1985, 1973 being the year Britain joined the European Economic Community (EEC) (see also Spoonley 2009). For New Zealand, Britain's EEC membership posed a significant economic challenge and led to a push to diversify its economy. Indeed, "founding EEC nations had agreed on a 'common agricultural policy,' which effectively excluded outside producers from the European market" (Nixon and Yeabsley 2010) and thus made it difficult for New Zealand to export agricultural produce to Britain. Britain managed, however, to secure a special arrangement for New Zealand (through the Luxembourg agreement), which limited the impact on New Zealand's economy and gave it time to diversify its market: "In 1970 Britain took more than 90% of New Zealand's butter exports and 75% of cheese exports. The Luxembourg agreement reduced the butter quota by roughly 17% and the cheese quota by roughly 68% over 5 years. Quantities were reduced further after 1977, to about half the 1973 levels. New Zealand continued to have butter quotas in the 1980s and 1990s – although at much reduced levels" (Nixon and Yeabsley 2010; see also Belich 2009).

Throughout these years, many elements also began to threaten the traditional representation of New Zealand society. Māori became more militant as well as more active in the practice of democracy, affirming their presence. Immigration increased and diversified with more intense links with Asia (for example, Smits 2010). This followed New Zealand's withdrawal from ANZUS (an agreement of military protection among Australia, New Zealand, and the United States) in 1984 because of its anti-nuclear convictions and its involvement in SEATO (the South-East Asia Treaty Organisation) (Bouchard 2008).

While the development of a national identity was always associated with imperial fidelity,[2] New Zealand altered its relationship with Great Britain in the 1960s and 1970s. However, to show the continuing symbolic importance of Great Britain, there is still a governor-general (or viceroy) in New Zealand and "God Save the Queen" has survived in parallel with the New Zealand national anthem "God Defend New Zealand." Today, there are also Māori words to the anthem, but the two songs are not translations of each other. The Union Jack is also still on the national flag. New Zealand, then, is situated within the framework of "continuism" (Bouchard 2008) – Belich (2009: 464) speaks of a "staunch New Zealand Britonism" – clearly differing from the United States, which developed from a stark rupture with Great Britain. Until 1986, "[the] United Kingdom parliament . . . retained the capacity to legislate for New Zealand" (Harris 2010: 92). According to Bouchard (2008), other countries of the Commonwealth, such as Canada and Australia, fall somewhere between the two in their relationship with the motherland (see also Sinclair 1986 and Belich 2009).

The Constitution Act 1986 – legally simply "a tidying up exercise" (Harris 2010: 93) – "terminated the right of the United Kingdom parliament to legislate for New Zealand" (93). In recent years, New Zealand also has reoriented its international relationships and network and now is developing more ties in the Asia-Pacific region.[3] Another important step toward still greater independence from Great Britain was the 2003 Supreme Court Act, which abolished the right to appeal to the Privy Council of London and created the Supreme Court of New Zealand, which is now the country's final appellate court (93). Up to now, however, New Zealand, unlike most countries (with the notable exceptions of the United Kingdom and Israel, Harris 2010: 95), does not have a "comprehensive codified written constitution which constitutes and gives authority to the organs of government" (91), even though the country does have a constitution founded on an "eclectic collection of United Kingdom and New Zealand statutes and the common law developed by the courts. Constitutional conventions also play an important role in the operation of the constitution" (91).

New Zealand was pressured to adjust its historiography and identity paradigm during the period of the forced rupture with Great Britain in the 1960s and 1970s. The mere presence of Māori and Māori artistic and literary expression was part of this new national character (Bouchard 2008; Allen 2002). Māori artistic and literary expression has been put forward as a distinct characteristic of Aotearoa/New Zealand and, since the 1970s and 1980s, biculturalism has been highly valued.[4]

The colonization period in New Zealand is generally defined as between 1769 and 1975.[5] Early contact occurred as part of a race among several European countries and the United States to colonize the Pacific and, according to Belich (1996: 121), the idea "[that] Britain monopolised early New Zealand contact with Europe is clearly a myth." From 1769, in comparison with the preceding 127 years of occasional contacts, expeditions came "thick and fast" (Belich 1996: 121). James Cook, who more thoroughly and carefully investigated New Zealand, played a significant part in the myth of the British monopoly on New Zealand and Britain's later control of its colonization. Cook visited New Zealand five times on three voyages: 1769–70, 1773–4, and 1777 (Belich 1996: 121; on Cook's voyages in the South seas, see also Salmond 2003). Many other British – as well as French, Spanish, Russian, American, and Austrian – expeditions followed.[6]

As a result, New Zealand was first conceived of as an economic annex to Great Britain in the Pacific. It was also seen as a solution to the problem of overpopulation in the mother country. In contrast to Australia, New Zealand was never a destination of exile for convicts, except for a small number who escaped from Australia. According to Bouchard (2008), the people who immigrated to New Zealand were part of the elite of the British working class and petite bourgeoisie.[7] The goal, at least in the formal myths of settlement, was to reproduce Britishness at its best or better. New Zealand was to be the Britain of the South, Better Britain, Greater Britain (Belich 1996). The New Zealand settler population was, thus, very homogenous for a long period of time.

In 1920, the Immigration Restriction Amendment Act was adopted and had important repercussions throughout the first half of the twentieth century, even as late as the 1970s and 1980s. Anti-Chinese feeling was common and linked to the so-called "Yellow Peril" of the gold rush period (1850–60) and has persisted for a long time (Bouchard 2008; Fleras and Spoonley 1999; Murphy 2003, 2009; Pearson 2009). Neighbouring Australia was, at the time, also seen as a threat because of a marked anti-British tendency among some of its settlers, and also because "Australians were too Irish, too convict and too digger" (Belich 1996: 317). Thus, until the mid-twentieth century, New Zealand tried to preserve its homogeneity and cohesion through discrimination and exclusion, sometimes violent, principally against Māori, but also against Asians and other foreigners. More generally, according to Belich (2009: 466) who quotes Price (1974), "[f]rom the 1880s to the 1960s, the British Dominions set up and maintained 'great white walls.'"

In October 1835, a Declaration of Independence was signed by thirty-four Māori chiefs, aimed at establishing a national Māori body representative of all tribes (for example, Belich 1996; Cox 1993; Durie 2001b;

Hill 1986). Even though it is not clear whether the declaration was mainly the product of an initiative of the British Resident James Busby or of the ongoing efforts of a number of Māori chiefs, "[not] only did it proclaim New Zealand's independence and assert Maori title to the soil, it prescribed a Maori parliament able to frame laws for the promotion of peace, justice and trade" (Durie 2001b: 464). This was short lived, however, and Britain's proclamation of sovereignty over New Zealand in 1840 put an end to any ambitions for a Māori legislature.

In 1840, the British Crown and Māori chiefs signed the Treaty of Waitangi. Many chiefs signed the Māori version of the treaty, but the meaning was significantly different from the original English version.[8] In the English version, Māori sovereignty was given up to the Crown (Belgrave, Kawharu, and Williams 2005; Durie 1998; Kawharu 1989b; Walker 1996), which was not the general meaning of the Māori version in which only the *kawanatanga* (governance) was lost. This ambiguity is at the very heart of controversies around the treaty. Some explain the difference between the versions as a deliberate strategy of the colonizers. They say that if Māori chiefs were to have read a version that made it clear they were signing a treaty that meant giving up their sovereignty, and in effect, their *mana* (spiritual power, authority, prestige, status), they would not have signed it (Awatere 1984; Durie 1998; Mulgan 1989; Orange 2011; Walker 1996).

Questions about interpretation of the Treaty of Waitangi persist today and lead to differing expectations from various parties (Levine and Henare 1994; Kawharu 1990; Williams 1997; Belgrave, Kawharu, and Williams 2005; Mutu 2010). Despite the highly questionable translation signed by the chiefs, the treaty was considered sufficient to give the Crown the necessary authority to make and administer laws and to establish a constitutional government in New Zealand. The Treaty of Waitangi was violated not long after its signature and Māori social and political marginalization began. In 1877, a judgment of the Supreme Court of New Zealand[9] made the treaty a "simple nullity."[10] In spite of the multiple negations of the Treaty of Waitangi, the New Zealand state has used the treaty as a symbolic expression when seeking to increase nationalist feeling (Durie 1998; Douglas 1991). Among other events, in 1940, the centennial of the treaty was marked by the opening of a carved meeting house at Waitangi (see Walker 2001 for details). In 1960, February 6, the day the treaty was signed,[11] was declared National Day. That day is known as Waitangi Day and in 1973 the New Zealand Day Act declared it a public holiday. For years now, government officials as well as Māori leaders pay a visit on Waitangi Day to Waitangi for celebrations. It is now regarded as a "tradition" that the visit begins with a *powhiri* (welcome ceremony) at Te Tii *marae*, a *marae* belonging to the local people in the area, outside the Waitangi Treaty grounds.[12] A range of family activities are also offered to New Zealanders of all backgrounds. However, before the Treaty of Waitangi Act 1975, the treaty had no legal validity. Only the English version of the Treaty of Waitangi was officially recognized in 1975 in an annex to the Treaty of Waitangi Act, while the Māori version was not recognized until 1985 when the annex was revised.

During the nineteenth century, Māori lands were either bought at low cost by settlers[13] or were confiscated under armed threat by the army when necessary.[14] As underlined by Boast and Hill (2009b: 6), "[a]s practised in Ireland and on the imperial frontiers, 'confiscation' was . . . linked with settlement, especially military settlement. It is no accident that the main statute relating to confiscation in New Zealand was the New Zealand Settlements Act 1863." The creation of the Native Land Court in 1865 and the Native Land Act 1872 further undermined the collective social organization of Māori by individualizing land titles and by accelerating the alienation of tribal homelands (Sullivan 2001; Belich 1996; Ballara 1998; Boast 2008). "[By] 1911, Maori held only 7 million acres, a quarter of the North Island. By 1920, they held 5 million acres, most of it leased to Pakeha, and only a fifth usable for Maori agriculture" (Belich 1996: 259). Here, however, Belich warns against "the picture of naive Maori victims succumbing to legal chicanery and the blandishments of cunning Pakeha land buyers and storekeepers" (259). Rivalry for *mana* (spiritual power, authority, prestige, status) among Māori was a good reason for selling, with the Land Court as an arena for expression of this rivalry.

During the land invasion, however, the British were faced with opposition and had to deal with a strong Māori resistance. From 1845 to 1872, there were several important armed uprisings against the British invasion – the New Zealand Wars.[15] "They were not, as is sometimes suggested, storms in a teacup or gentlemanly bouts of fisticuffs but bitter and bloody struggles, as important to New Zealand as were the Civil Wars to England and the United States" (Belich 1988 [1986]: 15). The wars drained colonial resources so much that they posed "a serious threat to European dominance" (Belich 1996: 253). At the end of the 1860s, some spoke openly of the likelihood of a Māori victory (256). Māori were brilliant raiders. Belich (1996: 297) also compares the trench and bunker system of the modern Māori *pā* (fortified place)[16] to those of the American Civil War, the Russo-Turkish War of 1877–8, the Second South African War, the Russo-Japanese War of 1904–5, and, importantly, to those of the Western Front in 1914–18. Māori have also been successful in maintaining multiple fronts and in surprising the enemy. The colonial forces won in the end because of their overwhelming numbers.

> Finally, while sustained by a tribal socio-economy, the modern *pa* system's capacity to thwart superior forces was not infinite. Using it, the Maoris could block continuous offensives by twice their own numbers, or sporadic offensives by six times their strength. But they could not block the continuous offensive of an army six times as great as their own. (Belich 1996: 298)

Māori opposition went together with an increasing fervour for greater autonomy. Among other initiatives, from the 1870s onward, Māori leaders turned to tribal and inter-tribal assemblies. The meetings helped to clarify the plight of Māori. If the treaty as such was not seen as at fault, it was decided that the New Zealand government was responsible due to its infractions to the treaty (see Walker 2004: 160). In the years following the meetings, a deputation of northern chiefs (1882) and King Tawhiao's deputation (1884)[17] travelled to England to request the Queen inquire into their grievances. In 1894, Māori were unsuccessful in attempting to have a Native rights bill discussed at the House of Representatives on the basis of the Declaration of Independence of 1835, the Treaty of Waitangi, and the New Zealand Constitution Act 1852 (Walker 2004: 168).

In 1892, Tawhiao, the second Māori King, established his own Convention for Chiefs, the Kauhanganui (Belich 1996; King 2003). The convention was intended to unite all Māori chiefs but was adopted mainly by those close to the Kingitanga movement. The convention apparently did not have a pan-Māori appeal (Durie 2001b: 465). It was a form of government that drew on Westminster principles, having a written constitution and making provision for a judiciary system. The convention was created in reaction to the proposal for a Legislative Council of Chiefs, which was rejected by the minister of Native affairs of the time.

In 1892, at an assembly at Waitangi that gathered together many unrelated tribes, the unity movement Te Kotahitanga o Te Tiriti o Waitangi was officially established (Hill 2004; see also Cox 1993 for a detailed account of the Kotahitanga movement). The movement was to be headed by a parliament, *Paremata Māori*, which sought Crown recognition. Belich (1996: 267) notes that the Kotahitanga movement was mainly supported by *kupapa* groups; that is, by pro-government Māori who reminded the government that but for their help, its authority over New Zealand would have ceased long ago. The government responded with the Māori Council Act 1900, which allowed state-supported Māori leaders to administer some Māori affairs at a local level (Durie 2001b). Durie writes that "[by] the beginning of the twentieth century, both tribal authority and Maori nationalism had been silenced, leaving few obstacles to an assimilated future; indeed with the total Maori population reduced by then to some 43,000" (466).

Note that in 1859, the Crown ruled that Māori communal land tenure disqualified them from the right to vote (Sorrenson 1986, appendix B-17 in Sullivan 2001: 479; Sullivan 2010). The measure prevented them from voting until 1867 when Parliament agreed to create four electoral districts for Māori and thus four Māori seats in Parliament: property qualifications for voting in these electorates were abolished.[18] According to Sullivan (2010: 254),

[t]the seats were a way of appeasing demands for political representation by tribes who had both supported and resisted the colonists during the Taranaki and Waikato Land Wars of the 1860s, and they could be seen as a means of undermining tribal authority and chiefly resistance to government. It was thought Māori representation could reduce Māori resistance to land sales: to land alienation.[19]

The Maori Representation Act 1867 provided for all Māori men (over the age of twenty-one years and excluding those with a criminal record) the right to vote (Sullivan 2010: 254), which granted them universal suffrage before European men.[20] The right was extended to all women, including Māori women in 1893 (Rei 1993).[21] The provision for Māori seats was first temporary, but "[in] 1876 the Act was extended indefinitely as European members began to fear that abolishing the seats would result in a flood of Māori voters onto the European rolls, thereby jeopardising the chances of European members in those seats" (Wilson 2010: 50). Despite this, the secret ballot was not considered desirable for Māori until the 1938 election and Māori voted on a different day than the European population until 1951.[22]

Note also that the Māori language as a language of instruction was banned in 1867 through the Native School Act (Sullivan 2001; see also Belich 2001; Simon 1998a, 1998b; Simon and Smith 2001). By the 1920s, the land remaining under Māori control was insufficient to provide an economic base. In 1933, this condition, together with the Depression, resulted in three-quarters of the adult Māori male population being unemployed. Once again, relief payments discriminated between Māori and non-Māori: Māori were paid at a lower rate and many non-payments were justified by the argument that unemployment was a normal situation for Māori (Sullivan 2001).

Many analysts insist that colonization had an extra impact on Māori women, who were and still are doubly marginalized and oppressed (for example, see Awatere 1984; Greenland 1991; Johnson and Pihama 1993; Pihama 1998; Salmond 1991b; Smith 1999). Furthermore Smith (1999: 46) emphasizes the idea that "[r]angatiratanga has generally been interpreted in English as meaning chieftainship and sovereignty which in colonialism was a 'male thing,'" whereas traditional Māori society has always recognized male and female chiefs and was ambilineal.

A number of Māori religious movements and prophets appeared at the end of the nineteenth and beginning of the twentieth century (see Elsmore 1999 [1989]; Belich 1996; Binney 1995; Walker 2001, 2004). Among these were the Pai Marire religion, also known as Hauhau, and many religious movements including the movement of Te Whiti and Tohu of Parihaka, the movements of Titokowaru and Te Kooti, the Tariao and Pao Miere movement, and the Te Maiharoa's movement. They each had a different approach to the problems facing the Māori. In the Depression years, for example, the leader of the Ratana Church, Tahupotiki Wiremu Ratana, made an alliance with the Labour Party to improve the extent and quality of welfare payments to Māori (Walker 2004: 184). In 1935, the Labour government finally equalized Māori and non-Māori unemployment benefits. Improvements were also seen in the areas of Māori health, housing, and education. Māori old age and widows' pensions, however, remained lower (Sullivan 2001, based on Orange 1987 and Sorrenson 1986).

From the second half of the 1930s, urban labour requirements and population growth created a movement of Māori into the cities in search of employment. This great Māori urban migration is often called the "urban drift" even if it can be more accurately described as a "'mass' Māori urban migration" (Williams 2010: 1).

Maori urban migration is generally thought to have been triggered by World War Two. Young Maori were encouraged by the state and their own war-effort organisation . . . to fill urban jobs on the expectation that they would return to their rural homes once the war ended. But there are signs that the big take-off in urban migration did not occur until about 1950. Auckland's Maori population grew at an annual average of 18.7 per cent between the 1936 and 1945 censuses, probably with a heavy loading towards the second half of the period. But growth then dropped quite dramatically to 10.8 per cent between 1945 and 1951, before taking off again in the 1950s. It peaked in the early 1960s when, despite continued high birth rates and plummeting death rates the *rural* Maori population actually dropped 14 per cent. Net urban migration continued less strongly through the 1970s, before dropping back towards stability in the 1980s . . . The World War Two "false start" tends to confirm that it was falling death rates and the resulting population explosion that caused urbanisation – not the other way around . . . The "push" from the country stemmed largely from population growth, but also from changing aspirations among the young. (Belich 2001: 472; emphasis in original)

As underlined by Williams (2010) concerning the people of Panguru, Northland, the process of migration to the city has also to be understood within a family frame:

It was within the walls of their family homes that parents acted according to their expectations and hopes for the future which, by the 1950s and 1960s, revolved around maintaining the household economy and finding access to a secondary education, better health facilities and employment for their children. More often than not, the migration of one, some or all household members to Auckland was a means of meeting those expectations. (53)

Kin also eased the transition from the country to the city and provided resources for integration on Māori terms (Harris 2007–8). This is still true in the context of today, as I illustrate throughout this book. Thus, with urbanization and modernization, "Maori did not cease to 'be Maori.' They sought out fellow Maori in social and other circumstances, such as at playcentres, in church congregations and sports clubs, and outside school gates" (Hill 2009: 39; see also Walker 1975). As urbanization became an important reality for Māori in the postwar years, they also became involved in cultural clubs in the city, youth groups, and voluntary associations.

In the early 1950s, Māori-run institutions were strengthened or created to meet the needs of urban-based Māori, such as the Māori Women's Welfare League,[23] the volunteer Māori wardens,[24] and the urban committees. Indeed, the welfare committee system (composed of 300 tribal committees [Hill 2009: 12]), which was created during the Second World War, nationwide, as part of the Maori War Effort Organisation, expanded after the war into new urban committees. These committees became part of and came under the authority of the Department of Māori Affairs (Hill 2009: 13), even if they were successful at "carving out their own autonomistic spaces" (52). Unofficial committees also flourished, sometimes operating largely outside the control and support of the Department of Māori Affairs, but sometimes also using the official system for their own purposes (19).

By around 1960, Māori were a predominantly urban people (Belich 2001: 472). The policy of assimilation continued until the 1960s. At the beginning of the decade, this policy became one of integration (with, in retrospect, the same assimilative goals, see Hill 2009: 93–4) following the *Report on Department of Maori Affairs* that became known as the Hunn Report (1961) after its chairman, Jack Kent Hunn. The report made far-reaching recommendations on social reforms concerning Māori people. Harris (2007–8: 144) summarizes its main dimensions: "Hunn saw opportunities for integration everywhere . . . Schools were the 'nursery of integration'; housing a 'strong force for it'; employment a means of 'comingling the races in all ranks of society'; and the object of land title reform was to imitate European titles" (for more on the Hunn Report, including on Māori and non-Māori reactions to it, see Hill 2009).

Seeking to boost Māori organizations in cities and towns, the Maori Welfare Act 1962 finally replaced the tribal committees that fell under the Maori Social and Economic Advancement Act 1945 (Walker 1975: 148). "The base of the new welfare system, the Maori committee, was defined non-tribally, being 'elected by the Maori public of a given area to administer matters of Maori interest.' In rural areas, however, its boundaries generally reflected marae-based organisation . . . In 1963, there were 477 flaxroots committees and 84 executive committees" (Hill 2009: 113). "[T]hey sought 'to promote harmonious race relations,' assist in 'physical, economic, social, educational, moral and spiritual well-being,' and 'help the Maori enjoy the full rights, privileges and responsibilities of

New Zealand citizenship'" (Walker 1975: 168 in Hill 2009: 121; for ethnographic details on their everyday working see Walker 1975). Among
other initiatives, Māori committees could also "constitute themselves
as Maori Tribunal Committees (commonly called 'Maori courts' or tribunals) with power to adjudicate on low-level offences" (Hill 2009: 130;
see also Walker 1975 for an ethnography). While the Māori committees were designed as a tool for Māori full integration, Māori have also
taken them in new and informal directions even when they have faced
significant challenges (Hill 2009: 119).[25]

The Maori Affairs Amendment Act 1967 allowed for the sale of the remaining remnants of Māori lands on the pretext they were needed for
economic use. The Act denied cultural values as well as collective ownership (Sullivan 2001). From that time on, diversity was to be tolerated
as long as it did not interfere with the governing framework (Harris
2004b, 2007, 2007–8; Sullivan 2001).[26]

The 1970s finally saw the official recognition of the Treaty of Waitangi through the Treaty of Waitangi Act 1975, which also set up the
Waitangi Tribunal.[27] This was in reaction to increasing Māori direct opposition to continuing colonialism, as well as to other factors such as
the worldwide postwar decolonization movement. The year 1975 has
been described by Schwimmer (1999) as the beginning of the miracle
of decolonization and by Orange (2011: 230) as "initiating a new phase
in Crown-Māori relationships." The Treaty of Waitangi has since been
largely interpreted as the founding document of Aotearoa/New Zealand, which confirmed the existence of two nations (Pearson 1991; Durie
2001b) or two peoples[28] (Sharp 1995) and established their partnership.

At first, the power of the tribunal was limited to claims concerning
violations of the treaty arising after 1975. In 1985, the government extended the jurisdiction of the tribunal, through the Treaty of Waitangi
Amendment Act, to investigate claims referring back to 1840 (for details, see Orange 2011). The tribunal redirected attention to the Treaty of
Waitangi and biculturalism.[29]

The claims brought to the Waitangi Tribunal at first concerned specific tribes and issues, but its activity over the years would come to
involve larger areas and a wider array of claims, ranging from land
claims involving much of the South Island to claims involving fisheries, the Māori language as an official language, and the fair allocation of
radio frequencies, broadcasting assets, and management rights in radio
spectrum (Orange 2011: 236). This led to the important 1990s treaty settlements (Sullivan 2001; Orange 2011; Hayward and Wheen 2004).

However, the creation of the Waitangi Tribunal was seen at times by some as a tool mainly serving the interests of the state (Webster 1998; Melbourne 1995; Durie 1998; Kelsey 1991). For Kelsey (1991: 108), this judiciary initiative corresponded to "a shift from overt contempt to a much more subtle and pernicious form of subjugation, and the evolution of the Waitangi Tribunal as a panacea which helped stabilise, and later actively legitimise, the Pakeha state." This tendency was more visible with the imposition of the fiscal envelope in 1994, to which I will come back (Durie 1998; Kelsey 1996; Cheater and Hopa 1997; Sharp 1997; Sullivan 1997).[30]

The decade of the 1970s was also marked by a resurgence of Māori activism and is recalled notably for protests by the activist group Ngā Tamatoa,[31] the Land March of 1975, the occupation of Bastion Point (1978) (see Mita 1981 documentary) and Raglan Golf Course (1979), and the disruption of the Springbok Rugby Tour (1981) to draw "attention to Pākehā hypocrisy in fighting for justice overseas but ignoring apartheid-like inequities at home" (Fleras and Spoonley 1999: 45; see also Harris 2004a for a historical overview of Māori protest). Waitangi Day also provided a new occasion for Māori protest that became a good barometer of the relationships between Māori and the Crown at the national level (see Rosenblatt 2005; McAllister 2007; see also McAllister 2011 on a local commemoration of Waitangi Day for a complementary perspective). "Challenges had begun with urban Māori groups in the 1970s; strident protest dominated Waitangi Day ceremonies, particularly between 1979 and 1983" (Orange 2011: 232).

At the beginning of the 1970s, Māori also expressed grave concern about the future of their language. In 1972, thirty thousand people signed a petition that was sent to the New Zealand Parliament asking for the Māori language to be taught in schools. The Hunn Report of 1961 had already described the Māori language as a relic of a past life,[32] and a national survey conducted between 1973 and 1978 showed that only 18 to 20 per cent of Māori could speak their language fluently, mainly people over sixty-five years old. However, Māori were not ready to agree with Hunn and decided to mobilize and engage in political and cultural actions.

This period is often called the Māori cultural renaissance and is now widely recognized as such (among others, see Allen 2002; Belich 2001; Webster 1998; Walker 2004).[33] The mobilization of the time was in large part under the intellectual leadership of highly educated young urban revolutionaries.[34] With the support of many others, they were an important force in the pan-Māori reaction to impoverishment and marginalization (Rata 2000; Allen 2002).

This political engagement, which continued into the 1980s, led to, among other things, the birth of language revitalization movements and the creation of the *kohanga reo* (1981) and *kura kaupapa Māori* (1985). The *kohanga reo* or language nests for preschool children (kindergartens) based on Māori principles are popular initiatives in Māori language and culture (see, among others, Durie 1998; Smith 1999; Smith 1997; Smith and Smith 1996; Walker 1996; Webster 1998). The *kura kaupapa Māori* are the equivalent of those preschool classes, but at the primary and secondary school levels.[35] The *kohanga reo* were at first the initiative of parents, but the New Zealand state later accredited them.

These programs are based on *whānau* (extended family) principles. They pursue three principal objectives: "First, they aimed to provide a vehicle for the promotion of Maori language; second, they wished to stimulate whanau centers which offered quality child care within tikanga [tradition, custom] Maori; and third, they sought to maintain a totally Maori environment by using immersion modes of learning" (Durie 1998: 64). The Māori language is seen as an important symbol of the Māori cultural renaissance and is very important in the Māori search for self-determination.[36] In 1987, Māori was finally recognized as an official language of New Zealand, along with the English language and, since 2006, the New Zealand sign language.[37]

The political activism of the time also led to a series of initiatives including the Maori Education Development Conference (1984), the Maori Economic Development Conference (1985), and the museum exhibition *Te Māori*, which travelled in New Zealand and to the United States (Greenland 1991; McCarthy 2011; Pearson 1991; Poata-Smith 1996; Smith 1999; Sullivan 2001; Mead 1984).

Arts and literature were also vital symbols of the Māori renaissance and still have an important place (Allen 2002; Williams 1997; Schwimmer 2004a; Webster 1998). Many traditional arts such as *kapa haka* (performing arts), *waiata* (songs), *taiaha* (traditional weaponry), and carving are taught in the family or in *marae*, and schools. Significant books and documentaries also came out during the period of the Māori renaissance: among others Grace (1975, 1978, 1980, 1986); Ihimaera (1972, 1973, 1974, 1986, 1987); Hulme 1986 (1983); and Mita (1981). Many of these writers and filmmakers gained international recognition.

Again, this Māori political activism of the 1970s and 1980s should be seen as linked to a worldwide movement of decolonization and political activism following World War II. The rhetoric of "Brown Power," which represented the rejection of New Zealand racist colonial institutions and values, was important during these years and remains so today among certain groups and in critical moments. Māori were also inspired by liberation movements in both the so-called third world and fourth world (Greenland 1991). These included, as I already mentioned, the struggles by indigenous peoples to create international forums and to have a voice in international organizations. Māori were and still are, of course, concerned by the debates around issues of the right of indigenous peoples to be recognized. Charters (2007: 152) writes that "a globalised world that includes international institutions provides Māori with avenues to resist state domination that would not otherwise be available." She adds that "globalisation is not confined to the proliferation of neoliberal market policies. It also includes better opportunities for indigenous peoples to coordinate" (148).

Some Māori leaders have been involved in the transnational indigenous movement almost since its beginning (Allen 2002; Maaka and Fleras 2005, 2006; Sissons 2005; Smith 1999; Tsing 2007). Many links with other organizations were established thanks to George Manuel, who was the president of the National Indian Brotherhood of Canada from 1970 to 1976 and who travelled to New Zealand in 1971 as part of a delegation of the Canadian Department of Indian Affairs to take a closer look at the Māori's place in New Zealand society (McFarlane 1993). A large gathering of indigenous peoples was subsequently organized by the American Indian Movement in which Māori representatives participated. They later became involved in the International Indian Treaty Council created in 1974, the World Council of Indigenous Peoples created in 1975, and the indigenous missions and forums at the United Nations (UN) and on the world scene (Allen 2002; Tsing 2007).

The international arena has been very important for the Māori strategy. Māori leaders have always been very active at the UN, taking stands, for example, with representatives of the First Nations of Canada and the United States and the Aboriginals of Australia (Minde 1996; Allen 2002; Smith 1999). Minde (1996) writes that, with American Indian leaders, Māori leaders are among those principally fighting for indigenous self-determination and control over/guardianship of the land and sea (see also Charters 2007).[38] Land is at the very heart of Māori identity and Māori sense of continuity: "[for] Māori, the basis of right and their claim to justice is the concept of *tāngata whenua*, people of the land, which expresses their original occupation of the land and their distinctive relationship to it" (Turner 1999: 410). Or as Rika-Heke (1997: 174) expresses it, "We are the land."[39] It should be noted that in Māori worldviews, the sea and seabed are thought of as an extension of the land and not as a border delimiting the continental zone (see, for example, Schwimmer, Houle, and Breton 2000). Like the land, the sea is central to Māori economic survival and identity. This view is shared by Pacific Islanders and by many other indigenous peoples around the world (for example, Hau'ofa 1994; Scott and Mulrennan 1999; Mulrennan and Scott 2000). The land is also the symbol of Māori alienation, colonization, and political subjection (Walker 1992, 2004; Greenland 1991). This is the reason why, since the year 2003, the foreshore and seabed have explicitly become a key issue in the Māori struggle for greater autonomy, as well as an important symbol of Māori affirmation. Again, Prime Minister Clark's reassertion of Crown ownership of the foreshore and seabed, reversing the Court of Appeal's ruling that tribes could assert customary rights through the Land Court (Collins 2003) was interpreted by many Māori as the worst land confiscation since the beginning of British colonization.

In the 1980s, various Māori political movements in New Zealand also focused on the rediscovery and revitalization of Māori culture (Van Meijl 1994, 1997). In response, the government rethought its Māori policy and administration along devolutionary lines (Barcham 1998; Durie 1998; Fleras 1989; Fleras and Spoonley 1999; Schwimmer 1995; Van Meijl 1997). "These devolutionary commitments dovetailed with the government's structural adjustment program, most notably in the restructuring of New Zealand's public sector along the market-driven lines of privatisation, deregulation, and corporatisation" (Fleras and Spoonley 1999: 123).

In the 1980s, New Zealand was seen as a laboratory for neoliberalism, given the state's economic objectives of reducing bureaucratic management and government protectionism in the aftermath of the oil shock of the mid-1970s (Belich 2001; Laliberté 2000; Sullivan 2001). According to Schwimmer (1995), the devolution system was also instituted following the state's realization that its systematic integration/assimilation policy of Māori, pursued since 1845, had been a great failure.

Barcham (1998) speaks of this period in terms of "re-*iwi*-isation," since *iwi* (tribes) became, under the new government policy, responsible for the local management of services such as the distribution of social benefits and numerous other services that were previously assumed by the state.[40] According to Sullivan (2001: 482), re-*iwi*-ization or retribalization "provided Maori with an opportunity to limit state paternalism, partly through a functional transfer of power from government to the tribes (devolution) and partly by limited self-determination." By the end of the 1980s, the Treaty of Waitangi had outlined a direction for a restructuring of the relationships between tribes and the government according to bicultural principles.

In 1984, at the Hui Taumata, a government-sponsored economic summit, Māori leaders advocated tribal control and delivery of services. Two programs were implemented with the aim of giving some control over delivery of services to Māori to individual tribes: the MANA Enterprise Scheme, designed to fund entrepreneurial development and, thus, Māori employment opportunities; the MACCESS Scheme developed to provide Māori Trust Boards with the means to set up and deliver skills-training programs to the unemployed (Sullivan 2001).

Some of the reforms made by the Labour government from 1984 to 1990 seemed to answer Māori claims for self-determination and self-management. In 1990, the Labour government passed the Runanga Iwi Act, which "provided the necessary legal authority for tribal entities to enter into formal contractual arrangements with the state" (Sullivan 2001: 483) or the private sector (Fleras and Spoonley 1999: 124). However, it was pointed out that, in practice, there was a wide gap between theoretical and real devolution. The tribes did not have enough competent people to respond to their diverse clientele. They did not have enough money and they did not receive the support promised during the transition. Furthermore, because the guidelines of the transition itself were not clear, Māori and government expectations differed (Fleras 1991; Maaka 1994). In effect, the tribal devolution "consisted of 'decentralising' delivery structures to the community level without leading to any fundamental change in the prevailing distribution of power in society" (Fleras 1991: 186). It left the Crown in control of tribal development (Carter 2003b: 127).

Dissension over the Runanga Iwi Act 1990 arose for several reasons, such as the imposition of non-Māori ideas about how Māori should organize themselves: this was done, for example, through the recognition of *iwi* as holders of *rangatiratanga* (governance), which raises issues of representativity, and with the eligibility criteria defining the tribes as legal corporate entities and legitimate inheritors of traditional resources and knowledge (for an extensive synthesis, see Carter 2003b). The *rūnanga* (council) authorities, composed of elected leaders – rather than traditional leaders chosen according to *whakapapa* (genealogy)

– would then be recognized by the government as the only authoritative voice of *iwi* (Carter 2003b: 126). Māori organizations then had to deal with issues of representativity. On several occasions since the nineteenth century, the Crown has attempted to co-opt the mechanisms of tribal self-government for its own ends. *Rūnanga*, which were originally based on inclusive tribal assemblies, but have been continually refashioned by Māori in response to challenges posed by the European influence and control, were targeted as the institution allowing for the implementation of "a far more ambitious scheme of indirect rule" (O'Malley 2009: 78–9) by Governor George Grey in the 1860s.[41] In the context of a planned individualization of Native titles, Grey outlined a comprehensive scheme of "village and district runanga, to be overseen by Resident Magistrates and Civil Commissioners . . . suggest[ing] that the district runanga should be empowered to decide 'the adjustment of disputed land boundaries, of tribes, of hapus [subtribes], or of individuals, and for deciding who may be the true owners of any Native lands'" (O'Malley 1998: 22). If the initiative was largely unsuccessful,

> Grey's rūnanga plan had set the ball rolling for finding ways for government to manage Māori, and the rūnanga plan was the beginning of the institutionalisation of Māori groups. It introduced the ideas [*sic*] of elected representation – trusteeship – the idea of shared territories and the consolidation of groups living within them into one central iwi or rūnanga body. It established through these ideas the membership criteria, and how each member could receive benefits from the central governing body. All these ideas re-emerged in the government policies that resulted in the Tribal Trust Boards. Ultimately the Runanga Iwi Bill was to continue the Māori management process instigated by Grey. (Carter 2003b: 134)[42]

The proliferation of "legal-bureaucratic" (Carter 2003b) tribal organizations competing with one another for limited resources can be seen as a direct result of the devolution and mainstreaming policies of the 1990s (Sullivan 2001; Rata 2000; Barcham 1998). The government's continual reference to the tribes has contributed to giving them a fixed form, which ignores the flexibility and changing nature of the "traditional" tribes (Maaka 1994; Schwimmer 1990). The new entity has also had lasting effects on the ways Māori relate to each other and to the natural and spiritual worlds, through the different layers of relatedness and cooperation – the *waka* (canoe),[43] the *iwi* (tribe), the *hapū* (subtribe), and the *whānau* (extended family) – by limiting the choice of participation in some of these layers (Carter 2003b). The static and rigid form the government attributes to the tribes also ignores new urban organizations. As I will show, since 1995, urban-based Māori have challenged legal-bureaucratic tribal entities through the courts, up to the Privy Council in London, in order to have their organizations recognized as "tribes." As Sissons (2005: 54) notes "the hegemonic force of *iwi* ideology is now so strong that urban groups have been forced to claim that they, too, are types of *iwi*."

However, many Māori tribal leaders supported the government, because they welcomed the opportunity to reinforce their tribal authority and to extend it to tribal members now living in the city (Van Meijl 1997; Carter 2003b). This authority was not always consciously pursued but "retribalization," combined with the creation of Māori tribal capitalist enterprises, has had the effect of generating new class structures within the tribes (Rata 2000). Moreover, it appears that the government supported some specific Māori leaders with the precise goal of achieving its agenda (Cheater and Hopa 1997).

The National Party government, elected in 1990, rapidly did away with the Labour government's devolution formula and "put in place new processes to limit tribal control, initiative, and autonomy over service delivery" (Sullivan 2001: 483). This period is considered the period of the mainstreaming of Māori affairs. Devolution was replaced by "contracting," which was seen as a delegation of limited power rather than of real control, as it implied considerable supervision from the government. Under this arrangement, the state contracted service delivery programs in health, education, and training to organizations such as the Māori Women's Welfare League, Māori Trust Boards, the New Zealand Māori Council, and some urban Māori organizations and authorities such as Te Whānau o Waipareira in West Auckland and the Manukau Urban Māori Authority (MUMA) in South Auckland (Gover and Baird 2002; Sullivan 2001; Rangiheuea 2010). This sector is flourishing today and the number of urban Māori organizations and authorities who have contracted with the government has increased considerably.

By 1994, in various development initiatives, there had been an increasing call for another shift in emphasis, this time to smaller groupings like the *hapū* (subtribe) and *whānau* (extended family). In other words, there was a move away from *iwitanga*, the way of the tribe, a vertical structural ethic, toward *whanaungatanga*, the way of the extended family, a horizontal kinship principle (Durie 2001a, who cites Puketapu 1994 and Dyall and Wauchop 1994). Both structural ethics seem to be at work today, either complementing or reinforcing each other in different areas. I will come back to this point. A major theme of this book is that of the *whānau* as a central site not only for economic development but also for the day to day affirmation of Māori identities and presence in the city and in society at large.

In the 1990s, the mode of representation of Māori in Parliament was also modified.[44] Since 1867, Māori have four seats in Parliament. In 1996, the number of these seats was readjusted to five, in accordance with the percentage of the population registered on the Māori electoral roll. This readjustment was made at the time of the transition to the new overall system of representation, a mixed-member proportional electoral system (MMP). The MMP is a two-vote system: one for the electorate, one for the party (see Sullivan 2003 and Miller 2001 for details). Under this system, nearly half of the 120 members of Parliament (MPs) are drawn from "party lists," the rest, both Māori and general seats, being voted into office by the electorate.

Some Māori also sit in general seats, which increases their representation in Parliament. An increase in the number of Māori MPs was also made possible under MMP by the introduction of the list seats; that is, the seats attributed according to the percentage of votes obtained by the party for the party vote. The percentage of Māori MPs is thus now much closer to the actual percentage of Māori in the New Zealand population. During the 1993 referendum, a large proportion of Māori favoured the MMP system, mainly because power-sharing was almost nonexistent in the previous system, based on "one person, one vote," since Māori are a minority in New Zealand (Levine and Henare 1994; Levine and Roberts 1997; Van Meijl 1998).

MMP has also introduced New Zealand to coalition governments. Changing the electoral system has radically changed the make-up of New Zealand governments. Previously, single parties (either National or Labour) controlled government, and party members, including Māori, were required to support their respective party's policies . . . For the Māori MPs, this was a position of potential conflict between their Māori constituency and their political party . . . Post-1996, governments have been determined by a coalition of the highest polling political party and a minor party. As a result, MMP governments have had to accommodate some of the demands of their junior partners.

The Māori seats at the 1996 and 1999 elections were pivotal in the formation of a government and the Māori members potentially had considerable influence. Both governments appointed more than one Māori to the executive – an unusual occurrence for New Zealand governments. (Sullivan 2003: 230)

In 1996, in the first election under MMP, five Māori seats were occupied by Māori MPs. With other Māori members of Parliament from different parties, a total of fifteen Māori MPs were elected. In 1999, the number of Māori seats was adjusted to six, for a total of fifteen Māori MPs. In 2002, the number of Māori seats was adjusted again to seven. "In 2003, Māori MPs held 15.8 per cent of the seats in Parliament, a figure comparable for the first time with their proportion of the population . . . The proportion increased slightly in the 2005 parliament that had twenty-one MPs who identified as Māori, while the number dropped to twenty MPs in the 2008 parliament" (Orange 2011: 259).[45]

In terms of local government councils, Māori have long been underrepresented, but legislative changes in 2001 and 2002 gave local authorities the means to improve Māori representation and allowed for Māori seats to be created at this level (Hayward 2010b; Sullivan 2011). However, as of 2011, the Bay of Plenty Regional Council is the only one to have guaranteed Māori representation (Sullivan 2011; see Hayward 2010b for how other options were applied in certain councils). Of particular interest to us is the most recent reform of local government that concerned Auckland. In 2009, the Commission on Auckland Governance – established by the New Zealand government because of concerns about the workability of the Auckland Super City Council[46] – recommended a provision of three Māori members on the council. Two of these would be elected by voters on the Māori Electoral Roll and one would be appointed by *mana whenua* representatives – that is, by the representatives of tribes and subtribes with customary rights and authority on Auckland. The recommendation was rejected by the National-led government, and in 2009 a *hikoi* (march) was held in protest, bringing together many thousands of Māori and large numbers of non-Māori in downtown Auckland to demonstrate their "condemnation of the Crown's refusal to acknowledge its Treaty obligation to actively protect Māori partnership rights of representation on the Auckland Council" (Sullivan 2011). The Local Government (Auckland Council) Amendment Act 2010 finally created a statutory Māori Advisory Board, which fuelled additional controversy (see Sullivan 2011 for details). The board is made up of nine Māori members: seven are *mana whenua* representatives and two are *mātāwaka* representatives, meaning they represent Māori who do not identify with the *mana whenua* groups and who are often referred to and identify as "urban Māori." According to the Auckland City Council website: "The Māori Statutory Board is independent of the Auckland Council. It aims to ensure that the council takes the views of Māori into account when making decisions." The board is expected to "[put] forward the cultural, economic, environmental, and social issues that are significant for mana whenua groups and Mātāwaka in Tāmaki Makaurau, and [en]sure that the council complies with statutory provisions that refer to the Treaty of Waitangi." "The Board will also: [g]ive advice to the Auckland Council about issues that affect Māori in Auckland, and [w]ork with the council to create suitable documents and processes to help the council meet its statutory obligations to Māori in Auckland."[47] The advisory board also has to appoint two members to each of Auckland Council's committees dealing with the management and stewardship of natural and physical resources, and to any other committees if requested by the council. As mentioned by Sullivan (2011), some critics have seen the mandatory committee members as a major threat to democracy despite that they do not have the numbers to outvote other members of the council committees. The Local Government Minister, Rodney Hide, "who threatened to resign if Maori were given seats on the Auckland Council, said he opposed the "race-based privilege" of unelected Maori Statutory Board members sitting and voting on council committees" (Orsman 2011). This is one example of the various tensions and issues of participation and political representation now emerging in the urban setting.

In the 1990s, treaty settlements became a priority. The Waitangi Tribunal, with the 1985 extension of its jurisdiction to 1840 "had led to substantial research and important findings; [it] had built a new jurisprudence; it had developed the reasoning and approaches taken up by the . . . courts" (Orange 2011: 249). At the end of 1991, negotiations on the Waikato-Tainui claim and the Ngāi Tahu claim, two major claims, were under way. The Waikato-Tainui claim was among the first to enter into the process of direct negotiation with the Crown (Orange 2011: 251; Mahuta 1995a). In 1992, the Deed of Settlement of Māori fisheries claims was signed and led to the Treaty of Waitangi Fisheries Claims Settlement Act, known as the Sealord deal. This settlement, which involved large compensation payments and fishing assets, gave rise to public resentment and much debate and conflict among Māori. According to Orange, it "emphasized the need for a clear policy on Treaty claims: consistency was required across all settlements, and the government wanted to establish a definitive and final sum" (253). Part of the solution was the 1994 treaty settlement envelope of $1 billion for full and final resolution of all Māori grievances relating to the Treaty of Waitangi, a cut-off date of 21 September 1992, to establish which claims fall within the limit and could be classified as "historical claims," with a timeframe of the year 2000 to settle all claims (253).[48] Sullivan (2001) explains that the "fiscal envelope" fit well with a policy of fiscal responsibility, and was the outcome of successive governments' liberal economic policies. The tribes unanimously condemned the package, which led to a number of land occupations and protest actions, some during the 1995 Waitangi celebrations. The most remembered protest actions of the period were the chainsaw attack of the lone pine tree on One Tree Hill in Auckland, by Mike Smith, on the anniversary of the signing of the 1835 Declaration of Independence in October 1994; the decapitation of the statue of the nineteenth-century politician Sir John Balance, in December 1995; and the following occupation of Pākaitore, a park also known as Moutoa Gardens in Whanganui, where the statue stands (for details, see, among others Harris 2004a; Mutu 2011; Poata-Smith 1996; Rosenblatt 2005; Walker 2004).The attacks on the tree and the statue were dramatic actions against symbols of colonization. The first one – which was quite controversial for several reasons – was intended to "recall the anticolonial resistance of [Mike Smith's] ancestor Hone Heke, who had chopped down a British flagpole in 1845" (Rosenblatt 2005: 118) in opposition to the state interference and imposition of British customs (Belich 1996).[49]

Later, the National-New Zealand First coalition government refrained from referring to the $1 billion envelope for treaty settlement (Sullivan 2001; Durie 1998).[50] However, "all settlements from 1996 to 1999 did appear to fit within the parameters of the $1 billion package" (Sullivan 2001: 484). In 1995, the Waikato-Raupatu Claims Settlement Act finally "included the return of around 40,000 acres . . . of land (much of it rented out) and monetary compensation. The total settlement was valued at around $170 million" (Orange 2011: 255). The Ngāi Tahu Claims Settlement Act 1998 had about the same value and, in both cases, the settlement included a clause according to which it was "full and final" (see Orange 2011: 256).

Despite the progress that has been made, the Waitangi Tribunal has been criticized on a number of matters: among other things, for the legal and research costs made by claimants, for the "old" historiography on which it relied, for the way it conducted historical research, and for its poor productivity (see, among others, Belgrave 2005a, 2005b; Belgrave, Kawharu, and Williams 2005; Orange 2011). For example, Hayward, writing at the closing of the 1990s, notes

there are approximately 850 claims registered with the Waitangi Tribunal. To June 1999, the Tribunal had produced initial and final reports on seventy claims, and had reported on an aspect of a further fifteen claims (with additional claims settled by direct negotiation or mediation). To 30 June 1999 there were 129 claims in hearing. (Hayward 2001: 495)[51]

Even if she recognizes the need to move more quickly, Orange (2011: 261) warns that "[t]he risks in speeding up the Tribunal's process for hearing Treaty claims has to be offset against the desire to settle claims as soon as possible. Reliable research and the chance for Māori to express long-standing issues, often at hearings on marae, contribute significantly to the achievement of full and final settlements."

Orange (2011) summarizes the situation of the Waitangi Tribunal at its entrance into the twenty-first century:

The year 2000 was the twenty-fifth anniversary of the Treaty of Waitangi Act 1975 that established the Waitangi Tribunal. Since 1985, the Tribunal had published thirty major reports: ten or more had dealt primarily with land, and two with fisheries (Muriwhenua and Ngāi Tahu); others covered an ever-widening range of subjects. A formidable information base had been developed through research, through many supplementary claims reports (in addition to final reports on claims), through a comprehensive research series known as Rangahau Whanui, and through a National Overview – a major effort towards streamlining the historical side of the claims process. By the end of the 1990s, several Tribunal hearings were running concurrently, and preparatory research was under way on a number of other claims. (260)

According to Barton (2011), since the 1990s most *iwi* have adopted what is known as "the fast track." This option means bypassing the tribunal to engage in direct negotiations with Māori. It was developed in the 1980s, when the tribunal started being seen as representing a real threat to the New Zealand state and to the majority population generally. Even so, "[t]he fast track has produced some impressive results, including the largest-ever Treaty settlement – the 'Treelords' deal with central North Island iwi in 2008" (Barton 2011).

But in spite of treaty information campaigns (for details, see Orange 2011: 263), increasing public resentment over the so-called privileges enjoyed by Māori has been perceptible, especially since the treaty settlements of the 1990s (see Miller 2005; Orange 2011; Van Meijl 2006a; Walker 2004). As I have shown, the foreshore and seabed controversy had the effect of further invigorating this resentment, which expressed itself in increasingly "racial" terms. This also had the effect of fuelling debates about the place of the treaty within New Zealand's constitutional arrangements.

In 2006, the Treaty of Waitangi Act was revised again. The Treaty of Waitangi Amendment Act 2006 amends section 6 of the Treaty of Waitangi Act 1975, setting a closing date of 1 September 2008 for the submission of historical treaty claims to the Waitangi Tribunal. The idea of establishing a closing date for submitting historical claims was one of the important issues at stake during the campaign leading to the general election of 17 September 2005, along with demands for (1) the eradication of race-based policy, (2) the removal of the treaty principals from legislation, and (3) the abolition of the Waitangi Tribunal and of the designated Māori seats in Parliament. On these issues, the Relationship and Confidence and Supply Agreement between the National Party and the Māori Party following the 2008 general election states

> [b]oth parties agree to the establishment . . . of a group to consider constitutional issues including Māori representation . . . The National Party agrees it will not seek to remove the Māori seats without the consent of the Māori people. Accordingly, the Māori Party and the National Party will not be pursuing the entrenchment of the Māori seats in the current parliamentary term. Both parties agree that there will not be a question about the future of the Māori seats in the referendum on MMP planned by the National Party.[52]

Historical claims were also defined in the Treaty of Waitangi Amendment Act 2006 as any claim relating to an act of omission of the Crown that occurred before 21 September 1992. This date was set because it was when Cabinet agreed to the general principles for settling historical Treaty of Waitangi claims. It has since been used to define historical treaty claims in settlements. The closing date of 1 September 2008 was chosen for lodging historical claims. While the one-thousandth claim was registered in 2002, their number has more than doubled with the final end date for historical claims (Orange 2011: 260–1). Since then, the

Waitangi Tribunal has continued to investigate historical treaty claims submitted on or before 1 September 2008, and has also examined contemporary grievances related to violations of the treaty on or after 21 September 1992.

With the National-led coalition government elected in 2008, the year 2014 has been set as "an aspirational goal" (Barton 2011) for the settlement of all historical claims. This deadline, combined with the fast track option, has produced results: "I've got an ambitious programme, I'm working very hard on it. We've signed as many deeds of settlement [13] in two years as Labour signed in nine," said Treaty Negotiations Minister Chris Finlayson on Radio NZ (Barton 2011, precision by the author).

However, some found that the Crown was rushing settlements and a number of groups said they have been left out or treated unfairly. Complaints have been heard since 2006: "[i]ssues raised included the Crown's policy of only negotiating with 'large natural groupings,' its method of mandating whom it negotiates with, how it decides on priority, and ensuring that Crown assets were available for redress and not sold off" (Barton 2011). This proved disadvantageous for smaller tribes and extended families with less money. It also led to important disagreements between tribes over resources (Durie 1998; Melbourne 1995; Webster 1998; Sullivan 2001; for a retrospective account of the Waitangi Tribunal, see Hayward and Wheen 2004).

If the whole history of Māori protests, struggles, affirmation, and resistance is to be understood in a global context, it is also important to consider recent world events. At the beginning of the third millennium, many observers saw signs of resurgence in activism. These included anti-capitalist and anti-globalization movements (especially since the World Trade Organization protests in Seattle in 1999), anti-war campaigns against military intervention in Iraq and Afghanistan in the aftermath of the events of 11 September 2001 (as well as protests against the resulting imposition of "anti-terrorist" measures), expanding environmental movements concerned about global warming and related ecological threats, and popular uprisings against dictatorial governments in the Balkan states in the years 2000 and, at the moment of writing, in Arab countries. I would expect that these movements have touched Māori, too, and that the new global context could in part explain their recent mobilization.

With the success accomplished by the indigenous movement worldwide in recent years,[53] including the adoption by the UN of the

Declaration on the Rights of Indigenous Peoples in 2007, the indigenous strategy has also now became more prominent among Māori and seems to be appealing to people beyond a very small group of leaders interested in indigenous issues and active in international indigenous forums.[54] Mason Durie (2005b: 15)[55] insightfully sums up the changes in the ways the Māori struggle is framed:

> Although the Treaty of Waitangi has become the focus for considering the Maori constitutional position, it is not always the most useful document to define the extent of indigenous rights. In contrast to the Treaty, where 1840 represented a new beginning, indigenous rights have a longer memory. 1840 is somewhat incidental to a set of customs and lore that evolved over some hundreds of years. Increasingly the state will need to be concerned about indigeneity as an issue that is related but not identical to the Treaty of Waitangi, and the indigenous voice will need to be heard alongside the Treaty dialogue. (see also Durie 2011)

But while the global situation is certainly relevant to understanding both Māori mobilization and the current relations between the majority and minorities in New Zealand, it cannot completely account for the specificities of their activism in local contexts. For that, I will examine the everyday struggle of Māori in the last few decades and the ways it has prepared them for the most recent wave of mobilization and protest.

2   Māori Lives in Auckland

This chapter is an introduction to Māori in the city. I examine the situation of Māori life in Auckland in all its diversity and the ways that Māori express their experiences – of the city and Auckland in particular, of their relationships with other Māori, and of the nation – and their sense of home in terms of comfort.

In terms of surface area, Auckland is a big, spread-out city, since most of its 1.5 million[1] inhabitants live in one-storey, single-family houses, although this has started to change with the current real estate boom. Auckland is New Zealand's biggest multicultural city, with large Asian and Polynesian populations. As the city with the largest Polynesian population, Auckland is often called the Polynesian capital of the world. Misa (2010a) notes that "[a]bout 67 per cent of 336,000 Pacific people are concentrated in Auckland, making up more than 14 per cent of the region's population. The next largest concentration (Wellington, with 13 per cent) is a long way behind. Samoan is the second most spoken language after English in greater Auckland, Waitakere and, of course, Manukau, where Pacific Auckland is at its most visible."

Auckland is the New Zealand city that attracts the largest percentage of immigrants – a percentage that is continually growing. According to Friesen (2010), in addition to its booming economy (in particular in the service sectors) in recent years, "Auckland's ongoing rapid growth can also partly be attributed to its role as a 'gateway' city, similar to other cities on the Pacific Rim such as Vancouver, Sydney and San Francisco." This influx of immigrants – which adds to a large internal migration, an increasing number of people identifying with ethnic groups other than European (in particular with the Asian, Pacific, and Māori ethnic groups) – and interactions between ethnic groups, such as intermarriages, has made the Auckland region increasingly ethnically diverse. Spoonley (2007) uses the label "superdiversity" to speak of Auckland, which "has more overseas-born than any other Australasian city." According to Statistics New Zealand, "[i]n 1991, 76 percent of the Auckland region's population identified with the 'European or other' ethnic group (which includes New Zealand European and 'New Zealander'), but by 2006 this had decreased to 64 percent."[2] Friesen (2008: 2) notes "the 20 years leading up to [the 2006] Census, following the introduction of the Immigration Act in 1987, witnessed one of the most dramatic transitions in ethnic composition that New Zealand has ever experienced." What the Immigration Act 1987 did was change the criteria for immigrant entry into New Zealand: the policy went from being based on countries of origin to being based on individual characteristics. Criteria such as age, educational levels or work experience, and ability to bring investment capital into New Zealand were prioritized, creating a shift in the relative importance of migrant countries of origin (3). Friesen adds that "the most notable aspect of this change has been the growth of the populations of Asian origin, although other populations have also grown" (2). The changes are very apparent in Auckland where nearly two-thirds of immigrants originating from Asian countries settle. According to Statistics New Zealand, the percentage of people identifying with an Asian ethnicity in the Auckland region increased from 6 per cent in 1991 to 19 per cent in 2006. As for immigration from the Pacific, though it has dropped with the changes to immigration rules, "the Pacific population has continued to grow, fed by higher than average birth rates" (Misa 2010a). Thus, Anae observes that "the browning of Auckland is unparalleled in any other city in the world" (in Misa 2010a).

These trends create new dynamics and distinguish Auckland from the other New Zealand cities and towns. These processes should be kept in mind as a wider backdrop for our understanding of Māori experiences of Auckland, Māori engagement in the city, and the ways they interact among themselves and relate to non-Māori others. When most of the data for this book was collected, in the years 2001 and 2002, these processes were already at work, and the situation has changed significantly a decade later.

Turning now to the Māori population, it forms 14.6 per cent of New Zealand's population, which is just over 4.1 million (2006 Census).[3] It has increased by 30 per cent in the past fifteen years, up from 434,800 in 1991 to 565,300 in 2006. According to the 2006 Census, 84.4 per cent of Māori live in urban centres,[4] and one-third of these (or just under one quarter of the entire Māori population) live in the Auckland region. Pool (1991: 157–8) shows how Auckland became the number one destination for Māori from the beginning of the mass urban migration. In 1966, for example, it was the place of residence of 20 per cent of Māori, compared to 8 per cent in Wellington, the capital city. According to the 2006 Census, 7.8 per cent of the Auckland City population identifies with the Māori ethnic group.

There is great heterogeneity among Māori who live in Auckland. As Durie (2001a: 4) rightly says, "Māori do not conform to a typical presentation either physically or psychologically." Smith (1995: 18 in Cram and Pitama 1998) explains: "Māori are not a homogenous 'whole' in terms of their social, economic and cultural situation, nor are they of a single mind in respect of their aspirations related to 'things Māori,'" a fact that is not immediately apparent in much research, which tends too often to generalize about "the Māori," giving the image of a rather uniform group.[5] As Cram and Pitama (1998: 131) state it, "our diversity has gone unnoticed by anyone other than ourselves: we have been seen as 'Other' in the eyes of a colonising group that now exists in the majority in this country of ours." Of course, this situation is not unique to Māori; Herzfeld (2001) reminds us that the myth of the homogeneous other is deeply entrenched and has a durable influence on anthropological theory. Poata-Smith (2004b) adds that the homogenizing tendency is emphasized by non-Māori as well as Māori whose interests are convergent:

[t]he notion that all Māori share an overpowering and innate attachment based on blood, culture and language has underpinned cultural nationalist political ideology and practice, which emphasises the fundamental commonality of Māori interests in contemporary capitalist society. In this way, the existence of contradictory class interests and the inequalities of wealth and political power that are entrenched within and across iwi [tribe], hapū [subtribe] and urban Māori communities are disregarded in favour of an approach that emphasises the primacy of cultural conflict between Māori and Pākehā. (69)[6]

The lived reality of Māori is thus far more complex, than a homogenizing literature would suggest (see also George 2010) and the Auckland Māori population among whom I worked is highly diversified. Māori come from varied extended families, tribes, and subtribes. These "traditional" social structures merit closer examination. First comes the extended family or *whānau*, the urban reality of which is the focus of most of this study. Today, the word *"whānau"* can be applied to an increasingly wide variety of categories and groups, as I will show. Persons and *whānau* then belong to the *iwi*, meaning people or individuals who make or constitute a community, tribe, or nation, depending on the context and the interlocutors. For the purpose of this book, I simply translate *"iwi"* as "tribe," which is the most common translation of the term today. *Iwi* are sociopolitical groupings defined by descent from a named ancestor. Ballara (1998) explains that descent groups are ambilineal among Māori:

> Māori reckon their descent through a system that recognises either a male or a female as the founding ancestor of the descent group, traces descent from that ancestor through either males or females or a mixture of both, and counts among the descent groups to which any one individual belongs the hapū and iwi of both parents, all four grandparents, all eight great-grandparents. Ties even further removed are sometimes recognised. Māori could opt to regard themselves as members of one or several of their potential descent groups through lineage, and could and did reside with the different communities of which these descent groups were part at different times of their lives. (32)

The traditional social structure also includes *hapū*. Schwimmer (1990: 297) has argued in 1978 and 1990 that *"hapū* 'subtribe' is not just a segment of a larger *iwi* 'tribe' but rather a subset of *iwi* members, domiciled in the same place or places, whose genealogies have been restructured so that all descend from a more recent, localised eponymous ancestor." He also shows the pertinence of a model of *hapū* membership

> which starts from a nucleus of local residents linked by descent to a common ancestor, but which admits in addition some other specifiable classes of associates. Such associates would include not only cases of migrants . . ., but also participants in a wide range of activities, sometimes including socio-political decision-making in a plurality of villages. (299)

For Webster (1975), the participation in activities came first as the principal marker of membership, rather than coresidence. According to Sissons (2010: 374), however, Webster (1975) does not challenge the idea, originating with Firth (1959 [1929]) that *hapū* is essentially a descent category. Indeed, as emphasized by Sissons, Webster (1998) and

Metge (1995), despite earlier disagreement, finally "conclude that *hapū* are descent categories, with membership defined in terms of cognatic descent, *and* descent groups comprising the active members of the larger categories" (Sissons 2010: 374). In his recent contribution, Sissons (373) insists that the criterion of cognatic descent is insufficient. Lévi-Strauss's (1987) comment on *hapū* is relevant. He specifies

> the *hapu* cannot be strictly defined as a local group, nor as a descent group, and that maternal links play a role in it that is principally explicable in political terms. A federation of frequently heterogeneous elements that come into being and dissolve as a result of migrations and wars, the *hapu* fabricates a genealogy for itself for opportunistic reasons, rather than being engendered by it. It is thus a dynamic formation that cannot be defined in itself, but only in relation to others of the same kind, situated in their historical context. (178)

For Sissons (2010),

> [d]escent, residence, and active participation are all equally means, or practices, through which groups identifying as *tangata whenua* (people belonging to the land) assert their independent identities. A *hapū* is not firstly an abstract mental or discursive entity produced through the application of descent rules and secondly an active group produced through other means. It is only a group created through multiple practices of representation, co-residence, co-operation, and allegiance. (374)

Sissons (2010: 374) specifies that "practices of representation today include, most significantly, the construction of meeting houses and the production of historical discourse in association with these," such as genealogies and narratives "about the actions of people who are claimed as ancestors by members of the contemporary *hapū* group" (375). Concerning cooperation, this criterion could be met through taking part in the maintenance of the *marae*, contributing food and helping in the kitchen during gatherings, and more generally sharing food with people associated with the *marae*. As for coresidence, Sissons indicates that it could be brief and temporary through regular visits "home" by those who usually live elsewhere (375).

With today's greater ease of movement, there is a looser correspondence between residence and descent (Schwimmer 1990: 309). Indeed, my data support a greater emphasis on current residence in the city as a significant criterion for group formation. Sissons's (2010) recent analysis of meeting houses and *marae* also supports this relatively new emphasis on residence among Māori:

> recent literature on the concept of the "house society" – a society organized most fundamentally as a relationship between houses rather than through rules of descent – raises the possibility of understanding contemporary Maori *hapuu* as houses and Maori society as a relationship between groups that have formed around *marae*, cognatic descent serving largely as a legitimating ideology . . . I argue . . . that Maori society became progressively more house-ordered during the period 1880-1950 as the number of *hapuu* meeting houses on rural *marae* dramatically increased. (373)

Sissons (2008:1) also added that since the 1970s, urban meeting houses have participated in further transformations of indigenous society that have seen tribalism both affirmed and rejected.

In this book, I will translate *hapū* as "subtribe," to conform to general usage in New Zealand, although Ballara (1998) has suggested that "clan" would be better since it avoids the hierarchical connotations of "subtribe." Webster (1975) and Ballara (1998) have both emphasized that most ethnologists have obscured spontaneous Māori usages of *"whānau,"* *"hapū,"* and *"iwi"* through their own bias, according to which *whānau* "become" *hapū* through normal growth, and *hapū* "become" *iwi*. They also point out that it is equally mistaken to say that *iwi* are divided into *hapū*, which are divided in turn into *whānau*. This last conception seems to imply that the larger groups, *iwi*, existed prior to *hapū* and *whānau* and were a centralized political body or a corporate group. Rather, it appears more likely that *iwi* have not always existed first (at least, serious doubts have been raised about this assumption), nor are they a unified corporate group, since the membership is quite changeable. Metge (1995) explains:

> Since the 1970s, . . . this usage [translating *"hapū"* as "sub-tribe"] has increasingly come under attack from scholars, who suggest on the basis of historical and linguistic research that the hapū was the key organisational group in Māori society until the mid-nineteenth century and that iwi did not become fixed groups of paramount importance until late in the nineteenth century in the course of dealings with the Crown (Orbell 1978: 115–16; Metge 1986: 36–7; Ballara 1995).

> During the 1980s national Māori leaders initiated a drive to establish the iwi/tribe as paramount in the Māori social order, as a result of which this

view was entrenched in the politics of government departments. In the 1990s, however, this interpretation is being challenged on the one hand by hapū and on the other by pan-Māori organisations such as the Ratana Church, the Māori Women's Welfare League and various Māori urban authorities. (317)

The politics of government departments referred to by Metge includes the juridification of Māori property, which took place in the early 1990s in a context of devolution and claims settlements. It is a complex process involving (1) the recognition by the New Zealand state of tribes as legal corporate entities and the concomitant active participation of the tribes' representatives in retribalization, (2) the reinforcement of the tribes' authority and legitimacy as inheritors of traditional resources and knowledge, and (3) the subsequent new emphasis on blood and ancestry as criteria for access to properties and benefits (Rata 2000, see also Poata-Smith 2004a, 2004b). Note that since the nineteenth century, the government has participated in granting more significance to tribes by giving recognition to tribal leaders to the detriment of *hapū* leaders, in particular through the activities of the Land Court. However, until now *hapū* identities have endured (Sissons 2010: 374).

Salmond adds that in precontact time, *whānau* and *hapū* were sometimes used imprecisely, as is apparently still the case today. This is due to "a constant negotiation between an array of genealogical possibilities and the necessity of practical choice, especially at the life crises of birth, marriage and death" (Metge 1995: 46, summarizing Salmond 1991b: 343). Schwimmer (1990) adds that *hapū* formation was and still is a very complex process of fission and fusion of existing *hapū* as well as of periodic restructuring of the genealogical basis, depending on historical challenges. Looking at Kawharu's case study (1975), Schwimmer identifies *mana* – which can be translated as spiritual power, authority, prestige and is in part inherited and in part achieved – as a criteria for "opening up" (299) the *hapū* or joining together to enhance solidarity or status and predominance.

Schwimmer (1990) points out the inherent and "traditional" flexibility of the Māori social system. Sissons (2010) also emphasizes this flexibility. Ballara (1998: 21) argues along the same lines, saying that the "Māori political and social system was always dynamic, continuously modified." Salmond attributes this feature of Māori groupings to four principles: "The unity of all phenomenal life through genealogical connection; the complementarity of male and female; the principle of primogeniture; all of which can be overcome by a fourth principle of competitive striving expressed in a language of war" (Salmond 1991b: 337 in Metge 1995: 46).

Looking again at Kawharu's (1975) case study, Schwimmer (1990) highlights two different principles that are at work in various circumstances and histories: (1) *whanaungatanga*, which is an inclusive kinship ethic and unites people "horizontally" as a "collective factor" and (2) *whakapapa*, an exclusive descent ethic or "vertical" principle that makes restructuring and thus the definition of boundaries possible or necessary depending on circumstances. Schwimmer adds that "[there] never was full independence of any politico-economic unit because the moral principles of *whanaungatanga* and *whakapapa* pervade the entire culture, including both *hapū* and *iwi*" (313). *Whānau*, *hapū*, and *iwi* are thus linked in a cybernetic (in contrast to a mechanical) type of system that is in dialogue with historical conjunctures (314). As Metge (1995) rightly says, the process of change and transformation continues, but even today, continuity remains and the system is reaffirmed in a cyclic way.

At the beginning of the century, Durie (2001a) identified a shift from *iwi* to *whānau*. The data I collected during my fieldwork in Auckland support this emphasis on *whānau* among Māori today, even as, during my last stay in New Zealand in 2011, it became clear to me that contextual factors, such as the importance given to the Treaty of Waitangi settlement process, have also put an emphasis on tribes. Many factors explain this emphasis on tribes: the mobilization and research necessary to present a claim to the tribunal and to represent the interests of the people; the support required to register as a tribal member; and the consultation process involved in the management of the settlement, including returned lands or natural resources when applicable, monetary compensations and other assets. This tendency is balanced, however, by other measures such as the Whānau Ora initiative. The scheme, which was championed by the Māori Party and approved by the government in 2010, is "an inclusive, culturally anchored approach to provide services and opportunities to whānau and families across New Zealand."[7] A special fund aims at "[building] whānau capability, [strengthening] whānau connections, [supporting] the development of whānau leadership and [enhancing] best outcomes for whānau." Some have commented that this initiative is not new since there are already many social intervention programs that target mainly *whānau*. But because this type of initiative is more within the grasp of individuals, "impacts are more directly felt and accountabilities are reinforced by the linkages stemming from known relationships, mutual interests, shared whakapapa . . . and blood ties" (Durie 2001a: 189–90).

However, once again, *iwi*, *hapū*, and *whānau* complement each other. As Durie (2001a: 189) explains, *iwi* and *hapū* "have greater relevance in connection with broader collectivities and issues of wider community impact – resource management, marae encounters, wānanga (learning institutes), service delivery, tribal politics, negotiations with local and national authorities, and the settlement of Treaty of Waitangi claims." *Whānau*, though, are more within the grasp of persons and groups through day to day experiences, in particular in the city; Auckland is typically one to eight hours' drive or more from tribal home(s) if on the North Island (and further if on the South Island; see figure 2.1).

Some tribes are today very large (for example, Ngāpuhi has 122,211 members, Ngāti Porou has 71,910, and Ngāti Kahungunu 59,946; see 2006 Census) while others are quite small; about 50 per cent of all tribes have fewer than 1,000 members (Durie 2001a: 13).

A certain number of Māori who live in the city or outside their tribal areas do not know to which tribe(s) and subtribe(s) they belong and do not have connections to a particular *papakāinga* (ancestral or village settlement). Some suggest that 15.4 per cent of the Māori adults in Auckland do not know (or do not want to identify) their tribe (Te Hoe Nuku Roa 1999: 88), while in the 1996 Census, some 20 per cent of all Māori respondents did not identify their tribe(s) of origin (Durie 2001a: 189). In the 2006 Census, 15.9 per cent of all Māori respondents did not identify their tribe(s) of origin.[8] These percentages are contested by some who think they could have been somehow manipulated by urban Māori organizations trying to be recognized as legitimate tribes and, thus, as legitimate inheritors of traditional resources and knowledge in the larger context of retribalization, devolution, and claim settlements. As Sissons (2004: 19) indicates, "[s]ome actively reject an identity that links them to particular ancestral lands and tribal traditions." He gives the famous example of John Tamihere, a former Labour MP and head of an urban Māori authority based in West Auckland that provides services for Māori in Auckland. Still, it seems that a certain number of Māori who live in the city and in Auckland in particular really do not know their tribe(s) of origin, although, I never met anyone who was in that position. Some cases of students in that position were reported to me, for example, by Māori primary and secondary school teachers (see also Van Meijl 2006c). In all probability, such individuals have a much more restricted family network than others.

Figure 2.1: Simplified map of Māori *iwi* (tribes) and approximate locations

Note: The information displayed on this map should be considered indicative only.
Sources: This map and the information it contains have been collated from the following sources: Appendices to the NZ House of Representatives 1870; Te Puni Kōkiri website, www.tkm.govt.nz; McCarthy 2007; Starzecka 1996.

Māori are further diversified in terms of their place of origin. Some belong to tribes that have their *papakāinga* (ancestral or village settlement) in Auckland, some belong to tribes that have been displaced (Belich 1996; Stone 2001; George 2001), and others are from tribal areas outside of Auckland. More than 83 per cent are descended from tribes outside the Auckland region (Taonui 2010). Although Māori migrants do live in the other major cities, these tend to be dominated by the *tāngata whenua* tribes – that is, by home tribes, tribes who have customary ancestral authority over the area. The situation of Auckland is unique among the rest of New Zealand's major cities since it has a higher concentration of Māori migrants coming from a higher number of tribal regions. This situation impacts Māori relationships in Auckland: it has participated in undermining the dominance of the *tāngata whenua* tribes there, in contrast to what occurs in other places. What is also unique in Auckland is how the *tāngata whenua* tribes have been completely disregarded in the country's metropolis until very recently – in the case of the Ngāti Whātua o Ōrākei, for example, "their presence was seen as a stumbling block in Auckland's progressive development" (Tapsell 2002: 145). Note also the extent to which they have been stripped of their lands. This situation has greatly affected their capacity to maintain their kin group identity and sense of pride, and to assert their *tāngata whenua* status over the Auckland area in welcoming Māori migrants. In the case of the Ngāti Whātua o Ōrākei, Tapsell (2002) shows how deeply they were affected in their capacity to assert themselves: when the first wave of Māori migrated to Auckland in the 1950s, the "Ngati Whatua's *tangata whenua* identity was at its lowest" (152) and "[f]or a time everyone but Ngati Whatua prospered in the post-War II boom years as tens of thousand of young Maori migrated to cities like Auckland" (152). Still according to Tapsell, this situation had a lot to do with the emergence of the nontribal *marae* concept, to which I will return in the next chaper – the first New Zealand non-tribally organized urban *marae* being Hoani Waititi *marae* in West Auckland. The nontribal *marae* concept, according to Tapsell, "marginalized Ngati Whatua's *tangata whenua* status in favor of battling for nationalized Maori (nontribal) rights" (153).

Returning to today's situation, some Māori have been in Auckland for two or three generations, while others are just arriving or are in transit. Some therefore have a large family network in the city, while others are on their own or have to establish a new network. Some keep strong relationships with their people in the country, while others do not or cannot rely on those relationships. Not only does the level of involvement with the *whānau* (extended family) vary, but also its quality. People are also differently involved in diverse kinds of groupings such as (1) traditional kin groups like the extended family, subtribe, and tribe; (2) Māori voluntary associations like the "urban tribe"; and (3) other types of organizations, not necessarily or entirely Māori.[9] Māori have varying degrees of knowledge of *tikanga* (Māori traditions) and the Māori language[10] and rely in diverse ways on this knowledge in their everyday life.

Māori also come to live in Auckland for different reasons. The choice can be driven by several pull factors related to Auckland's better economic and other opportunities including higher salaries, better working conditions, more suitable jobs, better education for both children and adults, better health facilities, and a greater diversity of activities in general and of cultural and artistic events (see the pioneering research by Kawharu 1968, 1975; Metge 1964; see also Williams 2010).[11] Push factors were also often cited by the research participants. Some leave the rural area because of tribal politics or because they feel under too much pressure to conform to *whānau* (extended family) or tribal norms of behaviour or ways of life. Some disagreed or fought with family members, while others leave following abuse of one sort or another from their partner, parents, or other relatives. Others simply seek new experiences.

The study of Māori in Australia by Hamer (2007) identifies many reasons for Māori migration to that country that correspond to the reasons for migration to cities reported by my Māori acquaintances. The main factors that Hamer identifies are economic opportunities, lifestyle (such as better climate, greater cultural diversity, better shopping, a greater range of entertainment and recreational pursuits), and family reunification. Escaping from negative experiences in New Zealand, such as gangs, drugs and crime, domestic troubles, and perceived prejudice toward Māori, are also mentioned. The desire to leave the family environment (negative attitudes toward success, pressure associated with control by elders and being answerable for the family) is another push factor identified by Hamer.

Moreover, Māori are diversified according to their educational background, health status, incomes, and work experiences. Māori who live in Auckland will have several different kinds of status or *mana* (spiritual power, authority, prestige, status) in their subtribe(s) and tribe(s), and they are also variously positioned in the Pākehā stratified system. Indeed, Māori are increasingly differentiated among themselves according to social class (see, for example, Chapple 2000; Poata-Smith 2004a, 2004b; Rata 2000). This class differentiation is related in part to the process of claims settlements, as I will illustrate in more detail later.

In Auckland, Māori are mixed in with the rest of the population and live all over the city. However, they are residentially concentrated in certain areas depending on such things as living standards, economic conditions, labour and housing markets, ways of living, shared networks, world views, and physical and cultural security (see, for example, Johnston, Poulsen, and Forrest 2005; Morrison, Callister, and Rigby 2002; Friesen, Murphy, Kearns, and Haverkamp 2000). To give a very general picture, in the north of the city are Māori with higher living standards who are bicultural in the professional sphere. The highest proportion of people identifying with the Māori ethnic group in the Auckland region live in the south of Auckland, according to the 2006 Census: 27 per cent live in the Papakura district and 15 per cent in Manukau city (see figure 2.2). In the southern part of the city, are the highest number of those who, generally, have lower levels of formal education, are economically disadvantaged to a greater degree, and face major social problems in their everyday lives (see the deprivation maps in Crampton, Salmond, and Kirkpatrick 2000). Māori who live in the west of the city are more stable economically and are at the forefront of the renaissance of urban Māori consciousness. Many of the successful and long-lasting Māori community action projects in education, health, and general culture have been established in the west, but similar and successful projects are also now widespread in the south side of the city.[12] In the city centre are the churches and universities – bases for the community action in which Māori students and other members of Māori social and political movements are heavily involved. The city centre is also the location of head offices or urban branches of many Māori businesses, tribal authorities, institutions, voluntary associations, and family or charitable trusts. This is also where the immediate postwar waves of Māori migrants first established themselves before moving to the new suburbs to the south and west (Metge 1964; Walker 2004; Williams 2010; see also Latham 2003). The Ngāti Whātua o Ōrākei, the tāngata whenua, the people who have ancestral rights on that part of the territory of Auckland, live near the city centre. Tapsell (2002: 143) describes them as an "urban-encircled tangata whenua group," since the city has grown around them. Ancestral rights are also accorded to and recognized in other groups in other parts of the city.[13]

Figure 2.2: Simplified map of Auckland and suburbs

In general, in New Zealand, there are important socioeconomic disparities between Māori and non-Māori. Even though Māori are highly diversified and there are significant differences among Māori individuals and families, the James Henare Māori Research Centre (2002, 1: 6–9) has found that, in education, for instance, Māori made up 45 per cent of those suspended or expelled from schools in 1998; by the end of the 1990s, about 40 per cent of Māori still left school without any qualifications; and only about 20 per cent of Māori students went on to tertiary education compared with 40 per cent of non-Māori. Among those who did go on to university, the retention rate for Māori at the University of Auckland, to take one example, was 70.0 per cent in 2002–3, compared to 87.6 per cent for all the students (Equal Opportunities Office 2003: 34).

Māori are much more likely to be unemployed than non-Māori, constituting 32 per cent of all registered unemployed in 1991. In 2001, the unemployment rates remained disproportionate at 17 per cent for Māori and 6 per cent for non-Māori whites (Office of Ethnic Affairs 2002 in Maaka and Fleras 2005: 69). In 2002, the Māori unemployment rate dropped to 12 per cent, but it was only at 4 per cent for non-Māori whites (Maaka and Fleras 2005: 69). By 2005, the unemployment rate fell to 8.6 per cent for people of Māori ethnicity – but to only 2.6 per cent among people of European ethnicity (Ministry of Social Development 2006: 47). Still in 2012, Māori have the highest unemployment rate, higher even than that of Pacific islanders. Māori household incomes are generally NZ$10,000 per annum lower than non-Māori households, and over one-third of Māori receive social welfare transfer payments (James Henare Māori Research Centre 2002). At the end of the 1990s, about 60 per cent of Māori children belonged to families that struggled to meet their daily financial needs (Hohepa 1997 in Cram and Pitama 1998: 146). This percentage is quite significant, given that more than one-third of the Māori population is under the age of 15 (compared to about 20 per cent of the non-Māori population, 2006 Census).[14] But the situation has been improving in recent years. For the period 1981–2006, "proportions of families with low incomes declined over the period for all family types" (Kiro, von Randow, and Sporle 2010: 24).[15] For example, 36.1 per cent of one-family households with two Māori adults (other than couples without children) were low income in 1981; in 2006, this had dropped to 25 per cent. "Multi-family households . . . saw the greatest decline, from 49.4 percent to 28.1 percent, but they saw the highest proportion on low incomes of all household types at every census point" (24).

In the field of health, there is roughly an eight-year gap in life-expectancy between Māori and non-Māori, and it is well known that Māori have a higher incidence of obesity, cancer, diabetes, flu, pneumonia, suicide, and motor vehicle crash injury.[16] These disparities between Māori and non-Māori populations hold as true in Auckland as they do elsewhere in New Zealand.

Many Māori, generally speaking, do not consider the city and its institutions, and Auckland in particular, as Māori places; for one thing, they do not "look" and "feel" Māori. The city is experienced by many, including some of those who were born or have lived there for years, as a "colonized place" where Māori in general feel alien and powerless, with little or no control of either their environment or their lives. They find the cost of living to be exorbitant. They often have difficulty finding work. They face various kinds of discrimination in the labour market and other areas. And they often have no alternative but to depend on social security payments. In addition, they do not always have a choice in their area of residence, since they must live with relatives or are assigned to state-owned social housing, or are restricted to areas where rents are low. The city, and this was particularly prominent during my first fieldwork in 2001–2, was clearly experienced by a large proportion of the Māori who participated in my research as somewhere that was not theirs, a place in which they had little or no place. Although, there is evidence that the situation has improved greatly in the past few years (see Carlin 2010; Kawharu 2008; Tapsell 2002; Taonui 2010). Nonetheless, this sense of not having a place has also been true for some *tāngata whenua* people, like the Ngāti Whātua o Ōrākei who, by the 1950s, were stripped of all their lands, evicted from their *papakainga* (ancestral village), and forced to burn their meeting house down (see Kawharu 1975; Tapsell 2002). As mentioned earlier, they "were never seen as part and parcel of the metropolis that encircled them" (Tapsell 2002: 145) and their situation "prevented Ngati Whatua from asserting their *tangata whenua* status over the wider Auckland metropolitan area" (Tapsell 2002: 147) until fairly recently.

However, this general feeling does not prevent Māori from making a home for themselves in the city, as I will show (see also Harris 2007, 2007–8; Williams 2010). The sense of not belonging has to be understood in relation to social class and the experience of inequalities, even if this does not explain everything. Poata-Smith (2004b: 63) reminds us that throughout the 1980s and 1990s, "Māori have been disproportionately represented amongst those in the first three quintiles and significantly under-represented amongst those on high incomes."

Moreover, a majority of Māori migrants, at least at the beginning, do not "feel good" in the city, because even if they have moved there geographically and socially, they have not necessarily and fully moved there cognitively (in another context, see Rapport 1998: 78). They dream of the homeland, the home *marae*, the idyllic and idealized country life, and they keep alive and hold on to those memories or ideas of a pre-colonization or premigration "dreamtime" (which takes on nuances of a pre-exile or even pre-exodus idyll for some), in ways very similar to transnational migrants.[17] This is not only true of new migrants, but also for some of those who belong to the second or third generation born in the city. They still hold on to ideas of a dreamtime, at least in certain political and socioeconomic contexts. This notion of the dreamtime was not used in everyday conversations among Māori and its use has nothing to do with its meaning in an Australian context and in studies on Australian Aboriginal peoples. The term comes from Ihimaera's novel *Whanau* (1974) and describes a particular mindset that impacts Māori ways of life, outlook, and engagement in and with the city. Ihimaera uses it to contrast life in the city with the perfect life in the time of the ancestors. The dreamtime was

> A time of prosperity when the land was still our own and the Whanau A Kai had pride. That was in the dreamtime before we were stripped of our dignity. The dreamtime . . .
>
> A dream built on other dreams. Built on pride and the obstinate need to believe that once there *must* have been a time when the village blazed briefly with beauty. There must have been, surely, somewhere, such a time. A time to look back to and to escape to from the shame and poverty of the present. (1996 [1974]: 16–17; emphasis in original)

Dreaming about the dreamtime constitutes an escape from today's difficulties and today's hard life in the city; it creates a refuge in an "age lost" (41), a "happy . . . time . . . The dreamtime; the long ago time" (42). Williams (2010) warns against exaggerating the extent to which Māori idealize and romanticize tribal homelands and rural life. She shows that what has been interpreted as Māori romanticism, sentimentality, or nostalgia has often been the product of cross-cultural misinterpretations and "the romanticised non-Māori perceptions of the tribal village" (208). She adds that there is danger in an oversimplification of much more complex relations between urban and rural milieus. The warning, of course, must be kept in mind, but I also cannot ignore them. Dream-time narratives came up often during my 2001–2 field research, and I will take a closer look at how and why they are used in a variety of contexts.

Dreamtime narratives sometimes indicate a refusal to engage in a struggle to make the present viable, pleasant, or even better. They voice a kind of resignation or sense of powerlessness. References to the dreamtime reveal a great deal about Māori discomfort, not only in the city, but in the nation, a nation that they describe or conceive of vari-ously as "alien," "besieged," and "colonized." It is also, for some, a rhetorical device to blame others for what is happening. I heard these kinds of dreamtime arguments many times on urban *marae* among young people. Whetu, one of the teenage girls in one of the families where I lived, used it often when she was bored and did not want to make an effort to improve her situation at school and at home.

Some Māori also use dreamtime arguments to differentiate them-selves from the Pākehā and today's world. Rapport (1998: 80), speaking about the sense of home among English-mother-tongue Jewish immi-grants to Israel (including himself), explains this kind of process: "by staying cognitively apart," people "remain at home in the old verbal routines of criticising and distancing [themselves] from the present." "We became at home in Israel, as we would in any other nation-state, by staying cognitively apart" (80). These Jewish immigrants found a home in staying apart and refusing to engage and, by implication, re-fusing to take responsibility in the wider society and, for the present, preferring instead to map out commonalities and communities with fellow English-speaking Jews. In the same way, dreamtime arguments among Māori allow for the establishment of commonalities among those who use this device, in opposition to the rest of the population. They also allow those who use it to withdraw or disengage from the larger world, which is mainly Pākehā but also includes certain Māori universes, to a more comfortable place where they can escape their re-sponsibility in and for today's living conditions.[18]

However, the dreamtime is not merely an excuse for withdrawal. It is also part of today's dream for a better and more perfect world. The dreamtime can be a motivation for some in setting goals and has inspired many I met, especially young people, to regain their lan-guage, *tikanga* (traditions), and knowledge of the past. As I will re-turn to throughout this book, working as a *whānau*, identifying with one's *marae*, learning the Māori language, and acquiring knowledge of traditional philosophy, spirituality, and religion are part of the dream-time motivation. People may invoke dreamtime arguments in order to criticize or resist mainstream society and ways of doing things, or to motivate others to regain traditional Māori knowledge.

Narratives about the dreamtime are also symptomatic of people's sense that "the grass is always greener on the other side of the fence" and is the sign of a very human coveting of one's neighbour's goods. So, while some urban-based Māori really struggle with life in the city and idealize the country life, their rural cousins dream of the city because they feel that life in the country "sucks." In Witi Ihimaera's novel *Whanau* (1996 [1974]), Hana's greatest wish is to leave the village of her ancestors:

> She looks around her at the village. What a dump. What a waste of her life living here. And trapped here, that's what she is . . . At home, her bedroom walls are covered with pictures of film stars ripped from magazines, showing the kind of life they have. Her radio is always on full blast, for only when it's on loud can she forget this hick town. She reads all the fashion books, wishing she could look like the women in them. And she envies her older cousins when they come back to the village from Auckland or Wellington. They tell her of the fantastic time they're having. And when they leave, she wishes she was going with them too.
>
> There's nothing here for her. Getting away from the village is like a fever. (14)

Some of the participants in this research made similar comments, recalling life before their migration to the city. They had moved with the idea that city life would open new doors for themselves and their children. While some migrants were happy with what they found in the city, many were disappointed. This emphasizes the idea that "Māori migrants both 'romanticised and vilified' their tribal homes from the city, 'usually in comparison to what was good or bad about city life' [Harris 2007: 56]" (Williams 2010: 208–9). This was true for Māori migrants of the 1950s and 1960s as well as for Māori city dwellers of today.

Life in the city is often idealized by country dwellers, just as life in the country is idealized by city dwellers. This twin idealization hints at a certain lack of communication between the two milieus, and a certain almost-shared solitude that is not expressed to the other despite ongoing connections. Fiona, one of the research participants, conveys well this reciprocal envy and idealization between rural and urban cousins:

I am very staunch when it comes to my *taha Māori* [Māori side] and yet, I don't maintain strong links with my own tribal community. I have strong links with the Māori community, the university Māori community. My partner and I don't maintain a strong link with our own tribes. And I think mainly that's because . . . I think mainly for myself it's because I wasn't brought up in my tribal area because my father was a school teacher and I was raised outside my own tribal area. When we did go back there . . . I knew my cousins and that but I wasn't brought up with them and when I go back, all of my cousins look very tight and very close . . . They never ever made me feel as an outsider, they always recognize me, but I think within myself I did feel like an outsider because I wasn't brought up with them. They, at some point in their life, they all lived with my *koro* [grandfather] and my *kuia* [grandmother] and I have never lived with my *koro* and my *kuia*. I sort of felt stink about that too, because it's a real traditional Māori value that. As a *mokopuna* [grandchild], you're raised with your elders and I wasn't raised with my elders, so . . . [. . .] I feel stink about that. A few years ago I went back to do a project with my *koro* and my *kuia* and one of my cousins made the comment that "Yeah! Some only come back when they need something," and I don't know if she was directly referring to me but I felt like she was, inside. I'm sort of the outsider [. . .] because, as I said, I'm very staunch in my *taha Māori*, but when I go back to my tribal area, I try to be very humble because I wasn't raised there and some look down on me or I don't know. It's actually interesting 'cause we had my brother's twenty-first a few years ago and all the family came. [. . .] and my cousin got drunk and she said to me "Cous, I'm very scared of you!" [laughter] and I laughed and laughed and I said "Why?" and she goes "We're all scared of you, you know, you're at university and got your degree." Really, there's only a few of us from my father's family who have actually come through university, so I thought about it and then I thought "Gee! All my cousins are scared of me and on another level, I'm scared of them because when I go back, I haven't been raised within our tribal area. (Fiona)[19]

Fiona's quote illustrates not only a certain solitude in each milieu, but also a necessary coexistence and interdependence between urban-based and rural-based Māori. On the one hand, the city dwellers necessarily situate themselves in relation to the family, subtribe, and tribe in the countryside, which still represent a very important ontological foundation and serve to situate urban dwellers and the urban *whānau* (extended family) or urban networks in the larger Māori system, whatever the changes that city life has brought about. The family in the country remains an important link with traditions and culture as well as with Māori resources. On the other hand, the rural dwellers need, at times, both the skills of their urban cousins in Pākehā spheres/universes of meanings and their support and engagement in Māori universes of meanings to survive and, indeed, thrive. Both sides need each other to affirm Māori ways, visions, and rights more effectively.

Alternatively, Māori may use dreamtime arguments to assert their own superiority or proximity to the dreamtime in comparison with others. This last usage sometimes creates conflicts, since some people see themselves as better than others at reproducing or living the dreamtime. A kind of power game can be played around dreamtime among those who supposedly aspire to or incarnate it more perfectly. I also noted tensions regarding this issue between young and old: for some older people, life in the past was far better than today, when everything is so superficial. According to many participants in my research, dreamtime narratives can indicate a refusal on the part of the older generation to live in today's world and accept, or at least acknowledge, what the young ones are doing to make things better for Māori or even to simply be Māori. Of course, this is not unique to Māori.

But all this is part of the rhetoric about Māori authenticity. For most of the participants in my research, the refusal to make a home in the city was also linked to Māori politics about what a "real," "proper," "authentic" Māori was. It could be a way to prove one's "true" Māoriness in the face of the rhetoric about "urban" versus "real Māori." For many Māori who live in the city, the power and impact of this rhetoric of "real" versus "urban," "Pakehafied," or "plastic" Māori in their daily lives intensified in the last two decades of the twentieth century. This was in part due to the juridification of Māori property and the concomitant retribalization. This essentializing or stereotyping process further intensified as retribalization progressed with its claims settlements, the capitalization of traditional means and modes of production, and the bureaucratization of genealogy.[20]

Urban-based Māori appealed to the Courts of Justice to establish their own rights to ancestral resources, thereby challenging the exclusive legitimacy of the tribes that had become established since the short-lived Runanga Iwi Act 1990,[21] which empowered tribal authorities to deliver government programs. The fisheries case is a well-known example of that process (see, among others, Durie 1998; Levine 2001; Hill 2009; Rata 2000; Schwimmer 2001a; Schwimmer, Houle and

Breton 2000; Sissons 2004; Orange 2011; Van Meijl 2006b; Walker 1996; Webster 2002).[22] The Treaty of Waitangi Fisheries Claims Settlement Act 1992 (the Sealord deal) disadvantaged urban-based Māori, because Te Ohu Kai Moana (the Fisheries Commission), which carried the burden of constructing an allocation formula, agreed that urban-based Māori had no rights to a fishing quota, leaving only the "traditional" tribes as beneficiaries. Urban-based Māori's claims then became increasingly forceful and they appealed to the New Zealand courts. In April 1996, the Court of Appeal ruled in favour of "urban Māori" saying that *iwi* (tribes) did not have exclusive rights to fishing quotas. Te Ohu Kai Moana then went to the highest arena of appeal, the Privy Council of London, in 1997. The case involved the definition of the tribe and the allocation of Māori fishing quotas. The Privy Council objected to the Court of Appeal's failure to define the tribe, as the whole case hung on this, and therefore sent the matter back to the New Zealand High Court trial judge for further hearing. The High Court ruled that the Treaty of Waitangi Fisheries Settlement Act 1992 had defined the word *iwi* unambiguously so as to exclude any urban organizations and required the commission to provide solely to tribes, or bodies representing tribes, when distributing the assets. In October 1999, the Court of Appeal decision confirmed the August 1998 High Court decision. A case involving the same issues went to the Privy Council again in 2002. This time, the Privy Council dismissed the appeal and confirmed the New Zealand court's definition that *iwi* meant traditional tribes only. The Māori Fisheries Act 2004, which came into force on 26 September 2004, implements the agreements reached in the 1992 Act. However, through the establishment of a distinction between "the distribution of benefits and the allocation of assets" (Durie 2005a: 128), the Māori Fisheries Act 2004 also recognizes the rights of Māori who are not linked to tribal networks. The Fisheries Commission

had favoured a model that attempted to balance the obligation to allocate quota to iwi, as the court required, and the expectation that all Māori should benefit from the settlement. Quota would be allocated according to both demographic and geographic principles; all inshore quota were to go to iwi according to the length of the tribe's coastline, whereas the deepwater quota were split on a 75:25 basis, the greater share (75 per cent) being allocated to iwi according to the size of their populations, and the remaining 25 per cent to be allocated on the basis of the length of tribal coastlines. Although most was destined for iwi, with a one million dollar minimum

for each iwi, a twenty million dollar fund for Māori who were not linked
to tribal networks was also established. (Durie 2005a: 125–6).[23]

The long struggle, which manifests itself particularly clearly over the
fisheries allocation, is summarized by Sissons (2004), as a struggle on
two fronts:

> on the one hand, with other Maori who maintain that Maori society is es-
> sentially tribal and that power and decision-making should remain cen-
> tred on rural *marae* (ceremonial meeting places with meeting houses and
> dining halls); on the other hand, with the imagination of New Zealand
> as both a bicultural nation, in which Maori belong as cultured individu-
> als, and a treaty nation within which tribes are accorded fundamental im-
> portance by the Government and its agencies. There is a struggle against
> mutually reinforcing definitions of Maori society and the New Zealand
> nation that have been in the making for more than a century. (20)

The struggle has allowed distinctions between tribal Māori on the
one hand and those who identify as Māori but not with a particular
tribe on the other to emerge and fossilize to some degree over the years
(see also George 2010; Williams 2010: 204–5). The essentializing rhetoric
of what was a "real" Māori became an "orientational device" (Ramstad 2003) for some of those who lived in the city, but who wanted to
differentiate themselves from "urban Māori"; that is, Māori "who do
not know where they come from," who have not been "brought up as
Māori," and have (partially) lost their connections to their tribe(s) and
subtribe(s) in the country.

In this context, experiencing the city as a cold and alien place was
considered to be an "authentic" and "normal" feeling for "real" Māori;
that is, Māori who know where they come from and who still have
connections to their extended family and tribe(s) back in the country.
Therefore – and this was particularly salient during my first fieldwork
in 2001 and 2002 because of the characteristics of Māori politics at the
time and the general political context – it was also *not* right, if it were
even possible, for "real" Māori to consider the city an exciting place
to live, although they may more or less secretly like some if not many
aspects of the city. It was felt that there was something suspicious and
superficial about Māori who liked city life too much or felt "too" comfortable in Auckland and other big cities. Such a norm could give rise to
ambiguous emotions and a good deal of stress for many people. Thus,

many Māori nurtured a dream – and also more concrete projects – of returning to the tribal area while also critically distancing themselves, at least as part of a rhetorical strategy, from the "new" place.

The rhetoric about "real" versus "urban Māori" has been one important site for resistance to Pākehā and more generally to Western dominance, but not the only one. It has also allowed for ambiguity, which has made people realize that life in the city was not necessarily damaging, as long as they managed to balance relationships with their extended family and tribe(s), and with their city dweller social networks. It was widely recognized that the city was an important place for particular categories of persons, such as Māori artists to gain support and recognition, Māori students to gain qualifications, and also Māori activists to be effective, since the city was an important locus of state power, an important site to establish alliances with other marginalized or activist people and groups, a crucial place to express differences and claim rights, and a place where one could "disappear" and "be forgotten" for some time. This did not prevent people from also supporting the rhetoric about "true" Maoriness. More generally, the status of "real", Māori was easily accorded to any Māori who successfully balanced his or her engagement in and with the city and his or her people in tribal areas.

For example, during *tangihanga* (funerals), Māori who managed this balance supported their urban fellows by having the funerals in an urban, pan-tribal *marae* in a private house, or in a community centre. Afterward they would take the body to the tribal *marae* in the country and then to the cemetery of the ancestors, which is of profound symbolic significance in the Māori tradition. In this way, the *mana* (spiritual power, authority, prestige) of both the city dwellers and the country dwellers was reinforced, while "authentic" Māori ways were respected. The rhetoric about "real" versus "urban Māori" is ambiguous, leaving much space for heteroglossic interpretations and actions.

If the label "urban Māori" carried (and carries) negative connotations, it should be said it was not rejected by all and at all times. The label has possibly even gained in legitimacy. Many Māori described themselves as "urban Māori" as a political strategy and as a strong assertion of their identity. It was the basis of many urban-based Māori projects and claims in the 1980s and 1990s, such as in the fisheries case (Durie 1998; Sissons 2004). However, during my first fieldwork in 2001 and 2002, I did not meet many Māori individuals who spoke of themselves as "urban Māori." Those who identified more strongly with the urban setting preferred to say that they were Māori and lived in the city and that they belonged to an urban tribe or family, if this was the case. Others, however, used the designation "urban Māori" for themselves, but it meant primarily that they lived in the city. "Urban Māori to me is . . . just living in the city" and "I do class myself as urban Māori because I have been brought up in the town, I have always been living in the city" (Debra).[24] That is why I use the expression "urban-based Māori" over "urban Māori" whenever possible. However, Debra also added,

> Māori living in the city . . . because when you go back to home, then you see how different you really are to our people back home [. . .] We're a bit more inclined to more material things . . . [. . .] And before I learnt my *reo*, I would have been even more urban Māori [laughter]. (Debra)

Debra's comments illustrate that even if Debra said that an urban Māori was simply a Māori who lived in the city, she did see urban Māori as being different from rural Māori. Her experience led her to make the following link: the less one knew about Māori *tikanga* (custom, rules) and the Māori language, the more one "qualified" as an urban Māori.[25] This adds weight to the rhetoric about Māori authenticity and reveals a depth of internalization. During my last stay in New Zealand in 2011, however, there were important signs indicating that the essentializing tendency might be lessening as the passing of time brought increased self-confidence to many individuals and more Māori successes. I observed an apparent waxing and waning depending on the times and the larger political context. The Māori Fisheries Act 2004, which acknowledged the Māori urban authorities, was very much part of a changing context. Keiha and Moon (2008: 2) emphasize that "Maori urban authorities are now a permanent feature in Maori society, and are an entirely legitimate form of association, in both a structural and cultural sense" (see also Rangiheuea 2010). The so-called foreshore and seabed controversy, including the rhetoric of race used by non-Māori during the episode, which was part of a larger conservative backlash (Barber 2008; Miller 2005), has also played a role in lessening the divisions among Māori. The feeling of unity stimulated the mobilization that led to the 2004 *hikoi* (march) and to the creation of the Māori Party, the first party to appeal to mainstream Māori opinion and cut across tribal and social class divides (Miller 2005; Smith 2010b). The party also had an important urban base and Pita Sharples, the party's coleader, was a well-known "urban" figure, involved for years in many Auckland organizations and voluntary associations. Among other things, he occupied numerous leading functions at Hoani Waititi *marae*, a pan-tribal *marae* based in West Auckland.

Hearing everyday Māori conversations, talking with Māori, and listening attentively to taped interviews, I soon became aware of the repetition and multiple contexts of words like "comfort," "comfortable," "uncomfortable," and "comfort zone." I was particularly struck by these words because of my francophone background. In French it is less common to express one's feelings in terms of comfort. Francophones would tend to describe or qualify more specific feelings, whereas English-speakers might use a generalized idea of "comfort." A whole range of physical sensations, moods, and states of mind can be expressed with the word "comfort" and its derivatives by English-speaking people, including, of course, Māori speaking in English.[26]

The concept of "comfort" is used by Māori to express their own experiences in different spheres and at different levels, such as, for example, their feeling of belonging to different groups, including the *whānau* and larger entities, and thus to qualify their relationships among "us" and with "others." It is also used to express their feeling of belonging to spaces or sites like *marae*, mainstream universities, and Auckland and New Zealand as a whole. As Radice (2000) explains, one's comfort in the world(s) says a lot about internal, external, and in-between or relational factors:

> it allies several different realms of experience, including "internal" factors like one's emotional state, sense of security, and knowledge; "external" factors such as the weather, available information, physical ease, and fellow city-dwellers' attitudes; and "in-between" ones like having room for manoeuvre (both literal and metaphorical), interacting with other people, being satisfied or not with one's material fortunes, and so on. "Feeling comfortable" is therefore the bridging concept *par excellence* between "inside" and "outside." (131)

For Māori, expressing oneself in terms of comfort speaks volumes about one's being (as a person or a group) and one's relationships with the immediate physical and social environment and the wider world. "Comfort" features in intersubjectivity and coexistence, and regulates relationships. In the context of Auckland, the comfort felt by Māori is one of the factors that make their relationships with others easier (or not). These "others" are not always non-Māori: they may be Māori too but from different tribes or other kinds of groups, Māori who do not share the same philosophies or ways of life, or Māori who are not part of the *whānau*.

Comfort also always implies its uncomfortable counterpart: it is always conditional, requiring constant negotiation to be reached or maintained. "One does not feel comfortable permanently" (Radice 2000: 131). The measure necessary to feel comfortable depends on personal needs and preferences, on particular circumstances and global forces, and on collective and cultural parameters, values, or principles that are intrinsic to the universe(s) of meanings in which one engages. Feeling comfortable is context-dependent: one can be comfortable or uncomfortable to varying degrees in particular situations or in response to the presence of a particular person, group, or element of the natural, social, or cultural landscape. Comfort or discomfort can also be felt through a combination of several factors in a given space/time. With this in mind, I will here enquire further into Māori sense of the city and its residents, as well as how they perceive it in terms of comfort.

Comfort and discomfort in Auckland is closely related to a sense of security or insecurity, which can be physical, emotional, or social. "Auckland drains me," said Kahu. That was her immediate answer when I asked her how she liked living in Auckland. She explained that the city is an austere place for Māori, but said that she did not really know why. "I am not too sure . . . I don't know what it is that makes it so draining. Honestly, though, if you look around the streets, they don't look relaxed."

According to Kahu, some areas of the city are worse than others, for instance, South Auckland, with its large Māori and Pacific populations. I often heard people comparing South Auckland with the Bronx, above all, because of the gangs that were active there and the (relatively) high crime rates. The comparison is quite surprising and, in my opinion, largely based on an outsiders' perception (see Borell 2005: 201). The area's poor reputation was related to a campaign of fear waged by the media, as well as to the history of local housing development and settlement (see Walker 1970). "By 1970 Aotearoa/New Zealand's suburbs were often seen as bland, monotonous and boring places of conformist activity, where leisure was typified by work on the house and section" (Perkins and Thorns 2001: 37–8). They were also seen as violent places because of the powerful stereotypes about the Māori/Polynesian presence in the mainstream press. A decrease in Māori purchasing power in the 1980s and 1990s (related to their very high unemployment rates in a context of neoliberal policies), resulted in many Māori families, mainly from a working-class background, moving into public housing in new estates such as Ōtara in South Auckland.[27] And this led to the stigmatization of the southern suburbs, which created racism in the urban housing market and caused a decline in Māori home ownership (Cram and Pitama 1998: 146; on Māori stereotypes and discrimination see also Metge 1964; Ballara 1986; Hill 2009). Those residential areas have also taken on largely negative connotations in the minds of the mainstream population, not only because of this ethnic predominance but above all because the state was heavily involved in the creation of these new suburbs (Perkins and Thorns 2001: 38), which attracted people with low incomes, including many Māori families. Belich (2001: 473) adds that "the effect was reinforced by 'white flight' in a cause-effect spiral" (see also Misa 2010b).

I should add that I heard the comparison from people who had never been overseas, let alone to the Bronx. In fact, crime rates in New Zealand, and in Auckland in particular, are relatively low compared to other Western nation states and capital cities.[28] However, this comparison with the Bronx is significant. The recourse to extreme images tells us much about the discomfort that some people feel in the city or with their everyday lives in general.[29] It also provides a way for Māori to contrast their negative feelings about the city with their equally extreme but very positive image of the peacefulness and "relaxedness" of the countryside.

I was always surprised when Māori told me how hard it was to live in the city, particularly in Auckland where they considered life to be too fast. I found Auckland to be calm when compared to many North American and European cities. Māori like to say that they live by "Māori time," meaning that, compared to "Pākehā time," they are more relaxed and traditionally, politically, and rhetorically more in tune with the rhythm of nature and the seasons. This is also part of the rhetoric of being Māori and the politics of differentiation.[30] However, all this does not negate that life in Auckland is experienced as much faster than Māori life in the countryside. Generally speaking, preoccupations such as working conditions and workload, social life and *whānau* (extended family) life are also of a different speed and general quality in the city than in the country.

In Auckland, one can feel very lonely, cut off from one's support network and, thus, from one's safety net. It often takes time before one "feels good" in the city, before one develops a new support network and is sufficiently at ease with the new environment to be able to relax.

Hiraina explained to me how Ruka and his family have helped her to, at last, feel comfortable in Auckland:

> Ruka has been somebody very important to me. He has been awesome and his family: his mum, his dad, his wife, his mother-in-law and his father-in-law. Ruka has done so much to encourage me to stay on, to hang out a little bit longer, I don't think without his help . . . even though he would probably say "I didn't do anything," but just being there and there . . . [are] a lot of things, he has done. He is really special to me. I don't think I would have been still here. (Hiraina)

When one is incorporated or adopted into a *whānau*, one feels more at ease in the city. Being part of a group or a family is very important in the development of a certain sense of comfort for Māori migrants to cities.

As illustrated by Hiraina, discomfort is also explained for many by the city experience being completely new: "I was a bit scared because it was my first time out and I didn't really know what it was about." The unknown, obviously, is an important source of discomfort and, conversely, experience and knowledge are a source of comfort. The *whānau* or support group, part of the realm of the known, is a great help for Māori migrants. This help is not only moral, emotional, and spiritual, it is also tangible, since the family network in the city provides an efficient channel to access jobs, churches, and all kinds of groups and services for Māori and for the general public in the city (for example, Metge 1964, Williams 2010). "Relatives eased the transition from school to work, country to city, Te Araroa to Auckland, Te Hauhanga to Whangarei. Relatives made big moves less lonely. They took new migrants to dances, helped them to find work, had them join the same rugby and netball teams and carpooled for visits home" (Harris 2007–8: 149). Having family in the city enables many Māori migrants to integrate faster in terms of finding employment and learning to use city networks, Māori or not.

Living in what was perceived as a "good" neighbourhood also increased the sense of comfort for the Māori I met, as was conveyed to me by July, Awhina, and Joana. Joana went so far as to speak of her network of neighbours as a new urban subtribe. As for Christine, she spoke about the suburb in West Auckland where she was raised and has lived for forty years as a *whānau*.[31] Both Joana and Christine know their neighbourhood and the people who live there very well and express a sense of control over their environment.

> You get to feel safe, it's like you know, when you're a baby in your own home, you know, you . . . you get the feeling of the place, you know you're safe here, you know. And that's how I feel. This is a safe place. I'm familiar with the surroundings, I'm familiar with the people, the community [. . .] Even though this place has been called a slum, and we had murders happen in this area, I just feel that this is a safe place to be, because I'm familiar with it, you know. (Christine)

What is implicit here is that Christine's engagement in her neighbourhood in the course of her everyday life has turned it into a familiar place, and thus into a comfortable one. A sentiment of safety and control has emerged from that engagement, to give her a sense of security and identity. Borell (2005) came to the same conclusions about Māori residents of South Auckland, as did Harris (2007–8: 146) about Māori migrants of the 1950s and 1960s based in West Auckland. Williams's (2010) analysis also raises the same idea. The sense of comfort, like the sense of being at home in certain places or with certain persons, changes through experience and engagement "in a repetition of habitual social interactions," or "in a routine set of practices" (Rapport 1997: 73), with "a good understanding of the communities" (Borell 2005: 202).

For some Māori, the city is the place where they can "stand tall," since they know it very well and know how to behave and interact with the different "others" that inhabit it. They are comfortable there, which is not necessarily or always the case on the ancestral *marae* and among its people, which may be rather unfamiliar. To return to Christine's sense of home, she has developed an almost umbilical relationship with her residential area, because she has engaged in/with it since birth. Her comfort extended to calling her residential area in Auckland her *tūrangawaewae*, which means "a place to put one's feet," a place to stand, a special connection to the land given through ancestry. It is a controversial and non-traditional use of the term:

> Well, you know, *tūrangawaewae* is . . . where our roots are and while my roots through my ancestors are in the East Coast area, the West Coast, and up north [. . .], I feel this is my *tūrangawaewae*, too, because I've grown up here and I'm really, really into West Auckland. (Christine)

Some contrast the spiritual home where their ancestors come from, the homeland or tribal area, with the *kāinga*, or the urban home of everyday life:

> Spiritually, my home is the origin of my upbringing because when I die, that's where I am going to go back to [. . .] But presently, and emotionally, my home is here, in Auckland, because I deal with life [here] on a day to day basis. (Pita)

Speaking about his place in Central Auckland, Matiu gave a definition of "*kāinga*":

> *Kāinga* is like a place of residence [. . .] like a home [. . .] I will call this my *kāinga* at the moment because I invested. When you start investing . . . oh . . . I don't know [. . .] If you have a *tane* [man, partner, husband] and you have a house and you share the housework . . . you have enough arguments and you have enough love time in the house, the house starts to take on that kind of . . . *āhua* [appearance, likeness, form, character], that kind of . . . You know how you can walk into some places and could feel warm and you could walk into other places and you can feel, you know, kind of cold. I think this place is a fairly warm place and I think it is because of the time that we have invested into the place. Yeah . . . *kāinga*. (Matiu)

Both kinds of home, then, are significant in terms of identity and as a source of inspiration (Ellis 2001: 9; see also Harris 2007, 2007–8; Williams 2010). The sense of home is thus plural for many Māori. Williams (2010) speaks about "co-existent home-places." A plurality of homes can develop following migration from the country to the city and a gradual engagement with the new urban milieu, or, on the other hand, for Māori from the city, following the discovery or reactivation of tribal affiliations or a reconnection to the ancestral rural spiritual home(s) and people(s). The plurality of homes thus emerges in the movement between places (Rapport 1997 and Rapport and Dawson 1998a, 1998b) and can develop in both directions; that is, from the city to the country or from the country to the city, along with comfort. The meanings of the home(s) themselves are in movement. The movements are physical as well as cognitive, and relations exist between both physical and cognitive movements (Olwig 1998: 226).

Another important point is that most of the time home and comfort are not about the individual, but about the *whānau*, the group, a "communal approach" (Harris 2007–8: 148). Home is where the foundations are laid for developing and upholding one's identity. "This is my home, this is my whanau," said Tama at his father's funeral, looking across the green fields toward his village in Ihimaera's novel *Tangi* (1996 [1973]: 187). This type of comment has come up again and again among the participants in this research. Home, then, is the family, living and dead, those who have passed away and those who have never left the land and who connect one to a *marae*, to a cemetery, and to the land. This increased comfort and self-confidence in the city, the result of being part of a group or *whānau*, also allows Māori to feel more comfortable in other sociocultural spaces.

The Māori sense of comfort includes embodied and spiritual dimensions and the quality of the *wairua* is crucial to whether Māori call a place home. Māori I met defined the *wairua* as the feeling that emanates from the place, its people, and the *tīpuna* (dead ancestors) or spirits who gather there. The *wairua*, "it's something that you feel" (Christine). "You know how you can walk into some places and could feel warm and you could walk into other places and you can feel, you know, kind of cold?" (Matiu). Talking about her place and the surrounding area where she has lived for forty years, Christine said: "I just love the feel of this place!" Manuka, a Māori research participant and a member of my research team, explained that the *wairua* has nothing to do with the fact that a house is flash or has fancy furniture, but relates rather to the people (living and dead) inhabiting the place (see also Ihimaera 1972; Grace 1986). The *wairua* is intangible, "something you can't really explain, but you know it's there" (Keita). Māori who talk volumes about comfort and discomfort are very sensitive to these feelings. "It's that sixth sense" (Keita).

The city is often described as a cold place by many Māori, in contrast to the warmth they perceive in rural communities in general. It is quite common for country people everywhere to experience the city at first as a cold place and urban dwellers as cold people. This is not peculiar to Māori. But what is interesting is their use of rhetoric about the city being a cold and alien place for "real" Māori, specifically. A rhetoric of discomfort is thus used with the aim of proving or asserting one's authenticity as Māori. Such rhetoric, not used by all Māori and in all contexts, is most commonly employed by Māori who live in the city but want especially to insist that "they know where they come from." I do not want to imply here that those who talk of the city as cold do not "really" experience it as a cold place. Many do. But many also refer to this feeling as an "authentic" and "normal" feeling for people who know who they are and still have strong connections to their extended family and tribe back in the country.

Feeling at ease with the rural area can also have a significant impact on (dis)comfort in the urban one. Comfort or discomfort in the city does not depend entirely on urban conditions, experiences, and feelings. Aroha, for example, explained her ease in most contexts, Māori or Pākehā, urban or rural, by reference to a strong grounding in her rural milieu:

> I am comfortable with most situations because I know where I am from and I have good *kaumātua* [elders] and good family which ground me to my *marae* [traditional meeting place and ceremonial centre] [. . .] Because I know I come from there, I feel quite full, I feel quite comfortable to go to different places as a visitor and I can let myself be welcomed by those people because I know where I am from [. . .] Spiritually, I know where I come from and I know there are greater beings than me. It's knowing where I come from, but it's also having that element of belief, of spirituality, of believing in the power of our ancestors, and believing in good [. . .] [and] believing that good prevails. And that's what makes me comfortable, that's what is comforting for me. (Aroha)

Knowing where one comes from is thus not only about oneself and one's own identity and self-confidence, but also about relating to others.

> There is a saying we have in Maoridom and it is *"No hea koe?"* which means "where are you from?" and that links you. It is called *whakapapa* [genealogy] and once you know your *whakapapa*, it is easy to fit in. Like for instance that man there, he is from up north and he said "do you know my uncle?" you see, and we all do that and then suddenly there is a commonality . . . and then you know who their *tīpuna* [ancestors] are and then you know where their land is, so it is a lot easier to work if there is an element of trust or an element of commonality. (Maxine)

According to Maxine, it is very important in the city to be able to establish commonalities and relationships and to (re)establish *whānau* connections. Achieving a sense of being part of a *whānau* is also one of the motivations behind many Māori initiatives in the city, such as workshops, tribal festivals, *hui* (meetings), and a wide range of social welfare and preventive programs.[32] It has important practical implications. In

Maxine's case, it was crucial both to survive in the business world and to get by as a single mother of four children.

Aroha's case also reveals a dimension of comfort and discomfort that has to do with connections to the spiritual world and that involves keeping certain beliefs alive or behaving according to them, and maintaining a positive attitude toward life in general and urban life in particular. Comfort and discomfort in particular situations are thus related to one's general level of well-being. Aroha's overall sense of ease was deeply bound up in the support she received from her family and tribe, in particular her *kaumātua* (elders). Most of them lived in her tribal area in the country rather than in the city, and they would come and visit her when they deemed it necessary. For example, when Aroha decided to begin research toward a PhD, they came to meet her PhD supervisor, to be sure that Aroha was in good hands and to confirm their feelings about the supervisor. They also came to bless the place where she was to pursue her research, to ensure successful studies.

Asking for their agreement, support, and blessing to undertake PhD research was very important for Aroha and is part of the *tikanga* (traditions) for many Māori students at the university. Māori students will consult their *whānau* about their choice of research topic, whatever the discipline, but especially if it is about Māori or concerns Māori in any way. This practice of accompanying or *tautoko* (supporting) family members for new studies, job interviews, public presentations, meetings, and so on is widespread among Māori and part of tradition (Durie 2001a). The family, which also includes non-kin friends, shows to the others present that the candidate is well supported and surrounded. This practice also shows one's *mana* (spiritual power, authority, status) in being a united family. In the city and within mainstream institutions, however, this demonstration of support, even if well intentioned, can also be a source of discomfort for candidates, who may feel embarrassed by their family's insistence on accompanying them at crucial moments when they know that it is not in "the culture" of the people and institution in question.

What is also crucial for Māori is to work not only for their own sake, but for the benefit of one or all of their extended family, tribe, or Māori more generally.[33]

To be honest with you, I don't want to do a doctorate. I can't think of anything worse, to sit around for three years and write about something. I would rather be on holiday, I don't know, shocking! On an island trip or I could retire and just be my husband's wife. I don't need to do this, it's not for me that I'm doing this doctorate, I don't get much of pleasure out of this stuff [. . .] The reason that I'm going to try to get my doctorate, it's so that I can be in a position to help people from my *iwi* [tribe] because we are in a bad situation at the moment and I know it's just my destiny. I'm on a boat and I can't get off [. . .] I just even know how I end up doing things sometimes because it's just come to me, like in a dream or something, it comes and I'm just told to do so. I mean I'm happy in my personal life with my husband, my family, my friends, I certainly have a very good life [. . .] This study and stuff [. . .], it's not for me, it's for the tribe, it's for other young Māori people [. . .], it's for all those families that don't have access to education and health and money and houses, decent clothing, decent food . . . This doctorate, although it's a doctorate, it's a *taonga* [treasure], it's some way of making life a bit better. (Aroha)

That Aroha is doing her doctorate for her tribe is comforting, and that is also what makes her comfortable in general both around the university and in her daily life with her immediate family. Because she has been told by her *tīpuna* (dead ancestors) through signs and dreams to engage in doctoral studies, she would feel immensely uncomfortable if she were not to follow what she calls her "destiny." She was *meant* to do a doctorate, she was *chosen* by the ancestors and by certain living elders from her tribe. Now that she has made the decision to pursue her PhD studies, she feels good, she has a positive attitude to life, and she is happy. Aroha does not deny that other factors influence her general sense of ease. She acknowledges that she and her husband have a good financial and professional situation, which helps her to be more positive and to feel comfortable in the city and elsewhere: "And I feel comfortable because I can afford a $10 in my pocket to pay for my lunch and I can pay my friends a cup of tea" (Aroha).

Being comfortable in the city, however, is not only created by the knowledge of where one comes from, the easy relationships with one's tribal area and its people, and a secure socioeconomic situation. The opposite is also true: some uncomfortable aspects of rural life can explain a sense of urban comfort. For Aroha, the city means freedom, in terms of being more independent from the extended family and the subtribe who live very closely together in the countryside. The city also means the freedom to go where she pleases without being glared at, as she was when she went to what she calls "the Pākehā side of the village." There is a certain anonymity in Auckland that allows more freedom; one is not as easily monitored. At the end of her studies, she wants to find a job in the city and does not want to go back to her tribal area. However, the *kūmara* vine (literally sweet potato vine, but "grapevine" in common English) also creeps into the metropolis, and people there, too, eventually hear almost everything.

Mihi moved away from her village specifically to leave an uncomfortable situation: she left an abusive husband behind. The city for her meant a new beginning, even if it was difficult to live by herself at first. Joana's *whānau* was crucial in helping her to feel comfortable and to recognize the new avenues opening up before her. For Pita and Jackie, Auckland also meant that they could live freely and openly as gay and lesbian, which would not be widely accepted by the family in the country. In the city, their identity as gay could at times become more important than their Māori identity and lead them to become more involved in the Pākehā gay scene or the Pākehā world in general. Or they also, in the city, have the possibility of combining their participation in Māori and Pākehā circles.[34]

Life in the city allows for more possibilities and more choices, since many diverse and sometimes conflicting worlds are present and can be experienced on a daily basis. The city can be felt to be a comfortable place by people whose lives were restricted in the countryside, or by people who in the city can choose more freely among diverse possibilities. This does not mean that one is completely free in the city; on the contrary, there is considerable pressure to conform to certain stereotypes or to limit oneself to particular choices, sectors of the city, social horizons, or universes of meanings. Life in the city is more expensive and has its own set of problems.

Some Māori I encountered found the urban setting to be a place that opened up possibilities of "play" in several semiotic spaces at the same time, depending on their particular needs and circumstances – an opening made available to them through their Maoriness. Of course, this implies a good knowledge of the different worlds and a certain mastery of the different codes and realms of interpretation. It also meant being comfortable enough with each universe of meanings to be able to code-switch when necessary, either consciously or not, if the code was well internalized. For Rongo, this capacity to move through both worlds was clearly seen as a political advantage: "The thing with Māori and Pākehā, Pākehā should be scared of Māori because they don't have any understanding of them [. . .] But we understand them!" Since many Māori face "other" worlds in the city on a daily basis and have no choice but to acquire a fluency and competence in their workings through habitus (Bourdieu 1977, 1980), life in the city helps to build this capacity to "play" in multiple universes of meanings.

Knowing how Pākehā or others in general "work" and react allows one to anticipate reactions, behave correspondingly and easily, and feel comfortable. The same is true when Māori are among themselves: they usually feel comfortable because they know exactly how things "work"; they are familiar with the internalized codes of the universe of meanings in play – that is, with what is tacit or unsaid (see also Harris 2007–8: 147–8).

But discomfort can also be experienced among Māori. Roimata explained to me how uncomfortable she felt when she went to Māori gatherings in South Auckland. She did not know the "right" way to present herself, as she was used to living in Central Auckland, mainly among well-off Pākehā, as she said. Factors such as differences in tribe, social class, status, gender, and schooling must be taken into account. The "us" is not always the "generic Māori."

At the national level, discomfort can be linked to a sense of exclusion and powerlessness, and the idea that everything is beyond one's own reach. "Good health [and comfort in general] is not compatible with political marginalization any more than it is with socio-economic deprivation," writes Durie (2001a: 54). Because Māori are overrepresented in the lower social classes (see Poata-Smith 2004b), they often feel marginalized and believe that they do not have a real say at the policy-making level, even if this perception is changing today with the breakthrough of Māori in Parliament, as well as Māori development and the numerous successes of tribal and non-tribal groups in the last past several years. The statistics are often confirmed by a daily experience of exclusion at the bank, at school, when looking for accommodation, and so on.

A vicious circle is created. Those Māori who feel alienated and excluded from the decision-making process increasingly disengage themselves from it and express negative, pessimistic feelings and thoughts about it. Many express no feelings or thoughts at all on the matter. This might also be true of tribal politics. Generally speaking "alienated" Māori do not keep themselves particularly well informed about what is happening on the regional and national political scenes either.

Some participants in my research suggested that this lack of interest was also often related to their preference to concentrate on staying positive in their own lives, knowing that the more they know about "the world out there," the more depressed and stressed they will feel. For others, making ends meet and making sure that the bills are paid took most of their energy.

The lack of concern with politics and social policy is perhaps exacerbated in the city, where people feel the negative and stigmatizing effects of "the statistics" more directly. It could also explain why some Māori withdraw from any social life beyond their close and extended families. They know almost nobody in the city and feel incompetent in and rather excluded from the larger environment.

But this withdrawal depends also on particular circumstances and contextual events, which can renew Māori interest for what happens on the regional or national scene and in public affairs. This was the case during the foreshore and seabed controversy described at the beginning of this book.

The notion of "comfort" and its use by Māori is complex. Home, like comfort, is created through relationships with the living, the dead, the past and the present, and through engagement within different places and spaces. When Māori speak about comfort, they also speak about their relationships with all these entities. Making oneself at home and making oneself comfortable is about "negotiating a complexity of relations, imagery from other contexts, which overlap with the home context itself" (Hirsch 1998: 164).

Comfort and home are in themselves always rather ambiguous ideas in constant flux and movement. What is home, then? "It all depends," replies Hollander (1991: 31). The same is true for comfort. A comfort zone is a blurred zone with blurred boundaries. Zones of comfort and discomfort cross each other constantly and the boundaries of comfort zones are constantly changing. And comfort, like home and "like any word we use to cover a particular field of experience, always begets its own negation. Home may evoke security in one context and seem confining in another" (Jackson 1995: 122–3).

Meanings of home and feelings of comfort and discomfort change through experience and specific contexts. They also are changed by engagement in particular universes of meanings, places, and spaces, which are in turn influenced by larger structures like the state, local and national events, and trans-national forces. Specific local circumstances or realities are experienced differently under changing regional and global conditions. Comfort and home should be understood as lived relationships and not as distinct realities, entities, or essences.

Many Māori living in Auckland feel a certain discomfort. They are nostalgic about their past in the countryside with their extended family.

They miss the close contact with nature. They do not necessarily have a strong or large network in the city for mutual assistance and friendship. They often feel alienated from their work and study environments. And they must often struggle against difficult everyday circumstances (such as poverty or a poor quality of life in their neighbourhood).

But, as already described, not all Māori experience the city as uncomfortable. Some enjoy the city. They feel very comfortable in it and build a home there. People have various reasons for migration to the city. The choice to migrate is often linked to economics, with Auckland apparently offering higher salaries or better work prospects and conditions. Auckland can also be seen to offer other opportunities such as better schooling for both children and adults and a greater variety of cultural and artistic activities. Others leave the rural area because of tribal politics or family disagreements or because they feel under too much pressure to conform to family or tribal norms of behaviour or ways of life. Some Māori migrants leave to escape abuse by a partner, parents, or other relatives or because they are simply looking for new experiences.

Despite such differences, life for Māori migrants in the city brings about important changes for them all. It becomes increasingly difficult in the city to meet obligations associated with the extended family and to share in its activities, especially when they take place outside the city. But new kinds of *whānau* groups and activities develop in the urban setting.

Whatever the circumstances of Māori in Auckland, comfort is a preoccupation, and there are no strict distinctions among those who achieve it and those who do not. Metaphorical or symbolic sites of affirmation as Māori and the resistance to the mainstream society, and the West more generally, vary and are interrelated in complex ways. Rhetoric about "real" versus "urban Māori" is one such site that attracts Māori engagement. The *marae*, the traditional Māori meeting place and ceremonial centre, is another to which I will now turn.

3 The *Marae*: A Symbol of Continuity

Central to Māori ceremonial and community life is the traditional Māori meeting place and ceremonial centre – the group of fenced buildings called *marae*. *Marae* stand traditionally on family and tribal lands but are now also part of the urban landscape. They constitute an important contemporary symbol of identity and continuity and have become a key site for collective cultural and sociopolitical affirmation.

It has long been noted that Māori belong to their *whānau*, *hapū* (subtribe), and *iwi* (tribe). They also belong to *marae*. New evidence put forward by Sissons (2010) has led to the idea that Māori society might be more fundamentally organized as a relationship between houses, rather than through rules of descent, even if both dynamics are at work.

Basically, "[t]he *marae* is a local ceremonial centre, dedicated to the gatherings of Maori people and to the practice of traditional rituals. Each *marae* has a meeting house, a dining-hall and other small buildings set in about an acre of land and fenced off from surrounding properties" (Salmond 1975: 31). Sometimes one can find a *whare mate* (house where the dead lie in state), a church, a *urupa* (cemetery), a *kura kaupapa Māori* (Māori immersion school), a *kohanga reo* (Māori language kindergarten), or other buildings on a *marae* or nearby. The meaning and use has evolved.

Traditionally, the term "*marae*" was only used to designate the expanse of lawn, the vacant area, directly in front of the chief's house[1] or the meeting house, the ceremonial courtyard, "an open space reserved and used for Maori assembly" (Metge 1976: 227).[2] This first meaning of the word "*marae*" is the definition that is still given in the Williams's *Dictionary of the Maori Language* (2000 [1971]: 180), an "[enclosed] space in front of a house, courtyard." Metge (2010: 70–1) specifies that "[s]ince the 1980s Māori have distinguished the courtyard in front of the meeting-house from the marae complex by adding the adjective ātea (without obstruction, open) but they do this only when it is necessary to avoid confusion." Metge (1976: 232) coined the appellation "marae proper" (see also Metge 2010: 70), also often used today to distinguish it from the whole complex of buildings, which is also referred to as a pā (fortified place) (Metge 2010; Salmond 1975; Tauroa and Tauroa 1986). According to Mead (2003: 95), the new usage of the word "marae" came about in the late 1960s "partly as a result of the publication by the Department of Education's School Publications branch of a book called Washday at the Pa, by Ans Westra. There were a lot of negative reactions to the book, after which the word pā [fortified place or village] became very unpopular."

The functions of the marae ātea (ceremonial courtyard) are to welcome visitors and provide a space to exchange speeches and express points of view (Tauroa and Tauroa 1986: 59). Most of the powhiri (welcome ceremony) takes place on the ceremonial courtyard, but it can also be held inside the meeting house when it rains or during the cold season.

The marae is first and foremost a meeting place, but, as Tauroa and Tauroa write, "[it] is the family home of generations that have gone before. It is the standing place of the present generation and will be the standing place for the generations to come" (19). This standing place from which people take their rights is referred to as their tūrangawaewae (literally translated as "a place to put one's feet"), the connection to the land, to Papatūānuku, the Earth Mother, who is represented by the ceremonial courtyard. Through their tūrangawaewae (connection to the land), Māori gain rights as tāngata whenua (people of/from the land). Note that the word "whenua" means both land and placenta. Marsden and Henare (1992) explain the relationship between Māori and the land in this way:

The Maori thought of himself as holding a special relationship to mother earth and her resources. The popular name of the earth is whenua. This is also the name for the "afterbirth." Just as a foetus is nurtured in the mother's womb and after the baby's birth upon her breast, so all life forms are nurtured in the womb and upon earth's breast. Man is an integral part of the natural order and recipient of her bounty. He is her son and therefore, as every son has social obligations to fulfil towards his parents, siblings and other members of the whanau [extended family], so has man an obligation to mother earth and her whanau to promote their welfare and good (17, quoted in Waymouth 2003).

The *tūrangawaewae* is also the connection to the ancestors who came before, who walked and cried on the *marae*, and who are now buried there. According to Durie (1999: 362), it is about identity, an identity that goes beyond a particular land and embraces wider environments distant in time, space, and understanding. It is thus also about inter-connectedness and unity: "connections over time, connections between tribes and peoples, connections which link secular and spiritual, temporal and ethereal" (359).[3] It is the spiritual home and thus a sacred place (Tauroa and Tauroa 1986: 23). It is figuratively "a base, a strong-hold" (Metge 1967: 180), the "standing place from where one gains the authority to belong" (Tauroa and Tauroa 1986: 166).

When valued as *tūrangawaewae*, the *marae* becomes "a place which can complement a personal identity and lead to a greater sense of purpose and continuity" (Durie 2001a: 79). It gives the right "to participate in determining the kawa [protocol] of the marae; to determine what functions can be held and when they might best be held; to define roles on the marae; and to ensure that hospitality is provided to others" (Tauroa and Tauroa 1986: 38). On your own *marae*, "no-one can boss you around" (Salmond 1975: 60). It also gives rights to shares in the land; that is, "rights *in* the *marae*" as opposed to "rights *on* the *marae*," which are privileges in its use (Metge 1967: 179).

There are different types of *marae*, but in the case of *marae* dedicated to one descent-group, the rights in the *marae* are inherited through *whakapapa* (genealogy), through both male and female lines (Metge 1967: 174; Salmond 1975: 60). The people who have those rights are the *tāngata whenua*, the "people from the land," in opposition to *manuhiri* (visitors). Genealogy gives rights, but also responsibilities and obligations as *kaitiaki* (guardian) of the land and the *marae*. In order not to lose them, these rights must be kept "warm" by means of residence or frequent visits, known as *ahi kā*, which means "a fire kept alight" (Salmond 1975: 60).

The meeting house, which is the extension of the ceremonial court-yard, is used for sleeping and speech making when the weather is bad or at night. The meeting house and the ceremonial courtyard are symbolically in a relationship of opposition but this opposition is complementary. Tū, the god of mankind and war, is associated with the *marae* proper, while Rongo, the god of agriculture and the peaceful arts, is

associated with the meeting house. These associations refer symbolically to the ceremonial courtyard as the place where hostilities between
hosts and visitors should be resolved through debate while harmony
reigns inside the meeting house. This ideal in practice does not always
hold true. One can often witness the most heated and exciting debates
inside the meeting house (Metge 1976: 231).

The *mahau*, the porch of the meeting house, is a liminal zone linking
both areas. It is often used as an extension of the ceremonial courtyards:
kaumātua (elders) frequently sit there during welcome ceremonies and
in some places the coffin rests there during funerals (Salmond 1975).

The meeting house can take different names depending on both
tribal area and usage. It can be called *whare puni* or *whare moe* (sleeping
house), *whare whakairo* (carved house), *wharenui* (big house), *wharehui*
(meeting house), and *whare rūnanga* (council house) (Salmond 1975: 35;
Tauroa and Tauroa 1986: 90). It can also be called *whare tipuna* (ancestral
house) and is usually named after an ancestor.[4]

It represents the ancestor in a symbolic way. It is his or her body
(Metge 1976: 230; George 2010). As Tauroa and Tauroa (1986) summarize:

> the tekoteko (carved figure) on the roof top in front represents the ances-
> tor's head. The maihi (carved pieces from the tekoteko extending toward
> the ground) represent the arms of the ancestor, held out in welcome to vis-
> itors. The tahuhu or tahu (ridge pole), which runs down the center of the
> whare from front to back, represents the backbone. The tahuhu is a very
> long and solid piece of wood, for when the backbone is strong the body
> is strong. The heke or wheke (rafters), joining the tahuhu to the poupou
> (carved figures) around the walls, represent the ribs of the ancestor.
>
> The poupou usually represent ancestors from the tangata whenua and
> other tribes. A person with an understanding of whakapapa (genealogy)
> will identify the relationship between the tribal poupou and the tangata
> kainga (people from that marae).
>
> The pou tokomanawa (uprights) – of which there may be two in the
> whare whakairo – support the tahuhu and represent the connection be-
> tween Ranginui, the Sky Father, and Papatuanuku, the Earth Mother. The
> act of entering the house is interpreted symbolically as entering into the
> bosom of the ancestor. (91)

Inside the house, one is surrounded and protected by one's ancestors
and by the gods (Allen 2002: 48).

But the house itself is considered to be a living being, a contemporary living person, and not only a distant ancestor. In speeches, the house is addressed as a living elder (48), as this example greeting illustrates:

Te whare e tu nei, The house that stands here,
  Tena koe. I greet you. (Tauroa and Tauroa 1986: 114)

When Māori address a *whare tipuna* (ancestral house), they use a personal pronoun, referring to "him" or "her."

If the house is either or both carved and painted, all the forms represent various significant ancestral figures, people, or elements.[5] Whereas the house symbolizes a specific ancestor and events of the past,

each of the carved slabs within the house represents a slightly more recent figure in tribal history, or offshoots from the main descent-line . . . The final presentation of ancestral figures in the house are the portraits hung about the walls, which represent the most recent kin of all. (Salmond 1975: 39–41)

The meeting house, then, is "an architectural history book of the people concerned" (Salmond 1975: 39; see also Ihimaera 1972: 117). According to Rosenblatt (2011), the meanings assigned to the parts of the house form a "grammar" that represents the identity of the group and participates in its constitution and definition.

Because of its ancestral and highly symbolic character, the ancestral or meeting house as well as the *marae* proper is *tapu* (sacred), whereas the *wharekai* (kitchen or dining hall) is *noa* (free of religious restriction, ordinary). The cemetery is the most *tapu* place and for this reason, it is kept separate and fenced off from the *marae* complex (Salmond 1975: 42–3).

The concepts of "*tapu*" and "*noa*" are also important within the meeting house itself. They are opposite but complementary principles, which cannot and must not be kept separate (Metge 1976; Salmond 1975: 42); the relation between *tapu* and *noa* things should be seen as a matter of relativity and not as absolutes (Metge 1976: 232). The English word "sacred" is often used to translate *tapu*, but this definition does not fit all contexts. The Williams's *Dictionary of Maori Language* (2000 [1971]: 385; italics in original) defines *tapu* as:

1. a. *Under religious* or *superstitious restriction;* a condition affecting persons, places, and things, and arising from innumerable causes. Anyone violating **tapu** contracted a **hara** [offence, sin], and was certain to be overtaken by calamity. As a rule, elaborate ceremonies were necessary to remove **tapu** and make anything **noa** . . . 2. *Beyond one's power, inaccessible* . . . 3. *Sacred.* (mod.) 4. n. *Ceremonial restriction, quality or condition of being subject to such restriction.*

Noa is sometimes translated in English as "common," but its meaning is also much more complex than this simple word. *Noa* is defined as:

1. a. *Free from* **tapu** *or any other restriction* . . . 2. *Of no moment, ordinary* . . . 3. *Indefinite* . . . 4. *Within one's power* . . . 5. ad. denoting absence of limitations or conditions, to be translated variously according to context. (a) *Without restraint* . . . (b) *Spontaneously, of oneself* . . . (c) *Gratuitously* . . . (d) *Without consideration* or *argument* . . . (e) *At random, without object* . . . (g) *Fruitlessly, in vain* . . . (k) *Quite* . . . (l) *Just, merely.* (222–3; italics in original)

People, places, objects, and actions can be described as *tapu* and *noa* (Metge 1976: 58–9; Salmond 1975: 42). The degree of *tapu*-ness or *noa*-ness varies from mild to intense and also according to context. Both *tapu* and *noa* possess positive as well as negative values or aspects, one being positive when the other is negative. Metge (1976) gives the following examples:

Where *tapu* implies the presence of supernatural power (whether good or evil) and attracts attention and respect, *noa* implies the absence of such power and attracts neither attention nor respect. On these counts *noa* has negative value while *tapu* is positive. But *tapu* also stands for danger, restrictions on freedom of action, and anxious introspection to detect slips. *Noa* on the other hand is safety, freedom from restriction, and relaxed, outgoing warmth. On these counts it is *tapu* that has negative value and *noa* that is positive. (60)

Durie (1999: 356), drawing on Hiroa (1949), also underlines the utilitarian view of the *tapu/noa* distinction by saying that dangerous activities or locations can be declared *tapu* to prevent accidents, calamities, or misfortune. In contrast, *noa* is used to denote safety. Durie (1999: 357) also speaks about the "laws of *tapu*" as having a function of social control, control that is great on *marae* where most of the activities and behaviours are sanctioned by rules.[6]

So, the whole *marae* complex is *tapu* in relation to the outside world, while a series of *tapu* and *noa* parts in relation to each other are found within its boundaries. And each of these sectors is differentiated again into *tapu* and *noa* parts.

Strict measures are in place to ensure that no *tapu* is infringed. For example, alcohol is prohibited on most *marae*, and it is also more and more common to have smoke free *marae*.[7] Cooking and ceremonial activities are kept strictly separate. Neither food nor shoes should be taken into the meeting house. And women and certain categories of men (the young, the "insignificant," younger brothers, and sons of a living father; Salmond 1975: 45) are forbidden to speak on the ceremonial courtyard (except in the East Coast districts and Northland where women of high rank are allowed to speak as honorary "men" [44, 127]).

In relation to the outside world, *tāngata whenua* (people of the place, people connected to the *marae*) are *tapu* and in caring for their guests, they engage in both *tapu* and *noa* tasks. As explained by Metge (1976: 234), the *tapu* tasks – *karanga* (ceremonial call of welcome), *whaikōrero* (speeches), wailing – are carried out on the *marae* proper or in the meeting house by people of *mana*[8] such as elders, also called the *tāngata kei mua* (the people in front). The *noa* tasks are undertaken in the dining hall, kitchen, and toilets behind the scenes by the *tāngata kei muri* (people at the back). *Noa* tasks are as essential as the *tapu* ones to the success of the event and they are valued and acknowledged as such. Visitors are also *tapu* in relation to their hosts, in particular those described as *waewae tapu* ("sacred" feet), who are visiting that particular *marae* for the first time. The welcome ceremony will modify the *tapu* and will allow for social contact between visitors and hosts (Metge 1976: 234). There are also important *tapu/noa* distinctions inside the *wharenui* (meeting house)[9] that differentiate the right side from the left side. So, *marae* constitute an ordered domain that is highly regulated with precise protocols (hosts vs. visitors; *tapu* vs. *noa*; right vs. left; men vs. women).

The welcome on a *marae* is a very formal process that consists of the following sequence of actions: *te wero* (the challenge), *te karanga* (the call), *te powhiri* (the welcome), *te whakaekenga* (the moving on), *ngā mihi* (the greetings), *ngā whaikōrero* (the speeches), *te koha* (the gift), *te tutakitanga* (the physical contact) by means of *hariru* (shaking hands) and *hongi* (pressing nose).[10] Once the whole sequence of welcome on a *marae* is completed, the *tapu* of the visitors (*manuhiri tapu*) is lifted and visitors are free to move everywhere on the *marae* and to take part in the welcoming of other visitors (Tauroa and Tauroa 1986: 89–90). As emphasized by Rosenblatt (2011: 418), after the welcome, the hosts and the visitors become one single group and their oneness is thought of as a temporary kinship that is enacted and strengthened for the duration of the gathering.

Each *marae* has its own *kawa* (protocol), which might vary. For example, protocol determines the exact places where different people (visitors and locals, men and women, elders and young people) sit in the meeting house and on the ceremonial courtyard and this varies from tribe to tribe (for more examples and a discussion, see Karetu 1978).

The kitchen or dining hall is very important on a *marae*. It is the symbol of service to others, from which *mana* is bestowed through shared acts of service or *manaakitanga* (Tauroa and Tauroa 1986: 28), which Durie (1999: 358) describes as "the process whereby *mana* (power, authority) is translated into actions of generosity." *Mana* is above all associated with collective responsibility rather than individual brilliance, so all *marae* members join together in their efforts.

When Māori were living in villages surrounding or close to the *marae*, it would be used as the extension of their living quarters. But now the vast majority of Māori do not visit or perform activities on the *marae* on a daily basis (Metge 1967; Durie 1999). This is all the more true for city dwellers who often live some hours away from their *marae*:

> [a]bout one fifth of the participants in a study of Māori households, *Te Nuku Roa*, for example, have no recourse to visit a *marae*, and one third do so on a regular basis (*Te Hoe Nuku Roa* 1998). However, because it is likely that within wider *whanau* (family) networks other members of the family are more regularly involved, their lives will not be totally divorced from *marae*. (Durie 1999: 352)

Even in the country, most people do not go to the *marae* every day. Metge (1976: 235) explains that while

> [no] longer a village living-room, the *marae* is used, firstly, for the same purposes as other local halls: for club and committee meetings, recreation and money-raising, for church meetings and services where there is no church, for political meetings, welcomes and farewells, and discussions of local issues. But it is also used for two distinctively Māori purposes: for staging gatherings that attract large numbers of visitors to stay for several

days (*hui*), and for the temporary accommodation, between *hui*, of touring sports and concert parties, stranded strangers, and the temporarily homeless.

Of all the gatherings held at a *marae*, the *tangihanga* [funeral] is the most important.

Some people are chosen or volunteer to take care of the *marae*. They work on a voluntary basis (Mead 2003: 101), bar a few exceptional cases. They may be the only ones to visit the *marae* every day. Among the exceptions who still visit *marae* regularly are participants in particular projects, including students of Māori-language programs that take place on a *marae*, or children and their teachers who attend a *kohanga reo* (Māori language kindergarten) or a *kura kaupapa* (Māori immersion school) based on a *marae*, or people working in facilities located on a *marae* providing for a large array of services, including health services, counselling, financial advice, and training in different fields.[11] The apparent decline in everyday attendance on *marae* does not mean that *marae* principles and values are disconnected from most people's everyday lives. As we will see, some Māori have applied the *marae* principles and values in houses in the city and the country.

Traditionally, *marae* were of two types: (1) *whānau* (family) or *hapū* (subtribal) *marae*, which are mainly used by the direct descendants of the person who founded it, and (2) *iwi* (tribal) *marae*, which are used by all the people from a particular tribal area. Sissons (2010) says that *marae* of the first type are a relatively new development. According to him, an increase in the number of officially recognized *hapū* from the end of the 1870s to the end of the 1910s (see Ballara 1998) was accompanied by the building of new meeting houses. These were subtribe oriented and differed from earlier meeting houses, which were mainly "settlement houses – that is, they were used by groups comprising more than one *hapuu* residing together on collectively owned land under the leadership of one or more *rangatira* (chiefs). These were not the houses of single *hapuu*, but instead served principally as buildings in which guests from outside the valley were accommodated" (Sissons 2010: 379).

He also shows that the number of meeting houses in rural communities dramatically increased during the period 1880–1950, in part due to colonization and Christianization. New meeting houses were built to "host large political gatherings and/or to symbolise alliances between groups in opposition to the colonial government" (Sissons 2010: 379), but also for religious considerations. For example, in the 1880s and

1890s, many new meeting houses were constructed by the adherents of Te Kooti's Ringatū Church[12] throughout the North Island. On the East Coast, *marae* complexes consisting of a meeting house, a church, and a cemetery were built by Anglican communities (see Sissons 1998, 2010; but also Neich 1993; Binney 1995). According to Sissons (2010), this new situation, which was marked by a process of community fragmentation, has contributed to making Māori society progressively more house-based, as discussed in the previous chapter. Rosenblatt (2005: 120) also argues that the end of internal warfare during the nineteenth century also contributed to emphasizing the kinds of activities associated with meeting houses: "[m]eeting houses, which are carved to represent both an ancestor and the genealogy of the descent group, were an alternate way of performing the hapū." This is how meeting houses have become the centre and defining feature of rural communities (Rosenblatt 2011: 414).[13]

Today, these types of *marae*, which are seen as traditional, can be found on Māori land, mainly in rural areas. But some are located in urban or suburban areas where an extended family, a subtribe, or a tribe have ancestral rights on the land and still own a greater or smaller number of acres of it. Some of these *marae* predate urban settlement and the city has simply grown around them.

Since the 1960s, however, new types of *marae* have been built, following the urban drift that led to most Māori living too far from their own *marae* to visit regularly and, therefore with few places to meet for funerals and other gatherings. The first *marae* of the new or "modern" (Mead 2003: 106) type were urban *marae* that could be either tribal or pan-tribal. Tapsell (2002) establishes an additional distinction between *tāngata whenua marae* (that is, tribal *marae* belonging to the home people, the people who have the rights on the land) and *taurahere marae* (that is, non-tribal and immigrant-tribal *marae*). For a group to establish a *marae* outside of its own tribal territory breaks with general traditional rules according to which kin groups build *marae* on their own land. For this reason, "tikanga [custom, tradition] dictates that the group wanting to establish a marae must negotiate with the tangata whenua [people of the land] of that region and obtain their permission. Once the approval is obtained the group then proceeds to establish their *marae* and take full ownership and responsibility for it" (Mead 2003: 107).[14]

In Auckland, the first urban *marae* opened in Mangere, South Auckland, in 1965 and was named after Te Puea, a distinguished female paramount chief from the Waikato tribe (Walker 2004: 201). This *marae* is a traditional Waikato kin-based *marae*, but it is open to all urban-based Māori migrants, whatever their tribal affiliations. To use Tapsell's distinction noted earlier, this *marae* is a *tāngata whenua marae*, since the Waikato tribe has rights over the land in that area. In comparison, a Tūhoe *marae*, Te Tira Hou, is a *taurahere marae*, an immigrant-tribal *marae*. It opened in 1973 in Panmure, a southeastern suburb of Auckland.

Another important *marae* in Auckland is Ōrākei *marae*, whose meeting house was erected in 1973 (Tapsell 2002: 148). Ōrākei *marae* has a long history of struggles with the Crown, since it is located on some of the most desirable real estate in New Zealand (see Waitangi Tribunal 1987; Kawharu 1968, 1975, 1989a; James Henere Māori Research Centre 2002; Tapsell 2002). The forced eviction of the Ngāti Whātua people of Ōrākei from their *papakāinga* (ancestral village) in 1950 – officially for reasons of flood risk and unsanitary conditions, as the city of Auckland grew – and their relocation up the hill above Okahu Bay "forced them to burn their tribal meeting house, Te Puru o Tamaki, rather than allow the Crown to desecrate it" (Tapsell 2002: 146). The new *marae* was built to replace the old traditional *marae* located near the cemetery down the hill. The new *marae* was erected by the Crown for the use and benefit of all Māori people irrespective of tribe (see Waitangi Tribunal 1987 and Kawharu 2008 for details) and the Maori Land Court decided that it would be multicultural in character: "only four of the sixteen appointed trustees were from Ōrākei, along with eight Pakeha and four Maori members of parliament" (Tapsell 2002: 148). As emphasized by Kawharu (2008: 56), the initiative heightened criticism and resentment among the Ngāti Whātua people of Ōrākei. They "had to endure the pain of living in the shadow of a *marae* to which they had no *tangata whenua* status or controlling authority: a *marae* built on their dispossessed lands that now officially belonged to all the people of Auckland" (Tapsell 2002: 149). After many protests and complaints to different courts and committees over the years, the 1987 Report of the Waitangi Tribunal on the Ōrākei Claim (WAI 9) recommended, among other things, that Ōrākei *marae* be returned to Ngāti Whātua. "[O]f all the Waitangi Tribunal's recommendations, the return of the marae reserve and its meeting house to the Orakei hapu [subtribe] of Ngati Whatua was the one they most anxiously awaited and in the event, applauded." (Kawharu 2008: 56). The control and ownership of the *marae* was finally acquired when the Ōrākei Act 1991 gave effect to the Waitangi Tribunal's recommendations. The Ōrākei *marae* had hardly ever served its "official" pan-tribal vocation.

In 1980, the meeting house of Hoani Waititi *marae*, an important pan-tribal *marae* (whose members were involved from the beginning in the Māori education movement and the creation of Māori schools), was inaugurated. Money for the *marae* project had begun to be collected in the 1960s, allowing for the opening of a first building, the dining hall, in 1974 (Rosenblatt 2011: 416). Located in Glen Eden, West Auckland, Hoani Waititi *marae* was the first in Auckland of its type – one that was founded by a group of people from different tribes with a pan-tribal project, and that fulfilled a pan-tribal vocation (Tapsell 2002; Rosenblatt 2002, 2011). Among Māori, it was not universally welcomed. Rosenblatt (2011) explains,

> an urban, multitribal marae like Hoani Waititi poses a threat to tribal groups because it creates a context for the formation of lasting, kinlike, communities. In so doing, it creates a situation in which a generalized "Maori" identity can compete with specific tribal identities, at least as a matter of everyday practice. In practice, very few Maori endorse the idea that an "ethnic" identity such as Maori should ever take precedence over a specific tribal identity such as Ngati Whatua or Ngapuhi. (416)

This corresponds to the experience I also had with the people of Hoani Waititi *marae* and of other pan-tribal *marae* in Auckland.

Some of these urban *marae* are also linked to a religious denomination (that is, run by churches) and are thus pan-tribal. A Roman Catholic *marae*, Te Unga Waka, for example, opened in Epsom in 1965.[15] There, church affiliation takes precedence over kinship principles, as it does on Te Whaiora *marae* at Ōtara, South Auckland, also Roman Catholic, and at Tatai Hono in Khyber Pass, Central Auckland, which is Anglican (Walker 2004: 201).[16] Salmond (1975) gives a clear description of how one church-based *marae*, Te Unga Waka functions:

> The Centre is run by a *marae* committee for the benefit of all Maoris in Auckland, but it is tacitly regarded as a Catholic "*marae.*" Because the Centre has no open space or *marae ātea* [ceremonial courtyard], and because its architecture bears little resemblance to a traditional *marae*, it cannot be considered a *marae* in the strict sense of the term, but a wide range of *hui* [meetings] including *tangi* [funerals] are staged there, and guests can be housed overnight. Traditional decorative elements are included in the decor to mark Te Unga Waka as a Maori place, and the Catholic Society functions as an adapted form of *tāngata whenua* [people of the place,

connected to the *marae*]. The key personnel are a priest, a female caretaker and a female warden, all of whom are members of Northern tribes, and Te Unga Waka has Northern as well as Catholic associations. The "*marae*" is fully-used, and as well as *tangi*, dances, receptions, twenty-first birthdays, weddings, conferences, acclimatisation courses for newcomers to the city and the meetings of many clubs are held there.

. . . Because the senior dignitary of the *marae* is the priest, the role of visiting *kaumātua* (elders) is sometimes uncertain, and for many ceremonial occasions, Auckland elders of different tribes are invited instead to act as *tāngata whenua*. Despite these minor difficulties, Te Unga Waka functions successfully as a *marae*, because it provides all the facilities of a traditional *marae* except the open speaking-ground, and *hui* can be staged there without too many radical changes from the rural pattern. (87–8)

This description indicates that people can accommodate arrangements of buildings that do not conform to the traditional *marae* complex, even if many do greatly prefer the traditional form (89).

In general, modern *marae* have fewer buildings and all their parts can be under the same roof, which does not mean their various parts are not still present and clearly marked (Mead 2003: 106). Salmond's description, just quoted, also shows that the values, protocols, and ways of doing things are not so different to those on traditionally shaped *marae*. Traditional Māori values, principles, and identity are reaffirmed in the urban context even if changes are introduced by the church and the membership is not (necessarily) kin oriented. This is also true for the other types of urban *marae*. Through a study of the community of Hoani Waititi *marae*, Rosenblatt (2011: 419) shows that cultural institutions such as *marae* "contain within their structure (or logic, grammar, or pattern), something of the cultural world in which they were formed, and, thus, reviving or perpetuating them can make possible the (partial and transformed) reproduction of that world." In the next chapter I discuss how the physical presence of a *marae* or its regular attendance is not always necessary for the universe of meanings associated with it to be operating.

The second new type of *marae* are those constructed in larger institutions, which are pan-tribal and used by the staff, students, and other users of the establishments. Penetito (2010) calls them "institutional *marae*." Since about 1970 (Webster 1998: 189), public institutions like hospitals, government departments, and especially educational establishments like schools and universities started to build this type of *marae*.

Most universities have a *marae* or symbolically equivalent place(s) for Māori students. At the University of Auckland, for example, the plans for Waipapa *marae* were hatched in 1976 and the carved meeting house, Tāne-nui-a-Rangi,[17] officially opened in 1988. The official raison d'être of the *marae* is as follows:

Waipapa marae is the meeting house on the University campus, and is symbolic of Māori in the University. It reflects participation by Māori students and staff in the University. Although Waipapa is the University's marae, the control over the process of the marae is laid down by the tangata whenua (local people of the land), Ngāti Whātua o Orakei.

The marae is used for a variety of purposes, such as hui (meetings), powhiri (ceremonial welcomes), noho marae (overnight stays), Māori culture club practice, and tangihanga (funerals). It is also used by other departments and faculties of the University for various teaching purposes and functions. (The University of Auckland 2003)[18]

The *marae* itself – not to mention the years of struggle with university authorities to have it built[19] – opened new doors to both cultural and career opportunities for Māori. The *marae* today is primarily a meeting place and "home" for all Māori students (Gagné 2009c). It has also become a home in a more intimate sense for some, like Fiona:

I must honestly say that I have more to do with the university *marae* than I do with my own tribal *marae* and that's very sad for me to say, but that's just a fact. And it's [. . .] where I work and being in the *kapa haka* group, we take our name from the university *marae*, and while I'm here at university [. . .], that's where I want to be. It's not my traditional *tūrangawaewae*, but while I'm here in the city, it does fulfil my foundational base on which I stand, so in that way it is sort of like *tūrangawaewae*, but not in a traditional sense of *tūrangawaewae* [. . .], the land that you associate with through your tribe. But while, as I said, while I'm here in the city it is a place for me to be and to identify with as Māori within the city construct and there is lots of times where I need time away from here, I'll ask for the keys and I will go and sit in the *whare* and just sit there and read and just to get away from the construct of the city with all the burdens of the city life, just for turning to Māori roots. Some of the people may say that the university *marae* is not a *marae*; I do personally take that *marae* as my *marae* while I'm here at university. As to . . . in the future? I'm actually thinking of when my partner and I do finally decide to get married, I would like to get married here at

the university *marae*. And a lot of students . . . past students they still come
here for Māori graduation and help in the kitchen. (Fiona)

What is also special about Waipapa *marae* is that it is not only pan-
tribal – the captains and priest-navigators of the canoes that brought
the ancestors of the different tribes to Aotearoa/New Zealand in the
fourteenth century are carved in the meeting house – it is also pan-
Pacific. Indeed, Tangiia, an ancestor who connects the major islands of
the Pacific with Aotearoa/New Zealand, features in the carvings of the
house (see Harrison 2008).

Concerning institutional *marae* in general, and in particular *marae* in
tertiary institutions, Penetito (2010: 212) writes that they can be seen "as
an example of mediating structure." He argues

> that such an institution exists as a "halfway house" for Māori students
> looking for sanctuaries within often unfamiliar and sometimes hostile en-
> vironments. It is also a "halfway house" for non-Māori students who are
> learning how to get involved in a Māori world, albeit a misplaced one in
> the sense of its being located in an unfamiliar location, out of context and
> growing out of unfamiliar roots. (212)

Today, there are approximately 1,300 *marae* in urban, tribal, and institutional settings throughout New Zealand.[20] Approximately twenty of
these are in Auckland (Rosenblatt 2011: 411). Durie (1998: 222–3) groups
all these different types of *marae* under three main categories.[21] (1) *Marae
tīpuna* (ancestral *marae*) are for the use of the families sharing a common
ancestor, are governed by *marae* trustees and serve as a focus for tribal
activities and planning; (2) *marae-a-rohe* (regional *marae*) are for the use
of Māori people living in a particular vicinity (usually urban), regardless of tribal origin, are governed by a *marae* management committee
and serve as a cultural enforcement for Māori urban dwellers; and
(3) *marae tautoko kaupapa* (*marae* supporting a plan/mission/project) are
for the use of Māori participants in non-Māori institutions, are governed by governors of the parent institution, and serve as a support for
Māori and others who use the institutions.

In this last case Durie (223) highlights the potential intrusion of the
state or other non-Māori authorities into the control, management, and
disposal of the *marae* and the other cultural resources associated with it.
Salmond (1975: 90) underlines that "[w]herever *Pākeha* are placed in positions of leadership in urban *marae*, resentment inevitably results" (see

also Walker 1970, but also Tapsell 2002 in the case of Ōrākei *marae*). She also adds that by its very nature, a *marae* require some sort of founding *tāngata whenua* group; that is, a group composed of the people of the place, people connected to the *marae*. This group cannot be replaced by a European-style board of trustees with a diverse membership. Salmond (1975: 90) also adds that "[f]actionalism and struggles for leadership mark [the pan-tribal *marae's*] history, and it is dubious whether the ideal of integration should ever be applied to the *marae*." Although written in 1975, when urban *marae* were really still quite new, her assertion is still true today: factionalism and struggles along tribal or family lines persist on the urban *marae* (plural) where I carried out fieldwork.[22]

The principle of affiliation, identification, or belonging to *marae* is the same as the principle that traces membership to family, subtribe, and tribe. Māori can opt to regard themselves as belonging to one or several of the *marae* of their parents, grandparents, and great-grandparents. As for their spouses, they are sometimes included and sometimes excluded from the host group on the *marae*, since "the *whānau* that constitute the *hapū* are ambiguously defined, sometimes including spouses, sometimes not" (Sissons 2010: 376). As Sissons specifies, "[m]ultiple practices of group formation centred on the *marae* bring together principles of descent, marriage, and residence as kin and non-kin become included and identified as *tangata whenua* – 'people of the land'/ hosts" (378). In the case of urban *marae*, both pan-tribal and tribal, institutional or not, participation in *marae* activities becomes a particularly crucial criteria for belonging or identifying with one or several *marae*, but the other principles are also at play. For example, at Hoani Waititi *marae*, people who are members of the "original" families who were prominent in the effort to have the *marae* built "have a kind of place waiting for them at the marae" (Rosenblatt 2011: 417).

Salmond (1975) suggests that from the early twentieth century to the present, *marae* seem to have increased in sanctity: "a marked revival in population and also cultural activity has occurred [following the announced extinction of the Māori], and leaders of the Maori people have fostered *marae* construction as a symbol of the renewed vitality of *Maoritanga* [Maoridom]" (50).[23] Sissons (1998, 2010), whose research points to a quite recent emphasis on meeting houses among Māori, comes to a similar conclusion, speaking of the "traditionalization" of the Māori meeting house, meaning by this "a process or set of processes through which aspects of contemporary culture come to be regarded as valued survivals from an earlier time" as "historical accomplishment"

(1998: 37). The *marae* is said to be at the very heart of Māori culture. In the 1920s, Apirana Ngata, an influential Māori leader,[24] focused on the meeting house as symbol of Māori identity, *mana* (spiritual power, authority, prestige, status), and tribal traditions in the cultural renaissance that was then beginning (Metge 1967, 1976; Sissons 2000, 2004, 2010; Walker 1987, 1996, 2004). The symbolic nature of the *marae* is also repeatedly stressed today by Māori operating in a variety of settings (for example, Rosenblatt 2005, 2011; Sissons 2010) and dealing with different state authorities.[25] *Marae* have been the focus of Māori struggles for political and cultural affirmation for a long time – since the nineteenth century (George 2010; Neich 1993; Salmond 1975; Walker 1970, 1987, 2008; Webster 1998; Williams 2010). As for recent developments, for Walker (1987: 147), "[t]he urban marae is the most powerful cultural statement the Maori has made in modern times."

The significance of the *marae* can also be seen in Māori novels written during the 1970s and 1980s by Witi Ihimaera, Keri Hulme, and Patricia Grace. They all

> present strategies for reclaiming a Maori self that necessarily involve re-creating or reforming, and in a sense re-defining, the Maori community. This end is achieved by the physical act of rebuilding the whare tipuna, the ancestral house, on the protagonists' home marae . . . . To rebuild the ancestral house means literally to rebuild the community's ancestor – its significant past – and the community's self – its significant present and possible future. (Allen 2002: 147)

In these novels, the rebuilding of ancestral houses is a collective rather than individual endeavour. As in Ihimaera's novel *Whanau* (1974), reconstruction revives the community by providing it with a common purpose. The same is true in Grace's novel *Potiki* (1986). In Hulme's novel, *The Bone People* (1986 [1983]), "[it] is only after Kerewin [the main character, a somewhat isolated and antisocial artist] rebuilds the whare tipuna on her home marae that she can reclaim her Maoritanga, rebuild her own house, and reunite with her family" (Allen 2002: 151). Allen (72) asserts that the essential spiritual and political functions of *marae* proper are to connect living kin with their ancestors and to provide individuals as well as the entire community with a place to stand.

The *marae* is thus considered to be a symbol of continuity with the ancestral past:

For our people, marae are places of refuge that provide facilities to enable us to continue with our way of life within the total structure of Maoridom. We, the Maori, need our marae so that we may pray to God; rise tall in oratory; weep for our dead; house our guests; have our meetings, feasts, weddings and reunions; and sing and dance. (Tauroa and Tauroa 1986: 19)

The *marae* offers to Māori a place to meet among themselves, apart from mainstream society. In 1972, Ihimaera wrote in his short story "The Whale" in *Pounamu, Pounamu*:

He sits, this old kaumatua [elder], in the darkness of the meeting house. He has come to this place because it is the only thing remaining in his dying world . . . This meeting house has been his heart, his strength . . . In this place lie his family and memories. (1972: 115)

Now, at the beginning of the twenty-first century with the successful revival of the Māori language and traditions and the establishment of Māori schools, this elder may not see his world as "dying." What remains true is that the *marae* is still seen as one place where Māori maintain their distinct identities and traditional culture in episodes "which carry [them] over from one special occasion to the next" (Salmond 1975: 210, quoted in Allen 2002: 10).

According to Tauroa and Tauroa (1986: 14), "it is when gathered on their *marae* that the Maori most fully express themselves as a people":

[T]he marae is the wahi rangatira mana (place of greatest mana), wahi rangatira wairua (place of greatest spirituality), wahi rangatira iwi (place that heightens people's dignity), and wahi rangatira tikanga Maori (place in which Maori customs are given ultimate expression). (17)

It is important to remember that even if many Māori experience the urban setting as a difficult, alien, and colonized place, a number of sites exist where Māori can affirm Māori ways, visions, and struggles against assimilationist forces. *Marae* are important places and spaces of affirmation and resistance for persons and groups, on a practical level as much as on the symbolic level. *Marae* themselves, as buildings, are also an important site of affirmation of the Māori presence in the city and in mainstream institutions. The *marae* is widely recognized as a symbol of the vitality of Māori culture and the continued Māori presence. As emphasized by Sissons (2010: 384), "while meeting houses and *marae* retain their local significance within rural communities, they have also assumed increased symbolic value for people living urban lives."

Finally, one may ask why, given the obvious importance of the *marae*, statistics regarding *marae* frequentation are so low. At the end of the 1990s, one third of all Māori had little or no contact with a *marae*, as had been revealed in a longitudinal study, entitled "Best Outcomes for Māori: Te Hoe Nuku Roa," which is tracking 700 representative households over a twenty-year period (1993–2013) (Durie 2001a: 55–6). Even if people tell anthropologists and other researchers that *marae* are the roots of their identity and the basis of Māori communities (Durie 2001a: 74), what does that actually mean if many people seldom or never go to *marae*, or do not go as often as they would like?

Perhaps people are finding alternatives. This is what I will now explore.

4   Ways of Life in a Māori House

Before I went to New Zealand, I had imagined myself walking down the streets of Auckland every day on a regular route, meeting Māori people on my way who could introduce me to their world and help me to understand how they maintain their identity in an urban setting. But the city is large and spread out. And Māori are not, generally speaking, the kind of people that you meet in public places.

I arrived at the end of February 2001 and immediately enrolled in Māori language courses at the University of Auckland, which gave me the opportunity to meet Māori faculty members and students. I had some interaction with Māori students in the breaks between classes. But as they tended to leave the university as soon as classes ended, lengthy conversations were difficult. When I asked Māori where they met, they answered: "We are not public people," or "We meet at home. My house is like a *marae*. There are always many people at home." But at the beginning of my stay, nobody invited me home. That would have been too easy. I can still hear my Māori friends laughing when I told them about my difficulties meeting Māori and integrating into Māori networks. One of them told me that they are not "café kind of people," they prefer drinking a cup of tea together at home or at their friend's or cousin's place.

It took some time before I was introduced to Māori family life and asked to come for dinner at the house that was to become my home in South Auckland for a great part of my fieldwork. I had been in New Zealand for eight months when Kiri,[1] a Māori mature student from the university, invited me to live with her family. I accepted with great pleasure. I really enjoyed Kiri's company and it was an excellent opportunity for me to learn more about and to become part of a place that people had described to me for so long and in quite intriguing terms. And as I became integrated into the daily life of Kiri's family – a family that would become in some ways mine, in a house that would be my refuge, as it was for most of the *whānau* members – I began to learn about the everyday worlds of Auckland Māori, the workings of the *whānau*, and the centrality of certain places in Māori city experiences.

I lived with them for about five months in 2001 and 2002 and for two more months in 2005, that time in the house of Kiri's sister, Rangi, who welcomed me again in her house for one week during a visit to New Zealand at the end of 2008. I was there once more for a visit in 2011 – outside Auckland that time, since Rangi and her children and grand-children moved back to her husband's tribal area just after he passed away in 2010. Feeling it was important for my research to experience Māori life in various parts of the city, I also lived in another, unrelated, household in West Auckland for a few months in 2002 and for a further month in 2005. I visited the people from that household during each of my subsequent visits to New Zealand.

But it started one Sunday evening, early in the New Zealand sum-mer of 2001–2 when I parked my apple-green 1987 station-wagon in the driveway of 30 Aroha Street in South Auckland. The car was full of my books, my foam mattress, my shaky desk and wobbly chair, my clothes, and my single houseplant, a gift from a Māori friend.

Since the door was wide open, I entered the house without knocking. Everybody was at home, except for Kiri who was still at work. Rangi and her husband Hoani were visiting. Some of the children were watch-ing television while others were playing in the backyard. Andrew, Ki-ri's Pākehā husband, said hello and began chatting with me while he prepared dinner. I asked two of the boys, David and Richard, to help me with my stuff. Andrew showed me which room would be mine, and there I was. There was no formal welcome and no explanation of the rules of the house, which I would have to learn by myself. I was just there, and from that time on I was made to feel part of the *whānau*.

When all my boxes and belongings had been unloaded and stacked in a room, I joined Andrew to help prepare dinner. When everything was ready, Kiri arrived home from work. She said *"Kia ora,"* we put everything on the table, everybody took their share, and we sat and ate. As it was to be for the next six months, we all exchanged our news of the day, we laughed, and we had moments of silence. The children ate quickly and returned to the television or went out to the backyard, coming back when the adults asked them to clear the table and do the dishes.

Gradually, certain patterns began to emerge. From one dinner to another, there could be anywhere from eight to seventeen of us around the table and sometimes even more. The children and teenagers often ate on the steps in front of the house or in the living room. David and his father William, the ex-husband of one of Kiri's sisters, often had their dinner in the shed behind the house where they had their living quarters with their two camp beds, a couple of chairs, and their personal belongings.

Kiri's mother was Teria and her father was Hiko whose roots were in different communities and in different tribes on North Island. All four grandparents were born in their respective tribal areas. Teria's father lived up north with Teria's mother but when he died, Teria's mother moved to Auckland with Rangi, Teria's daughter (her granddaughter), whom she *whāngai* (was bringing up). They travelled a great deal around the island, however, attending church meetings.

Hiko's mother and father lived for some of their adult lives in the city. Hiko's father, Rongo, even stayed at 30 Aroha Street for various periods while working in Auckland in the 1980s.

Hiko and Teria are the ones who first bought the house (see figure 4.1). At that time, it was new, stood on the street with just two others in a new development, and there was a farm nearby. However, the city soon grew around them. Hiko and Teria were young adults when they migrated to Auckland and Teria already had a son whom she brought with her. She also had a daughter, Rangi, whom she left in her mother's care "up north." Hiko and Teria met in the city. They were both members of a *kapa haka rōpū* (Māori performing arts group). They married and had all their children – Nina, Hana, the twins Ani and Kiri, and Hohi – in South Auckland on Aroha Street. In the early days, Hiko was a bus driver while Teria cared for the children and the house.

Rangi moved in with them when she was eleven or twelve years old. She recalls:

Nan died when I was eleven so in all that time I did not realize she was my nan, I always thought she was my mum until at the *tangi* [funeral] they told me who my mum was. All a bit of a shock, and worse to find out that I had sisters and a brother [. . .] So I was twelve or eleven when I came to stay with the new *whānau* [family] and it sure was tough not having things to myself and having to share with others as a whole. (Rangi)

Figure 4.1: Diagram of the family living at 30 Aroha Street

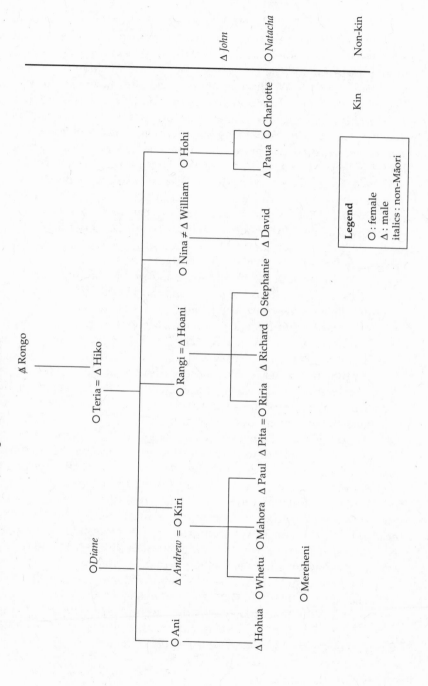

Rangi had five children in total: one born in Central Auckland, two born in South Auckland, one born in Wellington, and another one born on the East Coast. Rangi and her family have travelled quite a lot between Auckland and the East Coast. She lived in Auckland for a while and then moved to Wellington, then moved back to Auckland. When she married Hoani, a Māori man from the East Coast, they went to live there in his tribal area. For a time, she worked in farms there and then in a *kohanga reo* (Māori-language kindergarten). Since Rangi wanted to get a teaching diploma, her husband obtained a transfer to Auckland and they moved back there, but Hoani later returned to the countryside for work, and because he did not like Auckland very much. Rangi stayed in Auckland because she wanted to get her teaching qualification, and it was at this point that she moved back to 30 Aroha Street.

Kiri lived all her life in South Auckland, except for a brief stay in Central Auckland and four months when she worked in the far north when she was twenty-six. She has three children from previous relationships who are of Māori descent. Today she is married to Andrew, a Pākehā man, who has lived all his life in the neighbourhood and grew up just a couple of streets away from 30 Aroha St. All Kiri's children were born in Auckland. Kiri's daughters, Whetu and Mahora, were living at number 30 while I was there in 2001 and 2002, and Paul, her son, was living with his father on the East Coast.

At the time of my fieldwork, Andrew was working as a salesman in South Auckland and Kiri was working in a hospital as a care assistant. They were paying off a mortgage on the house.

When I got back from my New Year holidays in Quebec in February 2002, one of the main changes was that Rangi and her daughter Stephanie had just moved into the garage behind the house after Rangi's husband had to go back to his hometown, six hours' drive from Auckland. It was a nice surprise to see them living with us. The change was, as usual, taken completely for granted. Nobody told me why Rangi and Stephanie had arrived. I only learned the reason in the course of everyday conversations. It had an impact on our domestic organization, since Rangi took on the role of cooking most of the dinners and caring for the children by supervising their breakfast, homework, and after-school activities around the house. William, who must have felt rather intruded upon in the shed, was present much less often.

Dinner was the time that everybody did the same thing at the same time. The rest of the time, Kiri, Andrew, and the other adults were working elsewhere and most of the children were at school. As well as working, Kiri was taking university courses toward a bachelor's degree. During the first few months of my stay, Whetu stayed at home with her baby and then she also went back to school, while the baby was sent to a *kohanga reo*, a Māori daycare centre.

In the morning, everybody had a swift breakfast and by eight o'clock had left. When her work and university schedule allowed, Kiri used to sleep later than the others since she often worked far into the night, the only time when she found the peace and quiet to concentrate. Some people – like Whetu and (when he did not have a job) Rangi's son Richard – stayed at home most or part of the day. They watched television, took care of the baby, and did chores when they were asked. Whetu went back to school full time in February 2002 and Richard went away to live with his biological father for a couple of months soon afterward.

Usually, Kiri was at home one day a week. This was a time for her to enjoy playing with the baby, do some housework, go grocery shopping, study for university, and see friends or other members of the *whānau*. As she often said, she had "no time for social life during the weekend" because she was always working then. On her free day, Kiri also organized cultural activities for her Māori and Pacific Island clients at work. This day was very enjoyable for me, since I got the chance to meet and talk with many people and relax with them over cups of tea.

By three fifteen in the afternoon, the children were back from school and Whetu would look after them. If Whetu was not available, Kiri, Rangi, Riria (Rangi's oldest daughter), or occasionally somebody else, including me, would be there. Until dinnertime, the children played outside or watched television in the house or in the shed. Andrew, and later Rangi, were mainly responsible for preparing the dinner, but I was assigned days to cook too.

The time between four in the afternoon and dinner was quite busy. That is when Andrew or the older boys did some of their chores like mowing the lawn or cleaning the house. It was also the time when people came for a visit after work. Before she moved in, Rangi often used to come after school to look after the children and talk about what was happening at school with Kiri and the others. Sometimes a cousin, a friend, or a neighbour would come over for afternoon tea. Ani, Kiri's twin sister, would also sometimes drop by on the way home to her North Shore house. She usually had her son and her partner's daughter with her and sometimes they stayed for dinner.

After she moved in to 30 Aroha Street, Rangi often came back with Vanessa, the *kaiawhina* (teacher's assistant) from school who also sometimes joined us for dinner. They would talk shop about school, discussing children's behaviour, performances, activities, and so on. Rangi sometimes brought one or two pupils with her for dinner. They were generally children that she knew were not having a good time at home right then. One would sometimes stay over for the weekend or go with her on a trip to visit her husband down south.

After dinner, once a week, Rangi and Vanessa left the house for a Māori language and history class. On other occasions, Rangi gave a Māori language workshop at Vanessa's place for her pupils' parents. Rangi and Vanessa had parents' meetings, or meetings to plan fundraising activities to finance a school trip to rural *marae*. Most of the time they were very busy and very involved in school activities and planning, but sometimes for a treat on a Thursday or Friday night they would go to a housie, which is the term commonly used in New Zealand for bingo.

After dinner, the children cleared the table and did the dishes before being sent to bed. Andrew always made coffee for the adults. That was the time for a cigarette, a chat, and a gossip. Afterward, when everyone was busy again we just returned to our respective work or study for a couple more hours before going to bed. Those less busy might relax or watch television or surf the internet. Once a week, or more often just before performances or competitions, Kiri had a *kapa haka* (Māori performing arts) practice that I would always join. Sometimes, she also had meetings with colleagues from university or work.

Weekends were quite relaxed. Andrew usually did not have to work, or only on the odd Saturday morning. He was at home with the children, doing jobs around the house, playing computer games, watching movies, and relaxing with John, his best mate. John was over very often and slept at our place most weekend nights. He was Pākehā but seemed to fit in quite well with Māori ways and was pretty much part of the family for most of my stay. At one point, he did not have a place to stay, so he lived full time at number 30 until he left.

As for Kiri, she worked weekends as a care assistant, since she was at university during the week; the family needed her wages to cover the mortgage, her schooling, and all the *whānau*'s expenses. Kiri had taken on the family house quite recently, because she was the only one able to buy it and keep it in the family and open to everyone. Rangi, Richard, William, and myself paid a very reasonable price for our board (food, rent, bills, and other expenses included). This contributed to the financial security of the household and helped Kiri and Andrew make ends meet, which they could still sometimes do only with difficulty.

About once a month, Kiri's parents, Teria and Hiko, would visit from Hiko's tribal area in the country farther south. These visits were an opportunity for everybody – cousins, aunts, uncles, and friends – to come over and find out what was going on in the *whānau*, in the tribe, at the *marae*, and in the countryside in general. They were also a chance to obtain advice in relation to *tikanga* (custom, rules or right ways, see Metge 2010: 79) and ancestral knowledge, if anyone needed it. Sometimes, the visit was just a stopover in a longer trip to Teria's tribal area for a *whānau* or tribal *hui* (meeting). At other times, their visit to Auckland was their chance to enjoy the city and have some entertainment. The trip might also be a good opportunity for Kiri's youngest sister, Hohi, to come to the city with her parents and her daughter to see her son, Paua. Often, Teria and Hiko also would bring the twin granddaughters that they were *whāngai* (raising), since their mother, the eldest daughter, then lived overseas. These two girls are William's daughters and David's sisters.

Weekends were also the time when the children could have their friends stay over or could go to visit their cousins or aunts for a day or two. Mahora, Kiri's daughter, often visited her cousin Stephanie and her auntie Rangi for weekends until Rangi moved in. Because of her baby, Whetu stayed at home most of the time, but she often would have a friend to stay over, who was usually somehow related. The children were sometimes given money to go to the movies or shop, and they usually all went together. Even Whetu, who was sixteen years old, would take her ten year-old sister and seven year-old cousin with her when she went out with her friend(s). On rare occasions, she was allowed to go to a party at a friend's place.

Generally, Whetu had much help taking care of her daughter. If she was out in the street chatting with neighbours when people came home from work during the week, there was always someone to feed and look after her daughter. During the weekend, she could always count on someone to care for the child for a few hours while she took some free time. Everybody seemed to enjoy taking care of the baby. For many months she was the main attraction in the house for friends and kin from different branches of Whetu's *whānau*. Rangi regularly called in before she lived at the house just to see the little girl and feed her. At some point, however, Kiri, Rangi, and the other adults decided that

Whetu was relying too much on other people, so they decided to leave her more often to assume her responsibilities herself.

Friday and Saturday nights were when Andrew and Kiri invited friends over to play cards or chat. Andrew's mother and father, both Pākehā, and other friends often came around on card nights. Sunday evening dinners were also an important occasion when everybody would gather together for the usual pork roast. Even after I left to live in another household in West Auckland, I always came back for Sunday dinner. They only let me leave on the condition that I would come back at least once a week on Sundays! It was not difficult to keep my promise.

During the winter half-term and summer holidays, Kiri's son, who usually lived with his father about six hours' drive from Auckland, visited from a few days to a few weeks, as did another of Rangi's daughters, who lived in the same city with her father, Hoani, or, from time to time, with other Māori relations. Occasionally, Rangi's children came for a few days or more in their holidays. Richard, Rangi's oldest son, lived at Kiri's place for a couple of months before Rangi moved in, having had a disagreement with his parents. Likewise, some of the children from number 30 would go off elsewhere during their holidays, or occasionally if they had had a disagreement with one of the adults. Metge (1995) writes about this special relationship with a favourite aunt or uncle. She says that "[often], children sought refuge with an aunt or an uncle of their own accord, when they were in strife at home" (Metge 1995: 192). She also speaks of the mutual caring relationships between *mokopuna* (grandchildren) and *tīpuna* (grandparents). Riria and Whetu have this special bond with Teria and Hiko. Indeed, it is as if Riria and Whetu were chosen at an early age and have been exposed more than the others to *tikanga* (custom, rules) and various Māori teachings, sometimes in direct ways, sometimes in more subtle ways. Metge also mentions this practice (1995: 184–187).

Paua, Kiri's youngest sister's eldest son, who lived at 30 Aroha Street for most of my stay, sometimes went to visit his mother, who was living at her parents' place in their tribal area, or he would stay with his Tongan father who lived in another part of Auckland. On a few occasions, he stayed with his mum and his grandparents for many weeks and was registered at the school there. But his bad behaviour at school and at home got the better of his grandfather, and he was taken back to 30 Aroha Street.

Rangi and her daughter Stephanie went away from time to time to visit Rangi's husband (Stephanie's father) down south. At least once a year in the summer holidays Kiri, Andrew, and the children went south to visit Kiri's people in the tribal area where her father and her mother then lived. They also made the trip there for *tangihanga* (funerals) and other important *hui* (meetings). More rarely, they went up north to Kiri's mother's tribal area, usually for funerals and celebrations such as twenty-first birthdays and weddings. Very occasionally, Kiri, Andrew, and the children would do a special activity together on the weekend, like seeing family or friends, going to a restaurant or a movie, or visiting one of the city's attractions.

Everyday life, however, was not always easy in the *whānau*. There were fights and major or minor disagreements. There were personal problems, issues in relationships with kin, or financial challenges. There were concerns about the growing children who were increasingly exposed to the outside world and such potential dangers as bullying at school, violence, cigarettes, drugs, alcohol, and sex.

But what made this particular household especially interesting to me and relevant to my research was that Kiri and her siblings and children often compared their house to a *marae*. And because they did so, as did many other Māori people whom I met, when describing a certain type of city house, is part of why I was so keen to move in.

Kiri's sister, Rangi, explained why the house was like a *marae*:

The feeling in the house . . . pretty much like a *marae*. Everyone just becomes one. It is like a real unity, unity place [. . .] I think that the main [characteristic] is just the feeling inside it and the people. The first one will probably be how everybody respects the house by taking off their shoes. Pretty much like a *marae* basis. Everyone is sharing the jobs in the house. Everything is shared in the house. Yeah, pretty much like a *marae* basis: jobs, house duties, the looking after one another [. . .] Everybody belongs to everybody in the house [. . .] it has been blessed as our *wharenui* [meeting house] [. . .] It is just full with *aroha* [unconditional love] [. . .] We have had grandparents come through here. We have had aunties and uncles, cousins, nieces and nephews lived here, social welfare kids, sisters-in-law, brothers-in-law, we are still here. Yeah, I think it's just the way the house has been. Open to be [. . .] it has been like that as far as I can remember [. . .] We had family that would come from Wellington and like we had a twenty-first or we had a *tangi* [funeral] that was up north, this place will

probably be the centre for everyone to sleep over, catch up and you know
. . . travel on. (Rangi)

The house was open daily to everybody in the *whānau* (including
non-related friends) who were welcomed in for a chat, for a meal, for
advice about traditions, to help with the chores, or to look after the
children.

Whetu, Kiri's daughter, also stressed the idea of the house being a
home for many people:

> Everyone is welcome in this house. It is like . . . it's a homely house [. . .] It's
> like a *marae*, where there are people coming and going [. . .] You know how
> people like . . . go to *marae* and they stay there. They are from there and
> sometimes they are not from there, but it is like their home, it is like where
> they feel safe and where they gather to see *whānau* [. . .] People come here
> and it is very homely here for them. It is like another home [. . .] This house
> is a home for a lot of people. (Whetu)

For Kiri, her siblings, and the children who have grown up in that
house or lived there for a time, 30 Aroha Street was home, a place to
which they all returned at some point in their lives.

One *marae* quality that stands out clearly in Rangi's and Whetu's de-
scriptions of 30 Aroha Street is that the house is open to everybody: "We
have *whānau* going in and out of the house. You know, they come and
stay . . . just it's like everyone gathers. Our *whānau* come and gather and
you know, catch up with what's going on with the rest of our *whānau*.
Everyone is welcome in this house [. . .] It's like a *marae*, where there
are people coming and going" (Whetu). The house was thus a gathering place, a meeting place where information and news were shared.
"My house is a *hui* [meeting] point," said Tauni, who also described his
rented house in West Auckland in much the same way that the people
living at 30 Aroha Street described their place. This was particularly
true when grandparents were there for a visit or when there were visitors – cousins, uncles, or aunts – from the tribal area in the country or
when someone was just back from a trip there. That was when many
people dropped by, to hear about the happenings and gossip about kin
in the country.

More formal *hui* (meeting) were also called from time to time to discuss issues of family, subtribal and tribal lands, waters and *marae*, and
to establish the *whānau* position to be taken to tribal meetings. On their

way back from tribal meetings, the *whānau* representatives – in Kiri's *whānau*, Hiko and Teria and sometimes aunts or uncles – would also stop by to report to the *whānau* on what happened.

Tui, a mother of eight and grandmother of fourteen, also had such a house in South Auckland and made sure to have occasional meetings with the household members and other relatives in the city (brothers and sisters, aunts, uncles, and cousins) to catch up on what was happening with everybody, find out what was going on in their households, and to keep everybody informed about what was happening on the *marae* in the country, since she was on that *marae* committee. This particular type of house, like *marae*, thus becomes a meeting place to discuss serious issues as well as being an important place for relaxation and fun.

Speaking about his own house, Tauni said, "People come around to *hui* [meeting] at home and we've got a social life and we play a lot of games at night." However, activities were not always planned. People just turn up at the house to relax, watch television, play cards, and chat. Christine added: "We are quite sort of easygoing in our home. And we always sort of entertain people at home." These houses are good places for entertainment and play a central role in social life.

This is particularly true for the children who were "forever in and out" (Christine). For Tauni, "The house is yeah, totally for the kids, all about the kids." In Christine's *whānau*, they organized *whānau* activities to be with the kids: "Quite often, we have sports days. The family gets together and we organize sports. We play alongside them. We don't play apart from them. We'll play with them. They love it! When we have them all there, we probably have about forty children and that's just immediate family!"

For Joana, the children's importance in the house is "what makes our children be safe." She went on to explain that the children were considered everyone's children and were cared for as such, collectively and that this was a good way to prevent children from being abused. Everybody was responsible for them. This was particularly salient at 30 Aroha Street: Mereheni, Whetu's child, did indeed seem to be everybody's baby. In the same vein, Tauni's house was the children's kingdom since "I'd rather have my kids at home with their mates so I know where they are than having my kids out and not knowing what they do. So I guess that's the principle behind it." Metge (1995) writes that because of the Māori principle according to which anyone's children are everyone's children, *whānau* constitute safe environments for children, most of the time (see also Williams 2010: 100–1). In cases of crises or abuse, "intervention often took the form of a relative coming or being sent, without waiting for a request, to stay in the home and help until the crisis was over" (Metge 1995: 259).

If necessary, the *whānau* will call a meeting to discuss and deal with the internal problems. And if the *whānau* makes no move or is unable to stop a problem, the wider community will step in (Harris 2004b, 2007; Metge 1995: 269; Walker 1970). Metge (1995: 277) further specifies that in some cases, *whānau* do not have the skills or courage to deal with problems. This is especially true when the offence is committed by someone, or more than one person, who is of high *mana* – which can lead to a critical situation. She adds that if the offender or offenders and their *whānau* are merely ostracized by the wider community – as is perhaps the easiest solution if the offenders have high *mana* – children may be left unprotected from abuse. Thus, while the *whānau* is generally seen as a safety net and a springboard for emancipation, in some exceptional cases, instead of being the children's kingdom, the *whānau* can be experienced as a trap or a prison for some of its children or even adult members.[2]

Like *marae*, houses of this particular type are also places of learning, in which grandparents are extremely influential. Some grandparents live at the house. Others will visit from time to time. Figures from 1996 indicate that "one in five Māori (19 per cent) lived in multi-generation households compared to only 7 per cent of the non-Māori population" (Durie 2001a: 194).[3]

Metge (1995: 176) notes that "[w]hether Māori speak Māori or English, the terms *tīpuna* or grandparent, grandmother and grandfather are usually given a much wider range of reference than the English terms generally have. As well as a child's parents' parents, they are used to refer to a child's parents' siblings and cousins, to the latter's spouses, and to relatives from the previous generation if still living." It is principally these people who teach their grandchildren about *tikanga* (custom, rules, tradition), *whakapapa* (genealogy), *whānau* history and *marae*, *waiata* (songs), and *karakia* (prayers).

Grandparents see this as their duty: "I make it a responsibility. Yeah, we talk about how they can conduct themselves when they go to different places to different *marae*, that there are certain differences going on [. . .] Like at one stage, we were going to go down to the East Coast, my husband's cousin's son had his twenty-first birthday. Some of our kids wanted to go too, so we talked about roles" (Tui). According to Metge

(1995: 187), "[g]randparents rather than parents bear the responsibility for teaching children who they are, how they are related to particular relatives and how to behave toward them." And that is achieved through teaching genealogy and traditional knowledge to the children.

While I was at 30 Aroha Street, each time that Hiko, Kiri's father, came over, he always went through at least one *karakia* (prayer) or *waiata* (song) with the children. He also sometimes had them recite their genealogy and spoke to them a little in the Māori language so they could practise it. When he visited, he took on the responsibility of having a *kōrero* (serious talk) with any of the children who needed advice or a reprimand. He also made a point of congratulating those who had behaved well or performed well at school, at *kapa haka* (Māori performing arts), or in sports. The house symbolizes at its best the bond between grandparents and grandchildren, as well as cultural inheritance (Allen 2002; Ihimaera 1972).

The privileged bond between grandparents and grandchildren is very important among Māori.[4] According to Metge (1995: 176), this relation is often remembered as warm, close, comforting, and as a source of love and support. While grandparents do set strict standards for behaviour, especially concerning *tapu* (loose translation, restrictions) and *tikanga* (custom, rules), they are generally also more patient and more gentle in their corrections than parents can be. Grandparents are also remembered for their interest in their grandchildren's achievements, and for building up their self-esteem with praise and affection (182).

Whetu and Riria each experienced that very close relationship with their grandparents, Teria and Hiko. They were both *whāngai* (brought up, looked after) by them for some years when they lived up north in Teria's tribal area. For both Whetu and Riria, that area is their *tūrangawaewae*,[5] the spiritual home where they have their *marae*. This is different for Kiri, Whetu's mother, who identified more closely with her father's homeland down south, since, when she was young, she visited the *whānau* in the south more regularly than the *whānau* up north. Identification with *marae*, and also with the spiritual home, the *tūrangawaewae*, relies heavily on each person's particular life experiences and on his or her relationships with the various *whānau* members. Because of this special bond, when Whetu had her baby, her grandmother rather than her mother was with her in the delivery room, while her mother was with me, impatiently waiting outside.

As already mentioned, Teria and Hiko were bringing up William's twin daughters, as well as another granddaughter whose mother, their youngest daughter, still lived with them. They also took Paua from time to time. Whetu still visited them frequently and even stayed for longer sojourns when things were not going so well between her and her mother because of disagreements over Whetu's choices and behaviour.

Māori teachings are also passed on to the children by their parents. Kiri often taught what she learned at her *kapa haka* (Māori performing arts) practice to Whetu and Mahora. She took the children with her to the rehearsals, as did many other parents in the group. The children were always welcome to join in. Kiri learned the different actions for a song's words with the group and then they all practised the movements together at home. At Christine's house,

> We use the Māori language in the home as much as possible. We have *karakia* [prayers], we have . . . We should do this every night, but at least once a week we get together as a *whānau* and there is no TV allowed and we have *karakia* [prayers] and *hīmene* [hymns] and we have our children do their *whakapapa* [genealogy] and then we do *waiata* [songs] and . . . we do that for about two hours, usually on the Monday night. (Christine)

Tui's house became a *marae* during those special moments when she had *whānau* meetings, when teachings and information were passed on from one generation to the next, when everybody gathered at the house.

> My house is a *marae* when we have family meetings [. . .] once a month [. . .] Yeah, everybody comes and then my house is like a *marae*. Very much so, everybody is everywhere [. . .] It's because it's full up with people, people coming and going, and the kids all bring up something. They usually bring up . . . it's the pride of what I am bringing. It becomes a *marae*, because everybody comes and goes, everybody brings something, contributes and it really helps. (Tui)

This last quote raises two important ideas. First, these houses, like "real" *marae*, are all about sharing and the community, the group, the *whānau*. Second, like real *marae*, these types of houses and their principles are not necessarily part of everyone's daily experience. A house is not necessarily in a permanent state of being "like a *marae*." It could be so only on special occasions devoted to the extended family, in the same way that people go to *marae* for family or tribal meetings, celebrations, or "life-crisis *hui* [meetings]" (Tapsell 2002) such as funerals.

Central to these places is the concept that "everything is shared in the house" (Rangi). This also means that everyone takes on a role. "If there is a task that needs to be done, if you are capable of doing that task or capable of doing that role then you do it. It is the same as on a *marae*. If there is a role that needs to be filled and there is no one else to do it, it is your responsibility to do it" (Matiu). Typically different roles are attributed to specific members of the family, depending, for example, on their rank or predispositions for certain tasks. For example, Rangi explained how her sister Kiri had a different role than hers:

> I had the role ever since we were growing up. Being the eldest, my job was to cook, clean and care [. . .] She [Kiri] has a financial head, when it comes to making sure that bills are paid, there's food in the cupboard, where I will take the role of caregiver, caring for the kids, feeding the family, we sort of have our roles. So, she does take a big part on the financial side and I think me being able to take a part in the caregiver side, take a lot of pressure off her too. (Rangi)

So what makes a house similar to a *marae* is the sharing, the "joint effort" (Tui).

> For me, it's just about . . . it's just the common duties: respect, *aroha*, you know that word, love, just having love and respect and appreciation for people. And it's about . . . giving what you have to others, to those who don't have as much as you have, so you . . . It's the interaction, sharing of resources . . . intermingling of families . . . [. . .] My sister Gloria, what was the first thing she did when she came in? [. . .] Usually the first thing she does is go to the fridge. She always does and the children do it now too. They will do it at my sister's place too, they do it here . . . I'll go to her house. That sort of stuff. (Joana)

While people would usually bring extra food when they visited, there was no immediate obligation to reciprocate. "You're not obligated to take something or you don't have to" (Mihi). However, people expect to treat their visitors in the same way that they were treated when visiting them, and it can bother them if they do not see any chance for some sort of reciprocation in the long run.

Young people who come to the city intending to find a job will often stay for weeks with *whānau* members until they earn enough to live by themselves (Metge 1964: 245). This is also true of nieces and nephews who come to stay when they are on bad terms with their parents. These guests can become both a financial burden and an emotional or moral worry, since their parents will hold the hosts responsible for them. The young people then often move out to live in single rooms in an apartment or hostel and are therefore unable to reciprocate the hospitality. Sometimes the visitors are travellers or distant relatives with whom the hosts would not consider staying.

Metge (2002: 317; 2010: 67) explains that the imbalance created by the delay in returning the generosity keeps the relationship going in a cultural context where there is an obligation to return and indeed to give more than what one has received. Gift exchanges of all kinds forge and maintain these social bonds. Metge's understanding of this differs from that of Salmond (1991b), Patterson (1992), and Sahlins (1965), who insist rather on the importance of *balanced* reciprocity. Metge, drawing on Firth (1959), stresses the importance of the *im*balance via the practice of making a delayed return. Metge (2002: 320–1; 2010: 69–70) sees a close connection between *utu*,[6] the principle of reciprocity, and *mana*, spiritual power and authority. She explains that in "pre-colonial Māori society and to a varying extent in later years, there was a metaphysical dimension to the need for individuals and groups to continually strive to increase their *mana* by generous giving and to protect it against loss by repaying negative gifts in kind" (Metge 2002: 321).

In this statement, Metge underlines the existence of a negative as well as a positive side in the principle of *utu* (reciprocity). On the negative side, one (person or group) can suffer sanctions if one fails to return a gift, and bad things can happen, such as losing the chance for future exchange, losing one's reputation – and *mana* (spiritual power, authority) (Metge 2002: 321) – or even falling victim to *mākutu* (sorcery) (Firth 1959: 417, quoted in Metge 2002: 318). I did not hear about any sorcery as such during my field research (but then, nobody fell ill). However, I would confirm that if people did things that were wrong or did not fit with *tikanga* (customs, tradition), they did fear negative consequences from the supernatural world or expected, at least, some kind of warning from their dead ancestors.

But, in spite of the principle of *utu* (reciprocity), I did see conflicts and disagreements arising out of some people taking advantage of others' generosity. The context of sharing implies responsibility and obligation. The return did not need to be of the same nature. If one were hosted for a while at a relative's place, it would be possible to reciprocate, for example, by helping as much as possible around the house, giving a financial contribution toward the running of the house, or making one's car available for a collective use.

The workings of reciprocity can sometimes create tricky situations for homeowners, particularly those who own a house that has been in the family for generations and where all the siblings have been raised. Even if the family house is owned or rented now by one of the siblings, others might still consider that they have the right to come and go as they please. Some tend to take advantage, arriving whenever they like and staying as long as they like, without necessarily contributing to the day-to-day running and maintenance of the house. This issue was raised by the participants in my research, as well as by Metge (1964), many of whose Auckland informants complained that their country kin stayed with them for weeks at a time without making any economic contribution. Their rural cousins, however, also complained that "urban residents made a convenience of *them*, getting a cheap holiday at the busiest times of the rural year, Christmas and Easter" (245).

However, when visitors become a burden on the people of the house, it can be very difficult to tell them to leave. It goes against any Māori principle of hospitality. Infringing on these principles can create conflicts not only between the persons directly involved in the problematic situation, but also among other members of the wider family, thanks to the same principles, which include dimensions of mutual aid and reciprocity.

Still, staying with one's kinsfolk makes a lot of sense when one first moves to the city, as Rangi explained: "I think, when it comes to the crunch, a lot of family will probably end up doing that, to survive [. . .] If you have a big family that have come from the country to the city, you will find, [the] majority of the time, they will stay with someone until they are able to cope by going out, living on their own." The type of house considered to be like *marae* then becomes a transitory place, a place of passage. It is also a safety net in the city, which is sometimes experienced as an alien or dangerous place, a place not Māori. For Rangi, living with *whānau* gave her and her daughter more security:

> After coming from the country. Like . . . Hoani and I how we started off on our own when we came back to Auckland and we stayed in another house, it was very lonely. And like the only time that felt united was when it was a birthday or something and we came to visit. Yeah . . . Pretty much otherwise, it's lonely out there. Especially when you have been brought up as one, united family [. . .] if I was financially able to cope with a house, I was

financially less able to cope with food and travelling to and from school. And I did not want to put my baby at risk by going out and having a flat [...] I don't think I ever asked her [Kiri], she invited me for dinner one night and next day I moved everything into the shed and I was here to live [...] Just me and Stephanie and having no husband here, I think I would have felt insecure. Knowing the city, I don't think I would have been able to sleep [...] I have been out there and I don't like it, on my own. I find more security living with *whānau*. (Rangi)

Applying the *marae* principles to a house thus represents a way of coping with city life.

However, even if sharing is the "normal" thing to do in this kind of house, it is not always easy:

My house is their house and their house is my house. We sort of have this collective stuff going on. It's not about individuals. I could have something in the fridge that I bought especially for me and if somebody eats it, I will probably be a bit grumpy, but that's what happens when you have it within the fridge [laughter]. That's the purpose of it, that's what I mean, those values and beliefs: it's for everyone. So you buy for everyone. (Joana)

Sometimes, there are tensions between the collective and the individual in today's world where Māori principles and the *tikanga* (traditions, custom) of the *marae* are confronted by mainstream universes of meanings and values. Joana went on to say:

I mean, the doors are always open [...] Sometimes it's really difficult. Oh, just sometimes, I mean, I just don't want to do anything, I don't want to see anyone. You don't have that luxury, you don't have the luxury of just lying on the couch and just relaxing because people will visit [...] I mean, usually, I feed them and things like that [...] But it's good, I mean, I do like it. (Joana)

Even if Christine also appreciated living close to her family and always having a lot of people at home, she sometimes found it quite difficult.

We live closely together . . . but living so close together hasn't been that great in some ways. It has been great for the kids because they have got friends all the time, but . . . I suppose constantly being, you know, being

around each other, sometimes it got quite stressful and things that perhaps my sister and her husband will do with their children, I did not agree
with it because they are my nephews and nieces, you know, I become
quite upset about it and vice versa, you know [. . .] Of course Mum and
Dad are stuck in the middle and they don't agree with any of it, you know,
they got quite upset about . . . things that happen at home with grandchildren [. . .] There are some advantages of living like that, but on the other
hand it hasn't all been that great. (Christine)

Aroha also told me about how difficult it was to study when she was
living at her parents' place: "It was like a train station!" Everybody was
coming and going, there was always someone at home and that also
meant working to care for the visitors. When parents were occupied
with visitors, they could not give much attention to their children's
studies, either. Aroha said that she thought that this could cause problems for students, preventing them from studying. At least, she found
this to be the case for her when she was young; I observed a similar
situation where having a lot of people around often disturbed the children and young people in what they were doing, whether it was homework or housework.

Given her own experience, Aroha was not surprised to hear that
many Māori students do not succeed very well at school or do not finish their degrees. Even if Māori are making gains in their educational
achievement, "still around 30 percent of Māori are leaving secondary
education with no qualification" (Kiro, von Randow, and Sporle 2010:
47). Obviously, having a busy house is not the main reason for Māori
underachievement at school (see, among many others, Irwin 2002;
Johnston 1998; Smith 1997), but it can be a contributing factor. An over-
busy home life is one reason why Aroha chose to do her degree at a
university some distance away from her *whānau*, leaving her tribal area
for Auckland, where she now lives with her husband and her children.
She often has visitors, but not on a daily basis, since, for that, she lives a
bit too far from most of her *whānau* members. She does not describe her
house as being similar to a *marae*, nor does she want it to be like this, for
the sake of her children's achievement at school and her own achievement at work. Nevertheless, this does not prevent her from maintaining very good relationships with her *whānau* in the country and from
visiting them regularly, as often as once or twice a month depending
on what is happening in her own life, at the *marae*, and in her *whānau*
back home.

Aroha is not the only one who has favoured other principles in her house. Other participants in my research did the same. And some made compromises and specific provisions to be sure that the collective living arrangement would be viable in the long run.

> When we first got our house there [on her family plot of land], we have been at Mum's for breakfast and then at sister's for lunch and at my place for tea and then we'll have the children going back and forth . . . Actually it got too much. And . . . we chose . . . [. . .] we will have our own meals and things. But, ya, on special occasions, we'll always get together and have a meal. But the kids just come and go [. . .] They are forever running in and out. It's all right. I love having the kids around. (Christine)

Mutual sharing and reciprocity are the foundations on which the type of house compared to a *marae* is built. It is a symbol of the group and of unity and is central to social life and cultural inheritance. It constitutes a safety net for Māori on many levels, including economic ones, in the city and, more generally, in today's world. Like a *marae*, it is a place where one really belongs.

As Rangi put it when speaking about the house at 30 Aroha Street: "It's like this is our *kākano*, our seed. So, whenever we are stuck or we have a hiding or we are in trouble we always come back to the seed. Yeah, it's about the best that I can describe it, coming back to our seed." Rangi's description encompasses the sense of the house as being about identity and going back to who one is, and that it can be at the very core of people's identities. This notion of "the seed" suggests that the house is about the *whānau* (extended family), real or imagined. It is about the ancestors who have been there before. It is about memories kept alive in the house. Whetu recalled that a lot of people who came to 30 Aroha Street would often say things like: "Remember the memories in that room." She went on: "This house has been in our family for years and it's like a treasure as well. You know how a *marae* is a treasure to the people, yeah, that is just exactly like this house" (Whetu). Tapsell (2002: 143) emphasizes how the *marae* is the "ultimate *taonga*" of the people. Although, commonly translated as "treasure," Tapsell defines a *taonga* as "any tangible or intangible item, object, or thing that represents a kin group's genealogical identity in relation to its estates and resources and that is passed down through generations" (169). The *marae* has *taonga*-like qualities such as "ancestral warmth, presence, reverence, respect, *mana* (authority), *tapu* (restrict[ion]), *wairua* (spiritual presence), and *mauri* (life essence)" (143).

The house is the *manawa*, the heart of the family (Ihimaera 1972: 38). It stores memories, but also tangible family *taonga* like photos. In houses I visited that were identified by their members as being similar to *marae*, one could always find pictures of family members who had passed away, *taonga* like *patu* (hand weapons) and *pounamu* (greenstone), old woven flax baskets and other pieces of flax, genealogy books on occasion, and so forth. People cared for the house like they cared for a treasure. That is why some, like Kiri, felt a responsibility to keep it in the family, open to all.[7]

Marae-like house, usually, are not a single building or a single house. They are often a complex of buildings. In Auckland, Māori who speak about their house as a *marae* often have a sleep-out garage in their backyard that can accommodate visitors. Some others have several houses on the same block or plot of land. Christine recalled how it happened that she, her parents, and siblings came to live all together:

> We were living in our family house and then . . . I got pregnant to my first child and so I said to Mum and Dad, give me a piece of land, I wanna build my house, so they did. At the front of them folks, because they have quite a large crop of land [. . .] So I built a house there. It was just a small two-bedroom home [. . .] My sister and her husband and their children, they also built a house on the same section. So there is Mum and Dad's house, there is me and my husband and our children in the front of them and then in the side of Mum and Dad is the house of sister and brother-in-law and their children. But, Mum and Dad have got a big batch up north and they are up there at the moment and my sister who is a solo mother, her and her four children have moved into my Mum's house. (Christine)

This complex of houses on the same plot was also part of a network of houses in the neighbourhood. Close by was her husband's family house as well as those of his siblings. Christine also had cousins, aunts, and uncles who had their houses around and about.

> The other neat thing too is that my husband's family, the family home, have lived in that area as long as us. It's just across the park. The kids you know, just jump on their bikes and go over to nana's house. So, it's quite neat and all his nieces and nephews that I consider mine too. They all

know my nephews and nieces and they all treat each other like cousins. (Christine)

A similar thing happened at Vanessa's place:

Whaea [mother] Vanessa kind of lives like . . . in her household, she stays with her older brother, the older brother and his wife and their daughter who had a child lived in the house and then they have a sleep-out garage that *whaea* Vanessa and her mother share and then they have a little unit besides the sleep-out shed that houses the son and his girlfriend. So they pretty much live on a *marae* basis. (Rangi)[8]

When I visited Vanessa, there was also a foreign cousin who had just moved there.

Joana and Mihi's house was also part of a network of similar houses on their street. Joana's brother had a house on the same plot. Her sister lived up the road. Their Māori neighbours from other tribes also had their house as a *marae* and it was open to them. Joana explained:

It's like recreating a *marae* in a rural area and then just to adjust it into an urban area. It's like having the same basic values and beliefs that what I do reflects on my *whānau* and the same with my neighbours. And so if there is a death or celebration of some form in the neighbourhood, everyone goes to it [. . .] Like if somebody's child is turning twenty-one, it's not only us who will go, it's most of the Māori within the neighbours who will go 'cause we grew up together and . . . our children grew up together, they grew up with them [. . .] It was not about just being Māori; it was about being a new community. (Joana)

In an article about urban housing for Samoan immigrants in Auckland, Macpherson (1997) examines a popular solution to the problems of limited space for activities central to Samoan social organization: the use of garages as extensions to houses. Macpherson shows how housing in Auckland was designed to satisfy the needs of Pākehā families – that is, domestic groupings that typically correspond to nuclear family units, with a generally stable composition and only loose affiliations to various kinship and community groupings (151). Housing for "typical" low- and middle-income families was built to accommodate two parents (or one) and two children (155).

Like the Samoan migrants studied by Macpherson, Māori are more likely to live in larger domestic groupings that often extend beyond nuclear family units. The composition of domestic groupings is also more changeable and more tightly associated with the extended kin group. Like Samoan migrants, many Māori have taken advantage of government policy that encourages private home ownership for all New Zealanders and gives assistance for this purpose to low-income groups:

> Families with low incomes and little or no savings were assigned housing in various state-owned housing complexes. Rents in these complexes were related to income and were typically much lower than in the open housing market. A series of government policies encouraged families placed in these homes to save money in order to buy them or to buy private housing. Families with some savings were offered several incentives to purchase new homes. First, low-cost, long-term (typically longer than twenty years) mortgages were provided by a government home financing agency, the State Housing Corporation. Second, families were permitted to obtain cash advances on social entitlement such as the child allowance to enable them to meet deposit requirements. (Macpherson 1997: 153)

These housing complexes were typically located in low-cost subdivisions developed on the fringes of many cities. In Auckland, they include places like Ōtara, Papakura, and Manukau in the southside, which are now among the areas with the worse disparity statistics (see maps of urban disparities by Crampton, Salmond, and Kirkpatrick 2000).[9]

Houses designed for nuclear families soon created problems for Samoans and Māori. Houses built under the housing assistance programs were typically free-standing, single-storey, wooden, three- or four-bedroom homes with floor areas of around 100 square metres, set on a lot of between 750 and 1000 square metres (Macpherson 1997). According to Kiro, von Randow, and Sporle (2010), "there was an overall decline in household crowding between 1981 and 2006" (34).[10] The rates of crowding for multifamily households, however, were still particularly high in 2006: 58 per cent for households with one Māori adult and 55.9 per cent for households with two Māori adults (Kiro, von Randow, and Sporle 2010: 34).

In the case of houses that function in a *marae*-like fashion, frequent visits by *whānau* members, and more importantly their longer stays, put pressure on the regular house members since they often had to give up or share their bedrooms to accommodate visitors. At 30 Aroha

Street – a house that with its four bedrooms is bigger than the standard house – the children were the first to give up their rooms, according to status rules. In most cases, they were happy to do so and sleep on the floor in the lounge. But the situation occurred so frequently that it created occasional problems regarding the use of certain spaces, especially the lounge. Those who were sleeping there would have their sleep disturbed by the *whānau*'s regular activities, especially in the evening and the morning. When visitors came, there was a constant shifting of sleeping mats and bedding around the house: the lounge was cleared first thing in the morning to make space for daytime activities, and was packed again with mattresses at night. Mattresses were piled up in the rooms during the day. Of course, all this shifting put furniture and furnishings through considerable wear and tear: Kiri often complained about the deteriorating condition of her new couch and carpet.

As in the case of Samoan immigrants (Macpherson 1997), the garage is seen as a solution to problems of space at 30 Aroha Street and at Vanessa's home. At both places, the garage is used as a sleep-out area and indeed is occupied permanently by certain members of the *whānau*, who have their living quarters there. They decorate the garage according to their taste: Vanessa put *tukutuku* (woven panels usually found in meeting houses) on the walls; Rangi had her television, stereo, computer, couch, and refrigerator in the shed. The only thing that was missing was a bathroom and, for cold nights, some kind of insulation. When there were too many visitors in the house, the garage could provide extra beds. Rangi also had her own guests in the shed, such as Stephanie's friends or students from the school who sometimes stayed the night.

In Tauni's case, the garage was a *hui* (meeting) place for adults' social life and parlour games: "The *whare waka* [canoe house] or the garage is ours. It's the adult place; the house is the kids', so the kids know when to come in the garage 'cause that's our official place" (Tauni). The term *waka* is often used by Māori to speak about their cars, cars being today's Māori canoes. The garage is also the place where they will smoke a cigarette or a joint with adult friends at night. At Joana's place, sometimes her brother and nephew will also have a beer out in the shed. At the funeral of Joana's father, the garage was used as a complete outdoor cooking facility to feed all the visitors, while all the furniture in the house was cleared and stored in one bedroom to welcome the body and the visitors.

There were other space solutions. At one point, for example, Kiri and Andrew were thinking about buying a caravan to provide his friend

John with living quarters and so as to free up the lounge for everyone's use. Having John sleeping on the couch prevented Kiri from studying late at night in the dining room or lounge (there was no wall between the two rooms). She had to work in her own bedroom, which meant disturbing Andrew's sleep, while he had to get up at six thirty each morning. In this particular case, John's departure sorted out the problem until the next *whānau* member came to live with them. William and David felt that the shed became overcrowded when Rangi and Stephanie moved in with them, and they put up a cardboard wall to divide the space and to give everyone a certain degree of privacy. A mobile home was put beside Vanessa's sleep-out garage to lodge her brother and his wife. In Christine's *whānau*, they resolved their space problem by building new houses on their parents' plot.

Vanessa's garage was also used occasionally for school *whānau* meetings to plan fundraising activities and school trips, for example. This was also where Rangi gave Māori language lessons to her students' parents once a week, turning the garage into a "language nest"[11] (Macpherson 1997: 168). So garages, mobile homes, and caravans make useful and flexible extensions of the house. They are also relatively inexpensive when compared to buying a larger house or building an annex onto the existing house. As explained by Macpherson (160), larger houses were available in other districts but they were generally more expensive. Even if family incomes were sufficient to buy one of these houses, most Māori, like Samoans, are reluctant to move to areas dominated by Pākehā, and this is even truer for areas dominated by wealthy Pākehā.

The concentration of Māori in certain areas of the city can be explained both by the low cost housing and by their preference for areas where there are other Māori – and Pacific Islanders or both. This is what Johnston, Poulsen, and Forrest (2005: 177) call the desire for cultural (and physical) security. Moreover, Māori in general like to live near or not too far from their *whānau*. According to the participants in my research, their choice of place of residence is greatly influenced by where other *whānau* or *iwi* members live.

This kind of residential complex thus has marked similarities to traditional *marae*, where people's lives revolved around the *marae*, while their house would either be on the *marae* land or nearby. For many Māori, community life in the city revolves around a house, which they often compare to a *marae* and, for some, this supplements visits, regular or not, to the real *marae* in the country or elsewhere in the city. Johnston, Poulsen, and Forrest (2005) write that Māori's wishes to live in relatively separate areas may simply "reflect the dominance of communal property ownership in their cultures, as against the individual-istic culture of the New Zealand Europeans" (11). By observing Māori houses and living arrangements, one can learn much about changing *whānau* and social relationships, as Rodman suggests in Vanuatu, another Pacific context. "Like the social relations that produce them, houses change all the time" (Rodman 1997: 222). Housing, then, is seen as an active process that changes along with social dynamics. The way it is set out – and also the arrangement of furniture and objects inside the house – expresses something about the relationships within the *whānau* and with others. So, when a family expands as new people arrive in the house, the house also expands by adding annexes. These annexes are part of the house, but they stay peripheral to it.

Participants in my research said the *manawa* or the hearth will always be in the house and is usually in the lounge, dining room, and kitchen where most of the talking and collective activities take place. The annexes are seen more as sleeping facilities, even if certain members spend a good proportion of their time there and perhaps only come to the house for meals and to use the bathroom. There is a certain aura of privacy around most of the annexes, bedrooms and other sleeping rooms. Rooms such as parents' bedrooms, at least at 30 Aroha Street where Kiri and Andrew's bedroom were, are more or less off limits. The boundaries are not clear, but one sensed one could not freely occupy these rooms.

Sometimes, other houses are built on the plot of land of a family house so that people are dwelling on the same site but under several roofs. At Christine's house complex, the extra buildings were not primarily sleeping facilities. Each had its own hearth based on a nuclear family unit, although everybody came together on specific occasions for certain meals, and the children were free to move among houses. It appears to me that in this kind of complex, the members maintain a particular kind of attachment to the family house or the parents' house or the house in which they all grew up, the place that had been home to everybody. The hearth seems to stay there, as at Joana's place, even if other hearths also emerge as the family grows.

Many people have their house as a *marae* at certain times, but not at others. Why, how, and when is a "normal" house turned into a "little *marae*" (Metge 1967: 183) or conceived of as similar in many ways to a *marae*? The Māori I met replied with answers such as "I mean, it just comes naturally in our family, we just welcome people into our home"

(Whetu). "It just comes with your upbringing" (Rangi). Debra said: "If *whānau* turn up, ya, it's like a *marae*, ya. I think that's just the way we are, very . . . we don't mind things like that, *whānau* turn up, doesn't matter what time, it's always open."

Others told me that in the past, their house used to be open to everybody but through time, it changed. Keita said: "It used to be like that when my kids were here. Now it is just my husband and I and my daughter but we are never home. Like he is there and I am here and we are never home." People become preoccupied with work, studies, and other activities. They are at home less often now than when they had young children who have a lot to do with the comings and goings in a house. Children attract other children as well as their parents and grandparents. When the children leave, the house will not usually be as busy as it was until the next generation of children is born. However, the arrival of a baby can also be a reason to cap the number of visitors. This was the case for Moana, who wanted a stable and safe environment for her daughter's newborn. Many people still lived at Moana's place, but the door was not quite as wide open as it used to be, for the sake of peace and quiet for the baby.

For Tui, as I noted earlier, her house was a *marae* only in certain circumstances: once a month, when they had family meetings and all eight children and fourteen grandchildren came together for the Sunday barbecue and activities. "Yeah, everybody comes and then, my house is like a *marae*" (Tui). This was different from "normal" time during which "My house, it's my castle" (Tui). So, although a house can become a *marae* when it is full up with people coming and going, one single party held on one isolated occasion does not mean a house will be considered as a *marae*. To be considered as a *marae*, there must be something in the "spirit" of the house and its people.

There were often very practical reasons why a house was not like a *marae* on a daily basis, as was the case with Tui's house. Tui explained to me that at one time people had treated her house more like a *marae*, and would just show up. Over time, people learned that her husband slept during the day because he worked at night, and Tui was active with her church and in the evenings, since she was a member of her family trust management committee. People had learned to ring them up first to find out if it were okay to visit. During the week, Tui's household did not have many visitors.

Certain city houses can also be considered as *marae* during specific "typically" Māori occasions that traditionally take place on the *marae*, such as *tangihanga* (funerals). Unsurprisingly, these are infrequent. Such city houses may be considered as *marae* or not under "normal" circumstances.

The people who regularly visit houses described as being similar to *marae* are usually *whānau* members and friends who are also considered to be part of the *whānau*. Such a house would also be open for those in need. For example, Kiri and Rangi's grandfather, who used to stay at 30 Aroha Street, brought with him "social welfare kids" (young people whose families were in either emotional or financial crisis, or both, and who were in the care of social services). Whetu, talking about her own grandparents, Teria and Hiko, said: "They had a lot to do with people, also as a *whāngai* [adoptive] family looking after them. It just ended up that way [laughter]. I don't know, they brought up a lot of teenagers and family, like cousins [. . .] who came over and stayed, some for ages [laughter]." Rangi does the same today with some children from school who are in difficulty. Joana's sister, from another house also considered to be similar to a *marae*, used to bring residents of the geriatric unit where she works home for dinner.

Saying that the house is open to everybody is not exactly true, however. There is always some sort of filtering process in place. Rangi explained: "You would not get a complete stranger walk in with conflicts because they should not have been invited anyway." And Matiu said:

> We have not got qualms with people coming in but it is sort of like a filtering process to be like that to ones that fit in with our lifestyle and the ones that don't [. . .] Basically any one can come into our house but if they don't fit in with us then they usually get the telly bye bye [. . .] more than often the people that come around here are Māori and straight away it is a friendship connection. (Matiu)

This filtering process became very clear to me on one occasion at 30 Aroha Street when one of the teenagers brought home an unknown Māori young man of sixteen. At first sight of him, Kiri immediately asked the teenagers of the house to come and have a private talk with her. She and Rangi asked them who he was, where he came from, if he had a place to live, where they knew him from and so on. Receiving unsatisfactory answers to their questions, they asked the teenagers to tell the young man to leave, which they did not do. Kiri and Rangi kept a very close eye on the stranger during his entire visit. Kiri felt he was a threat to the girls – Whetu, Mahora, and Stephanie. Just before dinner,

Kiri decided to warn him in no uncertain terms that if he were there
to steal from them or to get close to the girls, he was not welcome. She
told him that he was being closely watched and that if the television or
stereo happened to be stolen or the girls were hurt, she would find him
and turn him in to the police. Then, she invited him to have a *kai* (meal)
with them and to leave afterward. After he left, Kiri warned everyone
that she and the other adults did not want to see that suspicious young
man around again unless they knew more about him and his *whānau*,
or unless he brought his aunt with whom he said he lived.

When people have reasonable doubts, they ensure that visitors respect the house and the people who live there. "Our home is open to
anybody as long as you respect our home" (Christine). Matiu, who was
from another house put forward much the same sort of idea:

> My house is a *marae* concept [. . .] You know the *marae* protocols and pro-
> cesses, I think you try to apply that to your own personal dwelling, so,
> you know, people who come in, you offer them a *kapu tī* [cup of tea], they
> could say they don't want it, but you offer them a *kapu tī* anyway and
> make them feel relaxed and you give them a *kai* [food, meal] and . . . yeah!
> My house is a *marae* concept.
>
> [. . .] It is the application of the things that you learn at the *marae*. Like . . .
> you don't sit on the tables, like the *tikanga* [customs, rules, tradition] that
> you learn on the *marae*, you use it in your home and . . . *Manaakitangata*
> [showing respect and kindness, hospitality extended to visitors] [. . .]
> Yeah, that's the *marae* concept that is used practically in the home. (Matiu)

There are some rules that are respected in the houses even if they do
not have nearly the same formality as real *marae*. For example, Mihi
explained that "they practise the concepts of *tapu*." But what does that
mean?

The precise practices explained in terms of *tapu* (that is, in terms of
restrictions for being either sacred or polluted and polluting) vary from
one family to another but many agree on the underlying principles and
some of the behaviour. At 30 Aroha Street, as in many Māori houses,
"everybody respects the house by taking off their shoes. Pretty much
like a *marae* basis" (Rangi). Rangi also insisted on the importance of not
washing tea towels (which touch food) with body towels. Food is considered *noa* (free of religious restriction, ordinary). What comes from
the body – hair, nails, and blood – is highly *tapu* (sacred) and should not
be left lying around. Rangi became quite upset when a Pākehā guest

trimmed his beard in the backyard and left the hair on the ground. When Māori have their hair cut, it has to be kept to be disposed of it in a clean and proper way. Rangi's favourite way to get rid of hair, for example, was to put it in a bag and bury the bag, which is not something that can easily be done in the city. She could also burn it, but that was also not easy in Auckland. So she choose to put the hair inside a bag, rather than have it loose and dispersed, and then put the bag in a secure garbage bin.

Some other *tapu* (restrictions) rules that I heard were don't put a hairbrush on the table; don't put a *taonga* (treasure) or a *tapu* (sacred) object like a *whakapapa* (genealogy) book, *patu* (traditional hand weapon), or a *pounamu* (greenstone) on a chair; and don't sit on a pillow. Salmond (1975) identifies some other *tapu* rules: "don't put your hat on the table (hat is *tapu* because it's been on your head; table is *noa* [free of religious restriction, ordinary] from food); don't leave toilet paper on the same shelf as food (toilet is *tapu*, food is *noa*); keep genealogy books out of the kitchen; never wash the baby in a basin you've had dishwater in (baby is *tapu*; dishwater has *noa* food in it), and so on" (49). Writing in 1975, she goes on to add that most families no longer practise these rules. My fieldwork suggests to me that certain practices were revived, along with the language and the Māori culture, during the Māori cultural renaissance.

My fieldwork also suggests that Māori today are more assertive about having their *tapu* (restrictions) respected and more self-confident in their ways of doing things. One night when I was in a nightclub with a group of Māori university students, one of them politely asked a young Pākehā woman not to sit on top of their table since they were Māori and it was important for them. She finally moved off, with some argumentative objection, and after considerable insistence from the woman of our group. Not long after the beginning of my fieldwork, we had to leave in a rush for a *marae* and the bathroom was busy. I was told off by a Māori woman for brushing my teeth in the kitchen sink. I should have known better and I did not make the same mistake twice. On occasion, knowledge (or lack of knowledge) of *tapu* rules can bring about conflicts or misunderstandings within the *whānau*, particularly in mixed households or when non-Māori are visiting. But, even Māori do not always know or practise the proper rules. Rangi told me, "Sometimes, we have a little bit of conflict, but I feel comfortable to talk to Andrew about things [. . .] Yeah, and it's good because it's open, it's an open house, you know, if something bugs him about me or about my child, he can tell me" (Rangi). And again: "If there is tension, it is mainly talked about, pretty much what happens on a *marae*. If there is a *raruraru* [problem], it's brought to . . . you know . . . to the *rangatira* [chief] or to whoever in the *whānau* and it is talked about. Pretty much here, in this case. If I got a *raruraru*, I will take it inside and I will sort it out there" (Rangi). The *marae* – and consequently the city house that is considered as a *marae* – is seen as a forum for people's expression and a place to sort out conflicts, minor or major.

Some houses are like a *marae* virtually full time and largely open on a daily basis to kin and friends. Others are like a *marae* only on particular occasions and, yet others, for a variety of reasons, cease to be like a *marae* for specific periods or forever. The closing of such a house would not necessarily disrupt a *whānau*. Houses in urban settings are legally private property and can be bought and sold and can sometimes become a point of friction among family members. Some will put pressure on the owner or the *kaitiaki* (guardian) of the house to keep it in the family and open to everyone.

Generally speaking, the house is already part of an existing larger network of houses based on similar principles, open to all the *whānau* members. When one is sold, or stops being like a *marae*, these other houses can take over and become a new link (or one of the links) between the *whānau* members in the city and those in the country. These houses are often the main connection to the real *marae* (plural) for the many people who cannot afford a visit to the country for financial or emotional reasons. This was true at 30 Aroha Street. In December 2004, two and a half years after my first stay there, I learned in an email from Kiri that they had just sold the house. She explained to me that she needed time and money for other plans. She wanted to finish her degree and go on a job placement in Europe, so that she could come back with new perspectives for her work with a Māori clientele. She also wanted to travel and buy some "luxury" things for herself and her immediate family. Despite this new situation, Kiri remained very much involved with her *whānau* and continued to work generally for the Māori cause. Among other things, she had more time to go back regularly to her tribe and to learn the Māori language.

By the time 30 Aroha Street was sold, Rangi had moved to a rented house a couple of streets away. Her husband Hoani then decided to move back to Auckland to be with her and the children. They took over the welcoming and caring role and turned their house into a *marae*. As well as Rangi and Hoani, the house welcomed their four children,

Riria; Jordin, who came back to Auckland with her father; Stephanie; and Richard. Over time, Riria's and Jordin's boyfriends moved in, as did Richard's girlfriend. Not too long afterward, three babies lived in the house and more were on their way. Some of Rangi's children decided to move out to their own place for a time . . . and then some came back. Whetu and little Mereheni also stayed at the house for short or long stays when there were *raruraru* (troubles) between Whetu and her mother. Mahora visited the house often, as did grandparents, cousins, friends, neighbours, workmates, and students who were having difficulties at Rangi's school. They even welcomed me again in 2005 and 2008!

When I discussed the idea with other people who could describe their own house in terms of similarities with *marae*, one participant, Tauni, preferred to use the term "*pā*" (fortified place or village). Metge (2012) mentions that "[u]ntil fairly recently the word marae was not used with reference to the marae complex in certain areas. Instead, the word pā was and is still used" (71). Others made a distinction between a *marae* and a *wharenui* (meeting house) and opted for the last expression: "When Dad got the place blessed, it was blessed 'the *wharenui*' [. . .] our house is pretty much a *wharenui*. It has open doors to anyone [. . .] Yeah, it is our *wharenui*" (Rangi). They said that their house is more like a *wharenui*, not like a *marae*, which is the whole set of buildings, since there is one single house. The main house, the *manawa* (hearth), is the core of these *marae*-like houses, even as some *whānau* members may sleep or spend a good part of the day in the garage or in a caravan behind the main house.

Not everybody liked to hear the word "*marae*" referring to a house. For many, there was a clear and significant difference between a house and a *marae*: they belonged to two completely different universes of meaning. Mixing the sacred aspects of *marae* with the profane connotations of a "house" was particularly shocking. When research participants spoke about their house being like a *marae*, however, they were not speaking about the building, as such, or the particular plot of land, but about the spirit of the house, its *wairua*, and its people. The house, then, becomes a symbol for the *whānau*, for the group. Speaking about real *marae*, Metge (2010) uses the term "*marae* community." She explains that "[j]ust as the marae ātea is subsumed in the marae complex, so the marae complex is subsumed in a larger conceptual package comprising the marae complex, a group of people who relate to the marae complex as tāngata whenua [people of/from the land, the hosts on a *marae*] . . .

If a name is needed for this larger package, I suggest 'the marae community.' A marae complex is given life by its people. Without them it is an empty shell" (71). In the urban context, when people say that they belong to the house, they are saying that they belong to the "community" that relates to the house, the *whānau* that inhabits the house, and all the ancestors who are associated with and within the *whānau* members, even if their bones are elsewhere at the traditional or real *marae*. The house is a safe place, a comforting place in the city where Māori are not alone and Māori can be and are Māori. It can also be a place where it is possible to maintain particular kin group identities.

There is no confusion with the real *marae*. But a house can be conceived of as an extension of the *marae* away from home in everyday life; the *tikanga* (custom, tradition) of the *marae*, without its highly sacred dimensions, is practised there on an everyday basis. The idea of the house as a *marae* does not challenge the rights of the *tāngata whenua* (people of the land or the group with a special relationship to the area, with a customary authority). All the participants in my research, without exception, acknowledged the ancestral primacy of the *tāngata whenua* in their area.

I should also emphasize that people who spoke about their house *as* a *marae* or *like* a *marae* did not have confused ideas about what a real or traditional *marae* was, nor did they think of both places as being one single thing. Similar processes happened in both places and they fulfilled similar functions in the life of the group, and the *whānau* network in particular. But "*marae*," when describing their houses, was used as a simile or metaphor. They said their house was *like* a *marae*. And in the absence of the real building or when away from it, the metaphor opens up the universe of meanings that governs everyday practices and relationships. The use of the term "*marae*" affirms this universe of meanings and helps to keep it alive.

In turning their house into a *marae* many challenge the Pākehā way of being and values. In the house, everything is managed collectively and belongs to everyone in the *whānau*, even if it is not actually owned in common in the legal sense of the Pākehā universe of meanings. The demands of the labour market and the capitalist economy, as well as the regulations regarding home ownership and the general requirements of ownership, have shaped the particular form that these houses have taken, which is that one person or a *whānau* couple will be the legal owner or renter of the house. In practice this does not prevent the group, the *whānau* or the collectivity, from being the main principle or value in the house at the very centre of everyday life.

There are some fundamental similarities when *marae* and houses are compared. Similar feelings can be expressed about each, similar activities happen in both, each fulfils similar roles or functions in the life of their *whānau*, and in both places similar values or principles are applied. For Manuka, a Māori research participant and a member of my research team, houses that are like *marae* could be summarized by two Māori principles: (1) *whanaungatanga*, which means "strengthening and enriching the bonds of family unity," and (2) *manaakitanga*, which means "befriending holistically and demonstrating extreme kindness with the utmost respect." These houses are places in the city where Māori can uphold *marae* values and principles while away from their own traditional *marae*.

Other analysts also suggest places that are not real *marae* can be called *"marae"* or described as such under particular circumstances. Tauroa and Tauroa (1986) write that "many people use the term *'marae'* for any place where they choose to welcome visitors, especially when they choose to use a format corresponding to that of a marae welcome. A room, therefore, may loosely, though acceptably, be referred to as a *marae* for the purposes of welcoming visitors" (141). The same could be said for a hall, an office, or a school car park, for example, if there is a *karanga* (call of welcome) and a *mihimihi* (exchange of greetings) (141). At Tauni's place, for example, some people performed *powhiri* (welcome ceremonies) when important visitors came or for special occasions. At the *tangihanga* (funeral) of Māta's newborn baby in her backyard, a *karanga* (call of welcome), *karakia* (prayers), and *waiata* (songs) were performed as well as a *whaikōrero* (speech). Some people present were also wearing leaves from a special tree as a protection against the contagion of death or maleficent influences, as would be practiced on real *marae* (Schwimmer 1965: 155).

What is important about calling a particular place a *marae*, as Tauroa and Tauroa (1986) suggest, is "that all such places belong to 'us,' not to 'me.' They are places where thoughts and ideas may be exchanged, and joy and sadness may be shared" (141–2). "Nothing is 'mine'; everything is 'ours'" (106). And this idea was clearly expressed by the participants in my research: "The house is home for a lot of people." "Everything is shared in the house." "The *whānau* feeling inside the house . . ." "The house is open to everybody who respects the house and its people." Like the *marae*, this type of house symbolizes group unity (Salmond 1975: 31). The real *marae* connects the group, composed of living and dead people, who belong to a particular land, to a particular *marae ātea* (ceremonial courtyard) (Allen 2002: 47). Houses or other informal *marae* also connect people. These people do not necessarily come from the same land but they share the same *kaupapa* (mission, plan, purpose, project) and consider themselves as a *whānau*, even if they are not necessarily related. With the concept of *whanaungatanga*, the inclusive kinship ethic that is part of both *marae* life and life in houses described as *marae*, everyone is responsible for the well-being of the others as well as for the whole *whānau* as a united group. Each adult becomes the parent of all the children of the house and, as such, has important responsibilities.

Metge (1967) explains how some Māori Community Centres are *marae* manqué mainly because "they are not available for *tangihanga* [funerals] or the overnight accommodation of guests" (184). Mutu (in Carter 2003a) also defines, to a large extent, a *marae* through its capacity to fulfil people's actual needs, and funerals are often the key events that determine how many people may need to be accommodated. According to Metge (1967), for a place to be considered a *marae* it should have the *tangihanga* (funerals) as an absolute priority over any recreational functions, should be equipped to provide beds and meals for mourners and for a large number of guests at a *hui* (gathering), and should be an open place for the group to debate and resolve their problems as custom demands. Tauroa and Tauroa (1986) underline that the *marae* is the place where "[every] emotion can be expressed and shared with others – shared not only with the living but also with those generations who have gone" (18).

For Metge (1967), what determines whether a place can be called a *marae* is the scope of its functions and much less "the form of *marae* buildings and the importance of inherited land ownership as the basis for status and authority on the *marae*" (186). According to her, this has become even truer in an urban context where not everybody has access to a *marae*. Therefore if a local *marae* is lacking or unavailable, urban dwellers will use their city house or other premises "as a little *marae*" (183), for a funeral, for example. Walker (2004) also refers to certain *whānau* that respond to a death by turning their city home into a "mini-*marae*" (200). The latter then writes that "[t]he living room cleared of furniture served as a meeting house where the body lay in state, and kinfolk and friends came to say farewell to the dead" (200). Walker suggests that funerals are the only circumstance during which a house can be considered as a "mini-*marae*." He explains that since Māori community centres in the city were not suitable for *tangihanga*, different groups formed to plan the construction of new urban *marae*. I think the lack of suitable places is also a reasonable explanation for why Māori turn their own homes into a "little" *marae* in everyday life. In times of death, they will today go to a real *marae* in the city if one is available and if they feel comfortable going there. Otherwise, they will have the funeral at home, at a relative's place, or in another Māori meeting place or community room.[12]

Joana's and Mihi's place in West Auckland hosted the *tangihanga* of Joana's brother. Joana recalled: "What happened is that when he passed away, before they even came back, Mum and that, the neighbours, all the neighbours had already set up a kitchen . . . removed all of the furniture out of the house, they had actually turned it into [. . .] a *marae* and then they prepared the *marae* for . . . that's what they do here, I mean everyone in the neighbourhood." The event lasted two days after which they took Joana's brother back to their real *marae* in the country. During these two days, "the whole thing, the whole cooking was done out there . . . people come in the house and speak . . ." (Mihi). On these occasions, people in the *whānau* or neighbours bring the extra equipment needed for the funeral: mattresses, blankets, tables, chairs, dishes, pans, tents. They also often bring food and money as *koha* (gifts).

Alternatively, with the impetus to renew links with their spiritual home, people increasingly take their dead to their traditional *marae* in the country. This last option would likely have been preferred if someone in Kiri's *whānau* were to have passed away. This would not necessarily prevent the family from first receiving those who wished to pay their respects in the city for a night or two, at the house or in another place, depending on who had passed away. Having a part of the funeral in the city before taking the dead to the country *marae* allows city friends who cannot travel to visit. This happened at the funeral of one of Kiri's aunties when I was back in Auckland at the beginning of 2005. Kiri's family first welcomed people at their aunty's church community room before taking her body up north to her *marae* where more mourners paid their respects.

In contrast to some other Māori who live in the city, Kiri and her *whānau* still had very good contacts with their *marae* in the country, particularly since Kiri's parents lived in Teria's tribal area for a few years before moving down south to Hiko's tribal area. Both Teria and Hiko have secured connections to their *tūrangawaewae* (standing place) for their children and grandchildren as well as themselves. Teria was also a trustee of her tribal trust board. For a couple of years from 2003 on, all the girls of the *whānau*, including Kiri herself, were also active members of the *kapa haka rōpū* (Maori performing arts group) of Hiko's *marae*.

Everybody travelled back and forth every weekend between Auckland and the *marae*, about fours hours' drive away, in preparation for regional *kapa haka* competitions. Rangi also went there on many occasions to support them. This helped strengthen their connections to their people as well as their *marae*.

Metge (1967), Walker (2004), and Mutu (in Carter 2003a) give a functionalist definition of the *marae*. This can be useful in understanding what happens on a *marae* but it is less useful for understanding its nature. That a house has never hosted a funeral does not stop its members from speaking about it as a *marae*. On the contrary, as Tauni's and Matiu's cases show, the house is like a *marae* primarily because of the symbolic meaning that the house takes on. The house is the *manawa* (hearth) of the *whānau*, symbolically and practically. "It is our *kākano* [seed]," Rangi said about the house standing at 30 Aroha Street. It symbolizes past and present generations, memories, histories, *whānau*, and cultural inheritance and thus, continuity through daily life. It is because of its symbolic meaning that those who have such a house feel a great responsibility to keep it in the family, as in Kiri's case.

At Māta's baby's funeral when the backyard was used as a *marae*, for example, some people took elders' responsibilities to do things according to the Māori ways and were supported in their songs and prayers by some of the people present. Tradition wasn't necessarily always followed – a male,[13] for example, did the *karanga* (ceremonial call of welcome) – but the acts of the *tangihanga* itself were more important than the exact way they were done. The important thing was to bring comfort by being together as a whole *whānau*. Māta's backyard, then, really became a *marae* for many people not because there was a *tangihanga* there, but because of the feeling that emanated from the moment – the sharing, the feeling of being together in that difficult and sad time after Māta's baby – everyone's baby – was born dead.

Certainly, some people were not very comfortable with the way things were done. The presence of many Pākehā also created some discomfort; people did not know how the Pākehā were going to experience the *marae* format. The hosts did everything possible to reconcile both world views and ways of doing things and the ceremony was part of this effort. I found these urban places to be spaces where different worlds meet because they do not have the same formality as real *marae*. Pākehā would not have necessarily attended a funeral on a real *marae*, but they felt able to be present at Māta's place. Because a house is a less formal, more relaxed place, it is easier for everybody to feel comfortable there, Māori or not.

The house is also important because it is where Māori feel safe, secure, relaxed, at home. Matiu emphasizes this by saying "this is like our refuge for us from the outside world." Because of the house and its particular character, its people feel they belong to a place and to a group, to a *whānau* in a city where one often feels lost, isolated, alien, and deterritorialized. I think it is this sense of group belonging that is meant when some Māori talk about places like the pub in terms of a *marae*, to which the connection is informal – "The pub is my *marae*" – the pub being their meeting place, the place where they find solace, the place where they find a *whānau*.[14] Metge (2002: personal communication) has expanded on her definition of a *marae* as a place where one can relax and recharge one's batteries. Mead (2003: 110) supports this view, but in a more specific sense, saying that *marae* are safe havens where Māori can recharge their *cultural* batteries. This dimension of the *marae* fits well with what Tauroa and Tauroa (1986) write:

> Just as people wishing to express their religious beliefs will go to church or to a place of worship, so will Maori people seeking fulfilment and reaffirmation of their identity go to their *marae* . . . There is an awareness of one's heritage; an awareness that one is accepted. It is a place of security and comfort.
>
> An analogy in the Pakeha world might be that of arriving home after a particularly busy and harrowing day. There is the sigh of relief – "thank goodness I'm home" . . . Everything is familiar: the faces, the surroundings, the noises, the conversation. At last you can truly relax. This is your home, and you belong. (20)

It also fits with what is described as essential for the people who qualify their house as a *marae*.

Church buildings and schools can be used as *marae*. They are meeting places where important decisions are taken, the members or the *whānau* group can host guests for meetings or to sleep over, or where they themselves can have a sleep-in. They have a kitchen and all the necessary utilities to provide for guests as well as themselves but, most importantly, they are places where one finds a *whānau*. Tui said of her church building:

> It functions every way like a *marae*, except we don't have . . . a forum where only men can speak. Women and children have the right to speak in this building. We don't have, as in a *marae*, you have your dead, you

bring your bodies there and you have things; we don't have that. We have memorial services [. . .] Why is it similar [to a *marae*]? Because it has the same . . . openness about who can come there, nobody is excluded, and it's Māori and everybody has the right to speak. (Tui)

Tui added that if it is *like* a *marae*, in many ways, it is not a real *marae* in many other ways: "It doesn't have the same formality that *marae* do. And we are not restricted by tribal etiquette, *kawa* [protocol], those things . . . the *kawa* in this place is the *kawa* of the church." Moreover, they do not perform a *powhiri* (welcome ceremony) for their guests on their church premises since it is not a real *marae*. If they need to welcome visitors, they will go to the real *marae* nearby, which is an urban pan-tribal *marae*. But, what makes it a *marae* is the *whānau* support: "Everybody knows everybody else. It's not like something new in the Church [. . .] It's very much a family [. . .] and we always eat at the church. We have service and then we have a lunch. Everybody brings something, we share the lunch" (Tui). Sharing and mutual support are very important:

We have reciprocal responsibility for many of our church members. Probably those who help me the most are the old aunties. I mean, some of the reciprocal stuff might simply be, my husband goes out fishing and comes home with half a dozen fish and we can't eat them all and I go and drop out two off, you know. As simple as that and it's not a big deal, but for some of them [. . .] something like that, it's really cool. (Tui)

And she added:

Support and comfort . . . I think if we use the two words together . . . Without support, I can't . . . my biological family has always supported me [. . .] and that is really good. And like my church family, most of them would help me with anything to do with the church or if I don't do something right and the other things it that, they don't . . . they will always offer some ways to do the things differently. I think that's help to build comfort. It's not just criticism [. . .] they're always there. (Tui)

Hiraina put the emphasis on the same *whānau* feeling, sharing and support, when she said, speaking about the resting area just in front of her store at the shopping centre where she works, "that's my *marae*!" She said that because when she goes there, she is among *whānau*: they share their problems, they support each other, they laugh together. It is the place where everybody converges; it is a good place to be and relax. "Here," she told me one time when we were sitting there, "you can put your feet up and it's all right!"

In his book *Tikanga Māori: Living by Māori Values*, Hirini Moko Mead (2003: 103)[15] acknowledges that the definition of "*marae*" has changed through history and he makes it clear that *tikanga* allows for innovation. The important thing, he writes, is that the main principles remain intact (106). He adds that if Māori were to stick firmly to what is generally recognized as a "traditional" definition of *marae*, urban and institutional *marae* – like school and university *marae* – could not be recognized as real *marae*, since the ownership of the land on which they stand as well as the *marae* themselves break with tradition in many ways. Mead (2003) thus gives additional credence to Māori who say that their city houses are like *marae*.

Not every urban-based Māori is involved with a *marae*-like house. Some are not at ease with the idea of an "open" house where people come and go and where everything is shared. Some need a certain degree of privacy to succeed well at school or work and so they choose not to turn their house into a *marae*. Others do not have access to this kind of world (or universe of meanings), either because their access to their *whānau* network is very limited, or because it is not in their "nature" to live in this way. They have not been brought up to live like that, or they do not associate with people who live like that. Others will be at ease with this kind of *whānau* and *marae* environment and will frequent the houses of kin or friends but will not have their own house turned into a "little *marae*."

For most of the participants in this study, however, this particular type of house was a place that was crucial to feeling comfortable in the city, to feeling that they belonged to a group or *whānau* and were supported.

Our analysis converges with Sissons's (2010) conclusions and adds to it by bringing ethnographic evidence into the urban context of today:

> Urban migration, which dramatically accelerated for Maori in the 1960s, made it more difficult for many people to participate in *marae* gatherings. However, while there are now large numbers of people who rarely return home to their *marae*, Maori society, insofar as it remains a distinctive field of meaningful interaction in New Zealand, remains house-focused. (383–4)

To come back to the question that arose at the end of the previous chapter – why, given the obvious importance of the *marae*, are statistics regarding *marae* frequentation so low? Part of the answer is to be found in the Māori city houses where *marae* principles are applied and they become homes away from home; homes that connect people and places, provide for comfort, and allow for Māori affirmation.

5 The *Whānau*, Past and Present

The "ordinary" homes in the city where "traditional" Māori principles and values are applied are key urban sites for maintaining extended family relationships and transmitting Māori principles that offer both continuity with the ancestral past and guidelines for change. They are places in the city where *whānau* members converge, where they secure connections to the past, to memories, and to ancestral worlds; transmit traditional knowledge and the Māori language; maintain links to the rural home, share news and gossip about the people and the *marae* in the country; and make important decisions about family, children, land, and politics.

Living with Māori families has given me an understanding of the principles that guide people in their interrelations and actions. It has given me a richer, more layered understanding of the word *whānau*, which does not always mean the same thing or apply to the same groupings. People and groups define the word in various ways and switch from one meaning to the other. Meanings of the word can expand and contract according to particular contexts, life-stages, persons, and sub-groups, as well as to wider socioeconomic structures, forces, and conjunctures. Family networks can sometimes be quite restricted and sometimes very large.

Apart from the fundamental meaning of the word "*whānau*," to "give birth" (Durie 2001a: 190) or to "be born" (Williams, 2000 [1971]: 487), Metge (1995) in her seminal work on Māori families in a typical rural context, identifies eleven other meanings for the word "*whānau*" that correspond to those I identified among the urban participants in my research.

First, it refers to a set of siblings; that is, brothers and sisters born from the same parents. Second, it can designate the descendants of a relatively recent ancestor through male or female links, regardless of their place of residence and their interactions with each other. Using classical anthropological terms this definition corresponds to the cognatic descent category. Third, it can correspond to the descendants of a relatively recent ancestor who interact and act together and who identify themselves as a group. In the anthropology of kinship, one would speak about a cognatic descent group. Fourth, it could designate a descent group with the addition of members' spouses and adopted children who act and interact together on an ongoing basis. One might equally say an extended family. Fifth, it could designate a descent group of much greater genealogical depth such as a tribe or subtribe. Metge (1995: 53) then adds that "[s]uch a usage is a metaphorical extension of the fourth usage above, used rhetorically to remind hapū and iwi members of their responsibilities and appropriate behaviour towards each other."

Added to these meanings are several new ones, which developed through the course of the twentieth century. The word "*whānau*" can thus be used in a sixth sense to mean a small family consisting of one or two parents and their children – that is, a modern nuclear family – or in Durie's (2001a: 194) terminology, the "whānau as households." Seventh, it could refer to a group made up of kin related in various ways who interact for common purposes and act as an extended family. In her previous work, Metge (1964: 166, 169–70) called this sort of group a kin-cluster. Eighth, "Māori who would normally apply the word to a group of limited size [could] stretch it elastically when it suits them to do so" (Metge 1995: 55). The word could cover anyone from close genealogical kin to all Māori. Ninth, the term could be used to express feelings of solidarity on specific occasions, for example to greet an assembly of people gathered for a common purpose. Tenth, the term could be used to speak of an "ad hoc *action-group* mobilised on behalf of a particular person to support him or her in a testing situation such as a job interview or a public speaking engagement" (55). This sort of group can include non-kin and even non-Māori friends. Eleventh, and finally, it could be used by a non-kin group as a reminder of *whānau* values to which a group aspires. The term could be used, for instance, by a group of non-related children and adults associated with a particular Māori school or a group associated with an urban *marae*, a sports team, or a church. Durie (2001a: 192) then speaks about "whānau as comrades."

The governing principles or values of the *whānau* – but also of the *marae* and the particular type of house that is often compared to a *marae* – serve as guides for Māori in their relationships among themselves as well as with others. These others can be other persons, *whānau*, tribes, the Pākehā, and so forth, depending on circumstances and the particular space/time.[1] These principles or values manage the inclusion and exclusion of members at the levels of *whānau*, subtribe, and tribe. They are based on *tikanga* (traditions, custom) and the space/time of the ancestors. The specific criteria governing each principle or value can vary from one *whānau* to another, one group to another, depending on particular experiences and relationships with others and intersubjectivity, as well as sensitivities related to particular histories and contexts.

Aroha: According to Metge (1995), the value that Māori name first is *aroha*,[2] which means unconditional, altruistic love and warm affection, especially for family members – including ancestors and supernatural beings – but also charity, compassion, or pity for those in need, unwell, or in trouble, and gratitude for kindness or gifts received. *Aroha* assumes caring acts. *Aroha* is also used to express approval or pride in someone. Today, Māori speakers and writers usually focus on the most comprehensive meaning of *aroha*, "stressing its connection with the divine, the generosity of spirit which puts others before self, and its refusal to impose limits or conditions" (Metge 1995: 80).

This raises the importance of another value, *te taha wairua*, or respect for the spiritual dimension, which completes and complements *te taha tinana* or the physical dimension. When seeking guidance, Māori acknowledge the signs and presence of their *tīpuna* (dead ancestors) and other spiritual beings. Most of them seem to recognize their agency and "generally agree on the desirability of seeking divine blessing and assistance in daily life, in crises and whenever they are gathered together, whether or not they do so themselves" (83).

Closely related to *te taha wairua* and *te taha tinana* are the complementary principles of *tapu* and *noa*. They are used to give or restrain access to the group/*whānau* resources (*taonga*, or treasure as in genealogical knowledge, arts or technical knowledge, natural resources, roles within the family according to rank, age and gender, and so forth). *Tapu* and *noa* principles help to maintain a certain control over persons, groups, and other resources; serious consequences (physical as well as supernatural) can follow from violating *tapu*/*noa* rules.

Whanaungatanga is the principle Māori value second in importance and is closely associated with *aroha*. *Whanaungatanga* means "strengthening and enriching the bonds of family unity," according to Manuka, one of the participants in this research. *Whanaungatanga*, from *whanaunga* or relatives, means kinship in its widest sense (see Kawharu 1975 for details). This principle, which is an inclusive horizontal kinship ethic, reinforces the commitment of all the relatives and reminds them of their responsibilities to their people, such as providing beds and food. It is also closely linked to the principle of reciprocity, *utu*. Māori must give without being asked so as to know how to be helpful. As Manuka explained, when you visit people, you bring *kai* (food) with you, which makes you feel good. *Whanaungatanga* is also commitment to one another in the *whānau*, the responsibility to help, support, and encourage – verbs translated to *awhi* and *tautoko* in Māori. This value allows for cohesion and mutuality (James Henare Māori Research Centre 2002, 3: 155). The danger of exclusion is always present if a person or a group does not assume the required responsibilities.

As already discussed, the principle of *whanaungatanga* also allows for the temporary acceptance of strangers in the group in particular circumstances, such as during celebrations and *tangihanga* (funerals) on *marae*. If some people present themselves as part of the *whānau* outside these specific moments, they will receive a discreet (or sometimes more explicit) warning.

Kotahitanga, another important principle, means "oneness" or "unity." *Kotahitanga* asks for the acceptance of differences within the group, confidentiality in contact with outsiders, responsibility for each other's actions, and prevention and control of damage or reparation to maintain or restore the *mana* of the *whānau* (Metge 1995: 102).

Mana is another important value, which has as its primary reference the spiritual power and authority that is made manifest in human experience (Metge 1995: 87).[3] Its second set of meanings can be translated into English as prestige or reputation. Both individuals and groups have *mana*, and every share or store of *mana* influences or affects the *mana* of the larger group, since *mana* is unitary and indivisible. *Mana* can be acquired through a combination of inheritance from ancestors, direct contact with the supernatural, and human achievement. Males and females also have their own special *mana*, seen as complementary, which entitles men and women to specific roles and responsibilities in the *whānau* and in relation to the principles of *tapu* and *noa* (for details, among others see Metge 1995: 91–8; Salmond 1991b; Durie 1994).

Because *mana* is acquired by inheritance from ancestors, genealogy, or *whakapapa*, it is highly valued. It cements *whānau* ties by developing pride and a sense of belonging to each other and to a common heritage. Genealogical knowledge – that is, the exclusive descent ethic or vertical ethic – also prescribes patterns of behaviour and roles according to birth order and generational level, enables *whānau* members to establish links with each other and with subtribe(s) and tribe(s), and enables relations with other groups to be traced. Genealogical knowledge is *tapu* and serves as a limiting or controlling principle.

Manaakitanga is another important value. It means "befriending holistically and demonstrating extreme kindness with the utmost respect" (Manuka). *Manaakitanga* begins when someone's guests arrive and finishes when the last person leaves. In my research, most of the participants identified *manaakitanga* and *whanaungatanga* as the two main overarching principles and they came up very often in informal and formal conversations on *marae* and in everyday situations. *Whanaungatanga* is identified as the domain of the self, the "us," while *manaakitanga* is rather the domain of the "others," who are temporarily included in the "us" or marked as the others by being cared for as visitors. The practice of *manaakitanga* is directly linked to the *whānau*'s *mana*. *Manaakitanga* can thus be used to make someone feel excluded from the *whānau* or as a stranger at home as opposed to one of "us." *Manaakitanga* can serve to establish a relationship but also to place a boundary between people.

Utu is the principle of reciprocity, "the principle that anything received should be requited with an appropriate return" (Metge 1995: 100). This definition implies a positive as well as a negative return, depending on what has been received. Metge (1995) identifies five important rules that underpin the *utu* principle: (1) "the return should never match what has been received exactly but should ideally include an increment in value, placing the recipient under obligation to make a further return"; (2) "the return should not be made immediately [. . .] but should be delayed until an appropriate occasion, months, years and even a generation later"; (3) "the return should preferably be different from what has been received in at least some respects: one kind of goods may be reciprocated by another kind, goods by services, services by a spouse"; and (4) "the return does not have to be made directly to the giver but may be made to the group to which he or she belongs or to his or her descendants" (100–1). Because of these rules, the principle of *utu* maintains an ongoing relationship among persons and groups. The imbalance of obligation is particularly crucial in maintaining the relationship (Metge 2002).

The principle of *utu* is also closely associated, again according to Metge (1995: 100; 2002: 320–1), with the principle of *mana*, since the store of *mana* is increased or diminished according to the holder's actions. *Mana* is increased by generous giving and protected against any loss by repaying negative gifts in kind, as Metge (2002) specifies:

> In contemporary Māori society offences against individuals and groups are in theory dealt with by the law of the land and it is well over a hundred years since inter-tribal warfare came to an end. Nowadays the obligation to repay "bad" gifts is not usually acknowledged openly nor acted upon outside the law by law-abiding citizens. Nevertheless, it still operates powerfully under certain circumstances. It can erupt in violence, for example, in relations between Māori "gangs." But in most cases those involved find other ways of securing *utu*, for example, in the Māori Land Court or the general law courts, on the Rugby field or in *kapa haka* "action song" competitions. (318)

I would add that *utu* is also secured through verbal exchanges and robust public debates, public lectures, or speeches on *marae*.

At the *whānau* level, members have obligations and responsibilities in relation to inherited *mana* and the leadership and guidance of the older members. The young are expected to respect what the *whānau* consider to be the right ways, to avoid actions that provoke criticism and, when their turn comes, to provide guidance to the next generation so that the *mana* of the *whānau* and the *mana* of the elders and ancestors will be maintained and even increased. If one person or a sub-group threatens the *mana* of the *whānau*, *utu* and *mana* principles combine and can be used as principles of exclusion. They can also serve as principles of inclusion when a person or a group can enhance the *whānau*'s *mana*.

The principle of *utu* is thus essential to the management of internal relations of the *whānau*. Those who have received affection, approval, support, care, protection, and respect are obliged to reciprocate generously without counting what it costs them (Metge 1995: 101). *Utu* is also closely related to principles such as *aroha* (100) and, in light of its importance for Māori today, *manaakitanga*.

In the case of "bad" gifts – dislike, jealousy, or abuses for example – the unity of the *whānau* can be protected by dealing with the problem collectively, resorting to mediators or *takawaenga*, or having a formal group discussion (101). A good gift can also halt the exchange of insults or injuries. If, in the long run, there is no, or not enough, reciprocity, the future of the relationship is endangered, which poses a limit to *whanaungatanga*.

Metge (103) also identifies negative values that are disliked and attract heavy sanctions in the *whānau*. Among others, any tendency to be self-centred and selfish or lazy is disapproved of. A tendency to arrogance, to look down on others, and for too much self-confidence is condemned. Two positive values that are highly encouraged and were mentioned repeatedly in discussions and meetings were the values of humility and respect for others. A Māori has to know his or her place and rank and show respect to others, particularly elders. A Māori's humility and respect are closely linked to his or her own *mana* and his or her *whānau's mana*. Trampling on someone else's *mana* provokes a counter-reaction, following the principle of *utu*, and serves to exclude one from the group. Metge (103–4) remarks that charges of being *whakahīhī* (arrogant) are sometimes unfair when addressed to people particularly gifted or marked out for leadership. These false accusations often arise from jealousy, which is another value identified as negative by Metge (104). Jealousy or backbiting can arise from envy or resentfulness of another or of another's possessions or advantages.

Whānau, the word, has various meanings and principles or values that govern it; it has great elasticity and covers many realities depending on context. Further distinctions can be made between *whakapapa whānau* (genealogical *whānau*, also referred to in English as *whakapapa*-based *whānau*), for which kinship and descent from a shared ancestor form the fundamental basis of connection, and *kaupapa whānau* (common-purpose *whānau*, also referred to in English as *kaupapa*-based whānau), which fulfils a common mission or a special purpose. This commonality could be in the form of a *kaupapa* (Metge 1995: 294; Durie 2001a: 192; Cram and Pitama 1998: 149) or could be that the members share a common bond such as a geographical location (Cunningham, Stevenson, and Tassell 2005) or a workplace (Williams 2010). In everyday life, people often identify with more than one *whānau* that could be a mix of genealogical *whānau* and common-purpose *whānau* (Cunningham, Stevenson, and Tassell 2005).

It is difficult to make generalizations about *whānau* life because of the wide variation over time, place, group, or tribe and because the meaning is so elastic. Among other things, different *whānau* have different degrees of knowledge of and reliance upon *whakapapa* (genealogy) and *tikanga* (traditions) (Cram and Pitama 1998). The *whānau* has evolved to meet new circumstances of urban life, but remains significant (Durie

1997, 2001a; Williams 2010), as my research confirms. Living with Māori made me realize, contrary to many analysts who see Māori people and culture as dislocated and fragmented in the city, that the *whānau* is still alive, well, and more active than many might think. Although *whānau* relationships are more often casual than formal, *whānau* probably have a greater influence than anything else on cultural identity. In daily life, people continually stress the importance of the *whānau* in various contexts.

Metge (1995: 17) argues that the *whānau* – along with the *marae* – has become a powerful symbol of Māori traditions and customs, even for those who are not currently active in *whānau*. This has triggered the emergence of new kinds of *whānau*, such as *kaupapa whānau* (common-purpose *whānau*). Durie (2001a) considers that the *whānau* is probably the single most common affiliation among Māori because it is part of their daily experience. Henare (1988, in Pihama 1998) describes the *whānau* as the basic social unit of Māori society. Kiro, von Randow, and Sporle (2010: 15) also remark that "'Whānau' has great policy currency, an example of which is the Whānau Ora Taskforce (2009–2010)." The meaning of the word *whānau* has changed with colonization and life in the city (Cram and Pitama 1998; Metge 1995; Durie 2001a), at the same time as the *whānau* might be the structure that has best withstood these forces (Cunningham, Stevenson, and Tassell 2005).

Major changes in the *whānau* are linked to historical changes. The British colonization of New Zealand, through warfare, legislation, and land confiscation, brought about important transformations in Māori ways of life. The loss of land in particular was a determining factor, according to Cram and Pitama (1998: 137). As a result, Māori became increasingly vulnerable to diseases associated with poverty, malnutrition, and overcrowding. Many were unable to sustain their *whānau* and had to enter the mainstream workforce to earn their living. Some chose to move to urban centres to find jobs in factories (Belich 2001; Metge 1964; Schwimmer 1968; Walker 2004; Williams 2010). Others moved to other subtribal or tribal areas with foreign protocols. This led many Māori to lose knowledge of *whakapapa* (genealogy), *tikanga* (traditions, customs), and *kawa* (protocols) and to adopt new ways of life.

The loss of land also brought about inadequate access to the *tūrangawaewae* (standing place where one belongs, the connection to the land), to cemeteries, and *marae* and, thus, fewer places for Māori to gather and discuss plans for survival. Williams (2010: 49) also explains that from the mid-1930s, changes in the Māori land development scheme and the individualization of Māori land titles affected the modes of socioeconomic organization: Māori farming was treated as an individual business and this eroded collective forms of economic development.

Christian missionaries also wrought changes on the structure of *whānau*. Generally speaking, their policies and practices had a particularly devastating effect on the traditional role and status of Māori women as well as on Māori parenting practices. With the missionaries' imposition of a patriarchal structure, Māori women found their traditional rank and birthright, their *mana* and position of authority undermined. According to Cram and Pitama (1998), the system of missionary schooling promoted "nuclear families, with the woman as the primary caregiver, and each woman looking after her 'own' children. This diminished traditional patterns of shared caring and parenting . . . Men were less involved as caregivers as they often had to work long hours (often shift hours) to earn an income that would sustain them" (138–9). The flexibility of child rearing inherent to the Māori practice of *whāngai* (for details, see Metge 1995; McRae and Nikora 2006) was further undermined by laws concerning adoption since the beginning of the twentieth century and, during the urban migration, due to housing policy for Māori "that turned children into things that had to be retained by parents in order to qualify for a home" (Williams 2010: 144). To qualify for state housing, the Māori practice of *whāngai* concerning children had to be legally registered as permanent adoptions.[4]

These new patterns of parenting and the redivision of domestic labour were based on a belief system closely related to capitalism and industrialization, which located women in the domestic and private sphere, fully responsible for the home and dependent on their husbands' earnings (Pihama 1998; Novitz 1982; Binney 1968; Smith 1992). Interestingly, Williams (2010) mentions, however, that in the urban postwar context in which "whānau utilised their homes as spaces of agency and identity empowerment," "the idea of mutuality . . . challenges the notion of the home as a rigidly gendered sphere occupied and maintained by women yet overseen by male breadwinners" (141). A mutual approach would be necessary to ensure the "cultural security of the home" (141).

Meanwhile, British education policies, "wrapped up in a cloth of superiority and racism" (Cram and Pitama 1998: 141), set the conditions for the minoritization of Māori language, culture, knowledge, and values, which has been another major factor of disruption of the *whānau*.[5] Even though many Māori, who increasingly live away from home, have reduced access to the *marae*, it is still recognized by Cram and Pitama (1998: 135) as one of the institutions that buffered the effect of colonization, particularly through the maintenance and reinforcement of *whānau* links. I would add that urban houses that are regarded as *marae* play a similar role in the city today.

The nuclear family and the *whānau* are not the same kind of unit, although the Western bias of many scholars has led to much confusion about this. As more Māori migrated to cities, the term *whānau* was applied to nuclear families or households because the wider links did not appear to be active or were greatly reduced in intensity, and there was no Māori word to describe the small nuclear family.[6] With urbanization, the networks of rural *whānau* houses in close proximity to each other gave way to small family units in single households dispersed throughout the city.

It is misleading to think that members of individual households are not part of a wider *whānau* system. When there is a need for it – for example in times of celebration or *tangihanga* (funerals) – *whānau* members cooperate and activate the extended *whānau* network.[7] At least, that is the case for a large proportion of Māori who live in the city today. *Whānau* relationships are also maintained, among other means, via the telephone, the internet, meetings and gatherings, and visits to Māori meeting places in the city, such as *marae* and family houses.

But because Māori are not very visible, do not often gather and express themselves loudly in public spaces, some analysts have drawn mistaken conclusions about the (lack of) vitality of Māori networks. Not being "café kind of people," to take an eloquent image used by some research participants,[8] meetings and negotiations among Māori are usually invisible to outsiders, in particular, "within the hustle and bustle of an urban environment dominated by Pākehā majority" (Williams 2010: 20).[9] Even as the Pākehā majority may be reduced, as the city has become more multicultural since the time of the first generations of Māori migrants to it, the idea of Māori invisibility still holds true today. The image of café culture – the public display of emotions, public disagreements, and even loud conversations and laughter – from which Māori distance themselves is revealing. Writing about Auckland migrants from Panguru from the 1950s to the 1970s, Williams (2010) notes an "etiquette of silence" that contributes to Māori invisibility in the city:

[i]t was a solution that suppressed openly negative opinions regarding Māori-Pākehā difference . . . Indeed, an etiquette of silence meant that

cultural negotiations between Panguru migrants and the other were often subtle. A mix of genuine and superficial politeness, mimicry, feigned understanding or sometimes incomprehension of the other's language, habits and desires was . . . a form of silent negotiation. (25–6)

Williams (2010) adds that it is "a cautious approach to living in the city that allowed . . . migrants to carve out their own community sites" (240). Even for Māori, it is difficult to find and meet Māori people when you do not already have a well-defined network in the city: "It is very lonely in the city" (Rangi), and one has to seek other Māori out. As underlined again by Williams, "'silence' has always been a culturally appropriate way for Māori to express 'dissent' or disagreement" (25).

Of course, Māori are out and on the street, and could be met in the city, but there is not an area that is recognizable as a Māori area. Māori are dispersed in the crowd and there are no or very few visible signs of a Māori neighbourhood, other than *marae* – which, although they usually have distinctive architecture and characteristic carvings, are infrequent and can also be situated in non-Māori neighbourhoods. Indeed, in the 1960s, a "pepperpotting" program was put in place in Wellington and Auckland by the Department of Māori Affairs to relocate Māori families throughout communities so they could adapt better and faster – that is to say assimilate – to city life and Pākehā ways (Cram and Pitama 1998; Durie 1998; Harris 2004b, 2007, 2007–8; Walker 1979, 2004; Morrison 1995; Trlin 1984).

Although criticised for accelerating the urbanisation process, the relocation programme seems to have been under-utilised compared to the thousands of Maori who were urbanising. In fact, the programme did not begin until 1961, so it could hardly be accused of pre-empting urbanisation for the purpose of manipulating it. (Harris 2004b: 204)

While some could not be convinced to leave their ancestral ways behind, with easy mortgages as an incentive, others showed active resistance to being "assisted" (Harris 2004b: 204). The scheme, thus, did not succeed in preventing Māori from being more concentrated in some areas than in others, but that is not easily visible to someone who, for example, is simply driving through the city or who is not familiar with the locality. In contrast to Chinese immigrants and their famous Chinatowns all over the world, for example, Māori do not mark urban space and do not affirm a political presence in it.[10]

Furthermore, Māori do not live in "Māoritowns" or clearly defined Māori districts. They live all over the city in apartments and one-family houses among the rest of the city dwellers. This situation contrasts with other Polynesian populations. According to an ethnic residential segregation study conducted in Auckland in 2001, while very few Māori lived in areas where at least 50 per cent of the population were Māori, 30 per cent of the Pacific Islanders lived in areas where at least 50 per cent of the population identified as Pacific Islanders (Johnston, Poulsen, and Forrest 2005: 123). However,

> when the two are combined into a single Polynesian group, the percentage living at or above the 50 percent threshold is over 40. Maori and Pacific islanders tended to be concentrated in the same areas. Indeed, some 20 percent of all Polynesians in Auckland in 2001 lived in meshblocks [the smallest geographic census unit] that were at least 70 percent Polynesian in their population composition, compared to figures of 0 and 10 for Maori and Pacific Islanders separately. (123)

It is still true today that Māori are dispersed throughout the city, although this effect was mitigated in subsequent decades by intensive building programs for low-cost public housing to meet the needs of the growing urban Māori population.

Difficult everyday conditions, often including inadequate housing, unemployment, and the social stigma of being Māori, continually put the well-being of *whānau* at risk (see Hill 2009). Paradoxically, it is also these very circumstances that often lead urban-based Māori to forge links among themselves, to take on other responsibilities with "new" *whānau* based on kinship or newly created connections based on a specific *kaupapa*, and improve their knowledge of cultural skills (Cram and Pitama 1998: 147).

Māori dislike of spatial concentration dissuades some Māori from living in stigmatized areas of the city, such as the southern suburbs. In rejecting the neighbourhoods that are labelled as poor, brown, and violent, some Māori aim to choose freely their ways of life and to avoid stigmatization in the workplace, social services, and the mainstream world in general. Furthermore, not living in Māori-concentrated areas is a way to inhabit the entire city and to assert rights to certain spaces not usually "occupied" by Māori or non-Pākehā. As much as some will not feel at ease in localities that are *not* predominantly Māori or Polynesian, others will not feel at ease in those that are and prefer to live in a more mixed neighbourhood. Among the participants in my research, Mere and Roimata felt this way and chose to live in Central and North Auckland, in neighbourhoods that were mostly Pākehā and rather affluent.

Social class[11] also helps determine the choice of place of residence. Many Māori professionals live in predominantly Pākehā neighbourhoods where the standards of living and housing are usually higher. Māori professionals are usually at ease with the mainstream environment, since they are familiar with its universes of meanings through their educational and professional achievements, and most of them are bicultural (Schwimmer 2003, 2004a). Moreover, Callister, Didham, and Potter (2005) have identified as a trend that well-schooled Māori are far more likely to have non-Māori partners than those with little formal education. They are also often more integrated into the mainstream population and do not have daily contact with their *whānau* network.

Māori professionals do not, very generally, turn their houses into *marae*; their occupations are usually rather time-consuming and, thus, they are less often at home. Some research participants also mentioned that they feel their non-Māori neighbours would not appreciate too much "traffic" around their house and would find the lifestyle of a house based on *marae* principles strange and inappropriate. The standard of living of Māori professionals is often higher and relies less heavily on *whānau* support. They tend to adhere more closely to the individualistic values of the mainstream universes of meaning and appreciate the privacy and the comfort of their homes.

Mere, for example, who was a student advisor in a post-secondary school, liked to keep her house as a private space to maintain a balance between the openness and sharing of the *whānau* at her workplace. She did, however, offer her home, upon invitation, to her students who had no place else to go. She needed to keep that balance "because I do come from two backgrounds. I do come from a Pākehā and a Māori background" (Mere). In the case of professionals, the choice of a place of residence appears to be more influenced by social stratification than by tribal affiliation and *whānau* network. From my observations, mixed origins, mixed marriages, and the milieu in which people grew up can add to or amplify the impact of social class on the choice of residence and the choice of home arrangements or principles.

Social class aside, the quality of local amenities in Pākehā neighbourhoods where the housing and living standards are higher can be very appealing. Some people live for a while in areas where the rents are lower to save money to buy their own house later, in a better neighbourhood with better schools and better services in general. Some Māori make compromises for a certain length of time to better their own and their family's living conditions and educational opportunities and, ultimately, their position and level of achievement in society. This was the case for Rena, who lived in South Auckland but drove her children to a "good" school in East Auckland every day. Meanwhile, she and her husband were saving to move to the neighbourhood surrounding the school as soon as possible.

Tribal affiliations and *whānau* networks also have an impact on the choice of places of residence. Even though most *iwi* (tribe) are represented across the whole urban territory, it is commonly understood that there is a high concentration of particular tribes in particular areas. If a person's *whānau* network is concentrated in a specific area, then this is likely to influence his or her choice of residence.

Those whose incomes are limited or who depend on social welfare payments often must live in areas where they can benefit from low-cost or state-subsidized rental housing. This can bring them closer to other *whānau* members in the same area or keep them apart from their *whānau*. Rua told me about her experience:

> I went into Housing New Zealand, and so I don't actually pay any rent, they just take it straight out of my benefit. I hate this place! It sucks! [laughter] Because you go outside and Mungo Mubs and Black Powers [two criminalized gangs] and . . . you got different nationalities and the kids . . . there is broken glass out on the street and the river, the creek is just behind us, really dangerous . . . And just the kids around here, they're so hard . . . swear a lot, it's the area, you know, it's South Auckland and it's like the Bronx . . . But people around here, beautiful people, but they struggle, they really, really struggle, and they're just like myself, they struggle and we never seem to further ourselves [. . .] they [Housing New Zealand] gave me three to choose from and the other two they showed us were big homes, more rooms, but when I went to look at them, the tenants that were there prior . . . had trashed the place [. . .] We decided to go with this one because it was the cheapest of the three and it was handy to the motorway. (Rua)

For those whose incomes are limited, another choice can be to move in with other *whānau* members, at least for a time. And, as already discussed, houses based on *marae* principles are important transition places and safety nets, even at the economic level.

Māori city dwellers have new obligations linked to jobs, children's activities, and schooling. They have to share their time with their new communities of interest or non-kin *whānau*. Life is more expensive in the city so they need to work harder and travel less. City life also offers many alternative lifestyles to *whānau* life. Their contact with Māori language and culture is often reduced, a situation that can cause discomfort back home at the rural *marae*. So they experience difficulties in fulfilling family and tribal obligations (Cram and Pitama 1998: 147). Funerals offer rare opportunities for people to go back to the rural *marae* and are occasions for maintaining contacts, reconnecting with people they have not seen for a while, finding out what is going on, and recharging their batteries.

If city life has brought about fundamental transformations in how Māori live, the experience of change also depends, among other factors, on the level of comfort felt in Māori and Pākehā worlds,[12] their access to each world, their capacity to adapt to the city and to build new relationships with Māori and others, their socioeconomic circumstances and degree of autonomy, and their *whānau* and support network in the city. The reasons they migrated to the city in the first place can also have an effect.

But it is unusual even for professional city-dwelling, middle-class Māori, to live entirely apart from wider family networks (Durie 2001a: 8). Each *whānau* is represented across the whole social spectrum and there is always someone in the *whānau* who keeps cultivating, even casually, relationships with the people in the country. The Māori world is, relatively speaking, quite a small world. Even in a city like Auckland with its 1.5 million inhabitants, people frequently discover that they are kin to people who seemed at first to be complete strangers.

There is no strict dichotomy between the rural and the urban milieus, and the urban migration is not an irreversible phenomenon. This was true in the 1950s and 1960s (Harris 2007, 2007–8; Walker 1970; Williams 2010) and still holds true today. The relationship between the two milieus is complex and constantly changing. Because urban *whānau* relationships are activated when needed, connections with home are kept alive in the city and relatives keep each other informed of the happenings and gossip when someone goes home. The same is also true in the country, where everyone knows what is going on among the city kin:

NATACHA: How do you keep the links with your *marae* and your people back home?

TUI: Through my sister. I have got a sister there [. . .] Yeah, and cousins
   come down, so we can catch up. The *kūmara* [sweet potato] vine, family grapevine, *kūmara* vine, one person knows something and everyone knows.
NATACHA: I know about that.
TUI: So you learnt about the *kūmara* vine, did you? [laughter] It's alive
   and well.

Some tribes, like the Waikato/Tainui and the Tūhoe, have a *marae* in
Auckland where their people meet regularly. In the 1970s, Tūhoe also
established an annual *whare wānanga* (school or learning) during which
they took young Tūhoe people from the city for a three week course
about their Maoritanga, their own tribal *kawa* (protocol) and traditions
on a tribal *marae* located in their tribal area. For John Rangihau (1975), a
Māori academic and prominent Tūhoe leader, .

> The only place we can teach these things properly is the marae. You get
> a whole feeling that descends on you there. Maoris have a saying that
> you walk into a meeting house and you feel the warmth of it because
> you know that meeting house is named after an ancestor. And you are
> amidst people who have passed on. [. . .] Beyond that, you're living in a
> valley where the young people have a history and where their ancestors
> have come from. And so you have a very different climate from that of
> a classroom. (226)

He explained further the reason behind this initiative:

> it seemed to us that we should try to take into the urban situation aspects
> of tribal living; aspects that would be real to them but which would also
> stand the test of urban pressures exerted on the members of the tribe. So
> we had to do something about Maori things [. . .] I also believe young folk
> can live with a greater amount of assurance if they know who they are.
> Then they can move into the Pakeha world full of self confidence because
> they have no difficulty about the question of identity. They recognise
> themselves fully because they know their history. (Rangihau 1975: 224)

Since the beginning of the 1970s, the tribe has held a three-day sports
and cultural festival at one of the tribal communities every two years,
which attracts around 25,000 tribal members from all over New Zealand and overseas (McGarvey 2009).

Other tribes or *whānau* have regular meetings, performing arts groups, or sports teams in the city. Some have urban representatives on tribal trust boards and *marae* committees. People also stay in touch by phone calls, letters, and increasingly by email, internet chat rooms, and Facebook. Some *whānau, hapū* (subtribe) or *iwi* (tribe) also have a newsletter (Metge 1995) or, today, social networks such as Facebook, websites, or blogs to keep everybody informed. The larger tribes, such as the Ngā Puhi, for example, also reach out to tribal members outside their region by organizing activities such as informational *hui* (meetings) in different cities where most of their members now live as well as an annual festival in Auckland. It is a way to keep their members informed about their tribal history and future directions. And some *whānau* also have a family house or little *marae* in the city. This kind of place makes *whānau* relationships easier to uphold. The house then, like a *marae*, becomes the heart of the family and allows bonds to be kept between *whānaunga* (relatives, kin, close friends) from different generations and places of residence.

During the last few decades, several factors have encouraged many Māori to renew or reactivate their relationships with people still living in their tribal area, to visit their ancestral land more often, to do genealogical research, to place more emphasis on their tribal identity, and even to move back. These factors include the pan-Māori cultural renaissance, which began in the 1970s; the 1975 Treaty of Waitangi Act, which recognized the treaty partnership between Māori and Pākehā and established the Waitangi Tribunal; the rise of biculturalism as an academic, popular, and state discourse; the 1985 Treaty of Waitangi Amendment Act, which established the tribes as the "social, political and economic institution of indigenisation" (Rata 2000: 25) and back-dated tribal claims for the restitution of lands and waters to 1840; and subsequent genealogical research, treaty settlements of the 1990s, and "retribalization," that is, the legal reinforcement of tribal entities.

It should be recalled, however, that retribalization has two complementary components. It began as a state program in the early 1990s through which the tribes were recognized as legal entities and as suppliers of services. Retribalization, in that sense, was synonymous with decentralization of the state. This is the meaning that I retain in this book. But retribalization is also the word used by certain analysts to describe the Māori return migration (for example, Barcham 2004; Scott and Kearns 2000; see Williams 2010: 205–6 for an analysis and a critique). Williams (2010) explains that in that sense, retribalization is the counter-process to urbanization, urbanization being often thought as having "fostered inauthentic and state-coerced forms of urban Māori communities and culture" (18); that is, cultural fragmentation. Williams (2010) insists that "[t]his view underestimates the portability of tribalism. It also exaggerates and oversimplifies the connections between return migration, geography-based tribal/culture and macro Māori cultural-politics. Some of the connections appear to have been a matter of timing; the radicalism of the 1970s and resurgence in Māori cultural and iwi-based politics coinciding with the long-term, life-course rhythms of post-war Māori migration" (206). Retribalization could also mean the revitalization of Māori culture, institutions, and principles through ideological practices that question Māori visions of their own identity in the light of the contradictions of their everyday experiences, and through practices that involve the learning and transmission of "traditional" knowledge (Schwimmer 2003). Moreover, in the journey back to their people and traditions, Māori in general have been influenced by global forces such as decolonization, the worldwide indigenous movement, other ethnic and nationalist movements, and movements of localization in reaction to processes of globalization (see, for example, Friedman 1994, 2003a, 2003b, 2008).

Specific events or experiences in many people's lives can also raise consciousness of their Māori identity. The experience of becoming a parent or a grandparent seems to be a determining factor. It is a turning point and gives one a focus in life, as several research participants, including Aroha, Kahu, and Rua, told me. For others, learning about Māori and New Zealand history at university, or indeed just studying in general, brings about changes in their identity and prompts them to undertake genealogical research and a "journey back home" as Māori often say. Many Māori education programs also emphasize the importance of students knowing their *whakapapa* (genealogy), and this has pushed many to explore their roots. One cannot learn the Māori language without learning the cultural fundamentals associated with it, such as how to recite one's genealogy and how to say a *karakia* (prayer). Learning the Māori language also implies learning to understand the concept of the Māori universe.

And sometimes, simple everyday experiences or confrontations with others raise people's consciousness of being Māori:

> I do come from two backgrounds. I do come from a Pākehā and a Māori background and I always knew, not always knew between the two, but for

the last ten years, I have. Before that it was mainly Pākehā. I was brought up more Pākehā because my mother is more Pākehā than Māori and in her attitude ... [...] I think you just notice these gaps and I guess it happens to everybody. It is the wanting to belong and to identify as somebody, makes you want to go back, and if you have your *whakapapa* [genealogy] then you are established and that is you. Because otherwise, for me, there would not be any other way that I could have because I don't have the behaviour or the symbolism that shows that you are Māori. (Mere)

Having a non-Māori partner and travelling are also factors that raise people's consciousness of their Maoriness.

It is often a highly emotional experience when people decide to make the "journey back home" and reconnect with their people after many years – or a whole life – in the city, with little or no contact with the rural base. The return home calls to mind painful memories embedded in the history of colonization, Christianization, and anglicization. It may also recall old personal or *whānau* disagreements or sad memories. It can also be a very spiritual experience and some people will begin to have dreams, be attentive to signs from the ancestors and the supernatural worlds, or experience unusual feelings and various pleasant or unpleasant bodily sensations.

The return "home" to an unfamiliar people and *marae* can be a very stressful experience for those who do not speak the Māori language fluently or for those who have a strong accent of an English speaker when speaking in Māori. It is stressful for those who do not know much about traditions and protocols and do not have someone there to guide them and introduce them to the others. Even if there are people who know about the returning person's family and elders, it is not always enough to put the returning person at ease. People back home may behave as if the person returning is a stranger and treat him or her as a *manuhiri* (visitor). The returning person can be made to feel unwelcome. A participant in my research, Tiana, told me how she had to tell people off and impose herself in the kitchen, as one of them. She could not accept being served like a visitor. This required, on Tiana's part, a good dose of self-confidence, courage, and a sense of being comfortable as a Māori and as a member of her *whānau* and tribe; not everybody has this foundation. These experiences seem to differ, in degree at least, from those of the postwar first-generation Māori migrants from Panguru, as described by Williams (2010: 209), whose ties with the people back home had not been "stretched" as much as those of some participants in my research. Aside from possible tribal differences,[13] this emphasizes the importance of intergenerational variances and underlines the notion that all Māori do not share a common politics of return (206).

The journey back home of the first generation of Māori migrants was also not without difficulty – practically (living conditions were often uncomfortable, for example), emotionally, and legally, particularly surrounding *whānau* lands. The "[r]eturn migrants could not successfully make the transition from a person back-home to one of the home-people until they demonstrated their commitment to the former" (218). This transition also involved collective dimensions that made it all the more complex since it was "about joining with hunga kāinga [home-people] to reaffirm home connections for absent whanaunga [relatives] and future descendents" (224).

For people returning home, as Durie (1999, 2001a) notes, *marae* encounters can help to establish and renew relationships among the person, the group, the ancestors, and the wider environment. Many things that happen at *marae* are expressions of connectedness and can help someone who is serious and shows good faith to reconnect to their people. *Tauparapara* (incantations) and *karakia* (prayers) as well as ritual chants locate the speakers and the listeners in terms of tribe and places and in relation to the heavens and the earth. Incantations, according to Durie (1999), "may be heard as a call for a union of the elements and terrestrial places (*tuia ki runga, tuia ki raro*); or the departed with each other (*tuia te hunga mate ki te hunga mate*); the living with the living (*tuia te hunga ora ki te hunga ora*); or the sky with the earth (*tuia te rangi e tu nei, tuia te papa e hora mai nei*)" (359). Prayers also have the wider purpose of creating a sense of unity among the living (person, tribes, and peoples), the ancestors, the environment, and the spiritual powers (Durie 1999: 359; Salmond 1975). "*Karakia* [prayers] lift preoccupations with daily existence to an elevated spiritual plane. They serve to both free people from threat of harm, and at the same time offer a degree of protection afforded by a link with a higher power" (Durie 1999: 359). *Marae* are recognized as sacred places where the potential to "find oneself" again exists. They are also very important places where conflicts can be openly discussed.

The move "back home" to find oneself or reconnect with others, or both, is also difficult and demanding for the "hosts" who never went away. Many people come with a desire to learn everything and expect that they will be taught genealogies, traditions, and other knowledge immediately. Those who stay behind may well feel like refusing to let strangers come and research them and their ancestral resources without having specific proof that they are related. They may have no interest in the returnees. They may also be angry with those who come back from time to time for holidays and when they need specific information or access to certain knowledge. Those who stay behind may feel as if they do all the hard work involved in keeping the *marae* warm, welcoming everybody back during funerals, and caring for the lands, the cemetery, and other peoples' properties. Williams (2010) describes, for example, how "[t]he number of tangihanga [funerals] alone placed a massive strain on home-people, especially on kaumātua and kuia [male and female elders], who were needed in both the kitchens and wharehui [meeting house] for an average of two or three tangi per month [in Panguru] between 1990 and 1999" (233). Those left behind are often the poor relatives of the city dwellers who have good qualifications and better access to well-paid jobs. As in most families, jealousy and backbiting also exist between rural and urban cousins. So, the reaction of those who stay behind is sometimes one of suspicion, since not all of those who came back in the past behaved as they should have done.

Many country folks are also tired of listening to the city Māori, whom they sometimes call "Wannabes" or "Know-it-alls," telling them how to do things better with their "shiny diplomas" from university. "Nobody will tell me what to do on my own land!" a *kaumātua* told me during a visit to an East Coast *marae*.

Another rural dweller from the East Coast, Rongo, explained to me:

> People who are living in the city and they come home, they are not liked at home. People are resentful towards them. Because, see, it works both ways. We look at these people that have had an opportunity to become a great lawyer or accountant or whatever and they have been living the high life and you sort of think, you are struggling, you, at home. These wankers come back with the suit and they are telling you what to do! You see, that's exactly what . . . the pathway any of them went through. They cannot come back with all these *kōrero* [speeches] about how to make things better for us. (Rongo)

On both sides, negative reactions also have to do with preconceived ideas about the other, as well as misunderstandings and misinterpretations of certain ways of being, particularly of gestures and specific spoken words.

Māori city dwellers are aware of the potential for negative reactions, and some will hesitate to go back home and participate in discussions on *marae* or elsewhere. Others will intentionally keep their city lives to themselves:

> When I go back home, I'm normal, I don't let them know [that I go to university]. I like to be on the same level as my people. Some of them know I am here [at university]. It doesn't make any difference. In fact, I think they sort of sneer at people that think they know it all. They will admire you if you don't come back and tell them what to do. (Keita)

The return home requires a lot of patience, humility, and respect for the local people and their ways of doing things. The person returning must prove good faith. It is important to go through the right channels and meet the right people as search guides and advisors about sacred things, places, and knowledge. Bad things, too, can come from the spiritual world, which causes some ambivalence for the rural dwellers. These is danger when city dwellers come back without having a deep knowledge of the "good" ways.

Some people, including my acquaintance Fiona, simply avoided claiming anything from people back home. She did not want to ask for a scholarship from her father's side, since her contact with that part of her family had been limited; she did not want to make people talk behind her back.[14] She was too proud and respected the people too much to ask for something that she felt others deserved more than her, since they grew up and still lived there. She would have liked to be closer to her grandmother, aunts, uncles, and cousins, but her father was working in another rural area and they did not visit as often as they would have liked during her childhood. It was a matter of humility, respect, and *mana* for her to come to know more about this part of her genealogy before asking for anything from them.

Despite the difficulties in reviving or maintaining *whānau* relationships with the rural home, the process of going back to one's people can also be very positive, and many are welcomed with open arms. This was the case for Christine. Since she was a Māori language teacher, she was seen as someone who could help the community regain the Māori language. The welcome may be far different in areas where the language is spoken by a large segment of the population and where a non-native speaker with the accent of an English speaker when speaking in Māori, English phrasing, or a different dialect learned through school might not be viewed favourably. Christine's *marae* committee was also in need of trustees at the time of her first approach, so the circumstances were ideal for her to take up with her people. This is an example of the home-people also depending on their urban network "to help provide the economic and human fuel to keep the fire burning back-home" (Williams 2010: 224).

The process of going back home can be a personal quest, but it can also be a *whānau* one, as is the case for the process of migration to the city (Williams 2010: 53). Rata (2000) describes an entire *whānau's* return to the tribal land.[15] The whole research process in preparation for the return, the teaching and learning of *waiata* (songs), *whakapapa* (genealogy), and *tikanga* (custom, rules), as well as the more practical preparation for the trip itself, is very often a collective process. Even if the return or visit to the tribal area is not collective, there are still usually many *whānau* members involved in the preparation. One of the participants in this research went back up North to her people for the first time when she was in her late forties, with many of her kin:

> It was a *kawe mate* [trip to bring a dead person back to her or his *marae*] for my mother's two sisters, so *tikanga* [custom, rules], and I have a cousin, a *tuakana* [older relative], he maintains this *tikanga* and the decision was made to go back and do it. We took back the spirits of my mother's two sisters who have died. That's *kawe mate*. Took them back to the *tūrangawaewae* up north. So, the decision was made to do it and then we just gathered to prepare to do it. People just played a role, find a bus, we fundraised, we learned *waiata* [songs], we learned the *kawa* [protocol] of our *marae* and we went [. . .] We spent about a month I suppose, maybe two months to fundraise, because we took our *kai* [food] from the city, we bought our *kai* . . . organised our bus . . . organised ourselves to be aware of the *kawa* for our northern tribe, to learn the *waiata*, probably two months, this time to prepare. It was the preparation that made it a good trip [. . .] It was my first time, and maybe for one or two others on the whole bus, it was not the first time for them. Very powerful as we were such a large *rōpū* [group]. (Rewa)

The return home is thus an important and powerful moment, often collectively experienced, which requires much preparation.

A central part of the return is the *whakapapa* (genealogy) that lies at the very heart of Māori identities. Genealogy ensures the continuity and transmission of institutions, values, practices, kinship roles, and responsibilities to relatives, as well as place and status within Māori society (Carter 2003b; Waymouth 2003; Mahuika 1998: 219). Genealogy also embodies notions of status, authority – that is, *mana* – and property (Carter 2003b; Waymouth 2003). According to the roles prescribed by genealogy, not everybody traditionally had access to genealogical knowledge. Some people were (and still are) chosen as inheritors of this knowledge, on the basis of their ability, commitment, maturity, and birthright. Young people are not usually taught deep and sacred genealogical knowledge.

Both traditionally and now, Māori introduce themselves by reciting their genealogy. According to Waymouth (2003),

> Whakapapa in its simplest definition is genealogies, or lists of names that act as keys to unlocking the way Maori understand the way the world operates and maintains stability . . . Everything in the Maori world, spiritual or physical, has a list of names that trace connections to a founding ancestor. The lists apply to humans and the physical world; things in the natural world such as trees, fish, rocks, stars, the winds, rain, sun, moon, seas and rivers; and the things in the spiritual world. All the thousands of whakapapa interact in some way and all the interactions take the form of relationships between "families." The family relationships are communicated through stories of events that explain how the relationships began. The stories show why the names are in the order that they are in the lists. They indicate the organisational processes that needed to be carried out in order to maintain the relationships among families, persons and the natural world.[16]

If *whakapapa* is accessed through a list of names, it is part of a living "integrated knowledge system" (Carter 2003b: 13) in which relationships exist among three worlds of *whakapapa* or three worlds of knowledge: *whakapapa atuatanga*, the spiritual world; *whakapapa tīpuna*, the ancestral or human world; and *whakapapa pūtaiao*, the natural world (see Carter 2003b for details).[17]

Today, in everyday situations and on a day-to-day level, when people recite their genealogy, they list their elders, sometimes more distant ancestors, tribe, subtribe, *marae*, mountain(s), river(s), and so forth. Here is a typical example of a *whakapapa* as taught at university, but also as learned in *Māori* workshops and seminars that I attended:

Ko X taku ingoa.
Ko Y taku papa. Ko Z taku mama.

Ko B taku iwi.
Ko A taku maunga.
Ko C taku awa . . .

My name is X.
My father's name is Y. My mother's name is Z.
B is my tribe.
A is my mountain.
C is my river . . .

(Notes, *Māori 101* course, University of Auckland, 2001)

In most cases, the identification with tribe, subtribe, and *marae* is not singular, fixed, or exclusive. The identifications and their importance change over time, depending on social and political contexts and on the intensity of ties. The spiritual home, the *tūrangawaewae*, the place to stand, the connection to the land, is thus part of the genealogy. It is necessary to the upholding of identity as Māori or as a member of a particular *whānau*, subtribe, or tribe. Again, the connection can be plural, depending not only on genealogy but also on experiences of a place, actual connections with the people, and parents' or elders' wishes. Māori also articulate different parts of their genealogy depending on the people with whom they are interacting. People can choose to affiliate to descent groups through links of either or both parents (Metge 1995). The genealogy is not gender marked, but a matter of choice.

By knowing and reciting their genealogy, Māori situate themselves in a particular universe. Nobody can question genealogy if the evidence is there and well demonstrated. This has been even truer in the recent years of retribalization, claims settlements, capitalization of traditional means and modes of production, and the bureaucratization of genealogy, which have led to a new emphasis on ancestry as a criterion for access to properties and benefits.[18] Poata-Smith (2004a) shows that this has had a direct impact on the contours of Māori identity. Waymouth (2003) explains:

Under the legislation [Runanga Iwi Bill 1990], the runanga [tribal council] were expected to establish beneficiary roles [sic, the correct spelling should be "rolls," meaning "lists"] to ensure that all members who met the criteria would be able to access the iwi's resources. In the Runanga Iwi Bill the criteria for beneficiary status was "a person of the Maori race of New

Zealand; and includes a descendant of any such person." This generalization of identity through ethnic descent stripped away the notion of kinship by descent that is tied directly to land [and] resources and managed through whakapapa relationships. The ethnic descent category provided an individual with a [sic] idea of being a member of an ethnic group without having to participate in the obligations and responsibilities inherent in a whakapapa relationship.

During this retribalization period, as shown, distinctions emerged between tribal Māori and those who identify as Māori, but not with a particular tribe; and other significant distinctions have also been reinforced, such as those between genealogical members of the tribe on the one hand and their spouses and *whāngai* (adopted, fostered) children on the other. While the latter are accepted as members of the *whānau* or the tribe for their commitment over the years and recognized as part of the group by people of status, their inclusion carries the possibility of exclusion, and this possibility is emphasized when dealing with access to ancestral lands, waters, and other resources. This creates very difficult and highly emotional situations between siblings or between parents and their children, for example, when one parent is not Māori, or from a different tribe, or Māori but with no particular tribal identification and is therefore excluded from certain parts of the *whānau* or tribal life (Rata 2000). The ever-present possibility of exclusion can be quite stressful and sometimes prevent people from full involvement in the group. Issues of power can also keep some people under pressure and force them to conform. Specific issues of power and control over resources and group leadership have clearly been at stake in the reinforced biological determinism and essentialism of recent years. All of this has contributed to "divorcing" (to a certain degree) the three worlds of *whakapapa* (see Carter 2003b for more details and examples).

However, in practice, there are always places for claims and challenges. Tensions, conflicts, and disagreements occur in *whānau* and tribes. They can sometimes bring about reconfigurations, as certain members or families decide to deactivate certain branches of their genealogy, while activating others. *Whānau* relationships change, expanding or contracting from time to time, and they always involve a certain degree of ambiguity and flexibility, as described in the discussion of the dynamics of tribe, subtribe, and *whānau*.

Many different factors are at play not only when claiming certain rights (to land, knowledge, or identity, for example), but also when contesting a claim. These factors can include (1) the (lack of) evidence of genealogical knowledge; (2) participation in family or tribal activities and chores; (3) the history of the relationships within the *whānau* or the tribe; (4) the struggle for *mana* (spiritual power, authority, prestige, status); (5) the (lack of) personal achievement and personal resources that may contribute to the family's or tribe's well-being; (6) any scarcity of *whānau* or tribal resources or, on the contrary, the sudden appearance of money linked to settlements of historical grievances; (7) jealousy and competition with other affiliations; (8) a (lack of) personal knowledge of genealogy, traditions, and protocols and (non-) demonstration of good faith and involvement; (9) emotional factors; and (10) signs from the ancestors or the supernatural worlds.

Claiming rights to lands, waters, or knowledge also implies the Māori notion of *ahi kā*, which can be literally translated as "(keeping) a fire alight" and actually means maintaining occupation of the land (Waymouth 2003; see also Williams 2010). This concept was used in several land claims cases considered by the Waitangi Tribunal.[19] For a tribe or a *whānau* to be able to claim land, they must demonstrate their continuous occupation of that land or at least their presence on it at certain periods, "keeping the home fires burning," as it were. The same concept is sometimes used in the case of individual or *whānau* claims inside or outside tribunals. Individuals are expected "to back up their claims with active participation in group affairs" (Metge 1995: 77). People sometimes "send home a child or grandchild to 'keep warm' . . . land inheritance and . . . group membership" (Metge 1964: 10; see also Williams 2010). This was a particularly common practice for women in the past, when patrilateral affiliation was more prominent. It is also common today to send children to their grandparents or uncles and aunts back home during the summer holidays or at certain other times, so they can come to know the history and the people and, very importantly, be known and recognized.

However, as Fiona explained, keeping the fire going was not always easy:

> When you have lived in the city you find it very hard to go back to your own home and you were raised outside the area, it's very hard. You always identify, you *whakapapa* [go genealogically] back to that area, but . . . We have this concept that we call *ahi kā, ahi kā* means keeping the domestic fire alight and often it's very hard for us to maintain our *ahi kā*. What happens is we have this concept of *ahi mātao*. It's when the fire is dying out,

so you're always trying to get back but there is the thing of some people, they look down on you because you don't come back or they think you're better because you live in the city, and la, la, la . . . But we feel stink 'cause we do want to go back, but there's no opportunity. It's one of the effects of urbanisation, as Walker says, you know going for the big opportunity, money, work . . . You gotta live your life! [sigh of discouragement] One of the consequences of living away from the tribal area. (Fiona)

Keita explained her strategy for her children to retain links to "back home":

KEITA: To me, home is where I was born and bred. That will always be my home because I will be going back there to be buried.
NATACHA: Is your husband going to go with you when he dies?
KEITA: No. We have already talked about that. He will go back to his area and I will go back to mine [. . .] It helps our children to link back to our tribes by us going back to our own places. Like if I was buried with my husband, I don't think my grandchildren will bother finding out where I even came from, so it is a means to retain the links of my people. You may be separated in body, but you will always be together spiritually anyway. It is so my grandchildren will know both sides [. . .] I thought about why the land is so important to Māori. I know when I go home, I know places and where my *tīpuna* [ancestors] are buried. I related to the land because all those ancestors are there so I said to my husband "I won't come with you when I go" and we talked about it how I said if we separate our grandchildren will connect to both areas and he agreed.

Specific criteria of occupation are changing, however, and differ from one family or tribe to another.[20] Once again, there is always implicit a kind of ambiguity that allows for flexibility around personal and circumstantial considerations. But Waymouth (2003) emphasizes that the generalization of identity through ethnic descent in recent years has played in favour of individualism, since it provided an individual with rights as a member of an ethnic group without having to participate in the obligations and responsibilities of any meaningful group *within* the ethnic group. This contradicts many traditional principles, one of which is the primacy of collectivism over individualism.

Traditional family systems worked at two levels of access to resources, places, and knowledge. Cram and Pitama (1998) identify

(1) the generational level, which uses age group distinctions to allocate work, attribute differences in attitudes, and promote respect between the different generations; and (2) the family descent-line level, which dictates land succession, genealogical rights (including knowledge and protocol), and tribal leadership. Not surprisingly, colonization and the implementation of Christian values and beliefs disrupted these transmission systems. For instance, Māori women, in particular, found their *mana* (spiritual power, status, prestige, authority) challenged.

Colonization and life in the city also make it increasingly difficult for new generations of *kaumātua* (elders), who are usually the eldest siblings, to assume their roles as cultural guardians and leaders. Many have an insufficient knowledge of the language and the necessary protocols. This can cause a great deal of shame and suffering for those unable to assume their roles. Many people of the age to be an elder, especially men who often need to be at the forefront in official meetings, told me with tears in their eyes that they feel *whakamā* for not being able to fulfil their obligations correctly and competently. The word "*whakamā*" is "used to describe a range of feelings from shyness through embarrassment to shame and behaviour involving varying degrees of withdrawal and unresponsiveness" (Metge 1995: 336; for details, see Metge 1986). It is often their younger siblings or even younger people from the next generation, who traditionally would not be of the right age to become elders, who replace the older ones, since they have had the chance to learn the language and traditions at university or in Māori schools.[21] The age distinction or the position in the family has thus become less important than it was a few generations ago, a situation that does not please many people and can lead to conflicts. However, it did also happen occasionally in the past that a younger sibling would take on an elder's role, if the younger one were more skilled for the task or if the eldest lacked the desire or personality for leadership.[22]

Even if Māori today define the roles and status of each person in the *whānau* and tribe less strictly, collective decisions about who should receive education in traditional skills, knowledge, and history are still taken in many families. Decisions depend on personal ability, achievement, and birthright, as well as signs received from the ancestors or the supernatural world. Certain persons are then invested with certain responsibilities and obligations on behalf of the group. To be chosen as caretaker of a specific kind of knowledge is a great honour, but it involves self-sacrifice. It demands a compromise between personal achievement and the collective well-being, in a wider world that tends to individualism, and where there are many attractions to and distractions by various other opportunities, particularly in the city.

Individuals themselves also look for the approval of the *whānau* in making decisions and undertaking projects. As shown in the case of Aroha, for many of the Māori graduate students I met at university, for example, it was essential to have the approval of their *whānau* and even their tribe for their choice of topic if they were studying Māori matters, and even other subjects like medicine or engineering.[23] It was a question of comfort.

So the *whānau* is important and clearly a crucial referential framework for Māori today, in the country as well as in the city. The *whakapapa whānau* (genealogical *whānau*, also referred to in English as *whakapapa*-based *whānau*) corresponds above all to the "extended family" of Metge's fourth definition. In this usage the *whānau* is ancestor-oriented and ambilineal; that is to say that it refers to a *kaumātua* (elder) from either genealogical line still living or recently dead. It is distributed among several households, particularly in the city, but acts together as a group on specific occasions (life crisis, caring for *whānau* property, and so on). It recognizes participation in *whānau* activities as a relevant factor of *whānau* membership. It has attached members, namely, spouses and *whāngai* (adopted, fostered) children. And it extends usually over three or more generations. However, this meaning of the *whānau* does not disconnect from its other components or levels:

> One component is related to Tipuna [ancestors] and whānau members who have passed on. This provides the spiritual and emotional well-being to the family. It is from the ancestors that Māori whānau develop their identity.
>
> The next component represents Whānui or tribal families. Most Māori people recognize the tribal names to whom they have links or ties.
>
> The third component is the whānau te rito – the closer family. This part of the whānau provides the immediate nurturance and the physical and emotional support. (Tukukino 1988: 70, in Cram and Pitama 1998: 150)

The recurring formal features of the *whānau* that distinguish it are visible through its core values or principles. Through their actions, interactions, and imagination, Māori reproduce the universe of meanings of the *whānau* in the city, but new contexts sometimes require adaptation, negotiation, and change to maintain overall continuity.

The *whānau* principles thus form a universe of meanings and a realm of interpretation that guide Māori in the countryside and in the city in their actions and relations with others. As explained by Metge (1995: 105), these *whānau* values and principles are all related in different and complex ways. They sometimes compete with each other and sometimes reinforce each other. All are flexible and can be adapted to particular circumstances. But it is worth repeating that while the *whānau* has changed with colonization and urban life, it is still very important for Māori. Even though it is highly time-consuming and emotionally and financially demanding, most make every effort to keep their *whānau* relationships alive in the city, despite and beyond the urban/rural divide.

6   A Practical Universe of Meanings

Living with Māori families made me realize the practical importance of the *whānau* in daily life and as a symbol of the affirmation of Māori identities and of the creation of their space and place in the city and greater society. The meaning, principles, and values of the *whānau* have changed through colonization and urbanization. But they have always remained important and continue to be so. And as the *whānau*'s principles and values have emerged and unfolded through the practices of daily life, its universe of meanings in relation to other Māori and non-Māori universes of meanings has been reaffirmed and negotiated.

During my field research, in conversations among themselves and in interviews, people continually stressed the importance of the *whānau*. They spoke of it as something central to their everyday worlds in Auckland, or, of course, central when talking about their family (immediate and extended), but also in reference to friends, colleagues, schoolmates, *kapa haka* (performing arts) ensembles, and other groups to which they belonged. *Whānau* (singular or plural) occupied not only their conversations but also much of their time and energy.

Whanaungatanga – that is, the principle of "strengthening and enriching the bonds of family unity" (Manuka), and more broadly, strengthening *whānau* ties and responsibilities (Durie 1997; Patterson 1992) – appeared to be *the* important value for Māori to practice and to work on, to make them strong, individually and collectively.

In the name of *whanaungatanga*, the Māori around me engaged in various projects such as learning the Māori language, doing genealogical research and working toward a university degree to improve the conditions of the *whānau* and of Māori more generally. Many were part of a *whānau* made up of the children of the *kohanga reo* (Māori language kindergarten) and their parents and grandparents. Others opened their houses to family members. And almost all Māori events whether public or more intimate emphasize the importance of *whanaungatanga* and have time in their schedule for *whakawhanaungatanga,* a moment entirely given over to the strengthening of *whānau* connections among participants.

In everyday life, therefore, the notion of *"whānau"* comes across as positive and inclusive. It is flexible but has boundaries, and it often takes a significant event to manifest both its principles or values and the limits of inclusion. *Raruraru* (troubles or problems) between *whānau* members, conflicts within the *whānau* or, very generally, disclosures of any type of offence by one or more members are especially revealing of the principles at work and they can ultimately bring about a *whānau's* reconfiguration.

A problematic situation marked the time I spent living with Kiri's *whānau* at 30 Aroha Street. It was a deeply emotional event, since the well-being of the *whānau* was at stake, and for many weeks it mobilized the entire *whānau* – including those not actually living at the house.

At the centre of the troubles were two members of the *whānau* and the house: David and his father William. William was the ex-husband of Kiri's sister Nina, and David was one of Nina's five children. Both of them had been living there for a couple of years. They had their sleeping quarters in the garage in the backyard.

On several different occasions, Kiri, Andrew, and I saw signs that somebody in the family was behaving inappropriately. And one day, David's behaviour became particularly disruptive. The *whānau* was already under stress when Kiri and her sister Rangi called a meeting of everybody in the house, including me, to look into a specific incident (details of which, at the request of this *whānau*, will not be disclosed).

It was not the first time that David had caused hurt to others. *Whānau* members had suspected for some time that his behaviour was escalating to the point of affecting all those around him including the *whānau* and the neighbours. Kiri, Andrew, and Rangi did not know what to do, nor did the other siblings, relatives, and the grandparents, who lived in their tribal area in the country but visited the house regularly. They thought that despite all the rehabilitation that the *whānau* had offered David through the years, he was perhaps too set in his erring ways to change.

Everyone knew that William and David needed a place to stay and that William was doing his best with his teenaged son. He was working hard as a carpenter's mate to provide for his son's needs and he had a "good heart," as did David, even if the boy had been "mucking around" for some time.

In the *whānau*'s intense and very emotional discussions, obligations were invoked in terms of *aroha* (unconditional love), *whanaungatanga*, *manaakitanga* (showing respect and kindness, hospitality extended to visitors) and *whakapapa* (genealogy) or kinship. Even if William was not related to them by blood and was now divorced from Kiri's sister, the *whānau* still had responsibilities toward him since he was the father of David and of Kiri's sister's other four children. The people of the family had considered him to be one of theirs for some time. They also felt, however, that William was too conciliatory with his child and not present enough and was not preventing his son from doing things that were negatively affecting the rest of the *whānau*.

The *whānau* members tried to make William understand that he should do something about David. William was offended. David's behaviour appeared to improve. But after a couple of weeks, he again became very defiant and his disruptive behaviour returned. Another *whānau* meeting was called and again nobody had any answers. This time, however, Kiri and Rangi directly confronted David. One of his cousins had told the adults about what David had done. David denied everything and William stayed silent.

Kiri, Rangi, and Andrew were extremely upset about the situation and had a discussion about what solution or reaction was *tika* (correct, morally just) in such circumstances. They sought a solution that was in accordance with *tikanga* (traditions). They thought about asking William to leave the house and find another place to stay. This would get rid of the immediate problem. But they would have also escaped their *whānau* obligations and "that was not right." Besides, given their considerations about their ancestors and the existence of possible supernatural *utu* – which is defined by Metge (1995: 336) as a "return for something received, whether good or bad" – they knew that one day they would have to pay for neglecting their duties. Māori in general are acutely sensitive to such issues and accord great power to the *wairua* (spirit, feelings of places, peoples, events) and the ancestral or supernatural worlds that manifest themselves through body feelings, emotions, intuitions, and dreams, among other things.

Furthermore, they felt an obligation to safeguard David's education and his rights as a biological member of the *whānau*, since one person's child is considered to be everybody's child. But they also admitted their own responsibility and powerlessness in dealing with David's behaviour.

Cutting ties with William could be easy to justify but it was much more difficult to do so with David. Either choice had wide implications. Asking William to leave was risky for the *whānau*'s future relationships with David, as well as for David's relations with his siblings and William's with his other children. As time went on, however, David's behaviour became increasingly selfish and lazy. He began to be very disruptive at school and in the neighbourhood and often avoided his chores.

And William, for his part, was away from home more often. He told me during an interview that he was *whakamā* because of his son, but he did not know how to deal with the situation. The word *whakamā* expresses a range of feelings from shyness through embarrassment to shame (see Metge 1986, 1995). In another discussion, William, who was truly anxious about the possibility of losing his son or being asked to find another place to live, cried because he would have no *whānau* whatsoever since links with his birth *whānau* were non-existent.

One morning, Kiri received a call from school telling her that they had not seen David for a couple of days. This was the last straw. She was already dealing with a full load of worries with work and university obligations and the other children. Given that William could not meet his responsibilities and even denied that David might be behaving badly, she decided the situation must end. Knowing that the *whānau* would support her decision, she drove straight over to see William and asked him to leave the house with David and to take all their belongings with them. She considered all the work that she and her *whānau* had done in terms of rehabilitation, and she knew everybody involved was exhausted.

Kiri explained to me later that what finally led the *whānau* to take this step was that, above all else, the *whānau*'s *mana* (spiritual power, authority, prestige, and status) was at stake at the school and in the neighbourhood because of a situation that had gone on for too long and in which she felt powerless. She was also afraid that David's behaviour was influencing the younger ones who would be encouraged in their bad habits by an absence of punitive reaction from her and the other adults.

Some important factors played against David. When the school representative called, the boy was already stigmatized by his defiant attitude and bad behaviour. He said that he missed his mother who lived in Europe and that he sometimes felt abandoned by his father who was often away from the house. Another factor was his *whāngai* (fostered child) status because he lived with his father but was cared for by Kiri and the other adults of the house. It often put him in the role of scapegoat. And Kiri was also highly preoccupied with a range of other pressing issues and demands at the time.

I was the only one at home with Kiri on the afternoon that she received the call from school. I saw on her face that something serious was happening. She left without saying a word. And after that day, I never saw William and David again.[1]

Throughout this incident, the *whānau's* role today in both the country and the city, as an important Māori universe of meanings, is vividly illustrated. Evident is the importance of practice in the construction of personal and group positionings, of personal and group agency, and of specific configurations within the *whānau*.

A "universe of meanings" is a set of principles and values that constitutes a realm of interpretation in which common specific moral rules, values, characters, actors, categories, and identities are recognized, particular significance is assigned to certain acts, ideas, and symbols, and particular outcomes and projects are prized over others. While valued acts and outcomes come across quite clearly in the example, the specific characters and actors recognized in the universe of meanings of the *whānau* were less obvious. The dilemma over responsibility for David's education and behaviour was also a dilemma over each person's role in the *whānau* and their relationships to each other.

In Māori tradition, because of the value of *whanaungatanga*, which means strengthening and enriching the bonds of family unity, those within the *whānau* must help and support the young and those in need. According to tradition, however, and particularly to the values of *tapu* (sacred or polluting) and *noa* (ordinary or relaxed), and genealogy and kinship, everyone should also respect and support their elders. Kiri, Rangi, and Andrew, and indeed everyone in the *whānau*, were in practice negotiating these values as well as other closely related *whānau* principles that were also part of the picture.

Whānau values or principles and codes of behaviour sometimes contradict and sometimes reinforce each other. And in this case they

worked in complex and interrelated ways to guide the *whānau*'s decision about David's (and William's) behaviour.

For a long period, the condemnation that one would expect of David's disrespectful attitude toward his *whānau* and elders was subordinated to values such as *whanaungatanga, kotahitanga* (oneness),
unconditional love, genealogy, and tradition. At some point, however,
something in the context changed so that the *whānau*'s *mana* and well-
being were threatened. This made Kiri react and take the ultimate and,
by then, obvious decision of asking David and his father to leave the
house and, at least for a time, to avoid the *whānau*.[2]

What exactly triggered this final act?

What I began to understand was that the value of *mana*, which refers
primarily to spiritual power and authority, is a very important motivation in the universe of meanings of the Māori *whānau*. Groups as well
as individuals have *mana* and every share of *mana* affects the *mana* of
the larger group, given that *mana* is a unitary principle. Thus, when
the *mana* of the 30 Aroha Street *whānau* was threatened, the *mana* of all
Māori was potentially threatened. This was particularly true in David's
case, since his behaviour began to be disruptive for people outside the
whānau and more precisely for non-Māori people and institutions. The
whānau tolerated David's non-respect of *whānau* values as long as his
behaviour only affected people within the *whānau*. But as soon as external forces, in the shape of the Pākehā school representatives, began to
intervene in the *whānau* regarding these violations, the *whānau* reacted
energetically and sorted out the situation.

Kiri explained to me that both David and William were guilty – the
latter because he did not do enough to correct his son's behaviour that
had affected not only the *whānau*'s *mana*, but potentially also the *mana*
of all the Māori related to the school, and of all Māori, living or dead.

By reacting strongly to signals from external (and powerful) forces,
Kiri (and her *whānau*) was also protecting, through the internalized
pan-Māori code, the *mana* of her elders and ancestors, relatives, and
other Māori as well as the *mana* of the multitude of ancestors that popu-
late sacred songs and prayers. She was thus moved by larger collective
forces, which she had internalized, but were also far beyond her.

The *whānau* reaction was all the more decisive since the violations
now not only affected daily life in the *whānau*, but had also become
part of a wider and highly political context in which power relationships between Māori and Pākehā in colonized space/time come into
play. And it is clear that external forces – here Pākehā, but they can also

be Māori – have the power to ruin the *mana* of any *whānau*.[3] Had the situation continued, the *whānau's mana* would have been diminished in the Pākehā school, the non-Māori neighbourhood, and in the non-Māori world more generally. The *whānau* would have suffered not only from a bad reputation for the actual events, but also from more general stereotypes about Māori that would have found support and justification in the behaviour of David and his *whānau*. The *whānau* is also likely to have been affected by malicious rumours among Māori defenders of the Māori national *mana*.

This case demonstrates the importance to *whānau* members of the *whānau*, with its values and codes of behaviour. Both for the sake of the *whānau's* survival and for the good of all Māori, action had to be taken. The *whānau* decided to exclude those who were threatening its survival and *mana*. The situation called for a circumstantial renegotiation of values, which were subsequently ranked according to contextual priorities. Thus, in these particular circumstances, *mana* took precedence over the other *whānau* values in the relationship with the *whānau* members at fault. This particular arrangement only emerged in practice as the best way of reaffirming *whānau* values with other *whānau* members and with all Māori, thereby securing the *whānau's* (and all Māori's) place in society at large, with the ultimate aim of getting things back to "normal." Indeed, all of the values or principles internalized through practice as habitus are flexible and can be adapted to particular cases or circumstances. Epa Huritau, one of Joan Metge's informants, explained this adaptability of the *whānau* well: "The Māori value system has the flexibility built into it to accommodate variation . . . If we know the principle, we can make adjustments" (Metge 1995: 105).

In social interactions, people behave according to cultural values that function as guides to behaviour. But they also have to make choices linked to their particular social positions or contexts. In doing that, they address specific interactions as and when they arise and improvise a response. This allows for both change and continuity. In this particular case, *mana* is clearly among the leading values and is not negotiable. The rest of the universe of meanings depends on it. A strong and immediate reaction to protect the core value effectively reaffirms the other values and principles, and thus the universe of meanings itself.

Different motivations among individuals, groups, and Māori as a people come into play to reinforce the positive values or principles and avoid the negative. These motivations include the desire to be accepted and admired; the fear of gossip and explicit and unspoken threats to withdraw support (Metge 1995: 105); the desire to regain knowledge of traditions, genealogy, or kinship; the revitalization of the Māori language; and the vision of increased autonomy for the group.

This *whānau* dilemma also illustrates that the more a situation is politicized (and conflictual), the less flexibility is allowed and the more self-conscious are the persons involved in the reaffirmation and contestation of the directional values and principles of the universes of meanings. The same forces are at work in the case of the rhetoric about "urban versus 'real' Māori." In the case of this *whānau* dilemma, the value of *mana* is non-negotiable in the city and in today's world where powerful forces are at play.

Mana is and has been equally important in other highly politicized cases in the country. Each situation, however, calls for a specific solution that emerges from a plurality of options that are linked, in turn, to many rhetorical and political possibilities, worlds in presence and ways of being Māori. Here, the decision was supported unanimously. It succeeded in preserving the unity that was threatened from both inside and outside the *whānau*. The case of David and William can serve to question any kind of absolutism, since it was both situational/circumstantial and cultural/structural.

My participation in the daily life of Māori and of this particular *whānau* was absolutely critical in my coming to understand this situation, even as I am well aware that my presence could not but have the disadvantage of influencing the situation. Had I not been participating in everyday *whānau* life, many factors would have escaped my attention, not only because of the Māori communicative style – they like subtlety, allusion, and ambiguity – but also because people do not reveal to a stranger internal family conflicts, money problems, or disagreements caused by visitors – it is not only against the principle of *mana*, but also against, for example, *manaakitanga, kotahitanga,* and *aroha*. I had access to a large part of what went on only because I was living in the house and because I was, at least to a certain degree, considered a member of the family.[4]

All universes of meanings are not on an equal footing in terms of power. In the case studied here, one universe of meanings – that of the *whānau* – is predominantly engaged by colonized people (the indigenous Māori minority), while other universes of meanings are closely linked to the members of the majority and their sociohistorical realm of interpretation. The universe of meanings of the *whānau* and any engagement in it must to some extent take into account[5] certain aspects of mainstream universes of meanings. People's and groups' internal dialogisms will inevitably include an internalization of key elements of the latter that are essential to survival in the present era. Individuals will thus necessarily act and imagine themselves in both the mainstream and *whānau* universes of meanings.

Māori today live in a globalized world in a capitalist economy in broad conditions of modernity, in a historically colonial nation state. Therefore, Māori, like other (if not all) minority populations and non-Western societies around the world, must take into account at least some of the aspects or fields of mainstream (dominant, Western) universes of meanings, such as the workplace, the welfare state, and commodities found in supermarkets or other businesses. Everyday, Māori are reminded that they need them for survival in today's world.

Access to commodities and cash has brought about important changes. I have noted how the *whānau* has changed with colonization, capitalism, and life in the city. But the *whānau* interpretative universe itself has changed, even while perpetuating itself, so as to accommodate contemporary obligations toward work, school, and recreation. The *whānau's* inherent flexibility has enabled its adaptation to life under new global conditions. For instance, the neoliberal policies of the fourth Labour government in the 1980s (which was part of a global trend) brought immense pressure to bear on a large part of the Māori population and, by extension, their *whānau*.

In my specific example, it is clear that money is important, since its abundance or lack impinges upon a *whānau's* everyday survival. David's disruptive behaviour resulted in unforeseen expenses that created enormous stress, since the *whānau* was already finding it hard to make ends meet. The situation around David touched on a sensitive issue, and even if the total amount of money utilized was not large, it could only exacerbate the situation. So, as well as illustrating disrespect for *whānau* values and conflict resolution in practice, this example also highlights the penetration of the capitalist world economy, and thus of another realm of interpretation, into the universe of meanings of the *whānau* and its everyday experiences.

First and foremost, the *whānau* dealt with David's and his father's behaviour because it contravened the values of the house and the universe of meanings it constitutes and put at risk the *whānau's* *mana* in a highly political arena. However, to a certain degree, their behaviour also put at risk the *whānau's* strong motivation to engage in another universe of meanings, that of mainstream New Zealand society and the capitalist West in general.

To survive, Māori today – even in the country – must rely on cash through work and social welfare, commodities, and the larger capitalist economy. The majority of the Māori participants in my research told me repeatedly that money and commodities matter little to Māori and their status in the community, *whānau,* or tribe and do not make one a person of *mana*. Yet in the practical "real" world, it is clear that mainstream commodity culture has a huge impact on interpersonal relationships. It allows people to display generosity toward guests, of course, but it also enables them to acquire the latest model of cell phone, the hottest computer game, the flashiest running shoes, or the biggest television set. Of course, these commodities do not have the same importance for everybody but they do have a certain significance, even for Māori (and especially young Māori). They allow one to acquire status.

Cash and commodities may not be ranked as highly in the value system of the *whānau* as in the mainstream world, and the same items or habits of consumption may not be valued in the same ways, but they are certainly not devoid of meaning. A person can increase his or her inherited *mana* through personal achievement. And success in the Pākehā world is often recognized as a *mana*-conferring form of personal achievement. The importance varies greatly depending on values, persons, and groups. Muru-Lanning (2004), in a study about Māori *rangatahi* (which could be glossed as "youth," but in practice can mean people anywhere between twenty-one and fifty years old) and their leadership, writes: "Higher education and wealth have become important factors in modern understandings of *mana*" (10). The same is true for professional success in mainstream society: money and commodities not only facilitate consumption, but also give access to schooling, professions, and positions of influence. Money and commodities enable appropriation (actual or symbolic) of places such as owner-occupied houses, universities, shops, and overseas tourist locations as well as of spaces of recognition and political power within society at large.

Maintaining and engaging with the universe of meanings of the *whānau*, then, implies also being able to comply with the basic requirements of the capitalist economy, since survival within one universe of meanings is rendered possible through survival within the other. To paraphrase Austin-Broos (2003: 130), "the economic" is not completely beyond "culture"; rather, it is part of it, even if there are always a variety of possible cultural responses to it.

The need for commodities and money can put a lot of pressure on the *whānau* and on the persons who are part of it. And the new exigencies of the modern world provoke other *whānau* dilemmas. *Whānau* obligations and responsibilities make substantial financial demands on the working members of the *whānau*, to provide everyone with food, clothes, shoes, furniture, leisure pursuits, and other necessities so that all members can succeed as individuals at school, at work, and among friends in the wider society, as well as fulfil their responsibilities on the *marae* and within the tribe.

Needless to say, caring for a large *whānau* is not an easy task. I have described some of the kinds of choices that people must grapple with in this process of engagement and negotiation with many universes of meanings. Some people withdraw from the *whānau*'s wider obligations while others attempt to fulfil all their responsibilities, putting themselves through a great deal of stress and suffering. This pressure to engage with and answer to many universes of meanings and *whānau* has been increased through the process of retribalization, here understood as the legal reinforcement of tribal entities by the government. It called for much genealogical research on the part of those who wanted to benefit from tribal resources and services and led many city-dwelling Māori to re-establish contact with their tribe.

Commodities and money are not only important among Māori, but also in their relationships with Pākehā and other New Zealanders. In daily life, Māori must show their success and "equality" by having great houses with great furniture, great outfits, and great cars. This relationship is true among neighbours, coworkers, friends, and students, and it is also a question of showing *mana* and the *whānau*'s *mana*. It is particularly important for Māori who are from middle-class backgrounds or live in middle- or upper-class neighbourhoods, where standards of consumption (and their impact on social relationships) are already well established.

This can put many Māori under considerable stress, which is all the more intense when they also have to respond to a *whānau*'s demands to maintain their relationship with it (or them, if they belong to more than one *whānau*). It is one of the reasons why some people prefer to live in poorer neighbourhoods but among Māori, rather than in "better" and "safer" neighbourhoods, as they often perceive them, among Pākehā.

Pākehā do not necessarily have the same standards of consumption as Māori and, in mainly Pākehā neighbourhoods, the balance of social power is clearly not in Māori's favour. The reverse is also true. Some

Māori are unable to tolerate the impoverished conditions in which some of their fellow Māori live, so they move to other, "whiter" areas, which can also be a way for them to enhance their prestige and status. Finally, dealing with *whānau* every day can simply become too difficult and moving to another neighbourhood is one way to avoid this particular stress.

Even traditional places like *marae* now need money to function properly (Salmond 1975). Hundreds of visitors cannot be fed without relying on cash and commodities. Everything has a price: the power and the gas used to cook the food, the new toilet installed, the new carpet laid in the meeting house, and so on. *Koha* (gifts) in kind are appreciated, but if everybody paid this way, there would be no money for bills and the *marae* would be in trouble. So *marae* now survive thanks to cash and quite utilitarian commodities. I heard several times of a group that stayed for a weekend workshop on an Auckland *marae* and gave as their present a carving. The craftwork was lovely and greatly admired by the people of the *marae*, but after the activity was over, they were heard wondering how it would pay for all the food, hot water, and heating that the visitors consumed over the weekend. Money would have been more appreciated in those circumstances.

This new reality has pushed many *marae* committees to set fees for visitors, according to the number of people, the length of the stay, the kind of food they want, and so forth. Although some people at first disagreed with such measures, arguing that they are against Māori principles and too similar to Western ways, in the end, *marae* finances meant they were not left with much choice.

The unbalanced – but unavoidable – relationship between mainstream and *whānau*/Māori universes of meanings also has an important political dimension. Politically, engagement with mainstream society is a way to improve the Māori situation and secure a place in the nation state. If the *whānau* dilemma, illustrated from my fieldwork, had happened in the 1960s or 1970s, just before or at the beginning of the Māori cultural renaissance and the Māori movement in education, very few Māori would have seen truancy from school as a serious fault. Māori truancy is a very old problem, and until fairly recently Māori parents have not dealt with it seriously.

This is less the case today.[6] To explain this change of attitude, I suggest, we must look beyond the *whānau* to sociocultural and political transformations and the struggle for affirmation and autonomy throughout Māori society. Māori leaders in the field of education did and still do a great deal to improve Māori perceptions of schooling and to set standards for Māori education and qualifications, as well as being, in many cases, good role models.

Māori schools first started as "'resistance' initiatives" (Smith 1997: 227) to combat Māori underachievement in mainstream schools and respond to the need for Māori language and cultural revitalization. These schools were incorporated into the state system as a result of the 1989 Education Act (227). The state gave Māori a measure of authority and rights and obtained in exchange some first-rate collaboration on many educational projects.

The first *kohanga reo* (Māori language kindergarten) was founded in 1981, and in 2000 there were 643 for 11,846 children throughout New Zealand.[7] The first *kura kaupapa Māori* (Māori immersion school) was established in 1987 (225), and in 2007[8] there were 68 schools throughout New Zealand (see Smith 1997 and Walker 2004 for the history of Māori schools). The 1990s also saw the creation of *wānanga* (Māori tertiary institutions) that are very successful and offer a wide range of programs. Three of these institutions are recognized today under the Education Act 1989. According to section 162 of the Act, "a wananga is characterised by teaching and research that maintains, advances, and disseminates knowledge and develops intellectual independence, and assists the application of knowledge regarding ahuatanga Maori (Maori tradition) according to tikanga Maori (Maori custom)."

Tribal and pan-tribal authorities have also done their part to encourage Māori schooling. For example, Muru-Lanning (2004) writes that the Waikato-Tainui tribal authority increased its spending on education during the 1990s: "While in 1990 only 26 tertiary education scholarships were given to tribal scholars, in 1995 the number increased to 588" (9). School and university authorities as well as Māori student associations have many initiatives to support Māori schooling and achievement, such as scholarships as well as various information and support programs (see Durie 2011; Gagné 2009c; see also Reilly 2011 on the development of Māori studies). The New Zealand state has also done a great deal to encourage Māori to carry on with or go back to school. More generally, as emphasized by Durie (2011: 73–4), "Māori involvement in all aspects of tertiary education, including student enrolment, curriculum development, and the management and strategies development of education institutions, has transformed New Zealand's education sector to the point where a palpable indigenous dimension can be felt both within and beyond the sector."

It is widely recognized among Māori that in today's world, Māori cannot better themselves as individuals, as *whānau*, as tribes, or as a people without education, be it Māori or mainstream. Education is as essential for their daily lives as it is for their collective participation in New Zealand society and their autonomy in the world at large. So perceptions of schooling and education in general have changed a good deal in recent decades and both are taken much more seriously by Māori today.

This is certainly the case in the *whānau* of our example, if not for all Māori. Kiri's *whānau*, including the children themselves, have been involved in educational initiatives for at least four generations. First, the great-grandfather, Rongo, set up a cultural enrichment program for urban youth dealing with youngsters with drug problems and nomadic lives on the streets of Auckland. Teria and Hiko were involved in building a *marae* in South Auckland, a project that had clear educational goals. Teria worked for a few years as teacher in the Māori language kindergarten when they moved back to Hiko's tribal area down south. Teria and Hiko took university correspondence courses in Māori studies and Hiko also worked as elder in a health organization. At the time of my fieldwork, Kiri was responsible for a Māori and Pacific Island cultural program in collaboration with a team of elders in a hospital. She was also a university student with dreams that her children would all go to university and get diplomas that would give them a good standing in society in general, but also put them in a position of influence for the future of Māori. Rangi, Kiri's sister was teaching in a Māori language kindergarten in her husband's tribal area but moved back to Auckland to study for a teaching qualification while working as teacher's assistant in a Māori bilingual unit in a mainstream primary school in South Auckland. Three of Kiri and Rangi's other sisters went to university, studying in different disciplines at undergraduate and master's levels. All five sisters were directing their schooling and future career toward a field in which they would work for or with Māori, or both. Last but not least, Whetu's daughter went to a Māori language kindergarten.

So this *whānau* took a particularly favourable view of schooling, and clearly recognized how important it was to obtain qualifications, not only for *whānau* members' own sake, but also for the good of Māori more generally. At 30 Aroha Street, schooling was important, but subsistence, primary care, chores, and the occasional "crisis" demanded a lot of attention, energy, and time. The children's schooling and homework did not always take priority. With all the worry of having a big *whānau* on top of a regular workload, the energy of the adults often went first to "fire-fighting." They dealt with critical problems and then, if they still had time, they went to parents' meetings at school, inquired about the children's school performance and, sometimes, reminded the children to do their homework. Rangi was clearly the one who kept on top of the children about this, given that she worked at their school and had time available. She also felt it was partly her responsibility.

While school was very important to Kiri's *whānau*, not all Māori are comfortable with it. Indeed, many of the participants in my research thought schools and universities were austere, hostile, and foreign to them and their identity. This could also explain in part David's behaviour at school. He may have wanted the school to pay the symbolic cost of his discomfort. But David had many reasons to feel uncomfortable in the family.[9]

Collectively Māori need schooling to participate in the nation as competent partners. The bicultural ideology of Aotearoa/New Zealand was built from the Treaty of Waitangi, the founding document of the New Zealand nation-state that recognizes an equal partnership between Māori and Pākehā. This treaty is all the more important in the universe of meanings of the *whānau* where the ancestors provide precedents for acceptable behaviours. Specific precedents, such as contracts, are binding for the ancestors' descendants (Patterson 1992: 82). Referring specifically to the Treaty of Waitangi, Moana Jackson explains:

> Because it was so ordained and acted upon by ancestors as a solemn agreement, it is a kawenata or spiritual covenant that cannot be lightly dismissed. This spiritual aspect does not mean that the Treaty is separate from the material world, but rather that the material rights are guaranteed and have spiritual sanction. Like the other acts of tipuna which came to be regarded as precedent, the Treaty was thus regarded as an affirmation of rangatiratanga and hence a confirmation of the authority implicit in that term to act on behalf of the iwi and to bind them in their future conduct. (Jackson 1988 in Patterson 1992: 82)

The treaty, then, has become a tactical (ideological) interpretative framework used to stage a potentially equal dialogue with the dominant population (Allen 2002). In spite of its long history of nonrecognition and nonrespect by the Pākehā or British party, the treaty has been taken as an ideological base for any consideration of Māori and Pākehā relationships in New Zealand society, in general, as well as in public institutions and government.

Indirectly, the problem of David not going to school is related to that bicultural ideology. His behaviour contravened the spirit of the treaty since by his absenteeism David was failing to prepare himself and his *whānau* to fulfil their role as treaty partners. The *whānau*, quite obviously, did not discuss the problem in these terms but the spirit of the treaty implies practical demands that are well internalized.

Treaty responsibilities and rights are asserted time and time again in public discourse and at various public and private meetings on *marae*, at school, at work, and elsewhere. It is common practice for all employers, not only those in the public sector, to offer their employees workshops on responsibilities and obligations emanating from the Treaty of Waitangi. It is also part of the curriculum to teach students about the treaty itself and the treaty responsibilities.[10] The reminders do not only come from Māori but from non-Māori people and institutions.

Again, the internalized pan-Māori code embodied as common sense pushed *whānau* members to react strongly and swiftly when the circumstances dictated. The norms and the new value of education for Māori were respected by the *whānau* as an internalized code for life under biculturalism. The code is made up of embodied, self-evident values that go "beyond the cognised sort common to intellectual reasoning" (Desjarlais 1992: 71). Thus, it is important to recognize that the universe of meanings of the *whānau* is influenced by the general history of both Māori and non-Māori and by the specific history of their relationships. It is in this context that I regard the final *whānau* decision to expel David and his father from the house. Although the course and outcome of the dilemma were not predetermined, they were preconstrained to a certain degree by overarching structures, universes of meanings, and sociopolitical and historical forces.

While it was obvious, for example, that David's behaviour was highly disturbing and that something was bound to happen, it was impossible to predict exactly what solutions would be adopted, how David (and William) would be sanctioned, and when these actions would become unavoidable and why. As shown by Schwimmer (1990), there is no simple dialectical relationship between the structural and the interactional but rather a "loose coupling" (53). A multiplicity of possibilities always exist, since the relationship is dialogical rather than simply dialectical. The resolution of a dilemma results not only from the dialogue between the structural and the interactional orders but also from the actors' interpretations, which are linked to their own personal experiences, projections into the future, and unconscious motivations. And it is linked, once again, to both general and particular histories and to the plurality of universes of meaning at play.

The solution might have been different had the Pākehā school been at fault or responsible in some way for David's truancy. Other authors have said that one possible response to a threat to the *whānau's mana* from outsiders is to unite and forget about internal quarrels (Pere 1982 in Metge 1995). And this *whānau* had not hesitated to criticize the school and stand up for its members when necessary, which happened on a few occasions while I was there. When Paua ran off from school and disappeared for a whole day, the *whānau* blamed the school for not giving him appropriate support for his behavioural and learning difficulties. Everybody was upset that he was neglected in this respect by his teacher, an educational psychologist and a social worker. Why did he stay outside the school when the bell rang? Why did nobody look for him, or even realize that he was not in the mainstream classroom to which he had just been transferred, because he was no longer allowed in the bilingual unit? Did such things happen only or mainly to Māori students? And if he had been Pākehā, would the teacher have noticed his absence? Once again, the *mana* of the *whānau* was at stake since, in this story, it was the parents who were accused of not doing enough.

I also remember that Kiri, supported by Rangi who was part of the school team, decided to withdraw two of the *whānau's* children, Paua and Mahora, from the school's annual trip to a series of *marae* in the country "up north" because she considered that the teachers and parents – even if they were all Māori – did not take enough responsibility for the children's behaviour and did not know enough about *marae* protocols. Having been part of the trip the year before, she thought that parents and teachers let the children do whatever they liked. That time, she did not want to be associated with the project and did not want the children to have such an experience. Kiri's reaction was again linked to the *whānau's* values. And the *whānau's mana* was once more the value that determined the final decision. If the *whānau's* children were seen on those *marae* behaving incorrectly or accompanying people who were behaving incorrectly, the *whānau's mana* was at risk of being diminished in the eyes of the people of these *marae*.

Rangi supported Kiri's decision, since she herself did not agree with the way things were going. But being a teacher's assistant and not a full teacher, she could not impose her view within the school team or with the parents. Kiri's intervention was also a way to alert the attention of the principal – a Pākehā woman – to certain negative dynamics in the bilingual unit and to ask for changes.

These various incidents and situations illustrate the complexity of the universe of meanings of the *whānau* and its codes and demonstrate its heteroglossia. Disagreement and power relationships are part of the dynamic not only between Māori and Pākehā, but also among Māori. Certain Pākehā can become very important allies, as happened in the case of the Pākehā school principal who finally made sure that the correct protocols were taught to the children and respected during their trip. This strategy was aimed at protecting the *whānau*'s *mana*, and serves to illustrate that *mana* can be protected or acquired in different ways.

The subject of finances is always present, and, doubtless, it is not a shock to find that money is essential for ensuring that the Māori political struggle continues. While I do not devote much discussion to political struggle in this book, it is, of course, important. Money is needed to pay for lawyers, advisors, Māori delegates to the United Nations, and trips around the world to build solidarity networks with other minority populations and indigenous peoples. Money enables Māori artists to exhibit or perform at international arts venues. At a local level, it is needed for organizing Māori festivals, performing at local venues, organizing workshops or seminars or *wānanga* (meetings called to discuss particular teachings or issues) about the Māori language, Māori traditions, and Māori arts and crafts. Money management is dealt with at different levels. Sometimes decisions are taken at the *whānau* level, sometimes at the *hapū* or *iwi* level and sometimes in pan-tribal organizations or other nontraditional Māori groupings.

Today's dominant universes of meanings have an impact on the *whānau*, but the latter also has an impact on other universes of meanings. The official recognition of the Treaty of Waitangi and the partnership that it implies, as well as other recent sociopolitical gains, would seem to demonstrate that the assimilationist and later integrationist policies of the various British and New Zealand governments through history have not completely succeeded.

The central importance of the *whānau* and its particular values and principles has also been acknowledged in various laws. For example, in the Mental Health (Compulsory Assessment and Treatment) Act 1992, family and *whānau* views are taken into consideration in applications for compulsory treatment, although in practice, the opportunities for families and *whānau* to participate in decisions to discharge patients to the care of relatives are limited (Durie 1997: 13). The Children, Young Persons and Their Families Act 1989 also "allows for *whānau* and *iwi* [tribes] to be involved in decisions about care, protection and youth justice processes" (13). Durie (13–14) also cites Te Ture Whenua Māori Act 1993 as one of a few examples of laws emphasizing *whānau* and tribal values in relation to Māori land and succession rights. In 2010, the government also approved the Whānau Ora scheme, as previously mentioned.

The labour market makes few allowances for the demands of the *whānau*, in particular in times of death. Today, many employers and government programs grant leave to attend *tangihanga* (funerals). However, people still sometimes hesitate to take their days off from work, either because of the stigma or because they just cannot afford to take days off. Their workload is too heavy, they want to show their good faith to their employer, or they simply need their full wages. The subsequent reactions of the *whānau* are then often difficult to deal with. Note that Māori funerals usually last for three days (see, among others, Ngata 1940; Hiroa 1949; Metge 1964, 1995; Schwimmer 1965; Sinclair 1990a; but also the novel *Tangi* by Ihimaera 1973).

That *tangihanga* now often take place in the city, on urban *marae* and in ordinary city houses as well as in the country allows for more flexibility. People from the city who cannot leave their job can pay their respects to the dead without feeling guilty or fearing reprisals from the supernatural world. It allows people to participate in the social group and fulfil their responsibilities and obligations as *whānau* members, without fear of losing their jobs in the city. It is also a privileged time for reaffirming their identity as Māori, since funerals remain an important symbol of Māori identity (McIntosh 2001; Sinclair 1990a) and "a key index of Maori culture in general" (Rosenblatt 2011: 419). They are an excellent occasion for resituating oneself in relationships to the living as well as the dead: "By supporting each other on the marae [or at the *whānau* house], the living are made aware of their place in life" (Tauroa and Tauroa 1986: 135). During funerals, many Māori that I met also organize a visit to country kin or volunteer their services for the work of the funeral. It was always a good opportunity to express their feelings and responsibilities to each other as a *whānau*.

In recent years, there has been a noticeable increase in the number of *tangihanga*, as Māori have returned to their own traditions of mourning and funeral rituals (Carter 2003a). They are an important political site for the affirmation of the Māori position in the wider New Zealand society as well as among Māori (Sinclair 1990a; McIntosh 2001).[11]

Despite all this, significant signs of backlash from the mainstream population have emerged (see, for example, Barber 2008; Gagné 2008a, 2008b; Miller 2005), in large part as a reaction to Māori achievements, including those within the mainstream universes of meanings where Māori have become skilful and successful "players," even as businessmen. This backlash has an impact (or will have, if it does not already) on *whānau* flexibility.

The urban Māori houses that are compared to *marae*, like "real" *marae* – including urban ones – allow Māori to reinforce solidarity within the group and thus shape and strengthen what "being Māori" means. The *whānau*, along with *marae*, has become a powerful symbol of *Māoritanga* and its flexibility has allowed for the extension of its realms of interpretation to include non-kin *whānau*, the *kaupapa whānau* (common-purpose *whānau*). And places like houses based on *marae* principles are a key site for affirmation and resistance, and are essential for assuring the strengthening and continuity of the universe of meanings of the *whānau* in the face of other powerful realms of interpretation.

7 At the Heart of a Politics of Differentiation

Since the 1970s, the Māori cultural renaissance and the global forces favouring indigenous and minority rights have renewed the *whānau* universe of meanings and transformed it into a powerful symbol. These dynamics also allowed non-kin *whānau*, also called *kaupapa whānau* (common-purpose *whānau*, also referred to in English as *kaupapa*-based *whānau*), to emerge. And they reinforced the conscious desire to perpetuate or to simply participate in the universe of meanings of the *whānau*, seen as central to Māori cultural identity, decolonization, and survival.

A dichotomy between Māori and Pākehā worlds emerges from Māori narratives. The boundaries between these worlds, apparently so solid and important in Māori narratives, are much more porous in practice. And at the heart of the reciprocal constitution of these universes of meanings, a politics of differentiation is at play.

The universe of meanings of the *whānau*, with its principles and values, is used to govern relationships both among Māori and between Māori and others. Family networks can at times be quite restricted, and at times rather large. They can extend to a person's entire tribe, to people of other tribes or, metaphorically, to the whole Māori people and can even include non-Māori or people beyond New Zealand. *Whānau* expand through experiences and practices when there is a need for cooperation, management of collective resources, or opposition to the state or the mainstream population. Family networks can also contract to a more selective group of persons, for example, when conflicts or divergences emerge, when abuses are revealed, when there is competition over resources, or when some persons or subgroups experience discomfort with others in the network.

But the *whānau* is not only ancestor-oriented, kinship-based, or genealogical. It can also be ideological and unite non-kin who cooperate to
achieve specific aims. To recap some elements of chapter 5, *whakapapa
whānau* are *whānau* for which genealogy – that is, *whakapapa* – forms
the fundamental basis of connection, while *kaupapa whānau* are *whānau*
groups established to fulfil a common mission or a special purpose
(which is what *kaupapa* means). For instance, neighbours, a performing arts group, or students from the same class might speak about their
group as a *whānau* and therefore respect extended family principles
and responsibilities in regard to it. Basically, the universe of meanings
is the same, but it unites non-kin.

The universe of meanings of *whānau* is inherently flexible. It has
adapted to new conditions in the city, for instance, where simply being
Māori has become an important basis for association (Walker 1970; Williams 2010). New Zealand's urbanization led to the development of
suburbs where large numbers of Māori live as neighbours.[1] In these
places, despite different tribal affiliations and regional origins, common
bonds developed around being Māori. Certain commonalties were
found. *Whānau* values and principles began to govern relationships between neighbours, by-passing "the customary requirements of kinship
and descent" (Williams 2010: 102). Research by Harris (2007, 2007–8)
and Williams (2010) on Māori in Auckland in the 1940s to the 1960s as
well as by Walker (1970) in the Ōtara of the second half of the 1960s at-
tests to this for the early period of Māori life in the city. Williams (2010),
for example, gives examples of "workplace-*whānau*" where there was
a critical mass of Māori workers and speaks of "surrogate *whānau*" at
the Department of Māori Affairs and at church-sponsored hostels that
welcomed Māori youth in the inner city. Similar processes are at work
today. Under certain circumstances and for certain persons, this identity becomes even more fundamental than their identity as a member of
a genealogical *whānau* or a tribe.

Belonging to a *kaupapa whānau* is a reasonably common experience
among Māori. The Māori households' longitudinal study "Best Outcomes For Māori: Te Hoe Nuku Roa," in which this type of *whānau* is
defined as any *whānau* not based on genealogy or kinship, revealed that
25 per cent of the respondents were members of one such *whānau*, another 17 per cent of two, and a further 14 per cent of three (Cunningham,
Stevenson, and Tassell 2005: 16).

But how do people speak of their relationships with different groups
as *whānau* relationships? Here Keita and her daughter Regan discussed

their group of friends in West Auckland, where they had lived for twenty-five years:

> KEITA: All my Māori friends are to me like my *whānau* [. . .] Because we have been so long together. With some of them, we have been long, long . . . more years than I have been with my own *whānau*, at home . . . in the North. I have been here for twenty-five years, it's longer than I have been up North, really.
>
> REGAN: See and I'm an urban child, I have been brought up here.
>
> KEITA: Yeah, she has been brought up with all my friends' kids from other tribes. So . . . you know, you get to know each other and share things, birthdays of your children, *tangi* [funerals] . . . The things you do with your own *whānau* back home, you're doing with your extended tribal *whānau*, yeah.

As for Christine, she simply said of the network of neighbours with whom she maintained daily relationships, "That's the feeling of being a *whānau!*"

Many members of a Māori performing arts groups considered their group as a *whānau*. Matiu explained how this came about:

> Especially at the university, there is a lot of Māori students who are disassociated with their tribal links and maybe *kapa haka* [performing arts] is a forum that they can find other Māori on campus who can understand how they are feeling and they are not alone, and *kapa haka* is the media where they can join together and share *waiata*, traditional Māori songs, and contemporary Māori music as a means of making them feel better and re-establish and create *whānau* feelings. (Matiu)

Mīria's performing arts group had been like a new family for her. Their support was very important and they were there for her when things went wrong with her partner or during her pregnancies. The group had also been very helpful in sharing child-care responsibilities. The common-purpose *whānau* is also a channel for cultural transmission and inheritance. Kiri's group was an important resource for learning about Māori performing arts and Māori *tikanga* (traditions, customs, rules).

The performing arts groups often have residential courses or activities aimed partly at strengthening bonds among the group. They also see each other on a daily basis at school or at home. And many group members stay at the *marae* or the Māori student room after their weekly activities, for the night, the weekend, or even the holidays. Some members of the group even have a house open to (almost) everybody.

In Māori immersion schools and kindergartens, the *whānau* is a model for education. As in a genealogical *whānau*, knowledge belongs to the group, the *whānau*. Pedagogical methods incorporate *whānau* values. Discipline is based on the authority of elders and the special roles of older children toward those who are younger. And the curriculum reflects the lives of the children, with plenty of opportunity for *whānau* values to be reinforced through content (Durie 2001a: 193).

In West Auckland, the *whānau* concept was the basis for the formation of an urban authority, Te Whānau o Waipareira (Durie 2001a: 193; Phillips 1999; Waitangi Tribunal 1998). At Hoani Waititi *marae*, Rosenblatt (2011: 411) emphasizes that the *marae* community represented and understood itself as a *whānau* in many contexts. The same idea of *whānau* is also promulgated among participants in Māori employment or language programs. The teachers emphasize *whānau* and tribal relationships as well as genealogy and kinship, but also speak about *whānau* support and unconditional love as often as they can. They reiterate the importance of "being a *whānau* to each other." They behave supportively toward their students and give to them unstintingly of their time and energy – even after school – on the *marae* where the programs take place or in their own house, which in some cases functions like a *marae* or as an extension of the school *marae* or classroom.

The *whānau* feeling also comes from the students' experience of learning together, of passing through challenging times together, and of being together every day for about a year. Tama expressed his feelings in the following way:

> We know each other so well, we work with each other every day in the program and course . . . When I go back home, to my own *marae*, I only see my family, I only see it once a year. So, the feeling is not the same. I have more feelings here than I do in my own *marae*. It's because I'm growing a relationship with these people. It's an everyday thing.

So, the daily sharing strengthens the family-like bonds. For Tama and many other students, this contrasts sharply with the genealogical network, which is mostly in the countryside far away from Auckland. Yearly or twice-yearly visits cannot compare to the everyday experience shared in the city in the common-purpose *whānau*.

When I was talking about being a family, we're not always going around kissing and hugging each other here on the *marae*. We actually show it in and outside this *marae* and that's what *whanaungatanga* is all about. Supportiveness and that's what family do, they go and support you wherever you go. You go walking, they come and support. That's what they're doing for me when they come to my boxing fights. I feel really special. I feel I'm really worth it. It's something very special in my life. (Tama)

However, this does not mean that Tama's genealogical *whānau* members don't also come to support him. His close family – father, brothers, and sisters – all flew out from the country to cheer him on at his last fight. But, in his everyday life, it is his common-purpose *whānau* from the *marae* that sustains him: "We keep each other safe, well" (Tama). So, he is also there for them when they need him. The relationship is one of long-term, balanced reciprocity. "Here, there is a lot . . . [of] support, love respect, everything is nice," Tama added. "Being here with all those people, it's just an experience of happiness, joy, love." It is thus also about being part of a group, about identity:

It gives you a sense of belonging. It gives you a sense of identity, of where you are, where you come from. Being among these people, you understand *whanaungatanga*, family, the feeling of being close to each other because we understand where we come from, who we are. We're Māori. I guess we're all proud of it. You know, being taught who you are, it's like your mum and dad telling you "this is who you are." Because we all started this together, we feel very close. (Tama)

Whānau is thus about sharing similar issues, problems, life experiences, and *kaupapa* (projects, plans).

Kahu considers her work team to be a *whānau* for very similar reasons, which were also identified by Williams (2010):

We have a hard-case bunch of people here. I mean, they are awesome to me [. . .] it is like a family. If something happens, they are all here. Like when my dad passed away, he passed away [. . .] a couple of months ago and my boss, he works hard here [. . .] he took some time off work and a few workers and took them to this little woop woop town where we buried my dad and that was really cool. I mean everybody would have come up, but some had to stay back and because I have my daughter as well and she can come up here if she was sick and stay here while I am working so

then when I have finished work, I can just cruise off home. It is just so relaxed. You do for them and they will do for you with a bit of extra. If I am
in trouble or if they have trouble, we can ring each other and plus, we have
got a good entertainment. You have to have the entertainment, but it is
because I have known them for quite a few years. We are all very comfortable around each other and now, our kids are starting to play with each
other. If they are all sick, they all come up here. (Kahu)

Common-purpose *whānau* members can become uncles and aunts for
the children of their neighbours or friends. People from younger generations call them "*mama*" and "*papa*," or "*whaea*," a term of respect
meaning mother, and "*matua*," a term of respect meaning father. The
oldest neighbours also become *kaumātua* (male elders) and *kuia* (female
elders) for the new *whānau*.

By us moving things from the rural to here, we did not have many cousins
around us, so our neighbours became our cousins [. . .] So it's kind of like
. . . adjust into the urban and still having a feel of the old, or what I believe
is the old . . . practices still happening even though it happens to be with
someone else out of my tribal area. The values are still there because . . . we
recreate [. . .] They are not, you know, like acquaintances, those are friends
and those friends that I have for forty years [. . .] They are like my family, they are part of who I am. So when they have a loss, I have a loss [. . .]
We did not have the blood ties. We still have the tie. For us it's a *whānau*
tie. (Joana)

Among young people, members of *kaupapa whānau*, such as performing arts groups or sports teams, the use of words like "cousin"
or simply "cous" and "brother" or "bro" is widespread. These forms
of address can also refer to those who share the same ideas or ways of
life, whether Māori or not. So, the use of terms like "cous" or "bro" is a
good indication of the context-dependent expansion or contraction of
the *whānau*. These terms are used particularly by certain categories of
people, namely, young people, gang members, and people from certain
subcultures like fans of rap, hip-hop, or reggae music.

Rewa, a woman in her late forties, who went home for the first time
only a few years ago, also uses these terms when she is among Māori
and among her people back home to accentuate her Maoriness and belonging to the group:

My *tuakana* [cousin of the same sex and generation in a senior line] told me
that one day [. . .] "I'm really surprised you're using language like that."
Like what? [. . .] I don't know. That's maybe their expectation for how I
should speak, because they use the "Bro." Because they don't want me to
use the "Bro language," Maybe they want me to use Pākehā language, because they called me Pākehā lady when I was growing up. (Rewa)

She goes on to say that she can be bicultural when she wants to and
adds, "I even talk differently. How I'm talking now with you is one
way. If you put me in a room of Pākehā people, doesn't matter the level,
and I will speak differently again. Only because if I have to speak at all,
I want my point to be clear" (Rewa). That is why she uses the "Bro language": she wants to make clear that she is part of the *whānau* – here
her genealogical *whānau*. The non-usage of "Bro language" can consequently serve to exclude those who are not considered part of the
whānau.

"Bro language" is closely associated with a Māori way of speaking
in the New Zealand media and public opinion. I have not done extensive research about its origins but it is clear that it is inspired by the
language used by Black Americans (and Black minorities in other countries) to distinguish themselves from the mainstream dominant society
and to express their solidarity, their fraternity, their particular identity.
Since the 1970s, Māori have been generally inspired by Black movements
and struggles for emancipation and empowerment. Rap, hip-hop, and
reggae music – and their messages – have a strong influence among
Māori. And some Māori will use "Bro language" to deliberately distinguish themselves from the elite, whether Māori or Pākehā, or to shock
"right-thinking" people. Manuka, who is a physically impressive and
even tough-looking man in his late forties, will sometimes greet a well-
dressed Pākehā that he does not know at all on the street with "*Kia ora*
bro!" Perhaps unsurprisingly, he generally receives no reply.

Some Māori, however, do not like this way of talking or moving in
ways emblematic of Black youth cultures in the United States and elsewhere. They say that Māori should find their own distinctive ways to
express themselves and should not identify too closely with Black minorities whose struggles are different. Others do not like this language
because it is synonymous in the mainstream media with the underclass
and gangs. They would prefer to show that not all Māori are like that,
that they are not all "dumb" and part of the "bad statistics." Finally,

some women pointed out that they do not like to be called "bro," since it is a male-oriented word that should be used by men talking to other men.[2]

People use *whānau* terms of address to speak to and about each other. These show the respect that Māori devote traditionally to older generations[3] and are a reminder of Māori values, traditions, and ways of relating to each other. Members of Joana and Mihi's urban *hapū* (subtribe) or *whānau* do this. But it is also how things generally work in places like Māori immersion schools and kindergartens (Durie 2001a: 193; Smith 1997), in Rangi's bilingual class, and in Māori performing arts groups.

To have *whānau* feelings with a group of people and to treat them as *whānau* members, the crucial criteria I found to be (1) mutual support and help; (2) a feeling of sharing similar experiences and interests; (3) unity, group feeling, or oneness; (4) a relaxed atmosphere, in the sense that one can truly be oneself; (5) the acceptance and inclusion of children as everybody's children; (6) personal and material support in times of death; and (7) reciprocity among the group. Many if not all of the genealogical *whānau* principles discussed earlier are at work in some way. These are all very important for *kaupapa whānau* and form the basis of their close association. In practice, if someone infringes on those principles they will be excluded, either little by little, or suddenly, in cases of serious *whānau* abuse.

The idea of the common-purpose *whānau* presupposes a kind of openness to everybody and implies some measure of equality among all members – aside from matters of *mana* (spiritual power, authority, prestige, status) and generational status. As Metge (1964) noted among Māori in Auckland in 1953–54, "[q]uestions of rank . . . seemed to be little discussed" (158).[4] Such issues were only occasionally raised, and always in private conversation, by people of a *rangatira* (chiefly) line.

Very often, however, divisive forces are at work. Some people in the *whānau* establish special relationships around particular interests or genealogical or tribal ties. This breaks the *whānau*'s unity.

> I just felt that they had that sort of little cliquey bunches of people and that we were an outsider. Because you had all those little *whānau* groups within the whole *whānau*, they were all little cliquey bunches and I'm not into that kind of stuff [. . .] and so, I said to my friend, I think I will move my kids [from the Māori immersion school]. I don't feel like, you know, there is a *whānau* concept here or feeling of being in a *whānau*. (Christine)

In the urban setting, as Api, one of my research participants, remarked and as I observed, the conflicts and alliances between tribe and subtribe are still alive. They change according to situations and larger political, economic, and social contexts. Tribal (cultural) differences are not as marked as in pre- and early colonial times, despite the retribalization process of recent years and the greater prominence and mediatization of tribal politics. And Māori are clearly capable of working together, as on pan-tribal *marae* where the underlying *marae* protocol is "*ngā hau e wha*," meaning that people from the four winds or from all around the island come together. However, there are still differences in ways of doing things and points of view. This can create conflict or misunderstandings in pan-tribal organizations and it is difficult to find a consensus. Every group or tribe has its own interests and preoccupations and sometimes people gather and join together according to tribes to pursue specific goals or projects. People also like to remind others of the tribal wars of the past. They remember and joke about battles lost and won but the jokes sometimes take a very serious turn and carry grave warnings about people's behaviour. Elders often recall past tribal alliances and conflicts in their speeches during *marae* ceremonies and public meetings of all sorts.

Like any *whānau*, a Māori performing group in which I participated had its fair share of tension. The members of the group were almost all more or less closely related to each other. At the very least, each person was related through tribal affiliation to someone else in the group, and this created some subgroups. Other subgroups followed simply from personal affinities or the length of time that members have been in the group. There was some tension between the "oldies" and the newer members. For example, the "oldies" wanted to learn new and more difficult action songs, while the recent recruits hardly knew the old program. Although the "oldies" were apparently sometimes bothered by the new members, they also promoted an open-door policy. They depended on new members for their survival as a group, since a few "oldies" dropped out every year because of new jobs, parental obligations, or just because they felt that it was time for them to move on. Some of the "oldies" or the "*kapa haka* [Māori performing arts] freaks," as Regan called them, could be very hard on those who had not done Māori performing arts before, who, for example, knew little about *haka* (posture dance)[5], and *poi*, which are flax balls on string used in posture dances. The stereotype that all Māori know how to dance and sing is persistent even among Māori. The pressure could thus be very heavy for new members. Sometimes girls were told they had "Pākehā hands," if they are unable to swing the *poi* (balls) properly. Such an accusation motivated some to learn fast and well, but also discouraged others so much that they gave up completely. There was also a great deal of competitiveness in the group, and in Māori performing arts in general, which was exacerbated by competitions at regional and national levels in which standards were very high.[6]

The level of knowledge of Māori language was another conflicting point. Some liked to show off their knowledge whenever possible and made quite offensive remarks about those who hardly knew the language. Kahu told me how this happened to her once. This event did not take place in the group that I was in, but I did hear of similar occurrences.

> I used to speak and one day [someone] said to me don't even bother if I couldn't speak it properly [. . .] and that was a real down for me and I was still learning but for me that was a big shifting for someone to say to you "Oh! Don't bother doing that because you are not good at it," if you get people like that, that put you down and that. You think to yourself, why even bother? And I found that was the problem of a lot of people. (Kahu)

Other problems within the group arose from jealousy and back-biting. For example, dances are performed in rows, with the women in front and the men behind. People would sometimes fight for the front row so that they can be seen and their talent admired. This was intolerable behaviour for those members who considered it to be against *whānau* values. A former member of the group told me once that all the fights were political. She had learned about *tikanga* (tradition, customs) from her mother and was taught not to be there for herself but to help and support people learning things:

> That's not the way to . . . you know, the talks . . . there is so much talk about the *whanaungatanga* [strengthening and enriching the bonds of family unity], but my mum taught me how . . . taught me *whanaungatanga* to other people, you know, and to *awhi* . . . humble, humble, and just to help, you know. And I think that's really important. (Regan)

Matiu explained a problem that arose in his group:

> There is problem with [our Māori performing arts *whānau*] in that we don't have any old people and every other group that I have been to they

have old people, like *koroua* [elders] and [. . .] those old people they are the
leaders of the group. They determine how the group functions and our
group we don't, see, myself now and Heather and Victor, we are probably
the oldest people in the group, we are like the old people for the group
and it is really hard because we are young as well [. . .] It would help
[to have elders] because we wouldn't be . . . like if there were problems
that arose in the group they would be the people that sorted it out [. . .] It
does work better in other groups because they have the old people. Every
group whatever culture, there is always a hierarchy. In the Māori side, the
old people, our *kaumātua*, they hold the knowledge and you expect them
to be able to sort out problems and stuff best. (Matiu)

Common-purpose *whānau*, lacking elders, therefore suffer from certain
problems that are unlikely to occur in genealogical *whānau*.

However, there is no dichotomy between the two kinds of *whānau*.
People can divide their time between both and be involved in one or
more genealogical *whānau* and one or more common-purpose *whānau*.
There are no inherent conflicts in being involved in multiple *whānau*,
since the values and principles are more or less the same. But people
sometimes have to choose between their various obligations or responsibilities, and subordinate some to others. This can create tension
in relations with other *whānau* members, who may pay the price for
someone else's choices, either having to compensate for other people's
withdrawal or rely on the arrival of new members. Pressure exerted
by members of one *whānau* can have various effects, from achieving
its intended purpose of exacting further commitment to alienating others, possibly to the point of breaking off relations with the demanding
whānau. In re-evaluating their involvement, some will try to balance
their individual needs with the wishes of the collective, but others will
simply quash their personal desires and give in to those exerting the
greatest pressure. Still others will be paralyzed by indecision. Nevertheless, many people succeed in combining their commitments to several *whānau*.

Being involved in a common-purpose *whānau* in the city can serve
as a safety net when one is far from one's genealogical *whānau*. People will negotiate their involvement in more than one *whānau* through
practice and interrelationships. The same processes are at work in the
case of multiple involvements in genealogical *whānau* networks. Once
again, the value of *mana* (spiritual power, authority, prestige, status)
plays a crucial role in regulating engagement, but so does the value of
genealogy.

What emerged from my participation in the lived worlds of Māori is that there is a hierarchy between the two types of association in practice, depending on social contexts and relations. Fidelity and first allegiance generally goes to the genealogical or kin-based *whānau*, except where it contains cases of serious abuse or really disruptive conflicts. The genealogical *whānau* is seen as a long-term and permanent *whānau* group while the common-purpose *whānau* "reflected the particular values and needs of a group . . . at a specific time and place" (Williams 2010: 185). Furthermore, the complex workings of the guiding principles and values of *whānau* are such that the common-purpose type has many features that distinguish it from the genealogical type; I have identified ten.

First, the force of the collective is not as strong as in genealogical *whānau*, since the *whakapapa* (genealogy) values do not apply, or at least not in the same way. Members are conscious of this weakness and of the vulnerability that follows from it. They may then hesitate to place too much emphasis on the common-purpose *whānau* because it does not benefit from the unifying power of genealogy; it is thus more fragile and has a more fluid membership since the membership is not automatically reproduced from one generation to the next. Many people will favour the genealogical *whānau* over common-purpose *whānau* when their time or energy is in short supply. To return to the *whānau* dilemma of the previous chapter, if David had not been kin, it is highly probable that he would have been asked to leave much sooner.

Second, in the common-purpose *whānau*, roles are less strictly defined than in the genealogy *whānau*. They are attributed on a voluntary basis and shift from time to time along with the membership.

Third, difficulties arise at the leadership level, since the members are often of similar ages, and a hierarchy does not naturally emerge through status related to age and experience. When elders are members, their participation helps structure the group, in terms of both relationships among its members and its activities. However, people do not always get involved for "good" or traditional reasons: some are there because of special personal or financial interests. Other members may be looking for power and status; many of the participants in my research call these people "*mana* munchers" (that is, munchers of spiritual power, authority, prestige, status), and they often disturb the structure of power.

Fourth, relatives can try to exercise power to favour their kin over non-kin, and can form cliques or subgroups that disturb the harmony of the group as a whole.

Fifth, limited resources (financial or human), as well as favouritism toward a subgroup, can compromise the accomplishment of the *kaupapa* (mission, project) of the group and thus its raison d'être.

A sixth issue is that the common-purpose *whānau* has no direct power of discipline. It does not have as strong a hold on individual members as the genealogical *whānau*, which chooses certain persons for specific roles. There is more room for negotiation in the common-purpose *whānau*, which also possibly means more opportunities for power struggles.

Seventh, the common-purpose *whānau* does not benefit from many other unifying factors. In most cases, it does not own land in common, for example, which would force people to come together for its management.

Eighth, when the mission or project is achieved, there is often insufficient reason to stay together and continue as a *whānau*.

Ninth, members have much greater freedom of involvement in a common-purpose *whānau* than in a genealogical *whānau*, which means that leaving the group is also easier. This liberty of choice is increased in the city, where there are more possibilities to choose from and more importance given to personal (as opposed to collective) experiences. This ease of leaving sometimes brings about extra work for those who stay and have to assume the leavers' responsibilities, which can in turn lead to further departures.

Tenth and finally, if the *mana* (spiritual power, authority, prestige, status) of a person's genealogical *whānau* is threatened by their involvement in common-purpose *whānau*, or by other external forces, the person will go back to invest more time and energy in their genealogical *whānau* to set the situation right and maintain the *whānau*'s *mana*.

The universe of meanings of the *whānau* has become an important element in the politics of differentiation. This is the case for common-purpose *whānau* and all organizations that "work" according to Māori/*whānau* principles, including Māori performing arts groups, Māori resource centres in mainstream institutions, Māori sports teams, Māori immersion schools and kindergartens, and bilingual units in mainstream schools.

City homes that function like *marae* are about being a *whānau* and thus about offering individuals feeling out of sorts an opportunity to be within community or simply to be themselves in an environment often conceived of as alien. The creation and maintenance of Māori places in the city, such as a *marae*-type house, are thus crucial for the coexistence of the universe of meanings of the *whānau* with the other universes of meanings of today.

The *whānau* then becomes an important symbol of "not being Pākehā."

To say that Pākehā are individually oriented and Māori collectively oriented is over-simplistic; it is preferable to avoid a strict dichotomy between the individual and the collective, but in general Māori people – like most indigenous peoples and peasant communities – place more value on the collective. The collectivity, the *whānau*, is at the very core of the traditional universe of meanings, as was made clear by the example of Kiri's *whānau*'s dilemma. In practice, Māori persons and groups have to deal with both sets of principles since Māori and Pākehā universes of meanings coexist and, to a certain extent, interpenetrate.

At the level of the nation state and New Zealand society, many factors combine to play a role in the politics of differentiation. Some government policies are directly related to this (re)emphasis on *whānau* (see chapter 1). After a decade (1984 to 1994) of Māori development policies centred on tribes, the emphasis shifted to smaller groupings, such as the subtribe and *whānau* (Durie 2001a: 189). Differentiation has also been further amplified by state decentralization and retribalization policies. In these processes, some (common-purpose) *whānau* organizations became major service providers (for example, Te Whānau o Waipareira in West Auckland).

Contextual factors have also favoured this (re)emphasis on the *whānau* within the larger politics of differentiation, including the growing awareness of the impact of colonization, the Māori cultural renaissance, and the experience of urbanization, often accompanied by a feeling of loneliness and discomfort in the city. Moreover, if Māori in the city are considered to be in a context of migration, then it is probable that the shock of experiencing the mainstream universes of meanings is less intense today than a few decades ago, thanks to technology, better working conditions, and better education. The internet, decent long-distance telephone rates, cell phones, and cheaper and better access to means of transportation, like planes, trains, and buses, all contribute to the maintenance of *whānau* links across the city/country divide and beyond the borders of New Zealand, with Durie (2001a: 194–5) alluding to the "virtual *whānau*." While this new context can allow for more fluid engagement in various universes of meanings, it also makes it easier for some to continue their engagement within the universe of meanings of the *whānau*. This is clearly the case for a good number of Māori university students who come from the country to study in Auckland universities.

In spite of that, many Māori (and this was very evident in 2001 and 2002) still experience the city as an alien place, a place that is not Māori. This feeling is reinforced when Māori experience a lack of recognition from and support in mainstream organizations. In accordance with the official policy of biculturalism, the government has made considerable efforts in recent decades to provide official publications, websites, and services in the Māori language as well as assistance and special programs for Māori. Earlier studies of Māori socioeconomic and health disparities (Durie 2001a; James Henare Māori Research Centre 2002) clearly established that Māori are both ill-served by and uncomfortable in mainstream institutions. This still holds true today for many. Some Māori will make all possible efforts to integrate into mainstream universes of meanings and to blend into the crowd. Others, on the contrary, will engage more actively with Māori universe(s) of meanings and put more emphasis on their difference.

The politics of biculturalism that stem from the treaty and a specific colonial history are linked to the politics of differentiation. The treaty was based on a fact of difference that colonization had sometimes tried to erase and sometimes re-emphasized until the "miracle of decolonisation" (Schwimmer 1999) happened. Since then, differences have been celebrated in a context of dialogue and change between the partners newly recognized through the Treaty of Waitangi Act 1975.

The present-day social and political environment, with its signs of resentment and backlash against Māori gains, favours an emphasis on symbolic competition[7] between both partners. This in turn feeds back into differentiation, and even increases polarization between the two parties. Their partner status, as recognized through the interpretation given to the Treaty of Waitangi, has also been directly threatened on several occasions. It is reasonable to think that this trend toward the polarization of New Zealand society may encourage a renewed engagement with the universe of meanings of the *whānau*. The *whānau* is considered to be a crucial site of resistance to the "peril of dilution," in particular in times of constitutional review and increasing ethnic diversification of New Zealand society. These processes generally benefit symbols of Maoritanga, like the *whānau* and the *marae*, but also today the *iwi* (tribe), giving them more symbolic power and visibility.

Within this general context, Māori often emphasize the idea that they participate on a daily basis in *two* different worlds, one being Māori and the other Pākehā or non-Māori. What emerged clearly from my research is that while Māori engage in many universes of meanings that coexist and confront each other, they do not always experience and conceive of their engagement in today's multiple worlds in a fluid way. Most participants put forward a more dichotomous vision in which everything seems to belong to either the Māori world *or* the Pākehā world. In many respects, various factors strengthen this experience and concept of "two worlds."

Māori university students told me that the *marae* and the Māori Studies Department constitute the Māori world, while "on the other side [of the parking lot]" was the Pākehā world. Margaret also explained to me that the only time she did not feel the existence of two different worlds was at international rugby matches, where everybody wanted the team representing New Zealand to win. As soon as the match ended, she said, everything returned to normal and you stopped talking and smiling to the Pākehā fellow beside you. In the car park, after the game, you can already feel that there are two different worlds, she said. The two worlds seemed to have an important embodied dimension: "You feel it!" Many boundaries between worlds are made visible through people's actions and reactions, the way they speak, the way they walk, their posture, and sometimes just the feeling of a place or the general atmosphere among people.

Cafés were clearly not part of the Māori world for many of the research participants, and this idea was particularly emphasized during my 2001–2 field research. This still holds true for many Māori, even as the New Zealand's "café culture" (Carter and Maynard 2001: 104; Latham 2003; Pearson and Kothari 2007) has begun to attract some followers from among the Māori in recent years. Notable, is a café in South Auckland where all the owners and the staff are Māori, as is the décor. However, the café serves no *kai Māori* (Māori food) with the exception of *kūmara* (sweet potato), so people often ask for boil-up nights to make it even more Māori.

Latham (2003) explains the emergence of a new urban public culture in New Zealand with the proliferation of cafés and fashionable bars and restaurants, which differs from the traditional, predominantly male public culture revolving around the public hotel (pub) and drawing on UK traditions. This new public culture now flourishing has emerged since the mid-1970s and early 1980s among young, socially liberal, tertiary-educated Pākehā. It is characterized by an aesthetics of consumption, but also by the virtues of "tolerance, diversity and creative energy" (1706). Discussing more generally how food is represented as nourishment for a multicultural New Zealand nation, Pearson and Kothari (2007: 54) speak of a "cosmopolitan chic," a "boutique multiculturalism [in which] ethnic difference becomes a resource for mainstream pleasure" (48). Among the "café culture" characteristics is clearly something to do with social class. Latham (2003) describes, for example, the process of gentrification of Auckland's inner suburbs referred to as the Greater Ponsonby – an area where the first-generation of Māori (and Pacific islanders) first migrated in the 1950s and 1960s – as one related to the development of the "café culture" and the housing boom. (See figure 2.2.) The outcome is that Ponsonby has seen a residential displacement of the older established – predominantly Māori and Pacific island – populations, and "had ceased to be a predominantly working-class community and had become a solidly middle-class one" (1706), predominantly Pākehā. The two main arterial roads of the area "are home to more than 90 cafés, restaurants and bars (or various hybrids of the three)" (1706).

The "two worlds" are also clearly part of the larger politics of differentiation in which people distinguish between people, things, and places that are (authentically) Māori and fall within the realm of the *whānau* and those that are not and do not. The emphasis on the *whānau* as a symbol of being Māori leads to the definition of criteria or markers that determine – more or less strictly according to the contexts – who (and what) is part of the *whānau* and who (and what) is not. This process involves some measure of essentialization.

Peoples' experiences and feelings must be taken seriously and the rhetorical processes as well as the practices that sometimes reinforce the dichotomy between the Māori and the Pākehā worlds and sometimes blur the boundaries or show how irrelevant they can be in certain contexts must be analysed. The boundaries between worlds (and their blurring) are not perceived or experienced in the same way by all Māori (or non-Māori). Perception depends on specific circumstances, on such factors as an individual's or group's personal and collective comfort in the different universes of meanings and in their stage of life, as well as on the larger sociopolitical context and on global forces.

Some Māori, for example, do frequent cafés. But often these are Māori from a specific socioeconomic background and are particularly used to and feel comfortable in places that are characteristic of a certain middle-class intellectual mainstream universe. Māori university students with whom I took Māori language classes also learn to frequent cafés, probably because it is part of a certain "student culture." Cafés have multiplied in recent years at university, as they have in the city more generally. From one semester to the next, I noticed that many of the Māori students who were among my first contacts at university began to enjoy going to cafés, first at university – they nearly appropriated the entire terrace of the café in the Human Sciences building for a semester – and then elsewhere in the city. It became an accepted way to relax with others and talk about university, work, personal life, and Māori events and news.

For many, it was a new experience. They were used to going out to suburban pubs and family restaurants, Chinese takeaways, and American fast food restaurants. Their reasons for going to cafés were not the same as their reasons for going to those other places. Cafés came to be mainly associated not with food and eating, but with "pleasure and a sense of well-being" (Stephens 1997, in Carter and Maynard 2001: 103). By frequenting cafés at university, the students began to internalize and embody the ways in which that type of place "works."

The dichotomy between the Pākehā and Māori worlds is also closely related to socioeconomic factors and to the social networks, places, and spaces in which people are engaged. According to their socioeconomic backgrounds, some places are not part of the Māori world for some people:

MIHI: Do you know Diane? She's from university.
JOANA: You'll know her. She is a fine looking woman, short hair. You know her, very healthy. I go to her place, she has a very, very beautiful home, very beautiful [. . .]
MIHI: I get nervous there. I, Mihi, don't feel comfortable in her home. Yeah, I spent most of the time outside, smoking cigarettes. I don't feel comfortable there. As much as I love her, you know, she's a really wonderful woman, but . . . no, I don't feel comfortable in her home.
JOANA: Just for me, it's very nice, they have like a separate dining room for formal dinners [. . .] and fluffy couch [laughter], very, it is very . . . I mean in the bathroom . . .
MIHI: Nice smelling toilet paper!
JOANA: [. . .] It's just because we are in different circles.

The situation is different for Aroha, Mere, and Maata, who are clearly at ease in mainstream worlds. They all either had or have had a Pākehā husband and benefit from socioeconomic conditions that allow them to buy what they class as "stylish" goods and clothes. They would not feel the same sense of being alien in, for example, Diane's house, and would not consider it as a different or Pākehā world, because it is also their world. So, the demarcation of the frontier between Māori and Pākehā depends on both a person's background and milieu.

The dichotomy is also linked to stereotypes and essentialist assumptions about how and what Māori should be: not too wealthy, not too slim, not too well dressed. As some Māori point out, it sometimes seems that the closer one's profile matches the statistics about, for instance, Māori poor health or precarious socioeconomic conditions, the more Māori one is, even if things tend to change with the multiplication of Māori success stories and the gradual and slow general improvement of their socioeconomic conditions. For other Māori, however, these criteria about appearances and wealth can disqualify someone from being a "real" Māori and qualify them as "urban Māori"; that is, as assimilated or fragmented Māori, as someone who is not "quite" Māori. Those who are not good enough at Māori performing arts, for example, not free enough for parties, too slim or too big to look "right," or not fluent enough in the Māori language, are sometimes excluded from the everyday life of the common-purpose *whānau*. I should specify, however, that "good" or "right" differ according to the context and the people.

I often heard comments such as "Look at her! She is dressed like a Pākehā!" This would be said about people who wear and enjoy fashionable clothing and sophisticated jewellery made of gold, for example, instead of only *pounamu* (greenstone), which has high symbolic value among Māori. In practice, being a "white Māori" or not having a "Māori look" can be used as a factor of exclusion even if someone can prove their genealogical connections and lives in most ways according to Māori principles and tradition. People who are the target of such comments often experience turbulent emotions. Some react with a strong assertiveness:

> There is this girl at university that I met. Awesome, very Pākehā-looking, fair as you, but she wanted her Māori side to come out so she would wear all the things in her hair: big long *pounamu* earrings, all the Māori-style clothing and she would wear that all the time so people would say "Oh no! She is Māori," even though she was blonde. (Mere)

So, by using Māori symbols, one will assert one's place within the *whānau* – here, the huge Māori *whānau*. Some use more specific symbols to assert their membership of more restricted groupings, like a particular Māori performing arts group or a specific tribe or subtribe. So many wear T-shirts, hats, or caps that associate them with particular groupings or with the Māori people in general. Others have traditional and contemporary tattoos that often contain the symbols of particular affiliations.

The Māori language has long been recognized as central to Māori identities. Tensions often arise between speakers and non-speakers and between those who have learned it in the countryside and those who have learned it in the city. Even the way that Māori speak English, as Kepa brought to my attention, has an effect on their recognition by others as Māori, as part of the *whānau*, and on their self-identification. Kepa explained to me, "There are those who look at me and tell [me] I am not a Māori because I don't have. I don't speak like a Māori." So he found that sometimes he adapted his mode of speaking to his audience:

> My language changes depending on whom I am speaking with, a range of modes of speaking, different modes of speaking [. . .] The whole idea of switching to different modes of speaking only came to me last year or the year before [. . .] It was an instantaneous switch and I had to switch and that is when I realised that yeah, I do change my mode of speaking. (Kepa)

These language factors seem to add to the existing tensions between Māori born in the country and raised in their tribe and Māori born in the city with, in certain cases, weaker ties with their tribe(s) and less contact with Māori tradition. But what exactly does it mean to "speak like a Māori"? Again, there are general stereotypes but the specific context of each situation is very important in determining the boundaries or markers of authenticity as well as the room for manoeuvre and scope for action – and interaction – among the people concerned.

I also found that people introduced themselves differently, depending on the addressee. They even used different names. Some take on new Māori names when they begin another period of their life during which they are particularly close to or in search of their *taha Māori* (Māori side). Some will use one of the Māori names on their birth certificate while others just take on a Māori name that is a derivative of their English name.

Starting to study the Māori language often appears to mark an important phase where many Māori decide to use a Māori name. This was the case for Fiona who began to use a Māori name and became known under that name. She wanted to make it clear that she was Māori and for her, her identity as Māori was related to her name, which is an external, public sign that tells everybody – Māori or not – that she is Māori. Reuniting with *whānau* or Māori relatives can also be the point when people take up a Māori name. The new name is part of a larger process of discovery or reconnection with their Māori side.

Matiu, who has Rarotongan (Cook Islands) as well as Māori ancestry, projected either one identity or the other, depending on the context:

> When I am with the Māori, a lot of the times, I just say "No, I'm a Coconut [nickname for Rarotongans], I'm Raro" and if I am in a situation that I can't understand, I will just go to my Raro and blame it on my Raro side, but I am a Māori when it comes to a Raro [. . .] If I stuff up and they say "you, Coconut!" where there are difficult situations, and it is easy for us to blame it on, not blame it, but you know, use your other side as a scapegoat. (Matiu)

This example also illustrates the other realities and complexities beside the dichotomous Māori/Pākehā worlds. In the Pākehā world, there would be no doubt that Matiu presents himself as Māori, but among Māori, he also sometimes plays on his Rarotongan identity. Schwimmer (2004a, 1999) convincingly highlights that Māori are skilled in operating on several different levels of meanings at the same time. They play on the potential for polysemy of words in both Māori and English, which allows them to respond to the main demands of all the universes of meanings involved. Then, depending on the space/time and circumstances, some aspects of the universes of meanings are favoured over others. The ambiguity inherent in many Māori narratives, acts, and discourses becomes a powerful resource in dealing with particular *whānau* members or wider forces, such as the New Zealand state.

One of the participants in my research often said that he lived in the Māori world while urban Māori lived in the Pākehā one, denying them, by the same token, a "true" or "real" Māori identity. He often called them *rīwai* or potato – that is, brown on the outside and white inside – meaning that the only Māori thing about them was the colour of their skin. The use of this expression is quite widespread by people who claim with a certain arrogance that *they* know the *true* way to be Māori. Other expressions in use include *Ngāti* Tupperware or *Ngāti* plastic. The prefixes "*Ngāti*," "*Ngāi*," and "*Ngā*" mean "of that person." They are used to connect traditional groupings to an eponymous ancestor. So the *iwi* descended from Porou, Whatua, Puhi, and Tahu will be called Ngāti Porou, Ngāti Whatua, Ngā Puhi, and Ngāi Tahu, for instance (Waymouth 2003). In that sense, calling people *Ngāti* Tupperware says that they have lost their ancestral affiliation, they do not know where they come from, they are a nobody in Māori terms. And "Tupperware," like "plastic," is used to emphasize the artificial or inauthentic character of a person in his or her identification as Māori. Others will say that these "inauthentic others" are "Pakehafied." These rhetorical categories are interesting to examine, since almost everyone – except for a few people of great *mana* (spiritual power, authority, prestige, status) who are widely recognized as embodying "true Maoriness" – is someone else's potato.

Such name-calling causes a lot of suffering. As emphasized by Sissons (2005),

> [the] requirements of authenticity can, in themselves, become oppressive. Oppressive authenticity operates primarily as a mechanism of exclusion; those who cannot be placed securely within one of two categories – "native" or "settler" – become people out of place. They do not properly belong in the official scheme of things; they are impure, inauthentic and too often become an excluded middle. (39)

People who are called these names – usually behind their back or in very subtle ways – are often deeply hurt. The unpleasant names often touch the sore points of issues that they have grappled with for years. When they become more self-confident and know more about Māori and Pākehā universes of meanings, however, they are not as affected by these names and by others' opinions about their Maoriness. Mere explained:

> But I can't be totally bicultural if I don't have the *reo* [Māori language], that is my personal view. I am going to be more Pākehā until that happens, that side is going to be stronger than the Māori side [. . .] I just have that feeling and then, I could be wrong. I have a strong sense of *tikanga* [tradition]. I don't know the *reo*, I can't speak *te reo*. I understand a lot, but I can't speak it. I am not a comfortable speaker, but I do embrace *tikanga* more, so I don't know if that makes me more qualified. I don't know, but being able to sit back and see both sides and having that balance and you know, when things don't upset you, but it doesn't mean you are any less Māori,

it just means that you are past that stage of worrying about those kinds of things [being told that she is Pakehafied]. (Mere)

Aroha had one explanation for certain persons or groups qualifying others as "Pakehafied":

I heard people say "Oh! You're pakehafied" [. . .] But . . . what is that? I think it's because I met . . . I can be with different people. I can get on with you, you're not a Māori. You come completely from a different place [. . .] Sitting with you, I feel comfortable [. . .] maybe it's because I feel spiritual, maybe that's why I feel so comfortable [. . .] It's knowing where I come from, but it's also having that element of belief, of spirituality, of believing in the power of our ancestors. (Aroha)

It does indeed seem that those who call others "Pakehafied" feel uncomfortable with these people who can move through different worlds so easily. They may feel jealous of this ease and will simply eject the bicultural person out of the "us," out of the *whānau*. Bicultural people can claim they belong to both worlds, to a certain degree, and can move more freely between the worlds than their non-bicultural relatives or colleagues. They are also the ones who can be most easily excluded from the *whānau*, being either too Pākehā or not Māori enough, and certainly something other than clearly identifiably Māori. Bicultural people can be very disturbing. In highly politicized situations, their allegiances are often doubted and they may even be accused of being traitors.

But bicultural people who are used to living, for example, in the central or northern sectors of Auckland are not necessarily comfortable in all Māori environments. Some of them will certainly not be at ease in parts of South Auckland where there is widespread poverty among Māori and where they will be regarded as *rīwai* (potato). For their part, South Auckland Māori can appear to some to lack enough pride to be "real" Māori, due to their physical appearance or poor housing conditions. They can also be perceived as acculturated because they never show up on the *marae* in the country for funerals or other events. Most of the time, however, this is not because they do not want to go, but because they cannot. They do not have a car or they do not have enough money to take the bus or they must stay in the city to look after their children or other dependants. And, they may feel that they will not be well received after such a long absence. It is a vicious circle. These are the people then perceived by others as potato or urban, acculturated or disconnected Māori.

Stereotypes and essentializing processes are not only created and affirmed by Māori, they are also and very importantly imposed in practice by the state and the media, including Māori-controlled ones. Various arms of the state, for example, require that Māori make their representations and projects "authentic" in order to be heard or obtain funding. In official political discourse, programs, and campaigns, certain Māori symbols and certain Māori ways are favoured, and these are then used by Māori to identify themselves and to present themselves to others.

This idea of an "authentic national culture," as Schwimmer (2003) underlines, has long roots in the modern doctrine of the "nation" according to which culture has an eternal essence. This doctrine invites – if not obliges – Māori leaders to personify and fight for this essence. The essentializing process is also reinforced by certain categories of people (Māori and non-Māori) who have economic as well as political interests in the processes described here, including anthropologists[8] and other social scientists.

Rata (2000) suggests that a rising Māori bourgeoisie was formed in the 1980s through the process of claims settlements, which imposed its agenda and took control of newly restored resources, at once controlling capital and maintaining the conical class structure. However, it is necessary to understand that the people who form certain types of elites[9] or leaders play an extremely important role in the relationships between Māori and the state as guardians of the social and symbolic order. Indeed, they do so through the cultural transmissions that they secure and that benefit all Māori.

Schwimmer (2003: 169) explains that the role of these elites or leaders is to share their knowledge with the general population as tools for resistance, and to convey the messages of the minority population to the state. In doing so, they must convince the state of the authenticity of (1) their status as representatives, (2) their ability to convey the popular feelings and desires of the minority population, and (3) their historical and cultural knowledge. This is also how certain Māori intellectuals, for example, who now form a Māori middle class (Rata 2000), have secured a specialized knowledge as well as an authority in particular fields of research and expertise (see, for example, Webster 1998; Rata 2002).

The almost unavoidable idea of a supposedly "authentic" or "more real" Māori identity and a tradition claimed and affirmed in different ways and different contexts by these various groups is a powerful political object and an important tool in negotiations among Māori. Most importantly, it also has a significant role on the public stage in the relationships of Māori with the majority population and the state. Friedman (2004: 76) rightly says that these elites or leaders "are, after all, the focal points for political unity and often political action as well, pivots in the competition for funding and rights." No doubt some Māori leaders today, like elites everywhere, deliberately use the essentializing ethnic discourse to conceal their own material and political interests, but this certainly was not (and is not) always or even often the case.[10]

Local leaders work hard in the field, often to the point of exhaustion, campaigning for years in voluntary associations, getting a university education, developing their professional skills, and building the ideological framework of their movement while trying to carefully balance their involvement in mainstream worlds with their commitment to the worlds of their family (including their genealogical and common-purpose *whānau*), tribes and neighbourhoods, through mutual obligations and responsibility. To be effective, they also have to balance local and global activism.

Māori leaders need the support of "ordinary people" who demand that their representatives be well grounded in local reality and genuinely connected to local issues, family, and tribe(s). This is how leaders can make the movement and its ideological framework relevant to people's everyday realities and capable of bringing them together. Schwimmer (2003: 167–8) reminds us that all the key events of the Māori sovereignty movement – for example, the 1975 Land March, the international museum exhibition *Te Maori: Maori Art from New Zealand Collections* (1984–5), the Māori language revitalization movement, the 2004 *Hikoi* in opposition to the Foreshore and Seabed Bill – had this unifying aspect in which the elite as well as "ordinary" people played essential and active roles.

Both Māori elites and "ordinary" Māori thus actively use stereotypes to promote particular kinds of Maoriness or ways of being Māori to make their world(s) more certain. This is an important part of the politics of differentiation that helps to further affirm the existence of "two worlds," one Māori, one Pākehā (or simply non-Māori). The essentialist dichotomy then functions as a political strategy and as a tool to exercise power, deliver ideological messages, and construct justifications. It aims sometimes at excluding others and sometimes at proving one's identity as Māori. The languages of indigeneity that have been more widely used by Māori in recent years are just another way to emphasize the dichotomy as part of the same political strategy, the same politics of differentiation.

With this closer look at the Māori and the Pākehā worlds and the boundaries between them, it becomes clear that they are not well defined. There are also other worlds, which leads to the idea of a multiplicity of possible universes of meanings, and the heteroglossic and changing ways that people can imagine themselves through these worlds. In listening attentively to Joana and Mihi, it would appear that "our" (Māori) world is the world of the *whānau*. The world of the *whānau* is not necessarily entirely Māori – just think of Kiri's house, which includes Pākehā and people of Chinese and Tongan descent. "Our" world is the intimate world of the "us," while the "other" world is everything outside the intimate circle or *whānau*. Joana and Mihi were not simply reaffirming the dichotomy between Māori and Pākehā. Rather, they revealed the fluidity, interpenetration, and complex character of the various worlds as they are lived.

> JOANA: Pākehā environment . . . [. . .] I don't have a lot to do with that. I mean, my friends are Māori, people I work with are Māori, I don't . . . I mean the environment is Pākehā, but it doesn't affect [me] like that because at the end of the day, the people I associate with . . . they are Māori. I don't see my life as being any different . . . all I see is that it's good for Māori to live in, among a group of other people.
>
> NATACHA: Do you feel like that too?
>
> MIHI: I don't know. I only know the same *whānau* in West Auckland. I don't know anyone else. Cousins, yeah.
>
> NATACHA: Like at university and . . .
>
> MIHI: All my friends are Māori there.
>
> NATACHA: So you don't consider me as your friend [joking].
>
> MIHI: I mean, yeah! [laughs]
>
> JOANA: But that's what we mean, you fit in. I don't look at things as a "Pākehā world," I don't look at you and say "You're not Māori."
>
> NATACHA: It's not separate like that.
>
> JOANA: No. It's not that black and white. It can't be, I mean.
>
> MIHI: I have never really thought about it.
>
> JOANA: But it can't be because . . .
>
> MIHI: Like for me, I have never really thought of that . . . you're white and we're all black kind of thing. I have never . . . I don't know . . .

JOANA: We keep into our world. It's like we live in different worlds and when we say that all our friends and everything we do is Māori, because those Pākehā who come over to this side, and it's our . . .
MIHI: And it's part of the life.
JOANA: It's part of this world.
NATACHA: Your world.
JOANA: Yeah, yeah, it's like we have created our world in another world, you know what I mean?
NATACHA: And you don't go out very often in the other one?
SIMONE: We don't need to. There is enough going on in our world.
JOANA: We just basically, we work, we socialize on the weekend, we have each other's children and that's our life. There is no . . . something else on the other side that I want to see. I don't make a point of going to places . . . that I don't know. Because they're not my friends, I don't have Pākehā friends! [laughter]

Thus, in addition and sometimes in contradiction to the classic dichotomy between "the two worlds," participants in this research referred to other worlds or other universes of meanings within the Māori world itself.

Many participants in this research mentioned that those who are intensely involved in the Māori world and entirely reliant on the *whānau* might encounter problems in the long run. Sooner or later, other members of the *whānau* might have their own preoccupations and problems or a common-purpose *whānau* might break down, which can lead to feelings of loneliness and isolation and the loss of a support network. There is a lot of pressure on *whānau* links in today's world, where people are pushed to perform as individuals. At the same time, this unavoidable individualistic tendency also allows *whānau* members to be more flexible in participating in *whānau* life and engaging in different universes of meanings. This flexibility also shapes their identities and the heteroglossic ways in which they engage in both the so-called Māori world and the wider society.

Ruka explained the choices he made to balance the Māori world of the *marae* and the *whānau* and the larger world in which he also participated with his family:

I used to be here [on the *marae*] just about every day [. . .] We were here on Tuesday night, Thursday night, Friday, Saturday, and Sunday nights, so in some cases my whole life was revolving a bit too much around the *marae*. Hence, I ended up going out and making affiliations with other groups and organizations. I just went and played rugby league for instance and went and did some sporting activities and that, just break up my weekly routine and that. Because I found a lot of people that I know here, friends and that I have on the *marae*, if you were to take the *marae* away from them, they would have nothing. So I am very much quite the person who likes to still interact with the rest of the community, which is why I went to play league for a season [. . .] The *marae* is very much a large part of my family's life, but it is not our whole life. We have other goals and other aspirations that we would like our children to achieve and for us to do that we need to interact with other parts of society as well as that to become a reality [. . .] I think it is for a lot of Māori on this *marae* anyway, the *marae* becomes that much a part of their life that when it comes time for them to head out and seek out their educational or vocational pathways, they are a bit intimidated by that side of the world because they have only kept themselves on this side of the world or on a *marae* side of the line and they are very intimidated by those responses, for the reaction they will get when they meet up again with the greater community, so with that sense I think it's very crucial that they grow up respecting the *marae*, but making it a part of their life and not their whole life. Because they could be setting themselves up for . . . a rude awakening later on. (Ruka)

Mere similarly felt that for Māori to be able to make positive changes for Māori, it was important for them to engage and balance their achievements in both worlds, a skill that is encouraged in many educational centres.

Usually, students come into an institute, they are very individualistic. They come in for themselves and "I am going to pass, no matter what. I don't care about the next person." And then, through coming to the resource centre, our concepts there are yes, we do that, but we don't put the qualification up there at the highest . . . we put being Māori alongside qualifications so we are walking in both worlds, but there is that balance and that is what we try to achieve, is a good balance. (Mere)

For some, having a Pākehā partner opens their eyes to their Māori identity, Māori particularities, and the Māori world in general. It also sometimes creates an urge to rebalance their lives in both worlds or address their Māori side if it has been neglected. This was the case for Mere, for whom cultural differences with her husband led to a separation:

> I spent a whole year once just *hui*-hopping around the place, just learning *te reo* [Māori language] and that was good. I learnt a lot in that year [. . .] Anything Māori . . . 1992 [. . .] the thing is when you are married in a mixed marriage. Before that there wasn't any obvious difference . . . well . . . between me and other people. Being in a mixed marriage, there were things that come out but you think . . . I don't believe this, there was a difference the way you think, the way you do things [. . .] The way you think about family it is different where it never came up before. It was never staring at you in the face, so it was different views [. . .] I think that was it. That probably was it that made me think I didn't belong here, not totally. Something is missing. Otherwise, I could have just gone on and on and I have Dick to thank for, yeah but I think the mixed marriage was the icing on the cake. (Mere)

Aroha, on the contrary, felt that having a Pākehā partner allowed her to balance her involvement in different universes of meanings. Her partner supported her in everything she did – Māori or not. He was himself engaged in the Māori world and actively participated in the life of Aroha's *whānau* and tribe. He was even chosen as a trustee of their land. Aroha explained:

> It was a little bit awkward at first [. . .], but now, he's their latest trustee on our land trust. The Pākehā is our last. They did not ask me, they asked him! [laughter] [. . .] she rang and asked him to be the new trustee. He had been elected on while he did not know he was nominated. They did not ask me! [laughter] At first, I thought it was so weird and it's like he's the only one that is not a direct descendant, he's Pākehā [. . .] He has always been helping and he feels comfortable with my own family, because he's a good person, he's a good man: fair, honest, integrity, hard-working, he would have been a good chief! Just the wrong colour. (Aroha)

This also demonstrates that Pākehā too, engage in Māori universes of meanings and that the boundaries are not always clear cut, at least up to a certain point. They become more visible, however, when situations are highly politicized or when resources, money, or a position of power or status are at stake. The recent reinforcement of genealogy criteria and the retribalization process have made this even clearer (see Rata 2000 for illustrations).

As part of a deliberate balancing of Māori involvement in the so-called Māori/Pākehā worlds, *whānau* have slightly altered the tradition of choosing certain people to take on specific roles or achieve specific goals.[11] Following traditional practice, some *whānau* members are chosen and raised as caretakers of the traditions of the universe of meanings of the *whānau*, but now others will be raised as bicultural persons, able to go from one world to the other. The latter will be freed of most of the everyday *whānau* responsibilities and will be supported in their career or studies or both. The particular mission that a person is given relates to the well-being of the *whānau* or Māori at large. It might be preparing to become the next chief or elder, or a good Māori lawyer, professor, or advisor for the *whānau* or for Māori in general. Having been thus mandated by the *whānau*, people in this position will feel a definite pressure to succeed in the Pākehā world.

Aroha was chosen in this way, and she was very sensitive to the desires of her *whānau*. However, she had also made choices for the benefit of herself and her own small family. She decided to leave her tribal area because the pressure to achieve was too high and she needed her own space. Her house was open to her *whānau*, but when her father came for a weekend and filled the house with people, she felt that it was too much. She needed to be in control of her physical environment, which was not always possible in a house in which *marae* principles are applied, for example – things will be broken or mislaid, personal space will shrink, if not disappear altogether. Similarly, for her *whānau*'s sake and for a certain time, Kiri had to abandon her dreams of redecorating and renovating her house with French doors, a barbecue area, a garden, and a big study all of her own.

Thus, when the workings of the *whānau* are examined, it becomes clear that while the universe of meanings of the *whānau* is a crucial element of Māori identity, it does not always and in all contexts have the same import. Nor is it significant for all Māori. Most, if not all, Māori combine engagements in at least two main universes of meanings, the one of the *whānau* and a Pākehā-oriented or mainstream one. Sometimes these realms of interpretations or worldviews also have components that seem incompatible. Dealing with or engaging in multiple universes of meanings often creates dilemmas.

According to actual circumstances and global forces, Māori will then privilege certain aspects of particular universes of meanings. They negotiate their multiple engagements through a complex combination of values and principles that unfold through practice and experience. It must therefore be emphasized that there is no real dichotomy between Māori and their realms of interpretation on one side and Pākehā and their realms of interpretation on the other, even if these realms are experienced as dichotomous by many people in various circumstances.

In practice, in the lived world, Māori and Pākehā people alike internalize multiple universes of meanings and develop multiple identities and ways of engaging within these worlds. Even if Māori are generally more bicultural, some Pākehā do internalize Māori universes of meanings, especially if, like Andrew, they actively participate in the daily life of a *whānau*.

Only fictional characters like the eponymous Potiki of the novel by Patricia Grace (1986) can exist simply within one universe of meanings – the universe of meanings of the *whānau*.[12] Even some mythical figures, like the little girl in the Witi Ihimaera (1987) novel *The Whale Rider* (as of 2002, also a film of international renown), negotiate their involvement in more than one universe of meanings in a heteroglossic way. With so many commitments to so many universes of meanings – taking in city life, work, parenting, and other responsibilities – the family network sometimes closes in on itself and the focal point for daily attention becomes the smaller family unit made up of the parent(s) and the children. This unit corresponds to the nuclear or single-parent families of the mainstream universe of meanings. For Māori, this smaller unit regularly includes one or more grandparent, and therefore grandchildren.

So, while the *whānau* works as an important and specifically Māori universe of meanings when there is a need for it, in other circumstances, conditions of everyday life often pressure Māori to concentrate on a more restricted kinship group and participate in the universe of meanings of the modern, mainstream family, which has different general characteristics and guiding principles and is based on other sociohistorical foundations and a different realm of interpretation.

The mainstream nuclear family(ies)[13] has had historical and cultural dominance over other kinship models in a colonized context such as New Zealand's, not least because it is the model apparently best suited to the guiding principles and demands of the capitalist, neoliberal economy. The mainstream family is thus linked to a global time/space that favours it, which illustrates again that universes of meanings are themselves part of larger power relations and can be subordinated to larger, even globalized forces.

For Māori who are involved in a *whānau* network – kin-oriented or not – and who take part in the public life of New Zealand or the Pākehā world by having a job, studying, or exercising their rights and responsibilities as citizens, tensions are, again, inevitable between the universe of meanings of the *whānau* and other mainstream universes of meanings, or simply between Māori and Pākehā worlds. Indeed, their participation in the larger society – especially as a worker or student – is very demanding in terms of time, performance, and availability. One cannot easily leave a workplace if a child in the *whānau* is sick or if an elder asks for assistance. Nevertheless, one is expected to do so as a member of the *whānau*, according to *whānau* values and principles.

Today, however, most people in the *whānau* understand that members have responsibilities and obligations not only toward the *whānau* but also toward their employers. They also understand that fulfilling their obligations toward employers guarantees regular incomes and thus, *whānau* well-being. Those who feel powerless to help their *whānau* members as much as they should or would like to often feel guilty about it, nonetheless.

The interaction between the *whānau* and the modern family is not, however, a place of constant and insurmountable struggle. Some succeed well in combining both or multiple engagements. The presence of different family models in today's world also allows some people greater reflexivity and heteroglossic possibilities. People's involvement, however, will vary according to a range of factors: personal choice, pressure to conform, life-stage, larger sociopolitical context, history of the relationships, mixed marriage, multiple belongings. Signs from the supernatural or spiritual worlds and the wishes of elders are also very important in engagement(s) in various universes of meanings.

For some, also, there is simply no choice and thus no negotiation possible between the modern family and the *whānau*, or the so-called Māori or Pākehā worlds. Because of their upbringing, they live entirely within the framework of the modern family. Their connections to their *whānau* are very limited or even nonexistent. At some point in their life, however, certain experiences can make them (re)discover the universe of meanings of the *whānau*, perhaps through marriage or friendship. For others, negative *whānau* experiences, such as abuse, or simply other experiences in the larger society may lead them gradually or abruptly away from the universe of meanings of the *whānau*.

Some contexts offer more space for reflexivity and freedom of choice than others, and some people and groups have more options to choose from than others. The habitus (Bourdieu 1977, 1980) also plays an important role in making participation in one universe of meanings or the other "natural," according to one's background and socialization. Those who participate in a house based on *marae* principles on a daily basis, for example, are usually much more involved in the universe of meanings of the *whānau*. Although they might sometimes like to have more personal space, or might sometimes feel under pressure to conform to mainstream universes of meanings, the world of the *whāanau* is a very real part of their everyday lives.

However, the political context also leads certain people and groups to favour one universe of meanings over another, sometimes in spite of the force of habitus. After the Māori renaissance, for example, which took place during a time of global decolonization, many who were socialized in the universe of meanings of the mainstream family wanted to "recover" or "reactivate" the traditional universe of meanings of Māori, so they worked hard to achieve that goal.

In this analysis, I have tried to avoid taking the strength of *whānau* links for granted. Other forms of belonging (gender, age, sexuality, social background, experiences from other places and other kinds of groupings) can eclipse the meaning of the universe of meanings of the *whānau* for persons and groups, either for a short time or for good. Genealogical or kinship links should not, therefore, always be seen as primary, and other factors and forms of belonging must be explored. These other factors can sometimes be just as important as genealogy in understanding engagement within diverse universes of meanings.

But in the confrontation with other universes of meanings, the *whānau* is still alive and well.

This was confirmed by the survey by Te Hoe Nuku Roa Team (1999: 89). The team found that during the twelve months preceding the survey, 48.8 per cent of Auckland Māori adults had made contact with their *whānau* (excluding members of their own household) "several times," and 32.5 per cent had made contact more than once a month. Over the same period, more than 50 per cent had stayed with their *whānau* a few to several times and more than 60 per cent had had their *whānau* to stay with them a few to several times (see also Cunningham, Stevenson, and Tassell 2005). The vibrancy and importance of the *whānau* is also illustrated by an expanded meaning, known as *kaupapa whānau* (common-purpose *whānau*), which includes non-kin.

The forces behind engagement in or disengagement from various universes of meanings are sometimes contradictory and sometimes convergent but are always complex and heteroglossic. The politics of differentiation both nourish and are nourished by government policies as well as by ethnic/cultural politics.

The attitudes of Pākehā (and others) toward Māori and stigmatization of Māori also accentuate the politics of differentiation on a large scale and may even contribute to a more active engagement in the *whānau* and a parallel retreat (which can only be partial) from other universes of meanings. The universe of meanings of the *whānau* is thus a critical and, I would add, effective site of resistance to state hegemony and mainstream universes of meanings, as well as an important space of affirmation and participation in society. To some extent, the politics of differentiation – and the larger sociopolitical context – have helped essentialize differences and boundaries between the universe of meanings of the *whānau* (and possibly other Māori universes of meanings)[14] and the mainstream universes of meanings and even between Māori and Pākehā.

But the boundaries are not clearly or neatly delimited. The limits of a universe of meanings are met in practice and depend on specific circumstances and the ordering of values linked to history, power relationships, and a broader ideological framework that is often internalized or embodied. The same flexibility and vagueness is characteristic of the universes of meanings themselves and of the identities of the people engaged within them.

This chapter has raised important issues of comfort. This is particularly salient when Māori discuss their particular relationships with the "other" world, the Pākehā world. What is fundamental for most Māori is the need to feel and be comfortable. For many, being comfortable simply means being Māori – which is therefore being "different." Being Māori implies a whole set of everyday relationships and ways of doing things. It means learning and performing traditional chants, songs, and "dance," traditional fighting arts, prayers, and so on. Being Māori is also translated through a way of walking, a way of talking, a way of looking at others, and a way of dressing with Māori symbols such as greenstones, Māori or tribal/*whānau* T-shirts, woven flax handbags, or backpacks.

Being Māori is most often not about an elaborate discourse or ideology. It is associated with everyday life and the embodiment or internalization of a set of principles, values, and meanings in a lived world. It is being part of a *whānau* and behaving as a *whānau* member – a brother, a cousin, a sister. This is not alien to the rhetoric about being a "real" or "true" Māori. The same is true for place-making, place-marking, and engagement with places. It is not disconnected from the nation of New Zealand at large and the ideology about the Māori place within the nation state. It is just another facet of it. This facet also connects with the politics of differentiation as expressed through the paradigm of the *whānau*.

Conclusion: Interconnected Places and Autonomous Spaces

The *whānau* and Māori houses in the city, along with *marae* and other Māori meeting places, are important sites and spaces for cultural recovery and affirmation, but they also allow for mobilization and engagement in the larger world. We have seen that Māori engage with the larger society on their own terms; that is, through the upholding of their identity as Māori and by affirming *whānau* values, Māori ways of being, and Māori places such as *marae* and houses based on *marae* principles. This affirmation is part of a larger movement that is creating places and spaces for Māori in the wider society, as well as allowing for more autonomy and decolonization.

The type of house that is referred to as being like a *marae* is a refuge for those who, by habitus, engage in the universe of meanings of the *whānau*, or for those who consciously want to regain the principles and values of what is, for them, something that has been lost. The houses are safe, secure, and comfortable places where a person is accepted for who he or she is, welcomed as a *whānau* member, and where a person can feel at home.

But these refuges cannot simply be seen as places of retreat and withdrawal from the larger society and the world. They are central to the expression and imagination of Māori identities. They are crucial to the consolidation of the group and of what *being* Māori means. Houses based on *marae* principles are a significant site for survival and continuity, but also for change. The security and comfort they provide in economic, physical, and emotional terms are important but so is the possibility they offer for thinking about being part of a group.

This type of house is where people negotiate and make collective decisions about *whānau* positions that will then be fed into tribal or school meetings, into sport or voluntary association meetings, into the ballot boxes of local and general elections, onto particular agendas for action in the workplace, into Parliament and, ultimately, into international forums such as indigenous transnational association conferences or UN meetings in Geneva or in New York. It allows for the engagement of *whānau* members in public beyond the *whānau* and gives them support as members of a group. And this group support is a significant factor in comfort.

A *marae*-like house is an important place for meeting *whānau* members, for exchanging news and gossip, and for keeping alive and maintaining social relationships among Māori who live in the city, between Māori city-dwellers and Māori who live in rural areas, between Māori who live inside and outside New Zealand, and between Māori and their non-Māori allies or relatives. If the relationships are not always face to face, they are at least symbolic. Places like these houses are very powerful. They make it possible for Māori to imagine and be something other than or something more than mere individuals in a larger society where they may not always recognize themselves and often feel uncomfortable.

Advances in technological tools of communication are important in strengthening these relationships, not only at a symbolic level, but also in a real and practical way. Depending on each *whānau*'s needs and possibilities, *whānau* members can use the telephone (landline telephone or mobile phone) and the internet to communicate and keep each other informed. These technologies bring greater immediacy to relationships with Māori who live in other areas or with Māori transnational migrants. They give a feeling of the absentees' presence to those who have stayed at home. The reverse is also true. The technologies give to those who are away a feel of home and of the *whānau*'s presence in their everyday life away from home.

There are also better possibilities for travelling, and thus for a real presence at the *whānau* house and *marae* from time to time. Technology also allows for better consultation processes and greater consensus in the everyday "workings" of the house and in other *whānau* experiences, as well as for effective official representations at different levels within and outside Maoridom. Coordination between different Māori places has been improved. The *whānau*, the group, the fact of being Māori

– even when one is physically absent from the *whānau* house, from the *marae*, and from New Zealand – is more immediate.

Since many of the participants in my research compared their city houses to a *marae*, it is important to consider the inherent character of *marae* as forums for discussion and, ultimately, consensus. Éric Schwimmer expressed this idea precisely in 1952. A young employee at the Ministry of Maori Affairs at the time, he described his view of the magazine *Te Ao Hou/The New World*, a government-sponsored publication of which he was the editor from 1952 to 1961.[1] He saw it as a "*marae* on paper" (Schwimmer 1952, see also Allen 2002, chapter 1; Schwimmer 2004b; Gagné and Campeau 2008; Kawharu 2008). He used the term "*marae*" to refer to a forum for discussion and exchange, an ideal of openness and inclusiveness (Allen 2002: 46). Schwimmer was thus using the word symbolically, evoking wider connotations than Durie (1998: 221), who says "the *marae* is the most enduring forum for debate and decision making," meaning a mode of discussion or a locus of interactions among kin, land, and ancestors. The emphasis on exchange and sharing seems to coincide with certain aspects of Tauroa and Tauroa's (1986) conception of *marae*. Durie (2001a: 72) adds that "[w]hat is important about a *marae* is not necessarily the physical structure, but the exercise of encounters and values that might otherwise remain dormant or seem at odds with the wider community." According to Schwimmer, the "*marae* on paper" allows for the staging of *hui* (assemblies, gatherings, meetings) – virtual ones – to bring together and exchange different Māori thoughts and opinions (Allen 2002: 46). "The concept of making the journal into a '*marae* on paper' (*Te Ao Hou* 1952) was aimed . . . at stimulating a cultural revival," Schwimmer (2004b: 11) wrote recently. In his view, the *marae* opened possibilities and new spaces. There must have been validity to Schwimmer's view, since the journal *Te Ao Hou/The New World* enjoyed great popularity among Māori during Schwimmer's editorship. Moreover, the permanent head of his department, who was a prominent Māori, let him continue (Schwimmer 2004b). Schwimmer was also guided by Māori who did not work for the government, people like Reweti Kohere, Wiremu Parker, and Pei Te Hurinui Jones, with whom he usually discussed the journal. "My role was a menial one: *Te Ao Hou* was made as much by these others who prompted me" (2004b: 12). *Te Ao Hou* thus endured due to warm responses from Māori outside and within the Department of Māori Affairs in spite of some Pākehā opposition (Schwimmer, unpublished note, April 2006, in Gagné and Campeau 2008: 17).

Graham Hingangaroa Smith (1997) wrote at the end of the 1990s that his own PhD dissertation "co-opts the 'marae' format, that is the values, rules and practices embedded in the formal public forum of the traditional marae context (traditional speaking arena). Thus the thesis becomes a 'marae' . . . to put forward a 'kauhau' (address) and to lay out a 'kaupapa' (a thesis)" (47). As such, a *marae* consists of the opening of a public forum, a public expression, and thus participation in the public scene where a *kaupapa* (plan, scheme, proposal) is put forward. The *marae*, interpreted in that sense, supposes a movement outward, an opening onto/of a larger space.

So when Māori compare their city house to a *marae*, they are speaking not only of unconditional love and reciprocity in a caring and warm environment, but also about responsibility, debates around all kinds of issues, consensus, and interconnectedness. The *marae* is, therefore, characterized by its openness. Durie (2001a: 90), writing about *marae* patterns of thinking and behaving, says the direction of energy on *marae* is outwards, away from smaller and toward larger levels, as compared with non-*marae* environments where the direction is inwards, toward smaller units. In a *marae*, the relationships are endpoints, while individualism is the focus in non-*marae* environments.

This emphasis on exchange and discussion in an open atmosphere corresponds to what I observed at 30 Aroha Street and elsewhere. Discussions and debates, particularly, took place when elders like Hiko and Teria were present. More people, then, converged on the house to discuss solutions to different problems that often reached far beyond the house and its people: the schooling of the children, involvement at the workplace, decisions about house or car maintenance, *marae* renovation, funding for a trip to Wellington to take part in a march or to visit a special exhibition at the Museum of New Zealand Te Papa Tongarewa, the tribe's claim to the Waitangi Tribunal, and even the master's thesis topic of one of the *whānau* members. Exchanges also often took place about the proper Māori way to do certain things, about traditions, and about how the *whānau*'s actions were going to make a difference for the group and for Māori at large. At the end of these discussions and debates, a consensus was generally reached on a *kaupapa* (plan, proposal, direction) to adopt, and people were already in agreement or rapidly moving into alignment with that consensus. Discussions were most often about places and spaces outside the house, or involved people, things, and actions in a wider space.

The *whānau* and Māori cosmogony, in general, suppose a high degree of openness. The interconnectedness of everything in the universe is emphasized: "From the mind-heart came darkness and the *kore*, the nothingness which yet holds the potential for everything to come. And from them came the *hau*, the breath of life, producing all forms of the world of light by genealogical engagement" (Salmond 2000: 40). So, everything in the cosmos is seen as related in some way to every other thing in a network of genealogical connection. All share the same *hau*, the same "wind of life" (38) or vital essence (Williams 2000 [1971]: 39). *Whakapapa* (genealogy), then, does not have as restricted a meaning as we give to it in the Western view of the universe (see also Carter 2003b; Waymouth 2003). As mentioned earlier, it is not only or mainly a list of names even if this list works as an entry to the network and associated "integrated knowledge system" (Carter 2003b: 13). Genealogy is founded on the Māori account of the creation of the universe in which "each form of life came together with another to make something new in a network of genealogical connection, [while] in the Christian account, God created the world by splitting its parts into binary sets. The deity was an analytic logician" (Salmond 2000: 42).[2] The image of the *kūmara* (sweet potato) vines is widely used today as an illustration of the persistence of this worldview (for example, Metge 1995; James Henare Māori Research Centre 2002). Māori are always looking for connections, whoever and wherever they meet. The same *kūmara* vines that allow information to circulate, also allow people to connect to each other. As explained by the James Henare Māori Research Centre (2002),

> the *whānau* is always remaking itself over time, growing and accommodating new relationships as old ones are transformed through marriage, birth, ageing, migration, separation and death. In this light, the lines of association through which *whanaungatanga* extends itself might be seen as tendrils of a *kūmara* vine, extending outwards to embrace new people and putting down roots to nourish new relationships of marriage, friendship and descent. (3: 43)

Whanaungatanga is defined, in the glossary of the James Hanere Māori Research Centre (2002), as "the processes by which *whānau* and other consanguineal and affinal links, cohesion and mutuality are maintained" (3: 155). In everyday life, the network of kinship and alliances emerges as a web of relationships between people, places, ancestors, and other living and inanimate beings. To describe any collective action or interaction is also to make a relational statement.

Salmond (2000: 52–3) explains, however, that relationships do not necessarily imply amity between the parties. On the contrary, as she illustrates, the relationship can be that of *hoa riri* (angry companion) as opposed to *hoa* (friend), and relationships will be managed through the relational principles of *utu*, which implies a return for something received, whether good or bad, reciprocity, compensation; *mana*, which means spiritual power, authority, status; and *tapu*, which implies restrictions in terms of sacredness or pollution. This book has shown these principles in action.

The *whānau* relationships and the language of kinship or genealogy are used to trace the relationships between people and the rest of the universe. If we look at the specifics of everyday life, Durie draws the same conclusion: the *whānau* (and I will add the house based on *marae* principles) connect people, places, and spaces and because of that are empowering for the people. The

capacity to empower, *whakamana*, is a *whānau* function that facilitates the entry of members of the *whānau* into the wider community. The *whānau* might be the gateway into the *marae*, or into sport, or to school, or to work. Rather than individuals negotiating the terms of their own entry, the *whānau* is able to exercise its wider influence to ease the passage, to advocate on behalf of its people. (Durie 2001a: 202)

The *whānau* has a long history of being effective. In manual occupations, entry was and is most often determined by *whānau*. In the migration to the city *whānau* have often played a key role in the transition and integration of its members into the job market and social networks (Metge 1964; Williams 2010), the *whānau* house being the transition place par excellence. The *whānau* is a practical link between places and people and the house is a gateway to other spaces and places, even as it reaffirms its central role in strengthening the *whānau* in the city.

Looking again at Kiri's house, I see that it is also a solid base where traditions and Māori teachings are transmitted to a larger *whānau*, that of the school that the children attend. Rangi taught at the same school in a bilingual unit. In preparation for the end-of-the-year show, Kiri and Rangi taught Māori performing arts to the students twice a week in front of the house and sometimes in the living room. In return, Rangi had helped Kiri organize cultural activities for her Māori clients at work and supported her in her attempt to implement a permanent Māori and Pacific Island cultural program. This meant giving her cultural advice, teaching her genealogy in the Māori language and also sitting beside her at meetings with the management committee. Indeed when there was a need for it, the whole *whānau* mobilized to support its members in their projects. There were obvious links between places and an inter-penetration of places given the open character of this particular type of house. And more than people moved between places. Knowledge too emanated from the house, widening the space of Māori affirmation.

All the previous examples are good illustrations of agency, self-determination, or autonomy at the personal, *whānau*, and cultural level in an environment where it is comfortable and safe to be Māori and where everyone feels supported and accepted as full members of the group. Kiri, like most of the participants in this research, spoke very lit-tle about politics as such. But she made every possible effort to change her world and the world around her. This meant studying Māori his-tory and culture by herself and at university, making phone calls to people who could help her, participating in different assemblies and meetings in South Auckland where she can find assistance, going back to her tribe for advice, spending her personal time and money to pre-pare cultural initiatives and activities involving many members of the *whānau* in her work, activities aimed at strengthening and enriching the bonds of family unity.

Many of the participants in my research attended informal or local sessions organized to pass on traditional knowledge on an occasional or regular basis, as a means of upgrading their skills and deepening their understanding of Māori traditions and custom. Many also did ge-nealogical research and shared and discussed their findings with the people around them. This is all about being Māori and being part of a *whānau*, a group in a highly political context where it is not enough to say one is Māori. A person must master the universe of meanings, rely on a certain knowledge of traditions, feel things and relate to others in a Māori way and as Māori, and know enough Māori words to be ac-cepted. This calls for a personal effort as well as a collective or *whānau* mobilization, since one needs recognition and support from one's *whānau*, genealogical or not, if one wants to affirm oneself as Māori. Being Māori is first and foremost a *whānau* thing, not an individual one.

Kiri said that she could not have implemented her cultural program a few years ago, because at that time she was not comfortable enough as a Māori. She did not know enough about Māori traditions and she did not have sufficient support from her *whānau* because she had distanced herself from it while going through a difficult period with ex-partners. The house with its *marae* principles had thus given her a resource centre to return to and help refocus her life. But it had also provided her with support in becoming more active in the larger society and more positive about her engagement in various universes of meanings, Māori and mainstream. The self-confidence she developed personally, as well as her *whānau* support, significantly helped her to become more comfortable in different places and spaces. The *whānau* gave her the strength to implement Māori ways at the workplace and obtain a bachelor's and then a master's degree at university.

Witi Ihimaera (1992–6), the Māori novelist, short story writer, anthologist, librettist, and retired professor of Māori, indigenous, and New Zealand literature at the University of Auckland is often considered the most prominent Māori writer alive. Writing about Māori writers who successfully put their creative power into their work and go out into the world (in New Zealand, Australia, and elsewhere), he says the *pito* (umbilical cord) informs their work, makes it Māori, and replenishes them. The *pito* is used by Ihimaera (1992–6, 5) to symbolize the Māori centre, the source of being Māori, which comprises the Māori language, *marae*, *kaupapa Māori* (Māori philosophy, plan, principle), Māori history, and *tūrangawaewae* (the place to stand, connection to the land). "[It] always reminds you that, wherever one goes in the world or whatever happens to you, you have a people and a place to return to; a life to which you belong, whether you know it or want it" (5: 17). In light of the present analysis, it seems that the type of house in the city based on *marae* principles is also part of the *pito* – or the *kākano* (seed), as Rangi suggested – and informs and allows for moves forward and outward. This is what allowed Kiri to be more involved in society. This is also what allowed Rangi to be a boundary breaker or crosser between Māori and non-Māori at school and in her neighbourhood.

Ihimaera speaks about a spiral that, at one and the same time, is going both forward and backward: it is a "constant going out and returning, *te torino heare whakahua, whakamuri*, possesses the kinds of tensions which can push our work, informed by *kaupapa Māori* [Māori philosophy, plan, principle], into a new form that is an amalgamation of both" (5: 17).

The *koru* (spiral) is an important iconographic element in such Māori arts as carvings – regularly found, for example, on carved meeting houses – and tattooing, and is widely understood to symbolize both harmony and growth or new beginnings from a solid foundation rooted in the past. The spiral form also comes under the "genealogical paradigm" (Schwimmer 1992: 65; see also Carter 2003b: 13) in which everything in the universe is connected.

Ihimaera then adds about Māori writers: "We are the writers of the spiral" (Ihimaera 1992–6, 5: 17). I would say that the people who "inhabit" the pages of this book are the survivors and the fighters of the spiral. The spiral movement allows Māori to participate in the larger society and to affirm themselves in the workplace, at school, and in the city. Their engagement in the universe of meanings of the *whānau* nourishes them, as does the power of places such as *whānau* house, *marae*, and *papakāinga* (ancestral settlement, home territory). They are also nourished in their engagements with other universes of meanings. It is this very multiplicity and diversity of universes of meanings, spaces, and places that they have internalized that allows them to be at ease, comfortable, and able to use their agency, creativity, and imagination both to engage in heteroglossic ways with the world, and to affirm themselves as Māori.

This is also what allows for different ways of being Māori. It allows Māori to be flexible in response to the demands of different contexts and circumstances. As Makareta – the chosen one who had the knowledge and the careful upbringing preparing her for initiatives, the one who carries her family's hopes – one of the three cousins in Patricia Grace's novel *Cousins*, said, "I realised . . . that having that knowledge, that security, that sound base, allowed me to reach out and to know that I could do anything else in the world that I wanted to do" (Grace 1992: 211). Schwimmer (2004b: 21) mentions that certain people might see the spiral movement as being essentialist. However he sees it as a local variant of a universal process of heteroglossia in which subjects submit their visions of the world to never-ending negotiations.

This is exactly the source of the motivation behind Mere's actions at the college where she worked:

> all this stuff about getting my qualifications and learning, it's all to do with being able to be some sort of change agent, making change within the bigger group [. . .] It's being able to use my skills enough to be able to make change for my family, my instant family, *whānau* [. . .] sisters, brothers, and then people that I work with. There are different levels of *whānau*: the staff I work with, they're a *whānau* group, the students I work with, they're a *whānau* group. To be able to be effective in what I do. (Mere)

Her efforts to feel more complete as a person, more comfortable as a Māori by learning about Māori traditions and language, help her implement comfort and *rangatiratanga* among her students; that is, "reaching the highest pinnacle, succeeding in what you do, being able to get to the level where you can determine your own future, you are not dependent" (Mere). And that is made possible by providing the students and the staff with support, with *whānau* feelings, with a comfortable Māori space, and with Māori-oriented services so they can engage in the larger society. In this way, Mere also contributed to opening spaces for herself, for her students, and for Māori at large.

The notion of comfort in relation to identity, to being Māori, played a huge role in the school *whānau* and in the involvement of the parents in the management of the bilingual unit and its activities, according to Maui, the teacher who founded it. He explained that:

> as soon as we started calling ourselves an enrichment unit, a Māori enrichment unit, as soon as we started calling ourselves that, well, some of the parents felt . . . they just seemed to come in and I think it was just because it was the name "Māori" in front and they were coming in. We started with about six parents coming in all the time and then it sort of grew from there and then they talked to another parent and now we sometimes have up to 20 parents involved in our *whānau hui* [assembly, gathering, meeting]. When you look at some of the things that happen in the school. They will get about three parents and this is for the mainstream. We might have an open day, we'll get about 20 parents in, other classes, about four. You see the difference . . . because they feel comfortable. (Maui)

And this feeling of comfort seems to be closely related to the parents being part of a *whānau* group. It thus seems to me that, when Māori feel comfortable, when they have places they call home or places they can call their own, places clearly identified as Māori, places in which they are part of a group and feel supported, many become involved in their *whānau* and in the larger community, and suggest actions or projects aiming at greater autonomy. The autonomy they look for often goes far beyond their personal autonomy and personal comfort.

Similarly, Māori with a good knowledge of the Māori language and culture appear to have greater self-confidence and to feel more comfortable in the city. Māori who know who they are, have good *whānau* support, and have a safe home seem to acknowledge more easily, for example, the non-Māori side(s) of their genealogy, even if they identify themselves primarily and proudly as Māori. I observed that they also engage more freely and more easily in different universes of meanings.

Māori who have a *whānau*, a support group at all levels – intellectual, spiritual, emotional, physical, and economic – and who can return home at night to real support, can be teachers, lawyers, politicians, engineers, or mechanics without compromising their identity as Māori. Even when away from home or away from the *whānau* house, they still feel supported, at least symbolically, because of *whānau* links. Those who succeed and are recognized in both worlds, Māori and Pākehā, are precisely those who keep alive their *whānau* engagement and support. At a time when *whānau* has become an important symbol of Maoridom and of "being Māori," being active members of a *whānau* allows them to succeed in the Pākehā world. Even if they return home less often, they will not be considered traitors.

Again, the house is neither the only place of comfort nor the only place in which family relationships are strengthened and given central importance. Other places such as "real" *marae* in the city, Māori schools, churches, sports clubs, Māori community centres, and Māori common rooms at university are also important sites that make both possible and easier Māori comfort, imagination, expression, autonomy, and participation in the public space at the local, regional, national, and even global levels. These places are interrelated and enable both cultural survival and change.

The particular type of houses described in these pages and its network of interconnected places and spaces are also important at the political level. They form a crucial site for upholding the universe of meanings of the *whānau*. This universe of meanings is a means and a strategy for affirmation of Māori in relationships with other Māori, but also with non-Māori. The universe of meanings of the *whānau* is a site of resistance to state power and to Western hegemony and to the power of the mainstream universes of meanings in a colonized and globalized context. Many participants in my research clearly said that it was, for them, an alternative way of life. The universe of meanings of the *whānau* is thus a means and a strategy for appropriating political, economic, urban, and state spaces and powers. It demonstrates solidarity with other Māori and affirms one's own Maoriness. It is a way of avoiding assimilation, of continuing the struggle for survival in an urban context that is often felt to be alien, and in a global context that is sometimes felt to be threatening.

While engagement in the public space is often the "work" of an elite through political organizations and parties, NGOs, activist groups, and social movements, "ordinary" Māori are also engaging actively in affirmation and resistance. They mainly operate within what is generally recognized as "private"[3] space, where they also fight assimilation and reinforce "traditional" Māori ways and values. Researchers, in most cases, have had difficulty seeing this "work," this engagement of ordinary Māori, since the struggle and debates take place in the privacy of the *whānau*, behind the doors of the house, the community centre, or the *marae*.[4]

Whānau members engage in many sites of struggle simultaneously and in various domains, such as Māori schooling, Māori health, Māori traditions and custom, Māori language, Māori representation in various governmental and non-governmental organizations, and land claims. They are active both privately and publicly, with much of the "work" taking place in the private space. Māori engagement in many sites is flexible and varies according to the stage of life, context, particular configuration of power relationships, and the persons and groups involved.

The spiral movements, the flows inwards and outwards, are not free of constraints. Movement is limited by external conditions, including the state and other sociohistorical global forces. Thus, the universe of meanings of the *whānau* both connects people who share and implement the *whānau*'s values and principles, and works as a boundary-marker between "us" and "others" who infringe on or threaten the *whānau* in any way.

Depending on circumstances and on power relationships, the *whānau* will contract, expand, or make distinctions between those who share its assumptions and those who do not. For example, the Māori experience of the Pākehā presence in New Zealand over the centuries has affected Māori categories and concepts. The vision of two worlds, one Māori and the other Pākehā, is surely a consequence of that experience even if, in reality, the boundaries are porous and allow for connections under a variety of circumstances.

Moreover, boundaries and connections change in nature over time (Cohen 2000: 11). It all depends on the larger context, which can be regional, national, or global; on the re-empowerment or dis-empowerment of categories of persons and universes of meanings; and on changing relationships between groups. Barth (2000) is right, in my judgment, when he emphasizes the fundamental importance of embodied experience and local circumstances and the significance of processes of social interaction, politics, and economics for shared conceptual categories and especially for their impact on particular patterns of social relations and engagement in places and spaces. Relationships and boundaries are also experienced and conceived differently depending on the person or group. "Those contingencies produce the effects from which people in turn reconceptualise boundaries (endowing the concept of boundary with what we used to call 'connotations') that derive from what actually happens along that particular boundary as a result of the connections that people spin by their actions and by the consequences of those actions" (Barth 2000: 31).

The Māori situation cannot be analysed without considering internal divisions including tribes, *whānau*, places of residence, and socio-economic factors. Nor can it be considered without taking into account their colonial situation and relationships with the dominant group in New Zealand and other growing populations in that country. The controversy about the ownership of the foreshore and seabed is a good illustration. Prior to 2003, the stress on Māori separatism and symbolic competition was less apparent. Since the Treaty of Waitangi Act 1975, the general mood had been one of conciliation and dialogue. But since 2003, the Pākehā response to Māori demands has changed and the Māori movement has put an ever greater emphasis on ethnic separatism. This strong reaction, which puts Māori indigeneity in ethnic terms, was partly caused by the perceived threat of multiculturalism in a demographic context where immigration, especially from Asia and the Pacific islands, is growing fast. Māori therefore fear they will become just another minority group (for example, Spoonley in TVNZ 2011). The danger was felt as being all the more immediate in the wake of the foreshore and seabed controversy, given the public debate about the abolition of all references to the Treaty of Waitangi, as well as the possibility of New Zealand becoming a republic and drafting its own constitution. In September 2011, in response to a Department of Labour report that found that Māori are more likely to express anti-immigration sentiments than any other ethnic group, Margaret Mutu (head of Auckland University's Department of Maori Studies) reiterated the call to limit white immigration to New Zealand. According to her, people arriving from countries such as South Africa, England, and the United States bring an attitude of white supremacy (TVNZ 2011). She explained that "Maori feel very threatened as more groups come in and swamp them" (Mutu in Neale 2011). Her call sparked controversy and many complaints were received by the Race Relations office. When invited to comment on Mutu's declaration, Ranginui Walker explained: "The problem of Maori under-performance in New Zealand – in terms of education and dependency on welfare – has not been resolved. If we can't solve our own internal problems, why add to those problems by bringing more people? It just doesn't make sense" (*Sunday Star Times* 2011). Interestingly, Smits (2010) reminds us that "in early 2007, the Māori party co-leader, Tariana Turia, [also] called for limits on European immigration to New Zealand, claiming that increases in ethnically white immigration was designed to stop the 'browning of New Zealand.' Māori party policy is now to encourage skilled immigrants irrespective of ethnicity, but to require all to complete a course on the history of Aotearoa/New Zealand and the Pacific region before being granted New Zealand citizenship" (73).

All these contextual factors have the effect of limiting the extent to which the Māori movement reaches out in its struggles. It seems to me to be crucial to inquire further into the British colonial structures that were set up in New Zealand to investigate their continued impact on Māori today (Gagné 2009b). These structures must still influence not only Māori relationships with the majority population and the state, but also the inward and outward turns of their struggle for decolonization and self-determination.

In spite of everything, and even if it is sometimes less vocal, more private, or subtle, *ka whawhai tonu rātou*[5] – the struggle continues for them, the Māori. It takes many forms and occurs in many places and spaces. Māori have been far from apathetic. The struggle is part of the internalization, under contemporary and urban conditions of life, of the various universes of meaning that allow for biculturalism and for "playing" with "traditional" Māori symbols and artefacts, as well as with symbols and cultural artefacts of mainstream universes of meaning, and for engaging in both worlds in heteroglossic ways. As Barker (2011: 21–2) reminds us, "'traditions' are conditional, . . . they are made meaningful and relevant again and again in the specific contexts in which they are articulated."

There are different strategies for being Māori in today's world, and not all support or agree with each of the various ways. The struggle is linked to their rights (economical, social, and political) as indigenous people in New Zealand. But it is also closely linked to upholding Māori identity and other cultural elements like the language, the *whānau*, and the *marae*. The character of each of these elements has changed and will continue to change. Indigenous worlds, visions, and ways of being are maintained and even strengthened through change and openness to the larger society (within certain limits imposed through colonization and by the state). The upholding of these elements is what mobilizes Māori and keeps the struggle alive, for example, through the teaching of the language, history, and values, and the maintenance of *whānau* networks in the city and beyond.

Two Māori anthropologists, in recent works, bring us back to the metaphor of the *marae* to foresee ways toward a future, ways that allow for reaffirmation of the Māori universe of meanings through change. First, Lily George (2010, 2011) revisits the symbolism of the main building of the *marae*, the *wharenui*, to speak of this constant "going out and returning" involved in the Māori cultural renaissance, which has participated in "pushing" Māori forward. She explains that "the *pou* (poles) found in the wharenui can be used as markers of time, and the Renaissance Periods likened to three of the *pou*" (George 2011: 171; English original): *Te Poutuarongo*, the pillar inside the house on the back wall is associated with Renaissance Period One (1870s to 1890s) and seen as being most encased in *Te Ao Kohatu* (The Ancient World); *Te Pouteaniwa*, the pillar on the front wall inside the wharenui, is associated with Renaissance Period Two (1909 to 1930s); and *Te Poutewharau*, the pillar outside the house, on the porch, joining the apex of the wharenui to the ground and supporting the *koruru* and *tekoteko* (carved figures representing noted ancestors), is associated with Renaissance Period Three (1970s to present). Of this last pole/renaissance period, George (2011) says,

> [i]t is more exposed to the light and metaphorical winds of change, requiring more movement outside of tradition and into the new world, while working to retain as much of Māori culture as possible. The innovation of tradition that occurred in relation to *marae* and *wharenui* can again be seen as an exemplar of the changes to *Māori* culture and society that was sometimes forced and sometimes deliberately chosen, often in response to those enforced changes. Of necessity was a move outside of tradition (which can be represented by the inside of the *wharenui*) and the incorporation of new ideas into our traditions and cultures that best served us in these new environments. While this can be and is seen by many as an indicator of the destruction of our culture and our traditions, it can also be seen as a sign of innovation and creativity demonstrating the potential to

re-create ourselves in new and exciting ways, leading to a celebration of our resilience and strength. (174; English original).

As for Merata Kawharu (2010: 236), she looks at the *marae* and its meeting house as a model to establish a socioenvironmental ethic. The *marae* – symbolizing *kotahitanga* (unity) between the human, material, and nonmaterial worlds – is the manifestation of a holistic ethos, a system of ordering the wider universe, events, and people (230). In regard to the domain that interests her most – the environment and the management of natural resources – Kawharu suggests that the *marae* and the meeting house can provide a set of practices and principles to face environmental challenges. "The environment may be considered as an extension of all that marae symbolises, and vice versa, marae as an extension of a wider environment" (227–8). The environment then may be interpreted as a "*marae* locale." Then, the principles governing the management of the environmental resources must be the same as those governing the relationships between people, particularly between kin, on a *marae*. This calls for the implementation of the principle of *kaitiakitanga* (trusteeship), which refers also to the notions of accountability, reciprocity, and guardianship, and to the key principle of *manaaki* (hospitality). Like people, resources should be "looked after and managed" (227). She insists on the idea that the ethic based on these principles is not simply environmental. It is rather a "socio-environmental ethic": "it weaves together ancestral, environmental and social threads of identity, purpose and practice" (227). And this represents an important challenge, "the challenge of the marae" (235), which includes, according to her, the re-establishment of *mana whenua* (customary rights and authority over land) and a "cultural footprint in a multi-cultural society" (235), the re-affirmation of credible tribal leadership; and the relearning and application of traditional knowledge and values, particularly by youth. From this proposition emerges again the idea of the *marae* as an "organising principle" (230) that allows for creativity (232) in today's contexts.

It is important to note that Kawharu's proposition is based specifically on tribal *marae* and a Māori tribal worldview and, as already shown, "for the perspective of tribal or sub-tribal identity, the environment provides markers or reference points that define one group from another" (221). If a *marae* is central to Māori identity, tribal *marae* and their relationships to a particular *maunga* (mountain), *moana* (sea), *wairere* (waterfall), *awa* (river), and so on, are central to tribal identity. The socioenvironmental ethic put forward by Kawharu thus does not apply, or at least does not apply in the same way to *taurahere marae* or "Māori immigrant *marae*" (Tapsell 2002) since they are on another tribe's ancestral land. However, what Kawharu (2010) emphasizes is the process of re-affirmation and reviving of tribal communities for those who suffered from the loss of lands (if not *marae*), such as hers, the Ngāti Whātua tribal community of Ōrākei (which holds customary rights and authority over parts of Auckland), and their reconnection with traditional knowledge and "the ancestral landscape that are now the farms, Crown lands, reserves, parks, and Auckland city" (235). This everyday struggle is also part of Māori realities in Auckland today, now that important legal and political gains have been achieved by the Ngāti Whātua (see Carlin 2010; Kawharu 2008; Tapsell 2002). It is also part of the process of reasserting themselves and renegotiating their relations with non-Māori as well as Māori migrants, Māori urban authorities, and other *tāngata whenua* communities. This is made possible through different forums. One such forum was the 2009–11 debate for Māori representation on Auckland's new Super City Council and committees.

In the decades before 2003, if Māori were less active in social and political groups and movements and resorted less often to public protests, sit-ins, marches, and demonstrations, they were not disengaged from the struggle for their rights and autonomy. They have made significant progress since the 1970s, and have secured a certain level of autonomy as a people, as *whānau*, and as tribes. We need only think of the Waitangi Tribunal, the decades of developments in education and language revitalization, the breakthrough of the Māori Party in Parliament, and many achievements in the arts and business.

The mobilization was there, but it took other forms and was expressed differently. The struggle took place, and still is taking place, on a daily basis at the *marae*, in *whānau* houses, in the rhetoric about real versus urban Māori, in learning Māori traditions and language, in bearing different signs of Māori identity, such as *whānau* and tribal T-shirts or stickers, and the traditional tattoo.

For leaders, the struggle has also taken place (and is ongoing) in the courts and through various negotiation forums at all levels of government and the bureaucracy. While important settlements have been reached, many claims are still waiting to be heard, and others are still being prepared. The period of the mid-1980s to 2003 was therefore one of active engagement and mobilization, but different from such activities in previous decades as well as from those in more recent years.

While "ordinary" Māori people can at first appear passive and dis-engaged, with no say in today's world, a closer look at *whānau* and at the lived worlds of everyday life soon reveals that this is a false im-pression. They are actively engaged in the interests of Māori. These everyday struggles established the conditions for the huge Māori mo-bilization of 2004 in opposition to the Foreshore and Seabed Bill, not to mention the creation of the Māori Party, which won four seats at the 2005 general election, five at the 2008 general election, and three at the 2011 general election along with the Mana Party, which gained one seat. The rising political consciousness among Māori also drew 7,000 people from all parts of Auckland to march on Queen Street in May 2009 in protest of the government's decision to exclude Māori seats from the proposed Auckland Super City Council (Hayward 2010b: 283). At the beginning of the year 2012, considering Māori achievements, I tend to agree with Smits (2010: 74): "collective Māori claims are likely in future to focus less on cultural recognition, and more on the political demands of self-determination."

However, many barriers still exist for Māori, including some signifi-cant socioeconomic disparities that slow down Māori access to public spaces and a better share of powers. Indeed many such barriers have been reinforced and new ones put in place. Certainly, new challenges have been posed by events around the foreshore and seabed debate between 2003 and 2008 that have been interpreted as a backlash (for example, Barber 2008; Miller 2005), as well as the emerging multicul-turalism and the coming constitutional review.

It is important to question the intentions and motivations of the ma-jority population. For instance, until recently at the government level, last-minute compromises were always (or nearly always) sufficient to silence people. The government will continue to test the thin line that separates peaceful coexistence from eventual disasters in the relation-ships between Māori and non-Māori in New Zealand. The media are also quick to qualify Māori as radical and to stress their lack of unity and insist on their internal conflicts, which inhibits many from speak-ing out. This appears to be less true among "ordinary" people since the 2004 *hikoi* (march); they seem to care less about labels, while lead-ing figures of the new Māori Party as well as other Māori leaders are obliged to be more careful in managing their image and in the way they stress Māori separatism. The relationships between government and a minority and between minority and majority populations are always precarious. There is a thin line between a situation where negotiation and coexistence are possible and one that could degenerate badly in unforeseen directions. Māori showed that they were ready to publicly unite and mobilize. If the government acts in ways that compromise the gains made by Māori in the past, it is right to expect that Māori will, at some point, react.

Before I finish, I think it is important for me to re-emphasize the fundamental character of the anthropology of everyday life, of the lived world, and of experience. Such anthropology demands time and deep involvement in a world where the pressure put on academics, not to mention the transformation of the university itself, do not always fit the requirements of long-term, in-depth field research.

And yet this kind of field research reveals the variety of sites where local identities are consolidated and expressed. The anthropology of everyday life allows us to see in finer detail the multiple and diversified effects of larger forces, such as the state and the capitalist economy, at the local level, and on the development and upholding of universes of meaning. It is also at the level of everyday life that the politics of differentiation and power struggles become visible, for example, in my research, between Māori, between Māori and non-Māori, and between Māori and larger forces.

Family and group solidarities are part of the struggle for affirmation, recognition, and autonomy. Engaging in the universe of meanings of the *whānau* is about actively facing, resisting, and engaging with global forces. It is about building relationships with others and the nation as a whole, in practice and through everyday experiences. It is for this reason that those non-kins who are integrated into the family are important allies of the family and its members. Concretely, then, the *whānau* can go as far as to include non-Māori and even complete strangers. Symbolically, the *whānau* can come to include all the populations of the Pacific and indigenous people all around the world. *Whānau* may expand to include members of the mainstream population or to deal with global forces when there is a need to manage collective resources and to cooperate with or oppose the state. *Whānau* contract in times of conflict or divergence, abuse, competition over resources, discomfort, or when the *whānau*'s *mana* (spiritual power, authority, prestige, status) and other important Māori principles are under threat.

The *whānau*, *marae*, and houses based on *marae* principles, by being central sites for strengthening the group and for just "being Māori," open doors on the world. Māori thus act in many places or spaces at once – both locally and globally, depending on situations, groups, and persons – and they mobilize in public when necessary.

Engagement at that level is also linked to national and global events, and to the history of conflicts and power relationships. Engagement or struggle on the international stage, for instance, is necessary when Māori hit the limits set by the state; that is, when they face important limits to their self-determination, freedom, and decolonization. There, it is a matter of taking a stance in a prestigious place to assert Māori or indigenous rights, or to point out that certain Māori rights are trampled upon.

Colonial and global forces have not succeeded in suppressing localisms, even though they exert a variety of pressures on the local. Local groupings are not passive and without resources, and this is another reason why the study of everyday life and lived worlds is important.

The study of the lived world of "ordinary" people, of their networks and of the ways they inhabit and mark urban and public spaces opens the way to a better understanding of how people conceptualize their identities and live their relations with each other, with the state, and with the majority population. It also reveals the ways in which people feel comfortable and uncomfortable in different settings – rural and urban, traditional and contemporary – and in their relationships to others, Māori and non-Māori.

Finally, it seems to me that Māori feel comfortable when they have places they can call home or places they can call their own, places clearly identified as Māori, places where the *wairua* (spirit, the sense of place, people, and events) is right. These places are crucial for cultural continuity, as well as for their transformation and autonomy.

The house based on *marae* principles is one of the most important sites in the city for cultural, ethnic, and political affirmation and resistance, including at the symbolic or metaphorical level. It is the urban place par excellence for the emergence and maintenance of the *whānau* universe of meanings as lived in daily life. It is a secure, comfortable, and comforting place – emotionally, culturally, spiritually, economically, and physically – that is sheltered from the powerful and potentially dangerous Pākehā and from the public eye.

This type of house is about how people show solidarity, support each other, and resist and struggle as Māori in a milieu which appears on the surface to be apolitical. It is also about going out into the world. That the *whānau* and other "traditional" aspects of Māori culture have changed is ultimately of little importance. What is really significant is the continued general attachment of Māori people to the idea of being Māori and to Māori identities.

Appendix: Profiles of Interviewees (2001–2002, formal interviews only)

Alias	Sex	Age	Area of Auckland	Principal tribal affiliation	Te reo*	Born in Auckland†	Occupation	Ed.‡
Alan	M	40s	Central	Eastern	+-	N, 1st	Student, designer	B
Alexis	M	60s	Outside	Northern	+-	N	Retired	HS
Andrew	M	20s	South	Pākehā	N	Y, 3rd+	Factory worker	HS
Api	M	30s	Central	Eastern	Y	N	Student	B
Aroha	F	30s	Central	Western	+-	N, 1st	Student	M
Christine	F	40s	West	Northern	Y	Y, 2nd	Teacher	B
Debra	M	20s	West	Northern	Y	Y, 3rd+	Service sector worker	HS
Donna	F	40s	South	Northern	+-	N, 2nd	Student	B
Fiona	F	20s	Central	Western	Y	N, 1st	Student, lecturer	M
Floria	F	30s	West	Eastern	Y	Y, 2nd	Educator	B
Georgina	F	60s	Central	Northern	Y	Y	Retired	B
Hepi	M	30s	Overseas	Northern	N	Y, 2nd	Construction industry worker	HS
Hiko	M	50s	Outside	Western	Y	N, 2nd	Retired	HS+
Hine	F	40s	South	Eastern	Y	N, 1st	Artist	HS
Hone	M	30s	West	Western	+-	Y, 1st	Student	B
Howard	M	70s	Central	Northern	Y	Y, 3rd+	Teacher	PhD
Ihaka	M	40s	South	Northern	Y	N, 1st	Artist, business woman	HS
Iranui	F	60s	West	Northern	+-	Y, 3rd+	Service sector worker	HS
Iritana	F	50s	South	Northern	N	N, 1st	Educator	+
Jack	M	40s	Outside	Eastern	+-	N	Lawyer	B

Jean	F	40s	South	Northern	N	Y, 2nd	Health care worker	B
Jessica	F	10s	West	Northern	Y	Y, 2nd	Student	B
Joana	F	40s	West	Western	N	N, 2nd	Student, health care worker	B
July	F	40s	South	Northern	+	N, 1st	Student	B
Kahu	F	20s	South	Northern	Y	Y, 1st	Media worker	HS
Keita	F	50s	West	Northern	Y	N, 1st	Student, researcher	B
Kepa	M	20s	Central	Eastern	+	N, 2nd	Student	B
Kiri	F	30s	South	Western	N	Y, 3rd	Student, health care worker	B
Maata	F	40s	Central	Northern	N	Y, 3rd	Health care worker	M
Manaaki	M	40s	South	Eastern	Y	N, 1st	Arts	B
Manuka	M	40s	West	Eastern	Y	N, 1st	Student	B-
Margaret	F	60s	North	Western	+	N, 1st	Student	+
Maria	F	30s	North	Northern	Y	Y	Educator	HS+
Mark	M	50s	West	n/a	N	N	Service sector worker	HS
Matiu	M	20s	Central	Western	Y	N, 1st	Student	B
Maui	M	30s	South	Western	N	N, 2nd	Educator	B
Maxine	F	40s	South	Northern	N	N, 1st	Businesswoman	B
Mere	F	40s	North	Northern	+	Y, 2nd	Educator	M
Merimeri	F	40s	Central	Western	N	N	Teacher	B
Mihi	F	20s	West	Northern	N	N, 1st	Student	B
Miro	F	30s	South	Eastern	N	Y, 2nd	Health care worker	B

(continued)

Alias	Sex	Age	Area of Auckland	Principal tribal affiliation	Te reo*	Born in Auckland†	Occupation	Ed.‡
Moana	F	50s	North	Eastern	Y	N, 1st	Teacher	M
Ngareta	F	40s	South	Western	N	Y, 3rd	Businesswoman	HS+
Ngawai	F	70s	Central	Northern	Y	Y, 3rd+	Retired	B
Niho	M	60s	South	Eastern	+-	N, 1st	Teacher	B
Nuku	M	40s	South	Eastern	Y	N, 1st	Service sector worker	M
Pania	F	60s	East	Western	Y	Y, 3rd	Retired	+
Patricia	F	20s	Central	Eastern	Y	N, 2nd	Student	B
Phil	M	20s	Central	Northern	N	N	Manager	M
Pita	M	60s	Central	Northern	Y	N, 1st	Student	B
Raina	F	20s	South	Eastern	+-	N, 3rd+	Service sector worker	HS
Rangi	F	30s	South	Northern	Y	Y, 3rd	Teacher's assistant	HS+
Rapi	M	60s	West	Western	+-	N, 1st	Businessman	HS
Regan	F	20s	West	Northern	N	Y, 2nd	Student	B
Rena	F	30s	South	Northern	N	N	Unemployed	HS+
Rewa	F	50s	West	Northern	+-	N, 3rd	Businesswoman	B-
Riripeti	F	50s	West	Northern	Y	N, 1st	Teacher	B
Robert	M	20s	South	Eastern	Y	Y, 1st	Student	B
Roha	F	50s	South	Northern	N	Y, 2nd	Cleaner	HS
Roimata	F	50s	East	Northern	+-	N, 2nd	Researcher	PhD
Rongo	M	40s	Outside	Eastern	Y	No, 1st	Construction industry worker	HS
Rose	F	20s	West	Northern	+-	N, 1st	Student	HS

Name	Sex	Age					Occupation	Education
Rua	F	20s	South	Eastern	N	N, 1st	Student, artist	B
Ruka	M	30s	West	Northern	Y	Y, 2nd	Teacher, artist	B
Sally	F	30s	South	Northern	N	Y, 2nd	Unemployed	HS
Sammy	M	40s	West	Northern	Y	N, 2nd	Teacher	HS
Tama	M	30s	West	Western	+-	N, 1st	Student	HS
Tauni	M	30s	West	Eastern	Y	N, 2nd	Teacher	B
Tepora	F	50s	South	Western	Y	N	Retired	n/a
Teria	F	50s	Outside	Northern	Y	N, 2nd	Unable to work through disability	HS+
Tiana	F	20s	South	Western	N	Y, 3rd	Unemployed	HS+
Tom	M	40s	Central	Central	N	Y, 3rd+	Artist	B
Tui	F	50s	South	Northern	Y	N, 1st	Student, researcher	B
Waerete	F	20s	Central	Eastern	+-	N	Student	B
Whetu	F	10s	South	Northern	+-	Y, 3rd+	Student	HS
William	M	30s	South	Southern	N	N, 1st	Construction industry worker	HS

* Māori language.

+- Partial knowledge of Māori language.

† When known, the number of generations the family has lived at least partly in Auckland: 1st = first generation to live in Auckland; + = at least that number of generations to live in Auckland.

‡ Formal education: HS = high school; B = bachelor's degree; M = master's degree; PhD = doctoral degree; + = plus some studies taken at a higher level.

Glossary

Māori language usually marks no difference between the plural and singular noun forms, which are inferred from the context. Glosses for nouns are generally given in the singular, but the plural may be intended throughout this book depending on context. The same word may also be a noun or a verb, as is often the case in English. All of the terms in the glossary are italicized in the text.

ahi kā: a fire kept alight, "literally '(long-) burning fire'; this term denotes the maintenance of the right to occupy land through sustained continuous occupation" (JHMRC 2002, 3: 152)[1]

ahi mātao: a fire dying out

ahu: to tend, to foster

āhua: appearance, likeness, form, character

aroha: unconditional love, caring, sympathy, charity, gratitude

awa: river

awhi: to embrace, to foster, to cherish, to support (as in, "we'll be there to *support* you, to *awhi* you")

awhina: assistance, help

haka: war dance

hapū: sub-tribe

hariru: shaking hands, as when greeting

hau: breath of life

heke, wheke: rafters (of a roof)

hīmene: hymn

hikoi: march

hoa: friend

hoa riri: angry companion (as opposed to friend)

hongi: pressing noses

hui: assembly, gathering, meeting

huia: gourd

iwi: tribe, but can also mean people(s) or persons composing a community, tribe, or nation

iwitanga: the way of the tribe, vertical structural ethic

kāinga: place of residence, home

kai: food, meal

kai Māori: Māori food

kaitiaki: guardian; "in regard to resources, person or group responsible for safeguarding the environment or tribal patrimony" (JHMRC 2002, 3: 152)

kaiawhina: teacher's assistant

kaitiakitanga: trusteeship, refers also to the notions of accountability, reciprocity, and guardianship

kapa haka ropū: Māori performing arts group

kapa haka: Māori performing arts

kapu tī: cup of tea, cuppa (colloquial New Zealand or British English)

karakia: prayers, "ritual chants" (Durie 1999: 359)

karanga: ceremonial call of welcome

kauhau: address, lecture, sermon

kaumātua: elders, or male elders when used in a pair with or as opposed to *kuia* (female elders)

kaupapa: plan, principle, scheme, proposal, mission, project

kaupapa Māori: Māori philosophy, plan, principle

kaupapa whānau: non-kin "families" based on a common mission or a special purpose

kawenata: spiritual covenant

kawanatanga: governance

kawe mate: bringing a dead person back to his/her *marae*

kia ora: greeting or salutation (used both on meeting and on parting), literally meaning "be well," "be healthy," or "be safe"

koha: gifts, presents, donation, "especially that given by visitors to their hosts during a hui" (Metge 1995: 333)

kohanga reo: kindergarten based on Māori principles, currently translated in Aotearoa/New Zealand as "language nests," that is "a whānau or community-based institution where children can be socialised through the medium of the Māori language" (JHMRC 2002, 3: 153)

kōrero: to speak, to give a speech; history, story, conversation, serious talk

kore: the nothingness

koro (abbreviation for koroua): male elder

koru: spiral

koruru: carved head (with no body visible) at the apex of the meeting house, who represents the ancestor after whom the house is named

kotahitanga: principle of oneness

kuia: female elders

kura: school

kura kaupapa Māori: Māori schools based on Māori principles

kūmara: sweet potato; the "kūmara vine" is a network for gossip, equivalent to "grapevine" in colloquial English

mākutu: sorcery

mahau: the porch of the meeting house

maihi: carved pieces from the *koruru* on a meeting house, extending toward the ground, sloping bargeboards, they represent the arms of the *koruru*

mama: mother

mana: spiritual power, authority, prestige, status

mana whenua: customary rights, Māori power and authority over a particular piece of land

manaakitanga: showing respect and kindness, befriending, hospitality extended to visitors, looking after people, entertaining

manawa: heart

māngere: lazy

māoritanga: "things that relate directly to the values and concepts of the Maori people" (Tauroa and Tauroa 1986: 161); Maoridom

manuhiri: visitor

manuhiri tapu: tapu of the visitors

marae: traditional Māori meeting place; "open space in front of a meeting-house; the combination of this open space with meeting-house, dining-hall and other buildings" (Metge 1995: 334)

marae ātea: ceremonial courtyard, open space in front of a meeting house

marae tautoko kaupapa: marae for the use of Māori participants in non-Māori institutions

marae-a-rohe: marae for the use of Maaori people living in a particular vicinity (usually urban), regardless of tribal origin

mātāwaka: Māori who live in the city and are not in a *mana whenua* group (Local Government [Auckland Council] Act 2009)

matua: father, siblings, and cousins of mother's generation; polite term of address for men older than oneself

maunga: mountain

mauri: life essence

mihi: to greet; exchange of greetings, speech of greeting

mihimihi: "frequentive form of mihi, hence sometimes used to indicate re-
    peated greeting speeches in welcome ceremony" (Metge 1995: 334)

moana: sea

mokopuna (often abbreviated as moko): grandchild(ren)

ngā: the (plural definite article)

ngā hau e wha: people from the "four winds"; that is, from all around the
    islands

Ngāti or Ngāi or Ngā: of that person

noa: free of religious restriction, ordinary, relaxed, common, the complement
    and antidote of tapu

noho marae: overnight stays

ora: alive and well in body, mind and spirit; life, health in the fullest measure

pā: fortified place or village

Pākehā: people of predominantly European ancestry; white New Zealanders

papa: father siblings and cousins of mother's generation; polite term of ad-
    dress for men older than oneself

papakāinga: ancestral or village settlement, "home territory, especially the
    land adjacent to a marae that is or could be used for residential purposes"
    (JHMRC 2002, 3: 154)

Papatūānuku: Earth Mother

patu: traditional hand weapon

pito: umbilical cord

poi: "light ball with a short string attached to it, which [is] swung and twirled
    rhythmically to the accompaniment of a song, the so-called poi dance"
    (Williams 2000 [1971]: 288).

pou: poles (in meeting houses)

pou tokomanawa: the central carved post in the meeting house

pounamu: greenstone, jade, which has great symbolic value among Māori

poupou: carved figures

poutuarongo: the pillar inside the meeting house on the back wall

pouteaniwa: the pillar on the front wall inside the meeting house

poutewharau: the pillar outside the meeting house, on the porch, joining the
    apex of the house to the ground and supporting the *koruru* and *tekoteko*

powhiri: welcome ceremony, to welcome

rangatahi: could be glossed as "youth," but in practice can mean people any-
    where between twenty-one and fifty years old

rangatira: chief, person of senior descent and high rank

rangatiratanga: "the capacity and right of a group to manage its own affairs"
    (Metge 1995: 334), chieftainship

raruraru: problem, trouble

reo: language

reo Māori: Māori language

rīwai: potato

ropū: group

rūnanga: council

taha: side

taha Māori: Māori side, "Māori aspect of life and behaviour" (JHMRC 2002, 3: 154)

taha wairua: the spiritual aspect of life

tahuhu or tahu: ridgepole, main pole supporting the meeting house

taiaha: traditional weaponry or fighting arts

takatāpui: this term has become synonymous with being non-heterosexual, either lesbian, gay, bi-sexual, transsexual, or queer

takawaenga: mediator

tamariki (singular: tamaiti): children

tane: man, husband, partner

tangata (plural: tāngata): man (men), person (people), human being(s)

tāngata kei mua: people in front

tāngata kei muri: people at the back

tangata whenua (plural: tāngata whenua): literally people of the land, indigenous people, first people of the land, "referring to a group with a special relationship to an area, region or marae by long-term occupancy, descent, or adoption by other tāngata whenua" (JHMRC 2002, 3: 154)

tāngata whenua marae: tribal *marae* belonging to the home people, the people who have the rights on the land

tangi: to cry, to weep

tangihanga (often abbreviated as tangi): funeral

taonga: treasure, "those things of value to a person that have been handed down through the generations" (Tauroa and Tauroa 1986: 164)

tapu: sacred or polluted, polluting; restriction, "quality or condition of being subject to such restriction" (Williams 2000 (1971): 385)

tauiwi: stranger, foreigner; originally, a person from another tribe (JHMRC 2002, col. 3: 155)

tauparapara: incantation

taurahere marae: non-tribal and immigrant-tribal marae

tautoko: support, to support

te: the (singular definite article)

te torino heare whakahua, whakamuri: constant going in and going out (spiral movement) *tekoteko:* the carved figure at the top of the meeting house

tiaki: to protect, to guard, to keep

tiakitanga: guardianship

tīpuna: dead ancestors, grandparents

tika: correct, morally just

tikanga: custom, rules, traditions, the way things are done

tikanga Māori: "the right Māori ways, rules or guidelines for living generally accepted as tika" (Metge 1995: 335)

tino rangatiratanga: self-determination, sovereignty

tipuna: dead ancestor, grandparent

tuakana: sibling or cousin of the same sex and generation in a senior line; older relative; senior

tukutuku: woven panels in the meeting house

tutakitanga: "the act of meeting with people, usually involving physical contact" (Tauroa and Tauroa 1986: 167)

tūrangawaewae: literally, a place to put one's feet; connection to the land; "standing place from where one gains the authority to belong" (Tauroa and Tauroa 1986: 166); "used to indicate a place (district, locality, or marae) where an individual or group can be and participate in community affairs as of right" (JHMRC 2002, col. 3: 155)

urupa: burial ground, cemetery

utu: "return for something received, whether good or bad" (Metge 1995: 336); reciprocity; compensation; price

waewae tapu: literally translated as "sacred feet"; "a person who is going onto a specific marae for the first time" (Tauroa and Tauroa 1986: 166)

wahi rangatira iwi: place that heightens people's dignity

wahi rangatira mana: place of greatest *mana*

wahi rangatira tikanga Māori: place in which Maori customs are given ultimate expression

wahi rangatira wairua: place of greatest spirituality

wahine: woman, female

waiata: song, to sing

wairere: waterfall

wairua: spirit, feelings of places, peoples, events; spiritual, spirituality

waka: great canoes of tradition that voyaged to Aotearoa from the ancestral home, Hawaiki; federation of *hapū* and *iwi*

wānanga: "the traditional school of higher learning, where esoteric philosophical, mythological, genealogical and spiritual knowledge was transmitted; now extended to include . . . : a tertiary institution education set up under the Education Amendment Act 1989 which engages in teaching and research in ways which reflect Māori cultural norms, and . . . informal or local sessions organised to pass on traditional (or other) knowledge to appropriate groups of people" (JHMRC 2002, 3: 155); meeting called to discuss particular teachings or issues; residential courses or workshops; Māori tertiary institutions

wero: challenge

whaea: mother, siblings and cousins of mother's generation; polite term of address for women older than oneself

whaikōrero: speech, speech-making; to speak, to orate

whakaekenga: the act of going onto a *marae*, the moving on

whakamā: "used to describe a range of feelings from shyness through embarrassment to shame and behaviour involving varying degrees of withdrawal and unresponsiveness" (Metge 1995: 336)

whakamana: capacity to empower

whakapapa: genealogy; an exclusive descent ethic or "vertical" principle

whakapapa atuatanga: the spiritual world

whakapapa tīpuna: the ancestral world

whakapapa pūtaiao: the natural world

whakapapa whānau: extended family based on kinship and descent

whakawhanaungatanga: strengthening and enriching the bonds of family unity

whāmere: word derived from the English word "family," used as synonym for *whānau* (Metge 1995: 336)

whānau: extended family (see chapter 5 for details); to give birth, to be born

whānaunga: relatives, kin, close friends

whanaungatanga: the way of the extended family; the principle of strengthening and enriching the bonds of family unity; "the processes by which whaanau and other consanguineal and affinal links, cohesion and mutuality are maintained" (JHMRC 2002, 3: 155); inclusive kinship ethic; horizontal kinship principle

whāngai: to feed, to nourish, to bring up, to nurture, to foster; adoption or fostering (formal or informal)

whanui: tribal family

whare: house

whare kura: school

whare mate: house where the dead lie in state

whare moe: sleeping house

whare puni: sleeping house

whare rūnanga: council house

whare tipuna: ancestral house

wharehui: meeting house

wharekai: kitchen or dining hall

wharenui: literally translated as big house, but used in this book to speak about meeting houses in general

whare waka: garage

whare whakairo: carved house

whawhai: struggle

whenua: land, afterbirth or placenta, earth, country

Notes

Introduction: Māori "Sitting at the Table"

1 The Treaty of Waitangi was signed between Māori chiefs and representatives of the British Crown and now generally considered to be the founding document of New Zealand, establishing a partnership between Māori and non-Māori.

2 See, for example, *New Zealand Herald* (2010b); Mulholland and Tawhai (2010).

3 See, among other examples, Durie (2005b, 2011); Maaka and Fleras (2005).

4 At the beginning of 2011, the Māori Party faced substantial internal conflicts that led to the resignation of Hone Harawira and the creation of the new left-wing Mana Party at the end of April 2011. Significantly, Hone Harawira opposed the Māori Party's position on the foreshore and seabed issue (*New Zealand Herald* 2010a). Hone Harawira won a by-election in June 2011 for the Mana Party and retained his seat at the 2011 election. He is still the only MP of the new party. Moreover, according to One News (2001), "the previous deal with National appears to have cost the party one MP with Rahui Katene tipped out of the southernmost Maori seat by Labour's Rino Tirikatene." Compared to the previous election, there was a low turnout of Māori on election day. Although low participation has always been characteristic of Māori, the significant decline since the 2008 election could be seen as a reflection of people's dissatisfaction with Māori fighting among themselves since the beginning of the year. Pita Sharples, the coleader of the Māori Party, had this to say after the election: "Our people don't like to see us and Mana fighting and I think that's been partly the reason for both of our parties to get a small party vote."

5 The agreement, among other things, demands welfare reform and includes the development of Whānau Ora, put in place at the initiative of the Māori Party after the 2008 elections, whose goal is to provide culturally sensitive services to families; the creation of a ministerial committee on poverty; the advancement of tribes (*iwi*) as housing providers through the Social Housing Unit; and the continuation of the constitutional review and the refocusing of Te Puni Kōkiri (Ministry of Māori Development) on Māori employment, training, housing, and education outcomes (Cheng 2011).

6 I will only briefly outline the main elements and moments of the controversy. For further details, see the numerous publications on the subject: among others, including those quoted, see Bennion (2005); Charters and Erueti (2007); Durie (2005a); Orange (2011); Palmer (2006); Walker (2004).

7 Controversies about the ownership of the foreshore and seabed and Native titles were not new and can be traced back to the establishment of the British colony (for details, see Ruru 2004). What was new, however, was that from 2003, the litigation took an ethnic or racial turn and the result was a polarization of New Zealand society along ethnic lines.

8 Ranginui Walker is Māori. He has a PhD in anthropology from the University of Auckland and is a specialist in Māori education. Among other functions, he has been professor at the Māori Studies Department of the University of Auckland and columnist for the *NZ Listener* and *Metro*. He has, since 2003, been a member of the Waitangi Tribunal. He has published many books and scientific articles. See his biography by Spoonley (2009).

9 As underlined by Van Meijl (2006), "[s]trictly speaking, the beach is not part of the foreshore, yet free access to the beach became the main subject of debate" (77; see also Ruru 2004: 68).

10 Note that the decline in Labour Party support can be attributed to a larger series of controversial bills, among them the Supreme Court Bill – which withdrew the right of appeal to the Privy Council of London and created a New Zealand Supreme Court – the Prostitution Reform Bill, and a series of announcements about schools fusions and closings (Miller 2005: 167).

11 For details on the circumstances of the creation of the party and its first years, see Durie (2005a); Miller (2005); Mutu (2011); Smith (2010a, 2010b); Walker (2004).

12 For further discussion on this process of unification beyond social class lines among Māori as well as the larger ethnic or racial polarization, see Barber (2008); Gagné (2008a, 2008b, 2009a); Miller (2005). See Smith (2010b) for a brief historical retrospective of key Māori political groups and parties; see also, among others, Cox (1993); Hazlehurst (1993); Durie (1998); Walker (2004).

13 For the text of the agreement, see Māori Party, "Confidence and Supply Agreement between Us and the National Party" (accessed 4 April 2011): http://www.maoriparty.org/index.php?pag=cms&id=153&p=national-party-and-the-māori-party-agreement.html. See also Mutu (2011).

14 See Te Puni Kōkiri, "Whānau Ora Fact Sheet" (accessed 15 March 2011): http://www.tpk.govt.nz/_documents/whanau-ora-factsheet.pdf.

15 New Zealand was – with Australia, Canada, and the United States – among the four countries who voted against the adoption, by the UN General Assembly, of the Declaration on the Rights of Indigenous Peoples on 13 September 2007.

16 The Act, however, contains limitations that have left some Māori dissatisfied, one being the necessity to prove continuous use and occupation since 1840. It is also in relation to this issue that the Māori Party MP Hone Harawira publicly challenged the party for its support of the National government's proposed bill in January 2011 in an interview published in the *Sunday-Star Times* (for example, Bennett and Donnell 2011). The event led to his resignation from the party at the end of February 2011 and later that year to the creation of the Mana Party. For a discussion on the background of the enactment of the Act, the changes it brought about, and its consequences on the development of the law in the area concerned by the new Act, see Boast (2011).

17 The case was made widely known through the internet, with photos and videos that supported that the "whole community was traumatized" (Mutu 2011: 180) after it was locked down and barricaded by police. The raids sparked controversy when the police sought to charge sixteen people – twelve of them Māori – under the Terrorism Suppression Act 2002. See Keenan (2008); Mutu (2011) for more details on this affair.

18 For an analysis of who some of those *iwi* (tribal) leaders are and their strategies – and a quite severe critique – see Rata (2011a, 2011b). In my opinion, these preliminary general overviews need to be more complex and complemented by more detailed qualitative studies.

19 A new Māori national television channel, Māori Television, was launched in March 2004. In March 2008, a second channel, called Te Reo, which literally means "the language," was launched. It is the first channel ever to broadcast 100 per cent in the Māori language. On Māori television, see Paul (2005); Smith (2011).

20 Poata-Smith (2004b) and Rata (2000, 2011a, 2011b) add some nuances to the analysis by pointing to important aspects of the situation to which we will return in more detail. They explain how, by the early 1990s, tribal corporation representatives and Māori business interests were able to

concentrate power and money in their hands, consolidating class structures within Maoridom.

21 The Māori Economic Taskforce is a symposium created in January 2009 as a result of the Māori Economic Summit hosted by the minister of Māori affairs, Pita Sharples, "to respond to the recession by looking at ways to grow the Māori economy and create employment" and "to embrace kaupapa Māori [Māori principles] in all that we do" (Sharples 2011).

22 For just one example among many, see O'Sullivan (2011). See also Rata (2011a, 2011b).

23 The transformations in the relationships between Māori and non-Māori are due to a set of factors, including, in no particular order, the state's actions and discourses, the actions and discourses of Māori elites, "ordinary" Māori's support for their leaders, the role of the media, and contingencies such as the foreshore and seabed controversy. For a fuller analysis, see Gagné (2008a, 2008b, 2009a).

24 See, among others, Durie (1995); Orange (2011); O'Sullivan (2007); Rata (2000); Schwimmer (1999, 2004a); Sissons (1992, 1993); Pearson (1991, 1996); Webster (1998); Smits (2010).

25 For a detail account, see Harris (2004a); Walker (2004).

26 Throughout this book, when referring to "activism" and "activists," I mean active involvement in social and political groups or movements at the community or broader levels. I do not imply, like particular New Zealand media, that activists are people whose actions are illegal; though some may be, they are certainly the exception.

27 The period of the "fiscal envelope" (1994–5) could be seen as exceptional. We will return to this episode.

28 McCormack (2012: 421) insists on the idea that "[a] surprising feature of neoliberalism is its amenability to socially liberal identity politics . . . ; neoliberalism appears to open spaces for indigeneity" (see also Edwards and Moore 2009; Lewis, Lewis, and Underhill-Sem 2009; McCormack 2011). In New Zealand, Māori recognition and official biculturalism seem compatible with neoliberal policies that favour changes toward devolution and privatization, including the transfer of state services to private or semi-private organizations, such as tribes. According to Rata (2000, 2003, 2011a, 2011b), these dynamics have given rise to what she calls "neotribal capitalism" and the "corporate tribes." For Māori perspectives, see also Bargh (2007b); Poata-Smith (2005).

29 According to Williams (2010: 18), the book by King (1975), *Te Ao Huri-huri*, "set an important yet problematic benchmark for both urban and rural Māori about what constituted 'authentic' Māori communities. With

the exception of Walker's essay on cultural continuity in urban areas, the implicit message contained in *Te Ao Hurihuri* was that the decades following World War Two had fostered inauthentic and state-coerced forms of urban Māori communities and cultures" (2010: 18). Harris (2007–8) also insists that "the Department of Māori Affairs consistently interpreted and measured Māori against the success or failure of their integration into mainstream society" (142). And Sissons (2005) highlights how "[r]acial and evolutionary categories continue to inform this process" (39). Prout (2011: 276) also draws attention to the role of social scientists in a similar "deeply contentious urban Aboriginal authenticity discourse" in Canada and Australia. Quoting Rowse (2000), she notes that "the notion of 'urban Aboriginality' is rarely simply a geographical categorisation. It is implicitly socialized. In part, . . . this social construction which equates 'urban' with 'assimilated' is the product of a powerful enduring assumption that consigns authentic Aboriginality to a traditional . . . past" (Prout 2011: 276; see also Lavanchy 2009 on the Mapuche of Chile). Prout (2008, 2011) also adds that if this assumption has received very little attention from social scientists, it speaks volume about why research has primarily focused on location "out there," largely in non-urban regions.

30 A few novels (Grace 1992, 1998; Ihimaera 1973, 1974) and short stories (Grace 1980; Ihimaera 1972, 1992–6; *Te Ao Hou* 1952–75) also give insights into the period of urban drift and the relationships between rural and urban dwellers.

1 An Overview of Māori and New Zealand History

1 On the Māori contribution to the war effort and its effect on their recognition by the state and in the nation, and on Māori consciousness, pride, and confidence, see, among others, Gardiner (1992); King (2001); Soutar (2008); Walker (2004).

2 On the development of New Zealand's national identity, see Sinclair (1986, 1990b); Hamer (1990). According to Sinclair (1990b: 5), "European New Zealanders first came to think of themselves as a nation in the period, approximately, 1890 to say 1914." Sinclair (1990b: 5) considers a crucial factor is that for the first time in 1886, according to the census, New Zealand-born Pākehā (the population of predominantly European ancestry) outnumbered immigrants. Among other factors, he stresses the importance of the South African war (1899–1902), also known as the "Boer war," as a stimulus to nationalism among New Zealanders as well as Canadians and

Australians. During that war, troops from the colonies of settlement fought for the first time alongside the British troops (Sinclair 1986: 125).

3 For example, on 7 April 2008 New Zealand signed a Free Trade Agreement (FTA) with China, as part of "New Zealand's objective of broadening and deepening relations in Asia and with China in particular, and advances our goal of strengthening our economic ties in the Asia-Pacific region" (*New Zealand Herald* 2008).

4 Rata (2000) attributes the bicultural project to liberal guilt and the subsequent emancipative idealism characteristic of the new middle class in postwar New Zealand.

5 In the historical division, I follow Schwimmer (2001b).

6 See Belich (1996), in particular chapters 5 to 11, for a detailed history of the European discovery of New Zealand and its colonization by the British (see also Hill 1986; Salmond 1991a, among many others).

7 Belich (1996: 297–312) adds some nuances and shows how the migrants were much more varied than some claimed: brides, governesses, carpenters and other craftsmen, gentry, invalids, and investors. These different people were attracted by different aspects of the myths of settlement (see Belich 1996 for details).

8 For a linguistic analysis of the treaty, see Biggs (1989). For more general discussions of the treaty's historical context, its interpretation, and its consequences, including on New Zealand's law and constitution, see, among others, Belgrave (2005a); Brookfield (2006); Durie (1991); Harris (2010); Hayward (2010a); Kawharu (1989b); Kelsey (1990, 1991); Orange (2011); Renwick (1991); Sharp (1991); Palmer (2008); Van Meijl (1994); Walker (1989).

9 The Supreme Court was created in 1841. It was renamed the High Court of New Zealand in 1980, in anticipation of the creation, in 2003, of a final court of appeal, which was called the Supreme Court of New Zealand.

10 The court's decision was taken in the case known as *Wi Parata v Bishop of Wellington*. For details on the factual background of the case and the insights it provides into Māori and non-Māori relations in the nineteenth century as well as into the legal position of the Treaty of Waitangi in New Zealand, see Williams (2011).

11 About 40 chiefs signed the treaty on 6 February 1840, and by the end of the year, there were about 500 Māori – including 13 Māori women – who had signed it (see Ministry for Culture and Heritage, "Signing the Treaty," in *New Zealand History Online* (accessed 20 June 2012): http://www.nzhistory. net.nz/Gallery/treaty-sigs/index.htm). See also Orange (2011).

12 This ceremony to the *marae* has become an important moment for Māori activists to express their grievances to the prime minister, other politicians,

and the media. See Rosenblatt (2005) for examples and a discussion. See also McAllister (2007).

13 The period between 1846 and 1853 is qualified by Belich (1996: 225) as the "golden age of Pākehā land buying."

14 On the confiscation of Māori land known as *raupatu* (see Gilling 2009 for details on the meaning of the word), in particular from the 1960s, see Boast (2008) and Boast and Hill (2009a). As mentioned by Boast and Hill (2009b) and Gilling (2009), the historiography of Māori land confiscations is very thin.

15 Among others, on the New Zealand wars, see Belich (1988 [1986], 1996, 2010); Durie (1998); Keenan (2009); Orange (2011); Sinclair (1957); Walker (2004); Ward (1995); Wright (2006).

16 See Belich (1996) for details on the adaption of the *pā* construction during the New Zealand wars.

17 The King movement (Te Kingitanga) began in the 1850s in an attempt to halt the sales of land and promote Māori authority in facing the British colonizers. A number of tribes supported the movement. They chose a Waikato chief, Pōtatau Te Wherowhero, as the first king in 1858. Pōtatau was succeeded by his son Tāwhiao in 1860. His kingship coincided with the Waikato war of 1863–4, after which he led his people into retreat in the lands south of Te Awamutu, which are known today as the King Country. The King movement thus became centred on the Waikato region and people. It still exists today. The Māori king since 2006 is Tūheitia Paki (for more details on the King movement and its history, see, among others, Belich 1988 [1986], 1996; Jones 1959; King 2007; Mahuta 1978, 1995b; McCan 2001; Roa 2010; Sinclair 2000; Van Meijl 1993; Walker 2004).

18 "The small number of Māori who owned individual freehold land were still allowed to vote in the European electorates. This 'dual vote' would survive until 1893 . . . Law changes in 1893 and 1896 completed the almost total separation of the Māori and European electoral systems. From then until 1975 only so-called 'half-castes' were allowed to choose which seats they wished to vote in." (Elections New Zealand, "Māori and the Vote," accessed 4 April 2011: http://www.elections.org.nz/study/education-centre/history/maori-vote.html.

19 They were already a precedent for special representation in the case of ex-soldiers and holders of a miner's licence (for details, see Sullivan 2010: 253). This provided an additional reason to grant Māori special representation: "The South Island warranted extra seats in Parliament because of the influx of gold miners, and provisions for two additional parliamentary seats to accommodate the Otago and Westland miners were going to alter

the balance of power between North and South Island parliamentarians
– providing three Māori seats in the North Island and one in the South island retained the status quo" (Sullivan 2010: 254).

20 See Elections New Zealand, "Māori and the Vote" (accessed 4 April 2011):
http://www.elections.org.nz/study/education-centre/history/maori-vote.
html.

21 The Election Act 1893 made New Zealand the first self-governing nation
in the world to grant women the right to vote in parliamentary elections.
However, women would only obtain the right to stand for Parliament in
1919. See Elections New Zealand, "Votes for Women" (accessed 4 April
2011): http://www.elections.org.nz/study/education-centre/history/votes-
for-women.html.

22 See History Group of the New Zealand Ministry for Culture and Heritage,
"Change in the 20th Century – Maori and the Vote," in *New Zealand History Online* (accessed 7 August 2008): http://www.nzhistory.net.nz/politics/
maori-and-the-vote/twentieth-century.

23 The Māori Women Welfare League was created in 1951. "Delegates were
from welfare committees established by Māori Welfare Officers under the
Māori Welfare Act 1945" (Hopa 2011; for more details, see also Hill 2009;
Walker 2004).

24 The first wardens were officially designated in the Maori Social and Economic Advancement Act in 1949, but Māori wardens began assuming leadership roles earlier. They were seen by the Department of Maori Affairs as
a "police force" for the tribal executives and committees. See Hill (2009)
and Walker (1975) for details.

25 Hill (2009: 53) remarks, for example, that "[i]n Auckland, as in other urban
areas, there were tensions within the system between old and young, and
many difficulties inherent in a situation in which leaders dealt with con-
stituents from a multiplicity of tribes. Their limited access, in a non-tribal
operating environment, to both coercive power and tribal sanctions was
just one of many problems." For further details on tribal and Māori committees, see Hill (2009); Metge (1964); Walker (1975); Winiata (1967).

26 Sullivan (2001) identifies four phases in the relationship between the New
Zealand government and Māori: (1) assimilation, from the conquest until
the beginning of the 1960s; (2) integration, from the beginning of the 1960s
until 1984; (3) devolution, from 1984 until 1990; (4) mainstreaming, 1990 to
the time she wrote her article.

27 For a comprehensive study on the place of the Treaty of Waitangi in New
Zealand history, see Orange (2011).

28 Referring to Māori, I will use the word "people," which avoids the debate and is used extensively by Māori themselves. This word has also been the subject of struggles in indigenous forums around the world, and especially at the United Nations, and Māori have been deeply involved in these struggles (see, for example, Gagné 2008c; Maaka and Fleras 2005; Smith 1999). It has been finally retained in the 2007 Declaration on the Rights of Indigenous Peoples. In contrast with the First *Nations* in Canada, to speak of Māori in terms of a "nation" has always been problematic, since the term has a Western origin and refers to a different cultural experience (Williams 1997). Durie (2001b) recognizes this, but still insists on the legitimacy of the word "nation" in speaking of Māori. However, this book as a general rule reserves the term "nation" to refer to the New Zealand nation.

29 For further discussion on biculturalism in Aotearoa/New Zealand, see, among others, Durie (1995); Kawharu (2008); Kelsey (1989, 1990, 1996); Levine (1999); Sharp (1995); Metge (2010); Mulgan (1989); O'Sullivan (2007); Pearson (1991, 1994, 1996); Rata (2000, 2005); Schwimmer (1968, 1999, 2004a); Sissons (1992, 1993, 1995); Vasil (2000); Webster (1998).

30 Note that the fiscal envelope was forgotten as soon as the Labour government came to power in 1999. Compensation payments follow the same norms as before, but without artificial limits.

31 This group, whose name means "The Young Warriors," aimed to challenge the Pākehā Establishment. The group was created at the University of Auckland and organized a series of programs in Auckland and Wellington to help Māori migrants seeking jobs in the city and to give legal advice to Māori who were summoned to court. The group also asked for the Māori language to be included in the school system. The members of Ngā Tamatoa included people such as Linda Tuhiwai Smith, Syd and Hana Jackson, Peter Rikys, and Donna Awatere (Walker 2004: 210–11; see also Spoonley 2009; Harris 2004a).

32 See Te Taura Whiri i te Reo Māori, "History" in *Māori Language Commission* (accessed 7 August 2008): http://www.tetaurawhiri.govt.nz/english/issues_e/hist/index.shtml.

33 It seems to me that George (2010, 2011) is right in emphasizing that there were many periods of cultural renaissance in the Māori post-contact history, and that each period has its own characteristics. In her discussion of the development of *marae*, she identifies three renaissance periods: a first one, associated with the New Zealand wars, from the 1870s to the 1890s; a second one, which followed the leadership of Apirana Ngata, from 1909 to the 1930s; and a third one from the 1970s to the present.

34 Note that a first generation of intellectual leaders, among them the well-known Apirana Ngata, Peter Hiroa (Buck), and Maui Pomare, did a great deal for Māori in the early nineteenth century. However, the context being different at that time, they were indebted to the Pākehā culture and people, and were in a position of compromise, which gave them less room for direct opposition than the later urban revolutionaries (Allen 2002). On contradiction in Ngata's thinking between tribalism and individualism as Māori roads for Māori success, see Sissons (2000, 2004). See also Walker (2001).

35 For a general overview of the development of Māori education since the end of the 1950s until the 1990s based on personal experiences, see Metge (2008).

36 See, among many others, Belich (2001); Cheater and Hopa (1997); Maaka (1994); Sissons (1993); Smith (1997); Walker (2004), on initiatives linked to the promotion of the Māori language by both Māori and the state.

37 See Te Taura Whiri i te Reo Māori, "History," in *Māori Language Commission* (accessed 7 August 2008): http://www.tetaurawhiri.govt.nz/english/ issues_e/hist/index.shtml.

38 Minde (1996: 227) adds the following point: "The Indian organisations focused almost entirely on the rights question, whilst their counterparts among the Sami came little by little to give most attention to cultural issues."

39 Note that the word *whenua* also means the afterbirth. We will come back to these different meanings of the word. In 2003, the associate Māori affairs minister, Tariana Turia, later supported by, among others, Ranginui Walker and Patu Hohepa, called for the use of *tāngata whenua* as more appropriate than "Māori" since "Māori" is a word to describe the collective of their people that came into use after the arrival of the colonizers (see, for example, Thomson 2003).

40 Note that there is a distinction between administrative and moral responsibilities. While *iwi* (tribes) are now responsible for different services, it does not mean that they are equally active in their role as guardian of Māori values and traditions. We will see throughout this book that *whānau* (extended families) are now mainly responsible for the transmission of Māori values and of culture more generally.

41 For details, see, among others, O'Malley (1998, 2009). Note that O'Malley (2009: 69) insists on seeing colonization as a complex process in which cultural change combines both processes of appropriation and dispossession.

42 "The trust board model had been pioneered by the Crown in the 1920s to allow tribes to manage compensation payments which had been

negotiated. The model was later developed to provide tribal representation for more general purposes. But trust boards also provided the Crown with a considerable degree of control . . . Even conservative pakeha, seeing the usefulness of boards as tools for accommodating and containing Maori counter-discourse, could approve of them. For tribes, however, . . . [t]hey offered opportunities for retaining or regaining a degree of autonomy in a generally unsympathetic socio-political environment. In the view of many board and tribal members, too, trust boards embodied a certain degree of state recognition of tribal authority. When controversy arose around systematizing and consolidating boards under the Maori Trust Boards Act in 1955, the desirability of the boards went unquestioned by tribal leaders" (Hill 2009: 47–8).

43 "The term refers to having descent from an ancestor who came on one of the settlement canoes in the distant past" (Carter 2003b: 11).

44 For an overview of Māori representation in the New Zealand government since colonization, see, for example, Sullivan (2003, 2010).

45 For more on Māori and Parliament, including their relation to political parties, the changes brought about by the MMP system, and Māori in Māori and general seats, see Bargh (2010). Note that after five elections under MMP, a referendum on the voting system was held with the 2011 general election (it was a pre-election promise of the National Party) (*New Zealand Herald* 2009). Voters had to answer two questions: (1) if they wish to change the MMP voting system and (2) what alternative system they would prefer among a list of five options (see http://www.referendum.org.nz/sites/all/themes/referendum/resources/Fact-Sheet_Whats_The_Difference.pdf). Some commentators – not necessarily in favour of Māori seats otherwise – have criticized the National-led government for gerrymandering the referendum by ensuring that every voting option except MMP will increase the number of Māori (for example, Newman 2011). A majority of voters (57.77 per cent) voted in favour of keeping the MMP voting system. In 2012, an independent review of MMP will take place and recommend changes that should be made to the way MMP works in New Zealand, but the size of Parliament and Māori representation will not be reviewed (the 2008 Confidence and Supply Agreement between the National Party and the Māori Party prevented any question on the future of the Māori seats during the referendum). For more details on the referendum, its results, and the review process, see Elections New Zealand website (accessed 22 December 2011): http://www.elections.org.nz/.

46 The new council combines seven existing city and district councils in the Auckland region into one "super council."

47 See Auckland Council, "Māori Relations" (accessed 13 January 2011): http://www.aucklandcouncil.govt.nz/EN/ABOUTCOUNCIL/HOWCOUN-CILWORKS/MAORI_RELATIONS/Pages/maoristatutoryboard.aspx.

48 For more details on the fiscal envelope and the related protest actions, see, among others, Durie (1998); Gardiner (1996); Harris (2004a); Mutu (2011); Rosenblatt (2005); Walker (2004).

49 Hone Heke was a Ngā Puhi chief who signed the Treaty of Waitangi, but who was later dissatisfied with British government. He had a very important role in the Northern War of 1845–6. Among others, see Belich (1988 [1986], 1996); Moon (2001); Walker (2004).

50 In 1999, a new coalition government, the Labour-Alliance government (McLeay 2001), was elected. The idea of a fiscal envelope was not reintroduced until the pre-electoral campaign of 2005.

51 However, Hayward (2001: 495) warns that these figures could be misleading in their raw form even if, in the past, there has been room for criticism of the tribunal's productivity.

52 See Māori Party, "Confidence and Supply Agreement between Us and the National Party" (accessed 4 April 2011): http://www.maoriparty.org/index.php?pag=cms&id=153&p=national-party-and-the-māori-party-agreement.html.

53 For a brief summary, see Gagné (2008c).

54 For more details, see Gagné (2011).

55 Sir Mason Durie is Māori. He has a PhD in Psychology from McGill University and is a specialist in Māori development, health, and social policy. He is professor of Māori research and development and assistant vice-chancellor (Māori and Pasifika) at Massey University. He has published many books and scientific articles.

2 Māori Lives in Auckland

1 The city's population hit a landmark 1.5 million in February 2012. Auckland's population growth has been fast since it hit "500,000 at the 1961 Census but crossed the one million mark by the time of the 1996 Census" (Tan 2012).

2 Statistics New Zealand, "Ethnicity," in *Mapping Trends in the Auckland Region* (accessed 22 December 2011): http://www.stats.govt.nz/browse_for_stats/people_and_communities/geographic-areas/mapping-trends-in-the-auckland-region/ethnicity.aspx.

3 For a statistical picture of Māori in New Zealand today, see Statistics New Zealand, "QuickStats about Māori" (accessed 7 August 2008): http://www.

stats.govt.nz/NR/rdonlyres/095030F8-BD62-4745-836D-0EF185619C37/0/200
6censusquickstatsaboutmaorirevised.pdf.

4 Note that the high mobility of Māori, due to their frequent journeys between places in the city and between urban and rural sites, and that many
do not have a stable residential address, often living at kin's places for short
or long stays, make the establishment of precise and reliable statistics difficult. For example, according to Statistics New Zealand, between 2001 and
2006, only 39 per cent of the Māori population in Auckland that had been
living in New Zealand in 2001 had not moved. This population is more mobile than the Pacific and Asian populations and Māori in general are more
likely than other groups to move inter-regionally. Among the participants
in this research, some think for Māori who live in cities that the reality is
closer to 75 per cent (25 per cent had not moved in that period). In 2001, according to Johnston, Poulsen, and Forrest (2005: 117), just under 20 per cent
of Māori lived in rural areas. In recent years, there have also been movements of return to the country (Rata 2000). However, the 2006 Census reveals that "in general the size of the outflows is very similar to the size of
the inflows, indicating a significant exchange of people between areas" (Statistics New Zealand, "Māori Mobility in New Zealand," accessed 26 August
2009: http://www.stats.govt.nz/Publications/PopulationStatistics/internal-
migration/maori-mobility/where-are-maori-moving-to.aspx). In each case,
the definition of who is Māori could also have had a certain impact on these
figures. This indicates also that the urban migration is not irreversible and
that urban and tribal milieus are interconnected.

5 Notable exceptions are Cheater and Hopa (1997); Cram and Pitama (1998);
Durie (1998, 2001a, 2001b); Durie, Black et al. (1994); Kawharu (1975); Liu,
McCreanor, McIntosh, and Teaiwa (2005); Metge (1964, 1995); Schwimmer
(2003, 2004a); Walker (1996); Webster (1998); all of whom have explicitly acknowledged Māori diversity. Poata-Smith (1996) and Spoonley (1991) affirm
that this also applies to Pākehā. They too are greatly diversified socially, economically, and ideologically. They are not a homogenous group confront-
ing Māori in a uniform, unified, and hostile way even if certain contexts
or recent events like those surrounding the so-called foreshore and seabed
controversy contribute to a polarization of New Zealand society along eth-
nic/racial lines.

6 See also Poata-Smith (2005) for a similar critique of Walker (2004).

7 See Te Puni Kōkiri, "Whānau Ora Fact Sheet" (accessed 15 Mars 2011):
http://www.tpk.govt.nz/_documents/whanau-ora-factsheet.pdf.

8 In the 2006 Census, "[a] total of 102,366 people of Māori descent did not
know their iwi. This is a decrease of 8.4 percent, compared with 2001,

and a 9.1 percent decrease since 1996" (Statistics New Zealand, "Quick Stats about Māori," accessed 26 August 2009: http://www.stats.govt.nz/ Census/2006CensusHomePage/quickstats-about-a-subject/maori/maori-descent-and-iwi-ko-nga-kawai-whakaheke-maori-me-nga-iwi.aspx). This can be seen as an illustration of the retribalization process and diverse types of networking initiatives put in place in the last years.

9 See Sharp (2002) for the different principles of association behind the diverse kinds of Māori groupings. The two last kinds of groupings could work in almost every aspect like extended families. Williams (2010) speaks of "surrogate extended family." We will come back to this kind of groupings more extensively.

10 In Auckland City, 20.3 per cent of Māori speak the Māori language, while it is spoken by 23.7 per cent of Māori nationwide (Statistics New Zealand, "Quick Stats about Auckland City," accessed 26 June 2012: http:// www.stats.govt.nz/Census/2006CensusHomePage/QuickStats/AboutA-Place/SnapShot.aspx?type=ta&ParentID=1000002&tab=Culturaldiversity &id=2000007).

11 Although statistical studies quantifying Māori internal migration exist (see, for example, documents by Statistics New Zealand, but also Bedford, Didham, Ho, and Hugo 2004; Bedford and Pool 2004), I have not come across any recent and comprehensive studies about the reasons for internal migration for Māori, even though this phenomenon is significant, since,· according to Statistics New Zealand, more than 60 per cent of the Māori population have moved at least once within New Zealand between 2001 and 2006.

12 For details on early and dynamic community action projects in Ōtara, South Auckland, see Walker (1970).

13 The following is the list of the Auckland *mana whenua* groups whose representatives were invited to a meeting (in July 2010) to form a selection committee. This selection committee's task was to appoint nine members for the statutory board to assist the Auckland Council in its decision making: Ngāti Whātua, Te Uri o Hau, Ngāti Whātua o Kaipara, Ngāti Whātua o Ōrākei, Ngāti Wai, Ngāti Manuhiri, Ngāti Rehua, Te Kawerau a Maki, Ngāti Te Ata, Te Ākitai. Ngai Tai ki Tamaki, Ngāti Tamaoho, Waikato-Tainui, Ngāti Paoa, Ngāti Whanaunga, Ngāti Maru, Ngāti Tamaterā, Patukirikiri, and Ngāti Hako. See Independent Māori Statutory Board, "What We Do" (accessed 15 January 2012): http://imsb.maori.nz/what. html.

14 For a more complete picture of the situation of Māori children and youth who live in the Auckland region, see Statistics New Zealand, 2001, *Tamariki*

Māori – Auckland Region and Rangatahi Māori – Auckland Region (accessed 15 January 2012): http://www.stats.govt.nz/browse_for_stats/people_and_communities/maori/maori-regional-reports.aspx.

15 "Low income" corresponds to those "whose equivalised gross income is less than 60 percent of the overall median equivalised gross household income" (Kiro, von Randow, and Sporle 2010: 23).

16 For education, health, and work and income statistics see the website of Te Puni Kōkiri (Ministry of Māori Development) (accessed 2 September 2009): http://www.tpk.govt.nz/.

17 See works on transnational migrants including Rapport (1997, 1998) and Clifford (1994).

18 I show elsewhere how colonial history and the state established the structural conditions that encourage spiritual separatism (Gagné 2009b). Disengagement from the larger society and world is thus not simply an individual question, but has powerful structural and collective causes.

19 When quoting interviewees directly, I indicate pauses and breaks in speech with ellipses. Omissions are indicated with ellipses enclosed in square brackets.

20 See Waymouth (2003), but also Rata (2000) for more details on the process.

21 The Act was repealed in 1991, but the model in favour of tribal distribution endured (see Carter 2003).

22 See also Maaka and Fleras (2005: 90–3) for the questions that provided a framework for the Fisheries Case debate and court cases.

23 For more details on the Māori Fisheries Act 2004, see Durie (2005a) as well as the Act itself: Parliamentary Counsel Office, "Māori Fisheries Act 2004," *New Zealand Legislation: Acts* (accessed 6 April 2011): http://www.legislation.govt.nz/act/public/2004/0078/latest/DLM311464.html.

24 This more general meaning is that which is used in the report *Well-being and Disparity in Tāmaki-makaurau* by the James Henare Māori Research Centre (2002).

25 Note that Maaka and Fleras (2005: 80) do not see "urban Māori" in the same way. They think the expression is a misnomer since "it does not pertain solely to those who live in cities," but also includes Māori who live in small towns and who keep contributing to the local Māori communities and maintaining traditions. Obviously, the expression "urban Māori" does not necessarily involve the kind of rupture that Debra mentions.

26 Social scientists have not paid much attention to how people use the concept of "comfort" to speak about themselves, their relationships with family and others, their everyday and new experiences, and their place in the

nation state. Two exceptions are Rybczynski (1986), who examined the history of domestic comfort and the home as lived by the French, Dutch, English, American, and Canadian middle and upper classes, and Radice (2000), who studied what made Anglo-Montrealers feel comfortable in the Montréal of the late 1990s.

27 "In 1965, 65 per cent of Otara schoolchildren were Pakeha. In 1980, the figure was 12 per cent" (Belich 2001: 473).

28 After adjustments for differences of definition and other standards between countries, New Zealand's total recorded violent crime rate is almost four times lower than that of the United States, 13 per cent lower than that of England and Wales, and 44 per cent lower than Canada's (see New Zealand Ministry of Justice, "Summary," in *International Comparisons of Recorded Violent Crime Rates for 2000* (accessed 8 August 2008): http://www.justice.govt.nz/pubs/reports/2002/intl-comparisons-crime/section-9.html).

29 Radice (2000: 113–15) reveals the presence of similar extreme images among Anglo-Montrealers likening the situation in Québec variously to war zones, "a Sarajevo situation," South Africa under apartheid, and Nazi Germany. Like me, she was surprised by such strong images.

30 This type of narration is common among indigenous peoples more generally. Sissons (2005) explains that this is part of a trend that he describes as eco-indigenism.

31 Walker (1970: 169) shows how people of Ōtara – mainly Māori, but not only – involved in voluntary associations came to speak about themselves as Ngāti Ōtara, the "new tribe of Ōtara."

32 As just one rather typical example, on the website of the 2011 edition of the Ngā Puhi Festival ki Tamaki Mākaurau, one can read, among other things, that the goals of the event will be achieved by "[b]uilding stronger whanau where people feel a sense of belonging and wellbeing" and "Wellbeing through 'Knowing who I am'" (see, accessed 14 March 2011: http://www.ngapuhifestivalkitamaki.maori.nz/node/7).

33 Such arguments are put forward by those who argue in favour of *kaupapa Māori* research; that is, research by Māori, for Māori, in accordance with Māori philosophy and principles (for example, Bishop 1994, 1996; Irwin 1994; Nepe 1991; Pihama 2005; Pihama, Cram, and Walker 2002; Smith 1997; Smith 1999; see a critical discussion by Rata 2004). In return, the success of *kaupapa Māori* research has encouraged more Māori to seek approval and support from their extended family and tribe(s).

34 On being *takatāpui* among Māori, which has become synonymous with being non-heterosexual – either lesbian, gay, bi-sexual, transsexual or queer – see, for example, Murray (2003) and Hutchings and Aspin (2007).

3 The *Marae*: A Symbol of Continuity

1 Meeting houses in collective ownership are not a precolonial institution (George 2010; Mead 1997; Sisson 1998). As we will see, the concept had developed in the contact with Europeans during the course of the nineteenth century. In the pre-European era, carved houses as well as ceremonial courtyards existed at the centre of Māori settlements, but the houses were the property of individual chiefs (Rosenblatt 2011: 414).

2 Walker mentions that "[t]he institution of marae as the open courtyard or forum where oratorical skills were displayed and consensus decisions arrived at in a community has deep roots in the malae of Polynesia" (1987: 143). *Marae* or ceremonial courtyards are indeed found throughout the Polynesian triangle (*malae* in Samoan and Hawaiian; *mala'e* in Tongan) even if their forms and uses vary. In French Polynesia, for example, the *marae* are defined as the spaces reserved for the ceremonial, religious, and social activities of the anciant Polynesians (Saura 2005: 163). Even though these types of sites vary in shape, size, and functions, they consist of two fundamental elements: (1) a rectangular space or courtyard comprising a *ahu* (platform) that is often referred to as a kind of altar for offerings, and (2) a set of stones erected along the platform and in the courtyard, which serve as a stand for deities and ancestors, and also as a backrest for ministers (Saura 2005: 163; see also Conte 2000). In Rapanui (Easter Islands), the word "*ahu*" came to designate the whole *marae* complex. Wooden structures and houses can also be found in the *marae* surroundings.

3 According to Durie (1999: 359), *karakia* (prayers), in particular those taking place on *marae*, emphasize the sense of interconnectedness and unity with a wider reality.

4 Most meeting houses are called after a male ancestor, except on the east coast of the North Island where, according to Metge (1976: 229), every second house is named after a woman. To symbolize the complementarity of the ancestral house and the kitchen or dining hall, the latter often bears the name of the wife, sister, or husband of the ancestor of the ancestral house. As noted by Sissons (2010: 377), *marae* "strongly objectify gender relations, particularly those between husband and wife."

5 Colonization brought about important and lasting changes to the architecture, size, and designs of meeting houses: they became larger and more artistic embellishments were added, whose symbolism and style also changed (for a historical synthesis, see George 2010). The fully carved meeting houses that appeared in the 1840s (see Neich 1993) were an important landmark in the development of meeting houses. However, by the early

twentieth century, the carving arts had almost been lost due to war and other factors (see George 2010), but a revival of these arts was championed by, among others, Apirana Ngata, which led to the creation of the Rotorua School of Māori Arts and Crafts in the 1920s, which contributed to giving a new impulse to carved meeting houses (for details, see Walker 2001, but also George 2010).

6 Because the *marae* traditionally refers to the land immediately in front of the meeting house itself, Māori generally say "on" rather than "in" or "at" *marae*. I have endeavoured to follow this use of prepositions wherever it does not impinge upon the readability of the text in English.

7 As well as for religious considerations this has to do with health issues, since Māori present the worst cancer statistics in New Zealand. A smoke-free nation has been a policy of the Māori Party since its creation. The government and various Māori organizations run many programs to reduce cigarette consumption. "According to Te Hotu Manawa Māori [a Māori health service provider], of the 918 Marae in Aotearoa/New Zealand, over one third (320 sites) have voluntarily declared themselves totally smoke-free. This is in addition to the 20 per cent (195 sites) that are smoke-free due to legal requirements, and a further 15 per cent (129 sites) that are partially smoke-free" (see Cancer Society of New Zealand, "Smoke-free Communities," accessed 16 March 2011: http://www.cancernz.org.nz/reducing-your-cancer-risk/smokefree/smokefree-community/).

8 Metge (1976: 64) distinguishes two sets of meanings for the concept of "*mana.*" Firstly, it is often translated into English as "prestige" or "standing," which implies power in a purely social and political sense. Secondly, and most importantly, relying on Schwimmer (1963), it signifies "power beyond the ordinary possessing and possessed by extra-ordinary individuals" (Metge 1976: 64). *Mana* can be inherited from the ancestors, depending on seniority of descent, sex, and birth order in the family, and it can also come from direct contact with the supernatural (Metge 1976: 64). Both individuals and groups can have *mana* (see chapter 5 for more details).

9 From now on, I will always use the expression "*wharenui*" to speak about the meeting house. This is only a personal preference based on my experience in Aotearoa where, among the people with whom I interacted, it was the expression the most in use.

10 For a detailed description of these processes, see Salmond (1975) and Tauroa and Tauroa (1986).

11 As we already said, this sector is fast growing.

12 The Ringatū Church was founded by Te Kōoti Arikirangi (1830–93). Te Kooti was deported without trial to the Chatham Islands during the East

Coast conflicts of 1864–8. During his captivity, he studied the Bible and held religious services mostly based on the Old Testament. Many of his codetainees converted to his new faith. In June 1868, Te Kooti and his followers seized a vessel and sailed back to New Zealand. Te Kooti was pursued by the colonial forces and fought a series of battles during the New Zealand wars (Belich 1988 [1986]). For years, he fled from the government, hiding out until his pardon in 1883. During all these years, his personal popularity and the popularity of his church continued to grow. Today, the Ringatū Church counts 16,419 members (Census 2006, Statistics New Zealand: http://www.stats.govt.nz/Census/2006CensusHomePage/QuickStats/quickstats-about-a-subject/culture-and-identity.aspx) (on Te Kooti and the Ringatū Church, see Binney 1995; Belich 1988 [1986], 1996).

13 For a good historical review and synthesis of work dealing with the development of the *marae* and meeting-house concept from the early days of Māori and European contacts, see George (2010).

14 See Tapsell (2002) for specific examples of consultation with *tāngata whenua*, including "failed" ones.

15 See Williams (2010, chapter 6) on activities that led to its building and the relations between the *marae* and the Auckland Māori catholic community. See also Harris (2007, 2007–8).

16 See Walker (2008) for details on this *marae* as well as other urban *marae* in Auckland and elsewhere in which the carver Paki Harrison was involved in the building.

17 For details about the meeting house Tāne-nui-a-Rangi, see Harrison (2008). For the specific and highly political history of Waipapa *marae*, see Walker (2008) and Webster (1998).

18 The University of Auckland, "Māori at University" (accessed 18 February 2004): http://www.auckland.ac.nz/cir_visitors/index.cfm?action=display_page&page_title=maori#marae.

19 Walker (1987: 145–6) reminds the reader that urban *marae* projects have often faced objections by non-Māori. Walker mentions that some of those objections – such as fears that they could become "booze barns," create traffic hazards, and attract gangs into an area – were often based on uninformed grounds, on people's ignorance of what constitutes a *marae*. Other objections were that *marae* would bring a devaluation of property in the area, block sunlight, or spoil the view.

20 See Te Puni Kōkiri, "Marae Development Project 2009" (accessed 16 March 2011): http://www.tpk.govt.nz/en/in-focus/marae/.

21 A new kind of *marae* has been built or is still under construction in Kaitaia, in the Northland of New Zealand, designed especially for the enjoyment

of tourists and to educate them about Māori meeting houses and culture (Carter 2003a). A tour operator is building the *marae* because he says he had trouble with the availability of traditional *marae* in the area, as they are sometimes booked at the last minute for funerals or other meetings. The project is highly controversial and some argue that a *marae* can only be truly traditional if its main raison d'être is to serve a particular group of people. Then the chair of the University of Auckland Māori Studies department, Margaret Mutu put it the following way: "If you can't have a tangi, then it can't successfully fulfill its role" (Mutu quoted in Carter 2003a).

22 For a detailed ethnography of this third type of *marae* and how it functions, see George (2010) on Awataha *marae*, a pan-tribal *marae* that caters for the people of Auckland's North Shore. See also Webster (1998) on Waipapa *marae*, the *marae* of the University of Auckland. Note also that factionalism and fights also occur on family, subtribal, and tribal *marae*.

23 Note that the government, through the minister of Native affairs, played a role in this process, since by subsidizing construction of *marae*, it "intended to advance much less radical political agendas. Foremost among these was an increase in Maori culture pride and social integration, both locally and nationally, in order that Maori might better adapt to European and capitalist society" (Sissons 1998: 37).

24 Apirana Ngata (1874–1950) was the first Māori to obtain a university degree. He was a lawyer, a member of Parliament (1905–43), and minister of Māori affairs (1928–34). Among his many other accomplishments, he was president of the Polynesian Society for nine years and devoted himself to ethnological research. For details, see his biography by Walker (2001).

25 Look at the websites of different state departments to be convinced.

4 Ways of Life in a Māori House

1 Kiri is a pseudonym, as are all the personal names used in this book.

2 For more on types of *whānau* that may be unable to take corrective action to ensure the safety of their members without external help, see Durie (2001a), chapter 7 in particular, and Durie (1997). I will only add here that many *whānau* problems are created through the confrontation of different universes of meanings: the traditional universe of meanings of the *whānau* and the Pākehā or mainstream universes of meanings. See chapter 5 for a detailed analysis of this type of confrontation.

3 The Census usual household composition categories used by Statistics New Zealand are couple only, one-parent family, one-parent family plus others, couple with children, couple only plus others, couple with children plus

others, two two-parent families with or without children, two-parent plus one-parent family, two one-parent families, three or more families (Kiro, von Randow, and Sporle 2010: 16). The categories do not account for multigenerational households. Let me mention, however, that according to the report *Trends in Wellbeing for Māori Households/Families, 1981/2006*, "[i]nteractions between social patterns such as demography and economic cycles impact on families and households by shaping the decisions that individuals, families and communities make, and thereby changing them. During times of economic recession, for example, it is more likely that families will group together in multi-family or multi-generational households" (Kiro, von Randow, and Sporle 2010: 15–16). In 2006, 8.3 per cent of Māori households were multifamily households compared to 4.7 per cent in 1981; 45.7 per cent were one-family households in 2006 compared to 68.3 per cent in 1981; and 34.4 per cent were single-parent families in 2006 compared to 13 per cent in 1981 (for a detailed table, see Kiro, von Randow, and Sporle 2010: 20).

4   This comes up very clearly, for example, throughout Ihimaera's work, especially in *Pounamu, Pounamu* (1972) and *The Matriarch* (1986), as underlined by Allen (2002). It is also central to *The Dream Swimmer* (1997), Ihimaera's sequel to *The Matriarch* (1986), as well as his play *Woman Far Walking* (2000). This is also true in Patricia Grace's work. See, for example, *Potiki* (1986), *Cousins* (1992), and *Baby No-Eyes* (1998). In all these works, the two figures of grandparent and *mokopuna* are in constant dialogue; each needs its complementary other.

5   As explained in chapter 3, this word literally means "a place to put one's feet; connection to the land"; "standing place from where one gains the authority to belong" (Tauroa and Tauroa 1986: 166). The term is "used to indicate a place (district, locality, or marae) where an individual or group can be and participate in community affairs as of right" (James Henare Māori Research Centre 2002, col. 3: 155).

6   Metge (2002: 320) argues that Mauss went beyond the evidence in his *Essai sur le don* (1925) in interpreting the concept of "*hau*" as "a purposive entity of retrospective aims." She rather suggests the concept of "*utu*" as the underlying concept of Māori gift exchange, as first suggested by Firth (1959) (see Metge 2002 for details).

7   We will see that the house is not literally open to "everybody." It is open to *whānau* members and friends who respect both the *whānau* principles and the house itself.

8   To show respect to persons of *mana* or simply to persons older than oneself, Māori use terms of address like *whaea* (which can be literally translated as mother) for women and *papa* or *matua* (literally translated as parent and

more precisely, father) for men. Certain other terms are also used depending on tribal area.

9 For statistics on home ownership for Māori from 1981 to 2006, see Kiro, von Randow, and Sporle (2010).

10 By crowding Kiro, von Randow, and Sporle (2010: 34) mean "living in dwellings that require at least one additional bedroom to meet the sleeping needs of the household." For example, for households with two Māori adults, the crowding decreases from 40.3 per cent to 25 per cent, and from 23.2 per cent to 12 per cent for households with one Māori adult.

11 This expression is widely used to speak about the *kohanga reo*, kindergartens based on Māori principles where the medium of socialization is the Māori language.

12 A funeral home is always an option, for a part or all of the funeral, if no other appropriate places are available.

13 That he was gay may explain this decision.

14 I heard this on a few occasions, other than in "Sad Joke on a Marae" by Apirana Taylor (1979), a poem that symbolizes "alienation from Maori tradition" (Allen 2002: 158).

15 Sidney (Hirini) Moko Mead is a specialist of Oceanist art and Māori language and culture. During his tenure as professor in Māori studies at Victoria University of Wellington, Te Herenga Waka, the university *marae* was built, a *kohanga reo* was established, and Māori studies became a department in its own right. When he retired from Victoria University, he established Te Whare Wananga o Awanuiarangi at Whakatane, a Māori tertiary education institution. Professor Mead was cocurator of the international Te Māori exhibition and is a consultant for world's leading art galleries and museums. He has written many books, articles, short stories, and a novel, and also composes poetry and music. He was appointed to the Waitangi Tribunal in 2003.

5 The *Whānau*, Past and Present

1 Note that if the *whānau* includes or excludes others, these others do not automatically become members of or are not automatically rejected from the subtribe and tribe. Each entity or grouping of Māori social organization seems to be autonomous, to a large degree at least, and context dependent. See also Sissons (2010).

2 Note that the importance or primacy of the values changes according to particular contexts; there is a complex combination and hierarchization of values in practice. The case study explored in the next chapter, for example,

illustrates how the value of *mana* can sometimes emerge in practice as the most determining factor in certain acts and events. For more details on the principles or values of the *whānau*, see Metge (1995), but also Metge (2010).

3 Keesing's (1984) analysis of the concept of "*mana*" suggested, through a linguistic comparative analysis, that *mana* was traditionally a stative verb meaning to "be efficacious, be successful, be realized, 'work,'" and, as a noun, it was not a substantive, which would have followed from an English reinterpretation of the term, but an abstract verbal noun meaning "efficacy," "success," "potency." However, since in the field among Māori and throughout the literature about Māori today, the concept of "*mana*" is widely used as a substantive noun meaning "spiritual power; authority stemming from the indwelling of spiritual power; prestige; the ability to do and get things done" (Metge 1995: 333), I favour this interpretation of the concept (see also Lévi-Strauss 1950; Patterson 1992; Metge 1986, 2010).

4 In the late 1980s, new regulations allow the practice of *whāngai* to exist alongside legal adoption (see McRae and Nikora 2006).

5 On New Zealand Native Schools see, for example, Barrington (2008); Simon (1998a, 1998b); Simon and Smith (2001); Stephenson (2006).

6 Durie (Te Puni Kōkiri 2003 in Cunningham, Stevenson, and Tassell 2005: 14) uses the expression "statistical *whānau*" to refer to a tendency in New Zealand publications to use the words "*whānau*," "family," and "household" interchangeably. This usage lacks rigour and makes analysing small collectives problematic.

7 Williams (2010: 51–2) quotes Hohepa (1964) to indicate that this predated the urban migration.

8 I will come back to New Zealand's café culture.

9 Williams (2010: 20) quotes the book *The Silent Migration: Ngati Poneke Young Māori Club 1937–1948* by Grace, Ramsden, and Dennis (2001) in which they show how Māori social transformations in the city could remain silent or invisible.

10 On the other hand, it is important to understand the lack of correspondence between Chinatowns and lived Chinese identity, including the general fact that only a tiny proportion of Chinese immigrant populations live in Chinatowns (see, for example, Anderson 1987).

11 When I refer to "social class" in this book, I refer to general socioeconomic conditions and living styles rather than to the Marxist definition in which the social classes are defined according to the extent of their control over the means of production.

12 Here, I do not intend to essentialize the distinctions between Māori and Pākehā worlds. See chapter 6 for more discussion.

13 More research needs to be done in these areas. See Emery (2008) for a perspective from a *hapū* (subtribe) of Te Arawa confederation of tribes.

14 Today, many tribal trusts offer scholarships to their *iwi* members, shareholders, or direct descendants of shareholders in lands within their tribal area. Each tribal trust has its own set of rules and priorities in awarding its scholarships.

15 See also Emery (2008). She looks at the reconnection or home-coming experience from the point of view of a rural subtribe that is concerned about cultural continuity, in part because of the dispersed or detribalized nature of their people, but also because of the declining number of elders and the relative lack of potential substitutes.

16 Note that the expertise of genealogy specialists is usually necessary to see and understand the relationships between different stories (Schwimmer, personal communication, April 2004).

17 Note that Lyn Waymouth and Lynette Carter is the same person.

18 I refer the reader back to chapter 2 for details.

19 Maybe paradoxically, the state legislation has also made possible for individuals to be entitled to access land regardless of the concept of *ahi kā* through land individualization and the establishment of tribe beneficiary lists (see Carter 2003b for more details).

20 According to basic Māori values, learning history and genealogy is part of *ahi kā* (keeping the fire alight), but today legal procedures and provisions often prevail upon more fundamental traditional values and ways.

21 According to the 2001 Census, nearly half of Māori language speakers are under twenty-five years old.

22 Faced with the incapacity of many men today to demonstrate enough *mana* to assume their proper role on *marae* and during Māori ceremonies in general, the coleader of the Māori Party, Pita Sharples, intervened in favour of a change in protocol to allow women of great *mana* (spiritual power, prestige, authrotiy, status) to speak on *marae*. Sharples suggested this change to save Māori *mana* and to ensure Māori continuity and affirmation, in cases where women are better versed than men in the language and *tikanga* (tradition, customs), especially in terms of local and genealogical history (Berry 2005). This happened following a controversy in November 2005, in which non-Māori female MPs refused to participate in Māori ceremonies held on *marae*, on the pretext that they would not lower themselves to sit behind men (for details on the controversy see Middleton 2005; Thomson 2005; and Curchin 2011; for an analysis of Māori male and female roles and *mana* spheres in the context of this controversy, see Gagné 2010 and Metge 2010).

23 The question of individuals' rights is interesting. Māori students, like any other New Zealand student, have individual rights. They have the choice between working as individuals or working as *whānau* members. If they recognize the authority of the *whānau*, they also give up certain individual rights. It is highly improbable that the *whānau* would forbid students from studying, for example, Russian language and culture, but they might then have to choose between the *whānau* and Russian studies, at least for a certain period of time.

6 A Practical Universe of Meanings

1 I had news from David, however, during my following stays in New Zealand. He kept in touch with his grandparents and siblings and occasionally saw his cousins, aunts, and uncles.

2 Harris (2004b: 200; 2007–8: 146) mentions the possibility of being sent away (with or without the support of relatives) as a Māori disciplining solution in the aftermath of disputes. Banishment from the community, according to Harris (2004b: 200), is the most severe punishment for offenders. She also reminds the reader that "Hohepa [1964: 84–93] recorded a number of instances in Waima, Hokianga, in the late 1950s where disputes within households resulted in offenders leaving home" (Harris 2007–8: 155).

3 If we look more globally at the concept of "*mana*," it is conceived of differently from one culture/people to another (see Lévi-Strauss 1950 and Smith 1974 for details). *Mana* is sometimes thought of as an innate character or nature, and sometimes as a quality that is acquired through life and one's actions. Among Māori, both concepts are significant but, according to Smith (1974), the innate character of *mana* is associated with the eldest son, while acquired *mana* is associated with the youngest son. In the example of the *whānau* dilemma discussed here, people are more preoccupied by the protection of acquired *mana*.

4 This raises the question of what might have been going on at an unconscious or unvoiced level. Past and forgotten personal experiences could have influenced the resolution of the dilemma, as could differences of status between the people involved, which were known but unspoken. The method of analysis I use here does not give access to the unconscious, but does take into account the specific as well as historical contexts in which an event is located. This helps shed light on certain aspects of the event at stake, including certain tacit elements.

5 Note that I am well aware that the vocabulary used here can give the impression that universes of meanings are autonomous entities endowed with

consciousness, but it is difficult to do otherwise. I reaffirm here the view according to which universes of meanings only "live" thanks to the persons and groups that reproduce and change them through history.

6 According to Te Hoe Nuku Roa Research Team (1999: 75), 43.9 per cent of Māori consider that mainstream education is extremely important and 47.5 per cent consider it important.

7 After a constant increase, their number has gradually decreased since 1995. In 1994, there were 800 kindergartens for 14,000 children. See Ministry of Education, "Review of the Relationship between the Crown and Te Kohanga Reo National Trust" (accessed 7 August 2008): http://www.minedu. govt.nz/index.cfm?layout=document&documentid=6158&data=l. This is not due to a fall in the birth rate. Some suggest that the system has reached saturation level, and that some Māori parents are questioning the pragmatic value of these programs in today's world.

8 Ministry of Education, "Kura Kaupapa Māori and Kura Teina Schools," in Education Counts (accessed 7 August 2008): http://www.educationcounts. govt.nz/statistics/data_cubes/quality_education_providers/3792.

9 During fieldwork, it was generally more difficult to interview or talk informally with young Māori men. Many young men that I was supposed to interview did not turn up at our meeting time. On the whole, Māori boys and young Māori men appeared to me to be quite shy and uncommunicative. Perhaps my position as a young, highly educated Western woman from a middle-class background partially explains this lack of rapport, which was not an issue with men over forty years old. In general, the relationships between men and women are very reserved, in particular in public and among strangers.

10 However, one can wonder how long these measures will continue to be applied in view of the constitutional review.

11 Funerals are also a key political site for Māori to resituate themselves in relationship to the New Zealand state and the former colonial powers of the West more generally (see, for one example, Gagné 2012).

7 At the Heart of a Politics of Differentiation

1 See Harris (2007, 2007–8); Walker (1970); and Williams (2010) for a description of lives and Māori organizations in these suburbs from the 1940s to the 1970s. More broadly, on how Māori organize themselves in diverse groupings in a quest for autonomy, with a focus on the urban setting, see also Hill (2009).

2 Note that some Māori also use "sis" for "sister." "Cous" for "cousin" naturally has no gender connotations.

3 For more on this, see Hohepa (1964) and Metge (1964, 1995).

4 Rank here refers to issues of inferior/superior descent in reference to the traditional stratified class structure (for example, Van Meijl 1997), while *mana* is more considered in terms of experience, education, ability, personality, popularity, and respectability (Metge 1964: 159). The generational status is very important, however, and elders (*kaumātua*) are acknowledged and given signs of respect (see Williams 2010: 183).

5 The term is currently translated as "war dance," but this is only one type of *haka*, since posture dance was also used traditionnaly for amusement, beguilement, and welcoming visitors (see, among others, McLean and Orbell 1975; Kaiwai 2003; Smith 2003).

6 For accounts about these competitions and their historical context, see, for example, Kaiwai (2003) and Smith (2003).

7 On the concept of "symbolic competition," see Schwimmer (1972). See also Gagné (2008a, 2008b).

8 See, among others, Barker (2011: 20–1) on Native peoples in the United States. More generally, see also Maaka and Fleras (2005); Niezen (2003, 2009); and Sissons (2005).

9 In general, the Māori with whom I talked do not much appreciate the label "elite." They far prefer "leader," which they feel is less pejorative and more political. As Shore (2002: 3) reminds us, in reference to Marcus (1983: 9), "elite" is typically a term of reference for others rather than a label of self-identification.

10 This is a reply to Rata (2005). See also Gagné (2009a).

11 This is a traditional way of doing things according to traditional *whānau* principles, which include attribution by the *whakapapa* of roles and responsibilities to the *whānau* members according to birth order and generation (see the novel *Cousins* by Grace, 1992, for eloquent examples, and Schwimmer's analysis of this novel, 2004b).

12 Thanks to Éric Schwimmer, for highlighting this point (personal communication, February 2004).

13 The plural indicates that many forms of family are possible beyond the typically modern nuclear family (see, for example, Dagenais 2000).

14 Consider, for example, the universe of meanings of Māori criminal gangs, which is in many respects similar to the universe of meanings of the *whānau*, but very different at the level of fundamental values or principles.

Conclusion: Interconnected Places and Autonomous Spaces

1 The editions of the magazine have been numbered and are now available online at (accessed 9 August 2008): http://teaohou.natlib.govt.nz/journals/teaohou/index.html. For details on Schwimmer's editorial work at *Te Ao Hou/The New World* and his vision for the magazine, see Schwimmer (2004b) and Gagné and Campeau (2008). For an intellectual biography of Schwimmer, see also Gagné and Campeau (2008).

2 On relational ontologies more generally among indigenous peoples, see Poirier (2008) and Clammer, Poirier, and Schwimmer (2004).

3 My research led me to question the dichotomy between so-called "private" and "public" spheres and spaces that is so often assumed in social sciences, particularly in relation to sociocultural contexts where the collective principle is central to everyday activities and practices. In colonial situations, for example, the group or the family is often crucial for engagement outside the circle of kin, in the broader society. The separation between private and public is thus not as sharp as it is generally conceptualized in Western thought, if it exists at all in these terms. This idea needs further investigation. For lack of better concepts for now, I use them here, but with caution.

4 If the *marae* is considered a "Maori public place" by Salmond (1975: 34), "and perhaps it is the last of these," it is not accessible easily or openly to those outside of the *marae* community, not to mention non-Māori. One has to be welcomed on the *marae* through an official welcome ceremony or another way. In this sense, the *marae* can also be seen as a "private place" for its members.

5 This is a wink at Ranginui Walker's (2004) book entitled *Ka Whawhai Tonu Matou. Struggle Without End.*

Glossary

1 JHMRC is the abbreviation used in the glossary for the James Henare Māori Research Centre.

References

Abu-Lughod, Lila. (Original work published 1986) 1999. *Veiled Sentiments: Honor and Poetry in a Bedouin Society*. Los Angeles: University of California Press.

Allen, Chadwick. 2002. *Blood Narrative. Indigenous Identity in American Indian and Maori Literary and Activist Texts*. Durham, London: Duke University Press.

Anderson, Atholl. 1989. "The Last Archipelago: 1000 Years of Maori Settlement in New Zealand." In *Towards 1990: Seven Leading Historians Examine Significant Aspects of New Zealand History*, ed. David Green, 1–19. Wellington, GP Books.

Anderson, Kay J. 1987. "The Idea of Chinatown: The Power of Place and Institutional Practice in the Making of a Racial Category." *Annals of the Association of American Geographers. Association of American Geographers* 77 (4): 580–98. http://dx.doi.org/10.1111/j.1467-8306.1987.tb00182.x.

Ansley, B. 2003. "Who Are You?" *New Zealand Listener* 190 (3305): 13–19. http://www.listener.co.nz/default,675.sm. Accessed 2 October 2005.

Ansley, B. 2004. "Stealing a March." *New Zealand Listener* 193 (3340): 15–21. http://www.listener.co.nz/default,1963.sm. Accessed 2 October 2005.

Austin-Broos, Diane. 2003. "Places, Practices, and Things: The Articulation of Arrernte Kinship with Welfare and Work." *American Ethnologist* 30 (1): 118–35. http://dx.doi.org/10.1525/ae.2003.30.1.118.

Awatere, Donna. 1984. *Maori Sovereignty*. Auckland: Broadsheets.

Ballara, Angela. 1986. *Proud to be White? A Survey of Pakeha Prejudice in New Zealand*. Auckland: Heinemann Publishers.

Ballara, Angela. 1995. "Porangahau: The Formation of an Eighteenth Century Community in Southern Hawkes Bay." *New Zealand Journal of History* 22 (1): 3–18.

Ballara, Angela. 1998. *Iwi: The Dynamics of Māori Tribal Organisation from c.1769 to c.1945*. Wellington: Victoria University Press.

Barber, Keith. 2008. "'Indigenous Rights' or 'Racial Privileges': The Rhetoric of 'Race' in New Zealand Politics." *Asia Pacific Journal of Anthropology* 9 (2): 141–56. http://dx.doi.org/10.1080/14442210802023665.

Barcham, Manuhuia. 1998. "The Challenge of Urban Maori: Reconciling Conceptions of Indigeneity and Social Change." *Pacific Viewpoint* 39 (3): 303–14. http://dx.doi.org/10.1111/1467-8373.00071.

Barcham, Manuhuia. 2004. "The Politics of Maori Mobility." In *Population Mobility and Indigenous Peoples in Australasia and North America*, ed. John Taylor and Martin Bell, 163–83. London: Routledge.

Barker, Joanne. 2011. *Native Acts: Law, Recognition, and Cultural Authenticity*. Durham: Duke University Press.

Bargh, Maria, ed. 2007a. *Resistance: An Indigenous Response to Neoliberalism*. Wellington: Hui Publishers.

Bargh, Maria, ed. 2010. *Māori and Parliament: Diverse Strategies and Compromises*. Wellington: Huia Publishers.

Bargh, Maria. 2007b. "Māori Development and Neoliberalism." In *Resistance: An Indigenous Response to Neoliberalism*, ed. Maria Bargh, 25–44. Wellington: Huia Publishers.

Barrington, John. 2008. *Separate but Equal? Māori Schools and the Crown 1867–1969*. Wellington: Victoria University Press.

Barth, Fredrik. 2000. "Boundaries and Connections." In *Signifying Identities: Anthropological Perspectives on Boundaries and Contested Values*, ed. Anthony P. Cohen, 17–36. London: Routledge.

Barton, Chris. 2011. "The Long Road to Settlement." *New Zealand Herald*, 5 February. http://www.nzherald.co.nz/nz/news/article.cfm?c_id=1&objectid=10704284. Accessed 7 April 2011.

Bedford, Richard, Robert Didham, Elsie Ho, and Graeme Hugo. 2004. "Maori Internal and International Migration at the Turn of the Century: An Australasian Perspective." *New Zealand Population Review* 30 (1–2): 131–41.

Bedford, Richard D., and Ian Pool, 2004. "Flirting with Zelinsky in Aotearoa/New Zealand: A Maori Mobility Transition." In *Population Mobility and Indigenous Peoples in Australasia and North America*, ed. J. Taylor and M. Bell, 44–74. London: Routledge Taylor and Francis Group.

Belgrave, Michael. 2005a. *Historical Frictions: Maori Claims and Reinvented Histories*. Auckland: Auckland University Press.

Belgrave, Michael. 2005b. "The Tribunal and the Past: Taking a Roundabout Path to a New History." In *Waitangi Revisited: Perspectives on the Treaty of Waitangi*, ed. Michael Belgrave, Merata Kawharu, and David Williams, 35–55. South Melbourne: Oxford University Press.

Belgrave, Michael, Merata Kawharu, and David Williams, eds. 2005. *Waitangi Revisited: Perspectives on the Treaty of Waitangi.* South Melbourne: Oxford University Press.

Belich, James. (Original work published 1986) 1988. *The New Zealand Wars and the Victorian Interpretation of Racial Conflict.* Auckland: Penguin Books.

Belich, James. 1996. *Making Peoples: A History of the New Zealanders: From Polynesian Settlement to the End of the Nineteenth Century.* Auckland: Penguin Books.

Belich, James. 2001. *Paradise Reforged: A History of the New Zealanders from the 1880s to the Year 2000.* Auckland: Allen Lane and Penguin Press.

Belich, James. 2009. *Replenishing the Earth: The Settler Revolution and the Rise of the Anglo-World, 1783–1939.* Oxford: Oxford University Press.

Belich, James. (Original work published 1989) 2010. *I Shall Not Die: Titokowaru's War 1868–1869.* Wellington: Bridget Williams Books.

Bennett, Adam. 2011. "Bonus Hint for Loyal SOE Investors." *New Zealand Herald*, 16 December. http://www.nzherald.co.nz/business/news/article.cfm?c_id=3&objectid=10773507. Accessed 20 December 2011.

Bennett, Adam, and Hayden Donnell. 2011. "Maori Leadership Open to Challenge." *New Zealand Herald*, 20 January. http://www.nzherald.co.nz/maori-party/news/article.cfm?o_id=265&objectid=10700861. Accessed 20 December 2011.

Bennion, Tom. 2005. "Lands Under the Sea: Foreshore and Seabed." In *Waitangi Revisited: Perspectives on the Treaty of Waitangi*, ed. Michael Belgrave, Merata Kawharu, and David Williams, 233–47. South Melbourne: Oxford University Press.

Berry, Ruth. 2005 "Let Women Speak says Sharples." *New Zealand Herald*, 18 November. http://subs.nzherald.co.nz/organisation/story.cfm?o_id=265&ObjectID=10355805. Accessed 15 October 2006.

Biggs, Bruce. 1989. "Humpty-Dumpty and the Treaty of Waitangi." In *Waitangi: Maori and Pakeha Perspectives of the Treaty of Waitangi*, ed. I. Hugh Kawharu, 300–12. Auckland: Oxford University Press.

Binney, Judith. 1968. *Legacy of Guilt: A Life of Thomas Kendall.* Auckland: Oxford University Press.

Binney, Judith. 1995. *Redemption Songs: A Life of Te Kooti Arikirangi Te Turuki.* Auckland: Auckland University Press and Bridget Williams Books.

Bishop, Russell. 1994. "Initiating Empowering Research." *New Zealand Journal of Educational Studies* 29 (1): 175–88.

Bishop, Russell, 1996. *Collaborative Research Stories: Whakawhanaungatanga.* Palmerston North: Dunmore Press.

Boast, Richard. 2008. *Buying the Land, Selling the Land: Governments and Maori Land in the North Island 1865–1921.* Wellington: Victoria University Press.

Boast, Richard, 2011. "Foreshore and Seabed, Again." *New Zealand Journal of Public and International Law* 9 (2): 273–86.

Boast, Richard, and Richard S. Hill, eds. 2009a. *Raupatu: The Confiscation fo Maori Land,* Wellinton. Victoria University Press.

Boast, Richard, and Richard S. Hill, 2009b. "Overview: Confiscation in New Zealand." In *Raupatu: The Confiscation of Maori Land,* Richard Boast and Richard S. Hill, 3–12. Wellinton: Victoria University Press.

Borell, Belinda. 2005. "Living in the City Ain't So Bad: Cultural Identity for Young Maori in South Auckland." In *New Zealand Identities: Departures and Destinations,* ed. James H. Liu, Tim McCreanor, Tracey McINtosh, and Teresia Teaiwa, 191–206. Wellington: Victoria University Press.

Bouchard, Gérard. (Original work published 2000) 2008. *The Making of the Nations and Cultures of the New World. An Essay in Comparative History.* Montréal, Kingston: McGill Queen's University Press.

Bourdieu, Pierre. 1977. *Outline of a Theory of Practice.* Cambridge: Cambridge University Press.

Bourdieu, Pierre. 1980. *Le sens pratique.* Paris: Les Éditions de Minuit.

Brash, Don. 2004. "Nationhood." http://www.national.org.nz/files/ OrewaRotaryClub_27Jan.pdf. Accessed 27 September 2005.

Brookfield, F.M. (Jock). (Original work published 1999) 2006. *Waitangi and Indigenous Rights: Revolution, Law and Legitimation.* Auckland: Auckland University Press.

Carlin, Darrell. 2010. "The Fall and Rise of Ngati Whatua." *New Zealand Herald,* 28 August. http://www.nzherald.co.nz/nz/news/article.cfm?c_ id=1&objectid=10667565. Accessed 12 January 2012.

Callister, Paul, Robert Didham, and Deborah Potter. 2005. "Ethnic Intermarriage in New Zealand." Statistics New Zealand Working Paper. Wellington: Statistics New Zealand.

Carter, Bridget. 2003a. "New Marae for Tourists, not Tangi." *New Zealand Herald,* 27 July.

Carter, Ian, and Angela Maynard. 2001. "Tell Me What You Eat . . ." In *Sociology of Everyday Life in New Zealand,* ed. Claudia Bell, 89–112. Palmerston North: Dunmore Press.

Carter, Lynnette Joy. 2003b. "Whakapapa and the State: Some Case Studies in the Impact of Central Government on Traditionally Organised Māori Groups." PhD thesis, University of Auckland.

Chapple, D.R. 1975. "A Timber Town: Some Aspects of Race Relations Between Maori and Non-Maori Immigrant Families in a Small, Single Industry Town." In *Conflict and Compromise: Essays on the Maori Since Colonisation,* ed. I. Hugh Kawharu, 187–211. Wellington, Sydney, London: A.H. & A.W. Reed.

Chapple, Simon. 2000. "Maori Socio-Economic Disparity." *Political Science (Wellington, N.Z.)* 52 (2): 101–15. http://dx.doi.org/10.1177/003231870 005200201.

Charters, Claire. 2007. "Māori and the United Nations." In *Resistance: An Indigenous Response to Neoliberalism*, ed. Maria Bargh, 147–65. Wellington: Huia Publishers.

Charters, Claire, and Andrew Erueti, eds. 2007. *Māori Property Rights and the Foreshore and Seabed: The Last Frontier*. Wellington: Victoria University Press.

Cheater, Angela, and Ngapare Hopa. 1997. "Representing Identity." In *After Writing Culture: Epistemology and Praxis in Contemporary Anthropology*, ed. Allison James, Jenny Hockey, and Andrew Dawson, 208–23. London, New York: Routledge.

Cheng, Derek. 2011. "Nats and Maori Party Sign." *New Zealand Herald*, 11 December. http://www.nzherald.co.nz/nz/news/article.cfm?c_id=1&objectid=10772529. Accessed 15 January 2012.

Clammer, John, Sylvie Poirier, and Eric Schwimmer, eds. 2004. *Figured Worlds: Ontological Obstacles in Intercultural Relations*. Toronto: Toronto University Press.

Clifford, James. 1994. "Diasporas." *Cultural Anthropology* 9 (3): 302–38. http://dx.doi.org/10.1525/can.1994.9.3.02a00040.

Coates, Ken S. 2004. *A Global History of Indigenous Peoples: Struggle and Survival*. Houndmills, Palgrave MacMillan. http://dx.doi.org/10.1057/9780230509078

Cohen, Anthony P. 2000. "Introduction: Discriminating Relations–Identity, Boundary and Authenticity." In *Signifying Identities: Anthropological Perspectives on Boundaries and Contested Values*, ed. Anthony P. Cohen, 1–13. London: Routledge.

Collins, Simon, 2003. "Maori Rush to Claim Foreshore." *New Zealand Herald*, 30 July.

Conte, Éric. 2000. *L'archéologie en Polynésie française: Esquisse d'un bilan critique*. Pape'ete: Au Vent des Iles.

Cox, Lindsay. 1993. *Kotahitanga: The Search for Maori Political Unity*. Auckland: Oxford University Press.

Cram, Fiona, and Suzanne Pitama. 1998. "Ko Tōku Whānau, Ko Tōku Mana." In *The Family in Aotearoa New Zealand*, ed. Vivienne Adair and Robyn Dixon, 130–57. Auckland: Longman.

Crampton, Peter, Clara Salmond, and Russel Kirkpatrick. 2000. *Degrees of Deprivation in New Zealand: An Atlas of Socioeconomic Difference*. Auckland: David Bateman.

Cunningham, Chris, Brendan Stevenson, and Natasha Tassell. 2005. *Analysis of the Characteristics of Whānau in Aotearoa*. Report prepared for the Ministry of Education, Palmerston North, Massey University.

Curchin, Katherine. 2011. "Pākehā Women and Māori Protocol: The Politics of Criticising Other Cultures." *Australian Journal of Political Science* 46 (3): 375–88.

Dagenais, Daniel. 2000. *La fin de la famille moderne: Signification des transformations contemporaines de la famille*. Québec: Presses de l'Université Laval.

Davidson, Janet. 1984. *The Prehistory of New Zealand*. Auckland: Longman Paul.

De Certeau, Michel. 1980. *L'invention du Quotidien*, vol. 1. Paris: Gallimard.

Desjarlais, Robert R. 1992. *Body and Emotion: The Aesthetics of Illness and Healing in the Nepal Himalayas*. Philadelphia: University of Pennsylvania Press.

Douglas, Edward Te Kohu. 1991. "Te Iwi Maori." *Pacific Viewpoint* 32 (2): 129–38.

Durie, Eddie T.J. 1991. "The Treaty in Maori History." In *Sovereignty & Indigenous Rights: The Treaty of Waitangi in International Contexts*, ed. William Renwick, 156–69. Wellington: Victoria University Press.

Durie, Mason. 1994. *Whaiora: Māori Health Development*. Auckland: Oxford University Press.

Durie, Mason. 1995. "Beyond 1852: Maori, the State, and a New Zealand Constitution." *Sites* 30: 31–47.

Durie, Mason. 1997. "Whānau, Whanaungatanga and Healthy Māori Development." In *Mai I Rangiātea: Māori Wellbeing and Development*, ed. Pania Te Whāiti, Marie McCarthy, and Arohia Durie, 1–24. Auckland: Auckland University Press and Bridget Williams Books.

Durie, Mason. 1998. *Te Mana, Te Kāwanatanga: The Politics of Māori Self Determination*. Auckland: Oxford University Press.

Durie, Mason. 1999. "Marae and Implications for a Modern Māori Psychology." *Journal of the Polynesian Society* 108 (4): 351–66.

Durie, Mason. 2001a. *Mauri Ora. The Dynamics of Māori Health*. Auckland: Oxford University Press.

Durie, Mason. 2001b. "Mana Maori Motuhake." In *New Zealand Government and Politics*, ed. Raymond Miller, 464–78. Auckland: Oxford University Press.

Durie, Mason. 2005a. *Ngā Tai Matatū: Tides of Māori Endurance*. South Melbourne: Oxford University Press.

Durie, Mason. 2005b. "Tino Rangatiratanga." In *Waitangi Revisited: Perspectives on the Treaty of Waitangi*, ed. Michael Belgrave, Merata Kawharu, and David Williams, 3–19. South Melbourne: Oxford University Press.

Durie, Mason. 2011. *Ngā Tini Whetū: Navigating Māori Futures*. Wellington: Huia Publishers.

Durie, Mason H., T.E. Black et al., 1994. "Māori Youth in Contemporary New Zealand." Youth Policy Seminar Series October 1994. Wellington: Ministry of Youth Affairs.

Dyall, Lorna, and Susan Wauchop. 1994. "The Pathway Forward–Directions for Māori Health: Views of the Hui Te Ara Ahu Whakamua Māori Health Decade Hui Rotorua 22–25 March 1994." *Social Policy Journal of New Zealand* 2: 142–50.

Edwards, Bryce, and John Moore. 2009. "Hegemony and the Culturalist State Ideology in New Zealand." In *The politics of conformity in New Zealand*, 45–64, ed. Elizabeth Rata and Roger Openshaw. North Shore: Pearson.

Ellis, Ngārino. 2001. "Home, Home on the Pa." In *Pūrangiaho Seeing Clearly*, ed. Ngāhiraka Mason and Mary Kisler, 9–19. Auckland: Auckland Art Gallery Toi o Tāmaki.

Elsmore, Bronwyn. (Original work published 1989) 1999. *Mana from Heaven: A Century of Maori Prophets in New Zealand*. Auckland: Reed Books.

Emery, Debra Joy Tepora. 2008. "E hoki ki tō maunga: The Quintessential Elements of Home." PhD thesis, University of Waikato.

Equal Opportunities Office. 2003. Annual Report Summary. Auckland: University of Auckland.

Firth, Raymond. 1959. *Economics of the New Zealand Maori*. Wellington: R.E. Owen.

Fleras, Augie. 1989. "'Inverting the Bureaucratic Pyramid': Reconciling Aboriginality and Bureaucracy in New Zealand." *Human Organization* 48 (3): 214–25.

Fleras, Augie. 1991. "Tuku Rangatiratanga: Devolution in Iwi-Government Relations." In *Nga Take: Ethnic Relations in Aotearoa/New Zealand*, ed. Paul Spoonley, David Pearson, and Cluny Macpherson, 171–93. Palmerston North: Dunmore Press.

Fleras, Augie, and Paul Spoonley. 1999. *Recalling Aotearoa: Indigenous Politics and Ethnic Relations in New Zealand*. Auckland: Oxford University Press.

Friedman, Jonathan. 1994. *Cultural Identity and Global Process*. London: Sage Publications.

Friedman, Jonathan. 2003a. "Globalizing Languages: Ideologies and Realities of the Contemporary Global System." *American Anthropologist* 105 (4): 744–52. http://dx.doi.org/10.1525/aa.2003.105.4.744.

Friedman, Jonathan. 2003b. "Globalization, Dis-integration, Re-organization: The Transformations of Violence." In *Globalization, the State, and Violence*, ed. Jonathan Friedman, 1–34. New York: Alta Mira Press.

Friedman, Jonathan. 2004. "Globalization, Transnationalization, and Migration: Ideologies and Realities of Global Transformation." In *Worlds on the Move: Globalization, Migration, and Cultural Security*, ed. Jonathan Friedman and Shalini Randeria, 63–88. London: I.G. Tauris.

Friedman, Jonathan. 2008. "Indigeneity: Anthropological Notes on a Historical Variable." In *Indigenous Peoples: Self-Determination, Knowledge, Indigeneity*, ed. Henry Minde, 29–48. Delft: Eburon.

Friesen, Wardlow. 2008. *Diverse Auckland: The Face of New Zealand in the 21st Century?* Auckland: Asia New Zealand Foundation, Outlook Series.

Friesen, Wardlow. 2010. "Auckland: The Drifters." *New Zealand Herald*, 26 August. http://www.nzherald.co.nz/nz/news/article.cfm?c_id=1&objectid=10667049. Accessed 22 December 2011.

Friesen, Wardlow, Laurence Murphy, Robin A. Kearns, and Edwin Haverkamp. 2000. *Mapping Change and Difference: A Social Atlas of Auckland*. Auckland: University of Auckland, Department of Geography.

Gagné, Natacha. 2008a. "L'analyse des relations entre minorités et majorités: retour sur la situation néo-zélandaise à l'aube des années 2000." *Anthropologica* 50 (1): 101–19.

Gagné, Natacha. 2008b. "On the Ethnicisation of New Zealand Politics: The Foreshore and Seabed Controversy in Context." *Asia Pacific Journal of Anthropology* 9 (2): 123–40. http://dx.doi.org/10.1080/14442210802023657.

Gagné, Natacha. 2008c. "Indigenous Peoples, a Category in Development." In *Introduction to International Development Studies: Approaches, Actors, and Issues*, ed. Paul Haslam, Jessica Schafer, and Pierre Beaudet, 425–43. Oxford: University of Oxford Press.

Gagné, Natacha. 2008d. "Le savoir comme enjeu de pouvoir: l'ethnologue critiquée par les autochtones." In *Politiques de l'enquête: Épreuves ethnographiques*, ed. Didier Fassin and Alban Bensa, 277–98. Paris: La Découverte.

Gagné, Natacha. 2009a. "The Political Dimensions of Coexistence." *Anthropological Theory* 9 (1): 33–58. http://dx.doi.org/10.1177/1463499609103546.

Gagné, Natacha. 2009b. "Penser la citoyenneté à l'aune des histoires coloniales: terrains avec les Māori et les Tahitiens." *Anthropologie et Sociétés* 33 (2): 81–100.

Gagné, Natacha. 2009c. "L'université: un site d'affirmation et de négociation de la coexistence pour les jeunes Māori de Nouvelle-Zélande." In *Jeunesses autochtones: Affirmation, innovation et résistance dans les monde contemporains*, ed. Natacha Gagné and Laurent Jérôme, 97–122. Québec: Presses de l'Université Laval.

Gagné, Natacha. 2010. "Structures et changement social dans l'interaction entre les mondes: Un commentaire à la lumière d'exemples maaori." In *Une anthropologue dans la cité: Autour de Françoise Héritier*, ed. Marie-Blanche Tahon, 75–87. Montréal: Athéna.

Gagné, Natacha. 2011. "La stratégie autochtone: ses trajectoires en Océanie." In *Destins des collectivités politiques d'Océanie, Volume 1: Théories et pratiques*, ed. Pierre-Yves Faberon, Jean-Marc Regnault, and Viviane Fayaud , 263–72. Aix-en-Provence: Presses Universitaires d'Aix-Marseille, Droit d'outre-mer.

Gagné, Natacha. 2012. "Affirmation et décolonisation: La cérémonie de rapatriement par la France des toi moko à la Nouvelle-Zélande en perspective." *Journal de la Société des Océanistes* 134: 5–24.

Gagné, Natacha, and André Campeau. 2008. "The Link between an Anthropologist and His Subject: Eric Schwimmer and the (De)Colonization Process." *Anthropologica* 50 (1): 13–22.

Gardiner, Wira. 1992. *Te Mura o te Ahi: The Story of the Maori Battalion*. Auckland: Reed.

Gardiner, Wira. 1996. *Return to Sender: What Really Happened at the Fiscal Envelope Hui*. Auckland: Reed.

George, Lily. 2001. "Different Music Same Dance: The Construction and Reconstruction of Iwi–Te Taou and the Treaty Claims Process." Undergraduate honour's thesis, Massey University, Albany.

George, Lily. 2010. "Tradition, Invention and Innovation: Multiple Reflections of an Urban Marae." PhD thesis, Massey University, Albany.

George, Lily. 2011. "Ka hao te rangatahi: Transformation et leadership dans la société māori." *Anthropologie et Sociétés* 35 (3): 167–87.

George, Lily. 2012. "Expressions of Māori Multiplicity in (Re)Connection to *Ngā Taonga Tuku Iho*." *Social Identities* 18 (4): 435–50.

Gilling, Bryan. 2009. "Raupatu: The Punitive Confiscation of Maori Land in the 1860s." In *Raupatu: The Confiscation fo Maori Land*, ed. Richard Boast and Richard S. Hill, 13–30. Wellinton: Victoria University Press.

Gover, Kirsty, and Natalie Baird. 2002. "Identifying the Māori Treaty Partner." *University of Toronto Law Journal* 52 (1): 39–68. http://dx.doi.org/10.2307/825927.

Grace, Patricia. 1975. *Waiariki*. Auckland: Longman.

Grace, Patricia. 1978. *Mutuwhenua: The Moon Sleeps*. Auckland: Longman.

Grace, Patricia. 1980. *The Dream Sleepers and Other Stories*. Auckland: Longman.

Grace, Patricia. 1986. *Potiki*. Auckland: Penguin.

Grace, Patricia. 1992. *Cousins*. Auckland: Penguin.

Grace, Patricia. 1998. *Baby No-Eyes*. Auckland: Penguin.

Grace, Patricia, Irihapeti Ramsden, and Jonathan Dennis, ed. 2001. *The Silent Migration. Ngāti Pōneke Young Māori Club 1937–1948: Stories of Urban Migration*. Wellington: Huia Publishers.

Greenland, Hauraki. 1991. "Maori Ethnicity as Ideology." In *Nga Take: Ethnic Relations and Racism in Aotearoa/New Zealand*, ed. Paul Spoonley, David Pearson, and Cluny Macpherson, 90–107. Palmerston North: Dunmore Press.

Hamer, David. 1990. "Centralization and Nationalism (1891-1912)." In *Oxford Illustrated History of New Zealand*, ed. Keith Sinclair, 125–52. Auckland: Oxford University Press.

Hamer, Paul. 2007. *Māori in Australia: Ngā Māori o te Moemoeā*. Wellington: Te Puni Kōkiri and Griffith University.

Harris, Aroha. 2004a. *Hīkoi: Forty Years of Māori Protest*. Wellington: Huia Publishers.

Harris, Aroha. 2004b. "Maori and 'the Maori Affairs." In *Past Judgement: Social Policy in New Zealand History*, ed. Bronwyn Dalley and Margaret Tennant, 191–205. Dunedin: University of Otago Press.

Harris, Aroha. 2007. "Dancing with the State: Maori Creative Energy and Policies of Integration, 1945–1967." PhD thesis, University of Auckland.

Harris, Aroha, 2007–8. "Concurrent Narratives of Māori and Integration in the 1950s and 60s." *Journal of New Zealand Studies* 6–7: 139–55.

Harris, Bruce V. 2010. "Towards a Written Constitution?" In *New Zealand Governement & Politics*, ed. Raymond Miller, 91–104. Melbourne: Oxford University Press.

Harrison, Paki. 2008. *Tāne-nui-ā-Rangi: 20th Anniversary Edition*. Auckland: University of Auckland.

Hastrup, Kirsten. 1995. *A Passage to Anthropology: Between Experience and Theory*. London, New York: Routledge.

Hau'ofa, Epeli. 1994. "Our Sea of Islands." *Contemporary Pacific* 6 (1): 148–61.

Hayward, Janine. 2001. "The Waitangi Tribunal." In *New Zealand Government and Politics*, ed. Raymond Miller, 490–8. Auckland: Oxford University Press.

Hayward, Janine. 2010a. "The Treaty and the Constitution." In *New Zealand Governement & Politics*, ed. Raymond Miller, 105–113. Melbourne: Oxford University Press.

Hayward, Janine. 2010b. "Local Government Representation." In *Weeping Waters: The Treaty of Waitangi and Constitutional Change*, ed. Malcolm Mulholland and Veronica Tawhai, 269–85. Wellington: Huia Publishers.

Hayward, Janine, and Nicola R. Wheen. 2004. *The Waitangi Tribunal: Te Rōpū Whakamana I te Tiriti o Waitangi*. Wellington: Bridget Williams Books.

Hazlehurst, Kayleen M. 1993. *Political Expression and Ethnicity: Statecraft and Mobilisation in the Maori World*. Westport: Praeger.

Henare, Manuka. 1988. "Nga tikanga me nga ritenga o te ao Maori: Standards and Foundations of Māori Society." In *The Royal Commission on Social Policy*. Wellington: Government Printer.

Herzfeld, Michael. 2001. *Anthropology: Theoretical Practice in Culture and Society*. Malden, Oxford: Blackwell Publishers.

Hill, Richard S. 1986. *Policing the Colonial Frontier: The Theory and Practice of Coercive Social and Racial Control in New Zealand, 1767–1867, Part One and Two*. Wellington: Governement Printer.

Hill, Richard S. 2004. *State Authority, Indigenous Autonomy: Crown-Maori Race Relations in New Zealand/Aotearoa, 1900–1950*. Wellington: Victoria University Press.

Hill, Richard S. 2009. *Maori and the State: Crown-Maori Relations in New Zealand/Aotearoa, 1950–2000*. Wellington: Victoria University Press.

Hiroa, Te Rangi (Peter Buck). 1949. *The Coming of the Maori*. Wellington: Whitcombe and Tombs.

Hirsch, Eric. 1998. "Domestic Appropriations: Multiple Contexts and Relational Limits in the Home-Making of Greater Londoners." In *Migrants of Identity: Perceptions of Home in a World of Movement*, ed. Nigel Rapport and Andrew Dawson, 161–79. Oxford: Berg.

Hohepa, M. 1997. "Te Kohanga Reo: Risk Breaking, Risk Taking." Paper presented at the Second Child and Family Policy Conference, "Enhancing Children's potential: Minimising Risk and Maximising Resiliency," University of Otago, July.

Hohepa, Pat W. 1964. *A Maori Community in Northland*. Wellington: A.H. & A.W. Reed.

Holland, Dorothy, William Lachicotte, Debra Skinner, and Carole Cain. 1998. *Identity and Agency in Cultural Worlds*. Cambridge: Harvard University Press.

Hollander, John. 1991. "It All Depends." *Social Research* 58 (1): 31–49.

Hopa, Ngapare. 1977. "Urban Maori Sodalities: A Study in Social Change." PhD thesis, University of Oxford.

Hopa, Ngapare. 2011. "Ngā rōpū – Māori Organisations – New Māori Organisations, Early 20th Century." *Te Ara – Encyclopedia of New Zealand*. http://www.TeAra.govt.nz/en/nga-ropu-maori-organisations/2. Accessed 15 January 2012.

Hulme, Keri. (Original work published 1983) 1986. *The Bone People*. London: Picador.

Hunn, J.K. 1961. *Report on the Department of Māori Affairs*. Appendix to the Journal of the House of Representatives 1960, Wellington.

Hutchings, Jessica, and Clive Aspin, 2007. *Sexuality and the Stories of Indigenous People*. Wellington: Huia Publishers.

Ihimaera, Witi. 1972. *Pounamu, Pounamu*. Auckland: Heinemann.

Ihimaera, Witi. 1973. *Tangi*. Auckland: Heinemann.

Ihimaera, Witi. 1974. *Whanau*. Auckland: Heinemann.

Ihimaera, Witi. 1986. *The Matriarch*. Auckland: Heinemann.

Ihimaera, Witi. 1987. *The Whale Rider*. Auckland: Heinemann.

Ihimaera, Witi. 1996 (Original work published 1973 and 1974). *Tangi &
Whanau. Two Classic Maori Novels*. Auckland: Secker & Warburg.

Ihimaera, Witi. 1997. *The Dream Swimmer*. Auckland: Penguin.

Ihimaera, Witi. 2000. *Woman Far Walking*. Wellington: Huia Publishers.

Ihimaera, Witi, ed. 1992–6. *Te Ao Mārama: Māori Writing*. 5 Volumes. Auckland:
Reed.

Ihimaera, Witi, ed. 1994. *Vision Aotearoa: Kaupapa New Zealand*. Wellington:
Bridget Williams Books.

Ihimaera, Witi, ed. 1998. *Growing up Māori*. Auckland: Tandem Press.

Ingold, Tim. 1996. "Hunting and Gathering as Ways of Perceiving the Environment." In *Redefining Nature. Ecology, Culture and Domestication*, ed. R.
Ellen and K. Fukui, 117–55. Oxford and Washington D.C.: Berg.

Irwin, Kathy. 1994. "Maori Research Methods and Practices." *Sites* 28 (Au-
tumn): 25–43.

Irwin, Kathy G. 2002. "Māori Education: From Wretchedness to Hope." PhD
thesis, Victoria University of Wellington.

Jackson, Michael. 1995. *At Home in the World*. Durham, London: Duke University Press.

Jackson, Moana. 1988. *The Maori and the Criminal Justice System, a New Perspective: He Whaipānga Hou. Part 2*. Wellington: Department of Justice.

Jackson, Moana. 2003. "Backgrounding the Paeroa Declaration." http://aote-
aroa.wellington.net.nz/he/paeroa.pdf. Accessed 2 October 2005.

James Henare Māori Research Centre. 2002. *Well-being and Disparity in Tāmaki-
makaurau*. Five volumes. Report prepared for Te Puni Kōkiri/The Ministry
of Māori Development. Auckland: University of Auckland.

Johnson, Pauline, and Leonie Pihama. 1993. "What Counts as Difference and
What Differences Count: Gender, Race and the Politics of Difference." In
Toi Wahine: The Worlds of Māori Women, ed. K. Irwin and I. Ramsden, 75–86.
Auckland: Penguin.

Johnston, Patricia Maringi G. 1998. "He Ao Rereke: Education Policy and
Maori Under-Achievement: Mechanisms of Power and Difference." Ph.D.
thesis, University of Auckland.

Johnston, Ron, Michael Poulsen, and James Forrest. 2005. "Ethnic Residential
Segregation across an Urban System: The Maori in New Zealand, 1991–
2001." *Professional Geographer* 57 (1): 115–29.

Jones, Pei Te Hurinui. 1959. *King Potatau: An Account of the Life of Potatau Te Wherewhero the First Māori King*. Auckland: The Polynesian Society.

Kaiwai, Hector. 2003. "Pūkana Rawatia: Mickey Mouse Does the Haka." Master's thesis, University of Auckland.

Karetu, Sam. 1978. "Kawa in Crisis." In *Tihe Mauri Ora: Aspects of Maoritanga*, ed. Michael King, 67–79. Wellington: Methuen Publications.

Kawharu, I. Hugh, 1968. "Urban Immigrants and *Tangata Whenua*." In *The Maori People in the Nineteen-Sixties*, ed. Erik Schwimmer, 174–186. Auckland: Longman Paul.

Kawharu, I. Hugh, 1975. *Orakei: A Ngati Whatua Community*. Wellington: New Zealand Council For Educational Research.

Kawharu, I. Hugh, 1989a, "Mana and the Crown, a Marae at Orakei." In *Waitangi: Maori and Pakeha Perspectives of the Treaty of Waitangi*, ed. Hugh Kawharu. Auckland: Oxford University Press.

Kawharu, I. Hugh, ed. 1989b, *Waitangi: Maori and Pakeha Perspectives of the Treaty of Waitangi*. Auckland: Oxford University Press.

Kawharu, I. Hugh, 1990. "Sovereignty vs. Rangatiratanga: The Treaty of Waitangi 1840 and the New Zealand Maori Council's Kaupapa 1983." In *Man and a Half: Essays in Pacific Anthropology and Ethnobiology in Honour of Ralph Bulmer*, ed. A. Pawlay, 573–581. Auckland: The Polynesian Society, Memoir no. 48.

Kawharu, I. Hugh. 2008. "Biculturalism and Inclusion in New Zealand: The Case of Orakei." *Anthropologica* 50 (1): 49–56.

Kawharu, Merata. 2010. "Environment as a Marae Locale." In *Māori and the Environment: Kaitiaki*, ed. Rachael Selby, Pātaka Moore, and Malcolm Mulholland, 221–37. Wellington: Huia Publishers.

Keenan, Danny, ed. 2008. *Terror in Our Midst? Searching for Terror in Aotearoa New Zealand*. Wellington: Huia Publishers.

Keenan, Danny. 2009. *Wars Without End: The Land Wars in Nineteenth-century New Zealand*. Rosedale: Penguin.

Keesing, Roger M. 1984. "Rethinking *Mana*." *Journal of Anthropological Research* 40 (1):137–56.

Keiha, Pare, and Paul Moon. 2008. "The Emergence and Evolution of Urban Māori Authorities: A Response to Māori Urbanisation." *Te Kaharoa* 1 (1): 1–17. http://tekaharoa.com/index.php/tekaharoa/article/view/10. Accessed 17 October 2012.

Kelsey, Jane. 1989. "Free Market 'Rogernomics' and Maori Rights under the Treaty of Waitangi: An Irresolvable Contradiction?" *Race Gender Class* 8: 1–19.

Kelsey, Jane. 1990. *A Question of Honour? Labour and the Treaty*. Wellington: Allen and Unwin.

Kelsey, Jane. 1991. "Treaty Justice in the 1980s." In *Nga Take: Ethnic Relations and Racism in Aotearoa/New Zealand*, ed. Paul Spoonley, David Pearson, and Cluny Macpherson, 108–130. Palmerston North: Dunmore Press.

Kelsey, Jane. 1996. "From Flagpoles to Pine Trees: Tino Rangatiratanga and Treaty Policy Today. " In *Nga Patai: Racism and Ethnic Relations in Aotearoa/New Zealand*, 177–287. Paul Spoonley, David Pearson, and Cluny Macpherson. Palmerston North: Dunmore Press.

King, Michael. 1977. *Te Puea: A Biography*. Auckland: Hodder and Stoughton.

King, Michael. 1988. *After the War: New Zealand Since 1945*. Auckland: Hodder and Stoughton and Wilson and Horton.

King, Michael. 2001. *Nga iwi o te motu: 1000 years of Maori History*. Revised edition. Auckland: Reed Books.

King, Michael. 2003. *The Penguin History of New Zealand*. Rosedale: Penguin.

King, Michael. (Original work published 2003) 2007. *The Penguin History of New Zealand Illustrated*. Rosedale: Penguin Books.

King, Michael, ed. 1975. *Te Ao Hurihuri: The World Moves On. Aspects of Maoritanga*. Wellington: Hicks Smith & Sons.

King, Michael, ed. 1978. *Tihe Mauri Ora: Aspects of Maoritanga*. Auckland: Methuen New Zealand.

Kiro, Cindy, Martin von Randow, and Andrew Sporle. 2010. *Trends in Wellbeing for Māori households/families, 1981–2006*. Research report. Auckland: Ngā Pae o te Māramatanga, University of Auckland.

Laliberté, Michel, 2000. "Le laboratoire du néolibéralisme au bord du gouffre? Les Néo-Zélandais en ont assez d'être des cobayes." *Le Devoir*, Tuesday, 8 February: B1.

Latham, Alan. 2003. "Urbanity, Lifestyle and Making Sense of the New Urban Cultural Economy: Notes from Auckland, New Zealand." *Urban Studies (Edinburgh, Scotland)* 40 (9): 1699–724. http://dx.doi.org/10.1080/0042098032 000106564.

Lavanchy, Anne, 2009. *Les langages de l'autochtonie: Enjeux politique et sociaux des négociations identitaires mapuche au Chili*. Neuchâtel et Paris : Éditions de l'Institut d'ethnologie et Éditions de la maison des sciences de l'homme.

Levine, Hal B. 1999. "Reconstructing Ethnicity." *Journal of the Royal Anthropological Institute* 5 (2): 165–80. http://dx.doi.org/10.2307/2660691.

Levine, Hal B. 2001. "Can A Voluntary Organisation Be A Treaty Partner? The Case Of Te Whānau O Waipareira Trust." *Social Policy Journal of New Zealand*, (17): 161–70.

Levine, Hal B., and Manuka Henare. 1994. "Mana Maori Motuhake: Maori Self-Determination." *Pacific Viewpoint* 35 (2): 193–210.

Levine, Stephen, and Nigel S. Roberts. 1997. "MMP: The Decision." In *New Zealand Politics in Transition*, ed. Raymond Miller, 25–36. Auckland: Oxford University Press.

Lévi-Strauss, Claude. 1950. "Introduction à l'œuvre de Marcel Mauss." In *Sociologie et anthropologie*, ed. Marcel Mauss, ix–lii. Paris: Presses Universitaires de France.

Lévi-Strauss, Claude. 1987. *Anthropology and Myth: Lectures, 1951–1982.* Oxford: Basil Blackwell.

Lewis, Nick, Owen Lewis, and Yvonne Underhill-Sem. 2009. "Filling Hollowed Out Spaces with Localized Meanings, Practices and Hope: Progressive Neoliberal Spaces in Te Rarawa." *Asia Pacific Viewpoint* 50 (2): 166–84. http://dx.doi.org/10.1111/j.1467-8373.2009.01391.x.

Liu, James H., Tim McCreanor, Tracey McIntosh, and Teresia Teaiwa, eds. 2005. *New Zealand Identities: Departures and Destinations.* Wellington: Victoria University Press.

Maaka, Roger C.A. 1994. "The New Tribe: Conflicts and Continuities in the Social Organisation of Urban Maori." *Contemporary Pacific* 6 (2): 311–36.

Maaka, Roger C.A., and Augie Fleras. 2005. *The Politics of Indigeneity: Challenging the State in Canada and Aotearoa New Zealand.* Dunedin: University of Otago Press.

Maaka, Roger C.A., and Augie Fleras. 2006. "Indigeneity at the Edge: Towards a Constructive Engagement." In *The Indigenous Experience: Global Perspectives*, ed. Roger C.A. Maaka and Chris Andersen, 337–60. Toronto: Canadian Scholars' Press.

MacAlister, John, ed. 2005. *A Dictionary of Maori Words in New Zealand English.* Melbourne: Oxford University Press.

Macpherson, Cluny. 1997. "A Samoan Solution to the Limitations of Urban Housing in New Zealand." In *Home in the Islands: Housing and Social Change in the Pacific*, ed. Jan Rensel and Margaret Rodman, 151–74. Honolulu: University of Hawaii Press.

Mahuika, Apirana. 1998. "Whakapapa is the Heart." In *Living Relationships: Kotahi Ngatahi. The Treaty of Waitangi in the New Millennium*, ed. Ken S. Coates and Paul G. McHugh, 214–21. Wellington: Victoria University Press.

Mahuta, Robert Te Kotahi. 1978. "The Maori King Movement Today." In *Tihe Mauri Ora: Aspects of Maoritanga*, ed. Michael King, 33–41. Wellington: Methuen Publications.

Mahuta, Robert Te Kotahi. 1995a. "Tainui: A Case Study of Direct Negotiation." In *Treaty Settlements: The Unfinished Business*, ed. G. McLay, 67–87. Wellington: New Zealand Institute of Advanced Legal Studies and Victoria University of Wellington Law Review.

Mahuta, Robert Te Kotahi. 1995b. "Tainui, Kingitanga and Raupatu." In *Justice and Identity: Antipodean Practices*, ed. Margaret Wilson and Anna Yeatman, 18–32. Wellington: Bridget Williams Books.

Marcus, George, ed. 1983. *Elites: Ethnographic Issues*. Albuquerque: University of New Mexico Press.

Marsden, Maori, and T.A. Henare. 1992. *Kaitiakitanga: A Definitive Introduction to the Holistic World View of the Maori*. Wellington: The Ministry for the Environment.

Mauss, Marcel. 1925. "Essai sur le don: Forme et raison de l'échange dans les sociétés archaïques." *L'Année Sociologique*, nouvelle série, 1 (1923–24): 30–186.

McAllister, Patrick. 2007. "Waitangi Day: An Annual Enactment of the Treaty?" *Sites: New Series* 4 (2): 155–80.

McAllister, Patrick. 2011. "Waitangi Day, Okains Bay: Contest, Co-operation and the Construction of Place in a Local Commemoration of Nation in New Zealand." *Anthropological Forum* 21 (2): 153–73. http://dx.doi.org/10.1080/006 64677.2011.582835.

McCan, David. 2001. *Whatiwhatihoe: The Waikato Raupatu Claim*. Wellington: Huia Publishers.

McCarthy, Conal. 2007. *Exhibiting Maori: A History of Colonial Cultures of Display*. Oxford and New York: Berg.

McCarthy, Conal. 2011. *Museums and Māori: Heritage Professionals, Indigenous Collections, Current Practice*. Walnut Creek: Left Coast Press.

McCormack, Fiona. 2011. "Levels of Indigeneity: The Maori and Neoliberalism." *Journal of the Royal Anthropological Institute* 17 (2): 281–300. http://dx.doi.org/10.1111/j.1467-9655.2011.01680.x.

McCormack, Fiona. 2012. "Indigeneity as Process: Māori Claims and Neoliberalism." *Social Identities* 18 (4): 417–34.

McFarlane, Peter. 1993. *Brotherhood to Nationhood: George Manuel and the Making of the Modern Indian Movement*. Toronto: Between The Lines.

McGarvey, Rangi. 2009. "Ngāi Tūhoe – Future challenges." *Te Ara - Encyclopedia of New Zealand*. http://www.TeAra.govt.nz/en/ngai-tuhoe/7. Accessed 16 January 2012.

McIntosh, Tracey. 2001. "Death, Every Day." In *Sociology of Everyday Life in New Zealand*, ed. Claudia Bell, 234–51. Palmerston North: Dunmore Press.

McLean, Mervyn, and Margaret Orbell. 1975. *Traditional Songs of the Maori*. Auckland: Auckland University Press.

McLeay, Elizabeth. 2001. "Cabinet." In *New Zealand Government and Politics*, ed. Raymond Miller, 88–105. Auckland: Oxford University Press.

McRae, Karyn Okeroa, and Linda Waimarie Nikora, 2006. "Whangai: Remembering, Understanding and Experiencing." *MAI Review*, (1), Intern Research Report 7.

Mead, Hirini Moko. 1997. *Landmarks, Bridges and Visions: Aspects of Maori Culture*. Wellington: Victoria University Press.

Mead, Sidney Moko. 2003. *Tikanga Māori: Living by Māori Values*. Wellington: Huia Publishers.

Mead, Sidney Moko, ed. 1984. *Te Maori: Maori Art from New Zealand Collections*. New York: Abrams.

Melbourne, Hineani. 1995. *Maori Sovereignty: The Maori Perspective*. Auckland: Hodder Moa Meckett.

Metge, Joan. 1964. *A New Maori Migration: Rural and Urban Relations in New Zealand*. London: Athlone Press.

Metge, Joan. 1967. *The Maoris of New Zealand*. London: Routledge.

Metge, Joan. 1976. *The Maoris of New Zealand Rautahi*. London: Routledge and Kegan Paul.

Metge, Joan. 1986. *In and Out of Touch: Whakamā in Cross Cultural Context*. Wellington: Victoria University Press.

Metge, Joan. 1995. *New Growth from Old: The Whānau in the Modern World*. Wellington: Victoria University Press.

Metge, Joan. 2002. "Returning the Gift: *Utu* in Intergroup Relations." *Journal of the Polynesian Society* 111 (4): 311–38.

Metge, Joan. 2008. "Māori Education 1958–1990: A Personal Memoir." *New Zealand Journal of Educational Studies* 43 (2): 13–28.

Metge, Joan. 2010. *Tuamaka: The Challenge of Difference in Aotearoa New Zealand*. Auckland: Auckland University Press.

Middleton, Julie. 2005. "'MP's Powhiri Anger 'Big To-do about Nothing.'" *New Zealand Herald*, 4 November. http://www.nzherald.co.nz/location/story.cfm?l_id=370&ObjectID=10353504. Accessed 15 October 2006.

Miller, Raymond, ed. 2001. *New Zealand Government and Politics*. Auckland: Oxford University Press.

Miller, Raymond, ed. 2005. *Party Politics in New Zealand*. Auckland: Oxford University Press.

Minde, Henry. 1996. "The Making of an International Movement of Indigenous Peoples." *Scandinavian Journal of History* 21 (3): 221–46. http://dx.doi.org/10.1080/03468759608579326.

Ministry of Social Development. 2006. *The Social Report 2006: Indicators of Social Wellbeing in New Zealand*. Wellington: Ministry of Social Development.

Misa, Tapu. 2010a, "Auckland: Pacific Power." *New Zealand Herald*, 28 August. http://www.nzherald.co.nz/auckland-tale-of-a-supercity/news/article.cfm?c_id=1502974&objectid=10667574. Accessed 22 December 2011.

Misa, Tapu. 2010b, "Otara: The First Polynesian Suburb." *New Zealand Herald*, 28 August. http://www.nzherald.co.nz/auckland-tale-of-a-supercity/news/article.cfm?c_id=1502974&objectid=10667583. Accessed 22 December 2011.

Mita, Merata, 1981. *Bastion Point Day 507*. Wellington: Documentary aired on TVNZ's *Contact* Program.

Moon, Paul. 2001. *Hone Heke: Nga Puhi Warrior*. Auckland: David Ling Publishers.

Morrison, Philip S. 1995. "The Geography of Rental Housing and the Restructuring of Housing Assistance in New Zealand." *Housing Studies* 10 (1): 39–56. http://dx.doi.org/10.1080/02673039508720808.

Morrison, Philip S., Paul Callister, and Jan Rigby. 2002. "The Spatial Separation of Work-Poor and Work-Rich Households in New Zealand 1986–2001: Introduction to a Research Project." Paper given at the New Zealand Association of Economists Conference, Wellington, June. http://nzae.org.nz. Accessed 2 October 2007.

Mulgan, Richard G. 1989. *Maori, Pakeha, and Democracy*. Auckland: Oxford University Press.

Mulholland, Malcolm, and Veronica Tawhai, eds. 2010. *Weeping Waters: The Treaty of Waitangi and Constitutional Change*. Wellington: Huia Publishers.

Mulrennan, Monica, and Colin H. Scott. 2000. "Mare Nullius: Indigenous Rights in Saltwater Environments." *Development and Change* 31 (3): 681–708. http://dx.doi.org/10.1111/1467-7660.00172.

Murphy, Nigel. 2003. "Joe Lum v. Attorney General: The Politics of Exclusion." In *Unfolding History, Evolving Identity: The Chinese in New Zealand*, ed. Manying Ip, 48–67. Auckland: Auckland University Press.

Murphy, Nigel. 2009. "'Māoriland' and 'Yellow Peril': Discourses of Māori and Chinese in the Formation of New Zealand's National Identity 1890–1914." In *The Dragon and the Taniwha: Māori and Chinese in New Zealand*, ed. Manying Ip, 56–88. Auckland: Auckland University Press.

Murray, David A.B. 2003. "Who is Takatapui? Maori Language, Sexuality and Identity in Aotearoa/New Zealand." *Anthropologica* 45 (2): 233–44. http://dx.doi.org/10.2307/25606143.

Muru-Lanning, Marama. 2004. "The Emergence of New Waikato-Tainui Subjects and Spaces." Paper presented at the Annual Conference of the Association for Social Anthropology in Oceania (ASAO), Hawthorne Hotel, Salem, US, February.

Mutu, Margaret. 2010. "Constitutional Intentions: The Treaty of Waitangi Texts." In *Weeping Waters: The Treaty of Waitangi and Constitutional Change*, ed. Malcolm Mulholland and Veronica Tawhai, 13–40. Wellington: Huia Publishers.

Mutu, Margaret. 2011. *The State of Māori Rights*. Wellington: Huia Publishers.

Nana, Ganesh, Fiona Stokes, and Wilma Molano. 2011. *The Māori Economy, Science, and Innovation*. Report commissioned by the Māori Economic

Taskforce, Wellington, Te Puni Kōkiri and BERL. http://www.tpk.govt.nz/_
   documents/taskforce/met-rep-ecosciinovate-2011.pdf.
Neale, Imogen. 2011. "Race Relations Complaint against Professor." *Stuff.*
   co.nz, 6 September. http://www.stuff.co.nz/auckland/local-news/5571191/
   Race-relations-complaint-against-professor. Accessed 12 Decembre 2011.
Neich, Roger. 1993. *Painted Histories: Early Maori Figurative Painting*. Auckland:
   Auckland University Press.
Nepe, Tuakana. 1991. "E Hao Nei e Teinei Reanga: Te Toi Huarewa Tipuna,
   Kaupapa Maori, an Educational Intervention System." Master's thesis, Uni-
   versity of Auckland.
Newman, Muriel. 2011. "Maori Seats Increase Undermines MMP Referen-
   dum." *NZCPR Weekly*, 1 August. http://www.nzcpr.com/Weekly288.pdf. Ac-
   cessed 22 December 2011.
New Zealand Herald. 2004a, "Hikoi Updates." *New Zealand Herald*, 5 May.
   http://www.nzherald.co.nz/section/story.cfm?c_id=1&objectid=3564583. Accessed 2 October 2005.
New Zealand Herald. 2004b, "Hikoi Size Estimates Range from 10000 to
   30000." *New Zealand Herald*, 6 May. http://www.nzherald.co.nz/topic/story.
   cfm?c_id=350&objectid=3564792. Accessed 2 October 2005.
New Zealand Herald. 2006. "Treaty Bill Passes First Reading But Won't Go
   Any Further." *New Zealand Herald*, 26 July.http://www.nzherald.co.nz/
   search/story.cfm?storyid=00024B30-4E64-14C7-928783027AF1010F. Accessed 24 August 2006.
New Zealand Herald. 2008. "Collective Welcomes Deed of Settlement and
   Legislation." *New Zealand Herald*, 25 June. http://www.nzherald.co.nz/sec-
   tion/1/story.cfm?c_id=1&objectid=10518365&pnum=2. Accessed 11 August
   2008.
New Zealand Herald. 2009. "MMP Referendum to be Held with 2011 Election." *New Zealand Herald*, 20 October. http://www.nzherald.co.nz/nz/news/
   article.cfm?c_id=1&objectid=10604317. Accessed 22 December 2011.
New Zealand Herald. 2010a, "Harawira Votes against Foreshore Bill." *New
   Zealand Herald*, 15 September, Available at: http://www.nzherald.co.nz/nz/
   news/article.cfm?c_id=1&objectid=10673658. Accessed 15 January 2012.
New Zealand Herald. 2010b, "Iwi Group to Hold Own Constitutional Review." *New Zealand Herald*, 14 December. http://www.nzherald.co.nz/nz/
   news/article.cfm?c_id=1&objectid=10694482. Accessed 12 March 2011.
New Zealand Institute of Economic Research. 2003. *Māori Economic Development: Te Ōhanga Whanaketanga Māori*. Wellington: New Zealand Institute of
   Economic Research. http://nzier.live.egressive.com/sites/nzier.live.egressive.
   com/files/Maori%20Economic%20Development.pdf. Accessed 19 July 2012.

Ngata, Apirana T. 1940. "Tribal Organisation." In *The Maori People Today*, ed. I.L.G. Sutherland, 155–81. Wellington: New Zealand Institute of International Affairs and New Zealand Council for Educational Research.

Ngata, Hoori M. 1995 (1993). *English-Maori Dictionary*, pocket edition. Wellington: Learning Media.

Niezen, Ronald. 2003. *The Origins of Indigenism: Human Rights and the Politics of Identity*. Berkeley: University of California Press.

Niezen, Ronald. 2009. *The Rediscovered Self: Indigenous Identity and Cultural Justice*. Montreal, Kingston: McGill-Queen's University Press.

Nixon, Chris, and John Yeabsley. 2010. "Overseas Trade Policy – New Zealand, Britain and the EEC." *Te Ara – Encyclopedia of New Zealand*. http://www.TeAra.govt.nz/en/overseas-trade-policy/4. Accessed 19 December 2011.

Novitz, Rosemary. 1982. "Feminism." In *New Zealand Sociological Perspectives*, ed. Paul Spoonley, David Pearson, and I. Shirley. Palmerston North: Dunmore Press.

Office of Ethnic Affairs. 2002. *Ethnic Perspectives in Policy*. Wellington.

Olwig, Karen Fog. 1998. "Epilogue: Contested Homes: Home-Making and the Making of Anthropology." In *Migrants of Identity: Perceptions of Home in a World of Movement*, ed. Nigel Rapport and Andrew Dawson, 225–36. Oxford: Berg.

O'Malley, Vincent. 1998. *Agents of Autonomy: Maori Commiettes in the Nineteenth Century*. Wellington: Huia Publishers.

O'Malley, Vincent. 2009. "Reinventing Tribal Mechanisms of Governance: The Emergence of Maori Runanga and Komiti in New Zealand before 1900." *Ethnohistory (Columbus, Ohio)* 56 (1): 69–89. http://dx.doi.org/10.1215/00141801-2008-036.

One News. 2011. "Maori Party Set to Have Key Role." *TVNZ*. http://tvnz.co.nz/election-2011/maori-party-set-have-key-role-4573756. Accessed 19 December 2011.

Orange, Claudia. 1987. *The Treaty of Waitangi*. Wellington: Allen and Unwin/Port Nicholson.

Orange, Claudia. 2011. *The Treaty of Waitangi*. 2nd ed. Wellington: Bridget William Books.

Orbell, Margaret. 1978. "The Traditional Maori Family." In *Families in New Zealand Society*, ed. Peggy Koopman-Boyden, 104–119. Wellington: Methuaen.

Orsman, Bernard. 2011. "Council Doesn't Have to Accept Maori Board – Hide." *New Zealand Herald*, 10 February. http://www.nzherald.co.nz/politics/news/article.cfm?c_id=280&objectid=10705294. Accessed 15 January 2011.

O'Sullivan, Dominic. 2007. *Beyond Biculturalism: The Politics of an Indigenous Minority*. Wellington: Huia Publishers.

O'Sullivan, Fran. 2011. "Harnessing the Maori Economy." *New Zealand Herald*, 11 May. http://www.nzherald.co.nz/economy/news/article.cfm?c_id=34&objectid=10724718. Accessed 20 December 2011.

Palmer, Matthew. 2006. "Resolving the Forsehore and Seabed Dispute." In *Political Leadership in New Zealand*, ed. Raymond Miller and Michael Mintrom, 197–214. Auckland: Auckland University Press.

Palmer, Matthew. 2008. *The Treaty of Waitangi in New Zealand's Law and Constitution*. Wellington: Victoria University Press.

Patterson, John. 1992. *Exploring Maori Values*. Palmerston North: Dunmore Press.

Paul, Joanna. 2005. "Challenges Lie Ahead for MTS in the Aotearoa Public Sphere." *Pacific Journalism Review* 11 (1): 42–6.

Pearson, David. 1991. "Biculturalism and Multiculturalism in Comparative Perspective." In *Nga Take: Ethnic Relations and Racism in Aotearoa/New Zealand*, ed. Paul Spoonley, David Pearson, and Cluny Macpherson, 194–214. Palmerston North: Dunmore Press.

Pearson, David. 1994. "Self-Determination and Indigenous Peoples in Comparative Perspective: Problems and Possibilities." *Pacific Viewpoint* 35 (2): 129–41.

Pearson, David. 1996. "Crossing Ethnic Thresholds: Multiculturalisms in Comparative Perspective." In *Nga Take: Ethnic Relations and Racism in Aotearoa/New Zealand*, ed. Paul Spoonley, David Pearson, and Cluny Macpherson, 247–266. Palmerston North: Dunmore Press.

Pearson, David. 2009. "The 'Majority Factor': Shaping Chenese and Māori Minorities." In *The Dragon and the Taniwha: Māori and Chinese in New Zealand*, ed. Manying Ip, 32–55. Auckland: Auckland University Press.

Pearson, Sarina, and Shuchi Kothari. 2007. "Menus for a Multicultural New Zealand." *Continuum: Journal of Media and Cultural Studies* 21 (1): 45–58. http://dx.doi.org/10.1080/10304310601103950.

Penetito, Wally. 2010. *What's Māori About Māori Education? The Struggle for a Meaningful Context*. Wellington: Victoria University Press.

Pere, Rangimarie. 1982. "Ako: Concepts and Learning in the Māori Tradition." Working paper no 17. Hamilton, University of Waikato, Department of Sociology.

Perkins, Harvey, and David Thorns. 2001. "Houses, Homes and New Zealanders' Everyday Lives." In *Sociology of Everyday Life in New Zealand*, ed. Claudia Bell, 30–51. Palmerston North: Dunmore Press.

Phillips, Hēni (Janie). 1999. "An Aspect of Maori Identity and Organisation: The Evolution of Te Whanau o Waipareira Trust." Master's thesis, University of Auckland.

Pihama, Leonie. 1998. "Reconstructing Meanings of Family: Lesbian/Gay Whānau and Families in Aotearoa." In *The Family in Aotearoa New Zealand*, ed. Vivienne Adair and Robyn Dixon, 179–207. Auckland: Longman.

Pihama, Leonie. 2005. "Asserting Indigenous Theories of Change." In *Sovereignty Matters: Locations of Contestation and Possibility in Indigenous Struggles for Self-Determination*, ed. Joanne Barker, 191–209. Lincoln: University of Nebraska Press.

Pihama, Leonie, Fiona Cram, and Sheila Walker. 2002. "Creating Methodological Space: A literature Review of Kaupapa Maori Research." *Canadian Journal of Native Education* 26 (1): 30–43.

Poata-Smith, Evan S. Te Ahu, 1996. "He Pekeke Uenuku i Tu Ai: The Evolution of Contemporary Maori Protest." In *Nga Patai: Racism and Ethnic Relations in Aotearoa/New Zealand*, ed. Paul Spoonley, David Pearson, and Cluny Macpherson, 97–116. Palmerston North: Dunmore Press.

Poata-Smith, Evan S. Te Ahu, 2004a, "The Changing Contours of Maori Identity and the Treaty Settlement Process." In *The Waitangi Tribunal: Te Rōpū Whakamana i te Tiriti o Waitangi*, ed. Jane Hayward and Nicola R. Wheen, 168–183. Wellington: Bridget Williams Books.

Poata-Smith, Evan S. Te Ahu, 2004b, "Ka Tika a Muri, Ka Tika a Mua? Māori Protest Politics and the Treaty of Waitangi Settlement Process." In *Tangata Tangata: The Changing Ethnic Countours of New Zealand*, ed. Paul Spoonley, Cluny Macpherson, and David Pearson, 59–88. Nelson: Thomson/Dunmore Press.

Poata-Smith, Evan S. Te Ahu. 2005. "The Veneer Is Radical, But the Substance Is Not." *Pacific Journalism Review* 11 (1): 211–17.

Poirier, Sylvie. 2008. "Reflections on Indigenous Cosmopolitics/Poetics." *Anthropologica* 50 (1): 75–85.

Pool, Ian. 1991. *Te Iwi Maori: A New Zealand Population Past, Present and Projected*. Auckland: Auckland University Press.

Price, Charles A., 1974. *The Great White Walls Are Built: Restrictive Immigration to North America and Australasia, 1836–1888*. Canberra: Australian Institute of International Affairs in association with Australian National University Press.

Prout, Sarah. 2008. "On the Move? Indigenous Temporary Mobility Practices in Australia." CAEPR Working Paper (48). Canberra, Centre for Aboriginal Economic Policy Research, Australian National University.

Prout, Sarah. 2011. "Urban Myths: Exploring the Unsettling Nature of Aboriginal Presence in and through a Regional Australian Town." *Urban Policy and Research* 29 (3): 275–91. http://dx.doi.org/10.1080/08111146.2011.578300.

Puketapu, B. Te T. 1994. "Hokia te Kōpae a ngā Pāhake: The Classical Māori Journey." In *Kia Pūmau Tonu: Proceedings of the Hui Whakapūmau Māori*

Development Conference, Department of Māori Studies. Palmerston North, Massey University.

Radice, Martha. 2000. *Feeling Comfortable? The Urban Experience of Anglo-Montrealers.* Sainte-Foy, Presses de l'Université Laval.

Ramstad, Jorun Broeck. 2003. "'Maori are Different, but We are Similar for Particular Reasons': Dynamics of Belonging in Social Practice." In *Oceanic Socialities and Cultural Forms. Ethnographies of Experience*, ed. Ingjerd Hoëm and Sidsel Roalkvam, 177–98. New York, Oxford: Berghahn Books.

Rangihau, John. 1975. "Being Maori." In *Te Ao Hurihuhuri: The World Moves On. Aspects of Maoritanga*, ed. Michael King, 221–33. Wellington: Hicks Smith & Sons.

Rangiheuea, Tania. 2010. "Urban Māori." In *Weeping Waters: The Treaty of Waitangi and Constitutional Change*, ed. Malcolm Mulholland and Veronica Tawhai, 187–206. Wellington: Huia Publishers.

Rapport, Nigel. 1997. *Transcendent Individual: Towards a Literary and Liberal Anthropology.* London: Routledge.

Rapport, Nigel. 1998. "Coming Home to a Dream: A Study of the Immigrant Discourse of 'Anglo-Saxons' in Israel." In *Migrants of Identity: Perceptions of Home in a World of Movement*, ed. Nigel Rapport and Andrew Dawson, 61–83. Oxford: Berg.

Rapport, Nigel, and Andrew Dawson. 1998a. "The Topic and the Book." In *Migrants of Identity: Perceptions of Home in a World of Movement*, ed. Nigel Rapport and Andrew Dawson, 3–17. Oxford: Berg.

Rapport, Nigel, and Andrew Dawson. 1998b. "Home and Movement: A Polemic." In *Migrants of Identity: Perceptions of Home in a World of Movement*, ed. Nigel Rapport and Andrew Dawson, 19–38. Oxford: Berg.

Rata, Elizabeth. 2000. *A Political Economy of Neotribal Capitalism.* New York: Lexington Books.

Rata, Elizabeth. 2002. *Democratic Principles in Teaching and Learning: A Kantian Approach*, Monograph/Research Report Series. Auckland: Auckland College of Education.

Rata, Elizabeth. 2003. "An Overview of Neotribal Capitalism." *Ethnologie comparée* 6. http://alor.univ-montp3.fr/cerce/r6/e.r.htm.

Rata, Elizabeth. 2004. "Kaupapa Maori Education in New Zealand." In *Citizenship and Political Education Today*, ed. Jack Demaine, 59–74. New York: Palgrave Macmillan.

Rata, Elizabeth. 2005. "Rethinking Biculturalism." *Anthropological Theory* 5 (3): 267–84. http://dx.doi.org/10.1177/1463499605055960.

Rata, Elizabeth. 2011a. "Encircling the Commons: Neotribal Capitalism in New Zealand since 2000." *Anthropological Theory* 11 (3): 327–53. http://dx.doi.org/10.1177/1463499611416724.

Rata, Elizabeth. 2011b. "Discursive Strategies of the Maori Tribal Elite." *Critique of Anthropology* 31 (4): 359–80. http://dx.doi.org/10.1177/0308275X11420116.

Rei, Tania. 1993. *Maori Women and the Vote*. Wellington: Huia Publishers.

Reilly, Michael P. J. 2011. "Māori Studies, Past and Present: A Review." *Contemporary Pacific* 23 (2): 340–70. http://dx.doi.org/10.1353/cp.2011.0039.

Renwick, William, ed. 1991. *Sovereignty and Indigenous Rights: The Treaty of Waitangi in International Contexts*. Wellington: Victoria University Press.

Rika-Heke, Powhiri. 1997. "Tribes or Nations? Post or Fence? What's the Matter with Self-Definition?" In *Not on Any Map: Essays on Post Coloniality and Cultural Nationalism*, ed. Stuart Murray, 170–81. Exeter, Devon: University of Exeter Press.

Roa, Tom. 2010. "Kīngitanga." In *Weeping Waters: The Treaty of Waitangi and Constitutional Change*, ed. Malcolm Mulholland and Veronica Tawhai, 165–174. Wellington: Huia Publishers.

Rodman, Margaret. 1997. "Conclusion." In *Home in the Islands: Housing and Social Change in the Pacific*, ed. Jan Rensel and Margaret Rodman, 222–33. Honolulu: University of Hawai'i Press.

Rosenblatt, Daniel. 2002. "'Titiranti is the Mountain': Representing Maori Community in Auckland." *Pacific Studies* 25 (1–2): 117–40.

Rosenblatt, Daniel. 2005. "Thinking Outside the Billiard Ball: Cognatic Nationalism and Performing a Maori Public Sphere." *Ethnohistory (Columbus, Ohio)* 52 (1): 111–36. http://dx.doi.org/10.1215/00141801-52-1-111.

Rosenblatt, Daniel. 2011. "Indigenizing the City and the Future of Maori Culture: The Construction of Community in Auckland as Representation, Experience, and Self-Making." *American Ethnologist* 38 (3): 411–29. http://dx.doi.org/10.1111/j.1548-1425.2011.01314.x.

Rowse, Tim. 2000. "Transforming the notion of the Urban Aborigine." *Urban Policy and Research* 18 (2): 171–90. http://dx.doi.org/10.1080/08111140008727831.

Ruru, Jacinta. 2004. "A Politically Fuelled Tsunami: The Foreshore/Seabed Controversy in Aotearoa Me Te Wai Pounamu/New Zealand." *Journal of the Polynesian Society* 113 (1): 57–72.

Rybczynski, Witold. 1986. *Home. A Short History of an Idea*. New York: Viking.

Sahlins, Marshall D. 1965. "On the Sociology of Primitive Exchange." In *The Relevance of Models for Social Anthropology*, ed. M. Banton, 139–236. ASA Monographs. London: Tavistock Publications.

Salmond, Anne. 1975. *Hui: A Study of Maori Ceremonial Gatherings*. Auckland: Reed Books.

Salmond, Anne. 1991a. *Two Worlds: First Meetings Between Maori and Europeans 1642–1772*. Auckland: Viking.

Salmond, Anne. 1991b. "Tipuna–Ancestors: Aspects of Maori Cognatic Descent." In *Man and a Half: Essays in Pacific Anthropology and Ethnobiology in Honour of Ralph Bulmer*, ed. Andrew Pawley, 334–47. Auckland: The Polynesian Society.

Salmond, Anne. 2000. "Māori and Modernity: Ruatara's dying." In *Signifying Identities: Anthropological Perspectives on Boundaries and Contested Values*, ed. Anthony P. Cohen, 37–58. London: Routledge.

Salmond, Anne. 2003. *The Trial of the Cannibal Dog: Captain Cook in the South Seas*. Auckland: Penguin.

Salmond, Anne, and Amiria Stirling. 1976. *Amiria: The Life Story of a Maori Woman*. Wellington: Reed.

Salmond, Anne, and Eruera Stirling. 1980. *Eruera: The Teachings of a Maori Elder*. Oxford: Oxford University Press.

Saura, Bruno, 2005. *Huahine aux temps anciens*. Cahiers du Patrimoine, Pape'ete, Service de la Culture et du Patrimoine de Polynésie française.

Schachter, Judith, and Albrecht Funk. 2012. "Sovereignty, Indigeneity, Identities: Perspectives from Hawai'i." *Social Identities* 18 (4): 381–98.

Schwimmer, Éric. 1952. "The Story of the Modern Marae." *Te Ao Hou* 2:23.

Schwimmer, Éric. 1963. "Guardian Animals of the Māori." *Journal of the Polynesian Society* 74: 149–81.

Schwimmer, Éric. 1965. "The Cognitive Aspect of Culture Change." *Journal of the Polynesian Society* 74: 149–81.

Schwimmer, Éric. 1972. "Symbolic Competition." *Anthropologica* xiv (2): 117–55. http://dx.doi.org/10.2307/25604875.

Schwimmer, Éric. 1978. "Lévi-Strauss and Maori Social Structure." *Anthropologica* xx (1/2): 201–22. http://dx.doi.org/10.2307/25605005.

Schwimmer, Éric. 1990. "The Maori *hapu*: a Generative Model." *Journal of the Polynesian Society* 99 (3): 297–317.

Schwimmer, Éric. 1992. "La spirale dédoublée et l'identité nationale: l'art abstrait traditionnel maori a-t-il une signification? " *Anthropologie et Sociétés* 16 (1): 59–72.

Schwimmer, Éric. 1995. "Les minorités nationales au Québec et en Nouvelle-Zélande." *Anthropologie et Sociétés* 19 (3): 127–50.

Schwimmer, Éric. 1999. "Les trois espaces de notre pays." Paper presented at the Annual Conference of the Canadian Anthropology Society (CASCA), Université Laval, Québec (Québec), May.

Schwimmer, Éric. 2001a. "General Report 1: Fisheries." Unpublished manuscript.

Schwimmer, Éric. 2001b, "Construire un monde pour la citoyenneté." In *L'éducation à la citoyenneté*, ed. Michel Pagé, Fernand Ouellet, and Luiza Cortesao, 305–17. Sherbrooke: Éditions du CRP.

Schwimmer, Éric. 2003. "Les minorités nationales: Volonté, désir, homéostasie optimale. Réflexions sur le biculturalisme en Nouvelle-Zélande, au Québec et ailleurs." *Anthropologie et Sociétés* 27 (3): 155–84.

Schwimmer, Éric. 2004a. "Making a World: The Māori of Aotearoa, New Zealand." In *Figured Worlds: Ontological Obstacles in Intercultural Relations*, ed. John Clammer, Sylvie Poirier, and Éric Schwimmer, 243–74. Toronto: University of Toronto Press.

Schwimmer, Éric. 2004b. "The Local and the Universal: Reflections on Contemporary Māori Literature in Response to *Blood Narrative* by Chadwick Allen." *Journal of the Polynesian Society* 113 (1): 7–36.

Schwimmer, Éric. 2009. "La citoyenneté double: le cas de l'autochtonie en 1965." *Anthropologie et Sociétés* 33 (2): 193–222.

Schwimmer, Erik, ed. 1968. *The Maori People in the Nineteen-Sixties*. Auckland: Longman Paul.

Schwimmer, Éric, Caroline Houle, and Yvan Breton, 2000. *La coexistence précaire de la pêche mondialisée et de la pêche coutumière: Le cas des Maori de la Nouvelle-Zélande*. Québec: Département d'anthropologie, Université Laval.

Scott, Colin H., and Monica E. Mulrennan. 1999. "Land and Sea Tenure at Erub, Torres Strait: Property, Sovereignty and the Adjudication of Cultural Continuity." *Oceania* 70 (2): 146–76.

Scott, Kathryn, and Robin Kearns. 2000. "Coming Home: Return Migration by Maori to the Mangakahia Valley, Northland." *New Zealand Population Review* 26 (2): 21–44.

Sharp, Andrew. 1991. "The Treaty of Waitangi: Reasoning and Social Justice in New Zealand?" In *Nga Take: Ethnic Relations and Racism in Aotearoa/New Zealand*, ed. Paul Spoonley, David Pearson, and Cluny Macpherson, 131–47. Palmerston North: Dunmore Press.

Sharp, Andrew. 1995. "Why Be Bicultural?" In *Justice and Identity: Antipodean Practices*, ed. Margaret Wilson and Anna Yeatman, 116–33. Wellington: Allen and Unwin.

Sharp, Andrew. 1997. "The Waitangi Tribunal 1984–1996." In *New Zealand Politics in Transition*, ed. Raymond Miller. Auckland: Oxford University Press.

Sharp, Andrew. 2002. "Blood, Custom and Consent: Three Kinds of Māori Groups in New Zealand and the Challenges They Present to

Governments." *The University of Toronto Law Journal* 51 (1): 9–37. http://dx.doi.org/10.2307/825926.

Sharp, Andrew, 2003. "Traditional Authority and the Legitimation Crisis of 'Urban Tribes': The Waipareira Case." *Ethnologie comparée* 6. http://alor.univ-montp3.fr/cerce/revue.htm.

Sharples, Pita. 2011. "Minister Congratulates Maori Economic Taskforce." Media Release, *Scoop News*, 5 May. http://www.scoop.co.nz/stories/PA1105/S00093/minister-congratulates-maori-economic-taskforce.htm. Accessed 20 December 2011.

Shore, Chris. 2002. "Introduction: Towards an Anthropology of Elites." In *Elite Cultures: Anthropological Perspectives*, ed. Cris Shore and Stephen Nugent, 1–21. London and New York: Routledge, ASA Monographs, vol. 38.

Simon, Judith A. 1998a. "Anthropology, 'Native Schooling' and Maori: the Politics of 'Cultural Adaptation' Policies." *Oceania* 69 (1): 61–78.

Simon, Judith, ed. 1998b. *Nga Kura Maori. The Native Schools System.* Auckland: Auckland University Press.

Simon, Judith, and Linda Tuhiwai Smith, eds. 2001. *A Civilising Mission? Perceptions and Representations of the New Zealand Native Schools System.* Auckland: Auckland University Press.

Sinclair, Karen P. 1990a. "Tangi: Funeral Rituals and the Construction of Maori Identity." In *Cultural Identity and Ethnicity in the Pacific*, ed. Jocelyn Linnekin and Lin Poyer, 219–36. Honolulu: University of Hawaii Press.

Sinclair, Keith. 1957. *The Origins of the Maori Wars.* Wellington: New Zealand University Press.

Sinclair, Keith. 1975. *Towards Independence.* Auckland: Hinemann Educational Books.

Sinclair, Keith. 1986. *A Destiny Apart: New Zealand's Search for National Identity.* Wellington: Allen and Unwin.

Sinclair, Keith. 1990b. *Towards 1990: Nation and Identity*, Hocken Lecture 1988. Dunedin: Hocken Library, University of Otago.

Sinclair, Keith. 2000. *A History of New Zealand,* 3rd revised edition. Auckland: Penguin.

Sissons, Jeffrey. 1992. "The Future of Biculturalism in Aotearoa New Zealand." In *Social Science and the Future of New Zealand*, ed. J. Morss, 15–24. Dunedin: University of Otago.

Sissons, Jeffrey. 1993. "The Systematisation of Tradition: Maori Culture as a Strategic Resource." *Oceania* 64 (2): 97–116.

Sissons, Jeffrey. 1995. "Tall Trees Need Deep Roots: Biculturalism, Bureaucracy and Tribal Democracy in Aotearoa/New Zealand." *Cultural Studies* 9 (1): 61–73. http://dx.doi.org/10.1080/09502389500490231.

Sissons, Jeffrey. 1998. "The Traditionalisation of the Maori Meeting House." *Oceania* 69 (1): 36–46.

Sissons, Jeffrey. 2000. "The Post-assimilationsist Thought of Sir Apirana Ngata: Towards a Genealogy of New Zealand Biculturalism." *New Zealand Journal of History* 34 (1): 47–59.

Sissons, Jeffrey. 2004. "Maori Tribalism and Post-settler Nationhood in New Zealand." *Oceania* 75 (1): 19–31.

Sissons, Jeffrey. 2005. *First Peoples: Indigenous Cultures and their Futures.* London: Reaktion.

Sissons, Jeffrey. 2008. "Leave Your Tribalism at the Door: Rematerialising Maori Society." Paper presented at the Annual Conference of the Association for Social Anthropology in Oceania (ASAO), Australian National University, Canberra, Australia, February.

Sissons, Jeffrey. 2010. "Building a House Society: The Reorganization of Maori Communities around Meeting Houses." *Journal of the Royal Anthropological Institute* 16 (2): 372–86. http://dx.doi.org/10.1111/j.1467-9655.2010.01630.x.

Smith, Graham Hingangaroa. 1995. "Whakaoho Whānau." *He Pukenga Korero* 1:18–36.

Smith, Graham Hingangaroa. 1997. "The Development of Kaupapa Maori: Theory and Praxis." Ph.D. thesis, University of Auckland.

Smith, Graham Hingangaroa, and Linda Tuhiwai Smith, 1996. "New Methodologies in Maori Education." In *Nga Patai: Racism and Ethnic Relations in Aotearoa/New Zealand*, ed. Paul Spoonley, David Pearson, and Cluny Macpherson, 217–34. Palmerston North: Dunmore Press.

Smith, Jean. 1974. *Tapu Removal in Maori Religion.* Wellington: The Polynesian Society.

Smith, Jo. 2011. "Postcolonial Māori Television? The Dirty Politics of Indigenous Cultural Production." *Continuum: Journal of Media and Cultural Studies* 25 (5): 719–29.

Smith, Kaapua. 2010a. "Māori Party." In *New Zealand Government and Politics*, ed. Raymond Miller, 509–21. Melbourne: Oxford University Press.

Smith, Kaapua. 2010b. "Māori Political Parties." In *Weeping Waters: The Treaty of Waitangi and Constitutional Change*, ed. Malcolm Mulholland and Veronica Tawhai, 207–17. Wellington: Huia Publishers.

Smith, Linda Tuhiwai. 1992. "Māori Women: Discourses, Projects and Mana Wahine." In *Women and Education in Aotearoa 2*, ed. Sue Middleton and Alison Jones, 35–51. Wellington: Bridget Williams Books.

Smith, Linda Tuhiwai. 1999. *Decolonizing Methodologies: Research and Indigenous Peoples.* Dunedin, London: Zed Books and University of Otago Press.

Smith, Valance. 2003. "Colonising the Stage: The Socio-Cultural Impact of Colonisation on Kapa Haka." Master's thesis, University of Auckland.

Smits, Katherine. 2010. "The Politics of Biculturalism." In *New Zealand Governement & Politics*, ed. Raymond Miller, 66–76. Melbourne: Oxford University Press.

Sorrenson, M.P.K., 1986. "A History of Maori Representation in Parliament." In *Report of the Royal Commission on the Electoral System*, app. B-1. Wellington: Government Printer.

Soutar, Monty. 2008. *Nga Tama Toa – The Price of Citizenship: C Company 28 (Maori) Battalion 1939–1945*. Auckland: David Bateman.

Spoonley, Paul. 1991. "Pakeha Ethnicity: A Response to Maori Sovereignty." In *Nga Take: Ethnic Relations and Racism in Aotearoa/New Zealand*, ed. Paul Spoonley, David Pearson, and Cluny Macpherson, 154–70. Palmerston North: Dunmore Press.

Spoonley, Paul. 2007. "He Iwi Tahi Tatou?" *Massey Magazine* 22 (April). http://www.massey.ac.nz/~wwpubafs/magazine/2007_Apr/stories/06-22-07.html. Accessed 22 December 2011.

Spoonley, Paul. 2009. *Mata Toa: The Life and Times of Ranginui Walker*, North Shore: Penguin.

Starzecka, D.C. 1996. *Maori: Art and Culture*. London: British Museum.

Stephens, A. 1997. "Food, Diet and Gender in the 21st Century." *Journal of the New Zealand Dietetic Association* 51:51–4.

Stephenson, Maxine. 2006. "Closing the Doors on the Maori Schools in New Zealand." *Race, Ethnicity and Education* 9 (3): 307–24. http://dx.doi.org/10.1080/13613320600807717.

Stewart-Harawira, Makere. 2005. *The New Imperial Order: Indigenous Responses to Globilization*. London, Wellington: Zed Books and Huia Publishers.

Stone, R.C.J. 2001. *From Tamaki-Makau-Rau to Auckland*. Auckland: Auckland University Press.

Sullivan, Ann. 1997. "Maori Politics and Government Policies." In *New Zealand Politics in Transition*, ed. Raymond Miller, 361–71. Auckland: Oxford University Press.

Sullivan, Ann. 2001. "Maori Affairs and Public Policy." In *New Zealand Government and Politics*, ed. Raymond Miller, 479–88. Auckland: Oxford University Press.

Sullivan, Ann. 2003. "Effecting Change through Electoral Politics: Cultural Identity and the Māori Franchise." *Journal of the Polynesian Society* 112 (3): 219–37.

Sullivan, Ann. 2010. "Minority Indigenous Representation." In *Weeping Waters: The Treaty of Waitangi and Constitutional Change*, ed. Malcolm Mulholland and Veronica Tawhai, 251–67. Wellington: Huia Publishers.

Sullivan, Ann. 2011. "Māori Representation, Local Government and the Auckland Concil." In *Along a Fault-Line: New Zealand's Changing Local Government Landscape*, ed. Jean Drage, Jeff McNeil, and Christine Cheyne, 59–74. Wellington: Dunmore Publishing.

Sunday Star Times. 2011. "Anger Building over 'Racist' Comment." *Sunday Star Times*, 11 September. http://www.stuff.co.nz/auckland/local-news/5602816/Anger-building-over-racist-comments. Accessed 12 December 2011.

Tahana, Yvonne, and Bernard Orsman. 2009. "Thousands March for Maori Voice." *New Zealand Herald*, 26 May.

Tan, Lincoln. 2012. "Auckland Hits 1.5m Population Milestone." *New Zealand Herald*, 1 February. http://www.nzherald.co.nz/nz/news/article.cfm?c_id=1&objectid=10782565. Accessed 1 February 2012.

Taonui, Rawiri. 2010. "Auckland: Urban and Angry." *New Zealand Herald*, 27 August. http://www.nzherald.co.nz/auckland-tale-of-a-supercity/news/article.cfm?c_id=1502974&objectid=10667603. Accessed 22 December 2011.

Tapsell, Paul. 2002. "*Marae* and Tribal Identity in Urban Aotearoa/New Zealand." *Pacific Studies* 25 (1–2): 141–71.

Tauroa, Hiwi, and Pat Tauroa. 1986. *Te Marae: A Guide to Customs and Protocol*. Auckland: Reed Books.

Taylor, Apirana. 1979. *Eyes of the Ruru*. Wellington: Voice Press.

Te Ao Hou/The New World. 1952–75. Wellington, Department of Māori Affairs.

Te Hoe Nuku Roa. 1998. *Baseline Study, Manawatu-Whanganui, Gisborne, Wellington, Auckland Regional Results*. Palmerston North: Massey University School of Māori Studies.

Te Hoe Nuku Roa. 1999. *Te Hoe Nuku Roa Source Document: Baseline History*. Palmerston North: Massey University School of Māori Studies.

Te Puni Kōkiri. 2003. *Proceedings of Whakapūmau Whānau: Whānau Development National Hui*. Wellington: Te Puni Kōkiri.

Thomson, Ainsley. 2003. "People of the Land Say Maori a Pakeha Name They Dislike." *New Zealand Herald*, 8 August.

Thomson, Ainsley. 2005. "MP Upset at Being Asked to Sit Behind Men," *New Zealand Herald*, 3 November. http://www.nzherald.co.nz/section/story.cfm?c_id=1&ObjectID=10353335. Accessed 15 October 2006.

Trevett, Claire. 2011. "Jones Backs Investment by Iwi in State Assets." *New Zealand Herald*, 16 December. http://www.nzherald.co.nz/politics/news/article.cfm?c_id=280&objectid=10773494. Accessed 20 Decembre 2011.

Trlin, Andrew. 1984. "Changing Ethnic Residential Distribution and Segrega-
tion in Auckland." In *Nga Take: Ethnic Relations and Racism in Aotearoa/New
Zealand*, ed. Paul Spoonley, David Pearson, and Cluny Macpherson, 172–98.
Palmerston North: Dunmore Press.

Tsing, Anna. 2007. "Indigenous Voice." In *Indigenous Experience Today*, ed.
Marisol de la Cadena and Orin Starn, 33–67. Oxford: Berg.

Tukukino, H. 1988. "Māori Families: The Support System." In *Māori Mental Health: A Resource Kit*. Auckland: Mental Health Foundation of New
Zealand.

Turner, Stephen. 1999. "A Legacy of Colonialism: The Uncivil Society of
Aotearoa/New Zealand." *Cultural Studies* 13 (3): 408–22. http://dx.doi.
org/10.1080/095023899335158.

TVNZ. 2011. "Maori Academic Slams 'White Supremacist' Immigrants."
TVNZ, 4 September. http://tvnz.co.nz/national-news/maori-academic-
slams-white-supremacist-immigrants-4382974. Accessed 12 Decembre
2011.

Van Meijl, Toon. 1993. "The Maori King Movement: Unity and Diversity in
Past and Present: Changing Political Relations." *Bijdragen tot de tāl-, land- en
volkenkunde* 149 (4): 673–89.

Van Meijl, Toon. 1994. "'Shifting the Goal Posts': The Politics of the Treaty of
Waitangi in New Zealand." *Cahiers des Sciences Humaines* 30 (3): 411–34.

Van Meijl, Toon. 1997. "The Re-emergence of Maori Chiefs: 'Devolution' as
a Strategy to Maintain Tribal Authority." In *Chiefs Today: Traditional Pacific
Leadership and the Postcolonial State*, ed. Lamont Lindstrom and Geoffrey
White, 84–107. Stanford: Stanford University Press.

Van Meijl, Toon. 1998. "Culture and Democracy Among the Maori." In *Pacific
Answers to Western Hegemony: Cultural Practices of Identity Construction*, ed.
Jurg Wassmann, 389–415. New York: Berg.

Van Meijl, Toon. 2006a, "The Paradox of Indigenous Rights Controversy." In
Public Policy and Ethnicity, The Politics of Ethnic Boundary-Making, ed. Elizabeth Rata and Roger Openshaw, 66–80. Houndmills: Palgrave Macmillan.

Van Meijl, Toon, 2006b, "Who Owns the Fisheries? Changing Views of Property and Its Redistribution in Post-colonial Maori Society." In *Changing Properties of Property*, ed. Franz von Benda-Beckmann, Keebet von
Benda-Beckmann, and Melanie G. Wiber, 170–93. New York and Oxford:
Berghahn.

Van Meijl, Toon. 2006c. "Multiple Identifications and the Dialogical
Self: Urban Maori Youngsters and the Cultural Renaissance." *Journal of the Royal Anthropological Institute* 12 (4): 917–33. http://dx.doi.
org/10.1111/j.1467-9655.2006.00370.x.

Vasil, Raj K. 2000. *Biculturalism: Reconciling Aotearoa with New Zealand*. Wellington: Institute of Policy Studies.

Waitangi Tribunal. 1987. *Ōrākei Report, Wai 9*. Wellington: Department of Justice.

Waitangi Tribunal. 1998. *Te Whanau o Waipareira Report, Wai 414*. Wellington: GP Publications.

Walker, Ranginui. 1970. "Maori in a Metropolis: The Social Adjustment of the Maori to Urban Living in Auckland." Ph.D. thesis, University of Auckland.

Walker, Ranginui. 1972. "Assimilation or Cultural Continuity." In *Racial Issues in New Zealand: Problems and Insights*, ed. Graham M. Vaughan, 54–61. Auckland: Akarana Press.

Walker, Ranginui. 1975. "The Politics of Voluntary Association: The Structure and Functioning of a Maori Welfare Committee in a City Suburb." In *Conflict and Compromise. Essays on the Maori since Colonisation*, ed. I. Hugh Kawharu, 167–86. Wellington: A.H. &A.W. Reed.

Walker, Ranginui. 1979. "The Urban Māori." In *He Mātāpuna: Some Māori Perspectives*. Wellington: Te Kaunihera Whakahaupapa mō Aotearoa.

Walker, Ranginui. 1987. *Nga Tau Tohetohe: Years of Anger*. Auckland: Penguin.

Walker, Ranginui. 1989. "The Treaty of Waitangi as the Focus of Maori Protest." In *Waitangi: Maori and Pakeha Perspectives of the Treaty of Waitangi*, ed. I. Hugh Kawharu, 263–79. Auckland: Oxford University Press.

Walker, Ranginui. 1992. "Maori People since 1950." In *The Oxford History of New Zealand*. 2nd ed., ed. Geoffrey W. Rice, 498–519. Auckland: Oxford University Press.

Walker, Ranginui. 1996. *Nga Pepa a Ranginui: The Walker Papers. Thought-Provoking Views on the Issues Affecting Maori and Pakeha*. Auckland: Penguin.

Walker, Ranginui. 2001. *He Tipua: The Life and Times of Sir Āpirana Ngata*. Auckland: Penguin.

Walker, Ranginui. 2004. *Ka Whawhai Tonu Matou: Struggle Without End*. 2nd ed. Auckland: Penguin.

Walker, Ranginui. 2008. *Tohunga Whakairo: Paki Harrisson. The Story of a Master Carver*. North Shore: Penguin.

Ward, Alan. (Original work published 1973) 1995. *A Show of Justice: Racial 'Amalgamation' in Nineteenth Century New Zealand*. Auckland: Auckland University Press.

Waymouth, Lyn. 2003. "The Bureaucratisation of Genealogy." *Ethnologie comparée* 6. http://alor.univ-montp3.fr/cerce/r6/l.w.htm. Accessed 15 January 2012.

Webster, Steven. 1975. "Cognatic Descent Groups and the Contemporary Maori: A Preliminary Assessment." *Journal of the Polynesian Society* 84 (2): 121–52.

Webster, Steven. 1998. *Patrons of Maori Culture: Power, Theory and Ideology in the Maori Renaissance*. Dunedin: University of Otago Press.

Webster, Steven. 2002. "Maori Retribalization and Treaty Rights to the New Zealand Fisheries." *Contemporary Pacific* 14 (2): 341–76. http://dx.doi.org/10.1353/cp.2002.0072.

Williams, David V. 2011. *A Simple Nullity? The Wi Parata Case in New Zealand Law and History*. Auckland: Auckland University Press.

Williams, H. William. 2000 (1971). *Dictionary of the Maori Language*. Wellington: Legislation Direct.

Williams, Mark. 1997. "Crippled by Geography? New Zealand Nationalisms." In *Not on Any Map: Essays on Postcoloniality and Cultural Nationalism*, ed. Stuart Murray, 19–42. Exeter: University of Exeter Press.

Williams, Melissa Matutina. 2010. "'Back-home' and Home in the City: Māori Migrations from Panguru to Auckland, 1930–1970." PhD thesis, University of Auckland.

Wilson, John. 2010. "The Origins of the Māori Seats." In *Māori and Parliament: Diverse Strategies and Compromises*, ed. Maria Barth, 37–71. Wellington: Huia Publishers.

Winiata, Maharaia. 1967. *The Changing Role of the Leader in Maori Society: A Study in Social Change and Race Relation*. Auckland: Blackwood and Janet Paul.

Woods, Megan C. 2002. "Intergrating the Nation: Gendering Maori Urbanisation and Integration, 1942–1969." PhD thesis, University of Canterbury.

Wright, Matthew. 2006. *Two Peoples, One Land: The New Zealand Wars*. Auckland: Reed.

Index

activism: terminology, 272n26 (*see also* resistance, Māori)

adoption (*whāngai*), 156, 173, 183, 291n4

ahi kā (keeping a fire alight), 174, 272nn19–20

Allen, Chadwick, 103

American Indian Movement, 35

Anglican *marae*, 98

Aotearoa/New Zealand: origins, 32

aroha (unconditional love), 150, 153, 181, 184. See also *whānau* (extended family)

assimilation, 31, 36, 104–5, 158, 276n26. *See also* biculturalism

Auckland: demographics, 48–9, 60, 62–3, 280n1, 281n4; location of Māori, *61*; *mana whānau*, 282n13; *mana whenua*, 41–2, 60; South compared to the Bronx, 74–5; urban *marae* in, 101; violent reputation, 75, 284nn28–9. *See also* urban-based Māori (Auckland)

Auckland Super City Council, 250, 279n46; Māori seats on, 8, 41

Austin-Broos, Diane, 188

Ballara, Angela, 51, 53–4

Barber, Keith, 6

Barcham, Manuhuia, 13, 36

Barker, Joanne, 247

Barth, Fredrik, 245

Barton, Chris, 44

Bastion Point (1978), 33

Bay of Plenty Regional Council, 41

"Beaches for All," 5–7, 270n9. *See also* National Party

Belich, James, 22, 23–4, 26–8, 30, 274n7, 275n13

"Best Outcomes for Māori," 105, 200

biculturalism: in Aotearoa/New Zealand identity, 23, 70, 193–4, 274n4; and Māori successes, 8; versus multiculturalism, 6; and neoliberalism, 272n28; as policy, 164; politics of differentiation, 205, 213, 220–1, 247; retribalization, 37; and standard of living, 60, 160; and Waitangi Tribunal, 9, 32; as *whānau* role, 228. *See also* assimilation; multiculturalism

Black American influences, 74–5, 205

Boast, Richard, and Richard Hill, 26

Anthropological Horizons

EDITOR: MICHAEL LAMBEK, UNIVERSITY OF TORONTO

Published to date: